CHEF'S BOOK OF FORMULAS, YIELDS, AND SIZES

CHEF'S BOOK OF FORMULAS, YIELDS, AND SIZES

SECOND EDITION

ARNO SCHMIDT

JOHN WILEY & SONS, INC.

New York   Chichester   Weinheim
Brisbane   Singapore   Toronto

Copyright © 1996 by John Wiley & Sons, Inc. All rights reserved.

Published simultaneously in Canada.

This publication is designed to provide accurate and authoritative information in regard to the subject matter covered. It is sold with the understanding that the publisher is not engaged in rendering professional services. If professional advice or other expert assistance is required, the services of a competent professional person should be sought.

Library of Congress Cataloging-in-Publication Data:

Schmidt, Arno.
    Chef's book of formulas, yields, and sizes / Arno Schmidt.—2nd ed.
      p. cm.
    Includes index.
    ISBN 0-471-28744-X
    1. Quantity cookery.   I. Title.
  TX820.S355   1995
  641.5'7—dc20
                             95-51688

Printed in the United States of America

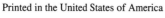
10 9 8 7 6 5 4 3

PREFACE

All foodservice operators, chefs, caterers, and dieticians are faced with the task and challenge of buying the right amount of food for an estimated number of meals. In order to accomplish this efficiently, they must assess yields realistically. Yields vary greatly. Obviously, serving size determines yields, but so does the accepted amount of trim and waste. The quality and size of the food purchased influence yields as well. In the case of fresh products, the time of the year can alter the yield. Cooking methods, care taken during the preparation, and the dishing-out process can also have a bearing on yields.

This book addresses these issues. It mentions, when applicable, the form(s) in which the food is available—such as canned, dehydrated, fresh, or frozen, and the packs and sizes most likely to be purchased by foodservice operators. It lists suggested serving sizes, and the number of servings that are reasonably obtainable from the most common packs and sizes.

All yield calculations are based on at least two average samples, and are always rounded down, to account for spillage, waste, and over-portioning. Meat and fish yields are based on tests done by an experienced butcher. All pieces were well trimmed and acceptable to a fine foodservice operation. A less experienced person might get lower yields than calculated in this book. On the other hand, some operators might accept portions with less trim and consequently get a better yield than indicated.

Since the measuring devices used in kitchens vary greatly, a series of entries listing the sizes and volumes of bottles, cans, scoops, steam-table pans, and the like is included. To make the book more accessible to foreign-born workers, all measurements are given in both U.S. and metric measurements. An ounce is calculated as 28 grams; a fluid ounce is 0.029 liter. Decimals were rounded off.

In response to current concerns about nutrition, the calorie counts for the suggested serving sizes are given when possible. The book also lists formulas for commonly prepared items that are composed of ingredients requiring measurement or scaling for best results. Good examples are dressings and simple bakery items. Yields are always included with these formulas. Since this is a book of formulas, it is assumed that methods for basic preparations are not needed.

To round out the information, important but hard-to-access miscellaneous data are included, from the skirting lengths needed to drape banquet tables, to a simple formula for estimating uniform sizes, to yields of beer kegs.

All entries are listed alphabetically, except certain items that are listed in groups. For example, all beef information is listed under Beef, all clam information appears under Clams. The following is an outline of a standard entry.

ENTRY NAME
SPECIFIC FOOD TYPE
FURTHER FOOD TYPE
DIFFERENTIATION (IF
NECESSARY)
Season

      Pack
      Sizes (as packed)
    Kitchen Yields
      Cooking recommendations
      Waste
      Counts (in terms of yield)
      Serving size
      Calories

This book is based on a lifetime of foodservice experience. It combines easy-to-understand formulas, yields, sizes, and quantities in one volume. It will serve as the most useful, ready reference on the shelves of any operator.

ACKNOWLEDGMENTS

So many friends and colleagues helped me collect the information contained in this book that it is impossible to remember them all. A remark made by a salesman, a question asked by a food server, and even a mistake made by someone in the kitchen have all triggered at different times the curiosity that led to additional information. I thank everyone who has accidentally or consciously helped to shape this book.

Special thanks go to my wife, Margaret, who encouraged me to write this book, and who provided valuable editorial comments and suggestions. When I needed help, she provided it. Without her, this book would not have been possible.

A

ABALONE

Large gastropods with beautiful shells, harvested in the Pacific Ocean. Big producers are Alaska and Mexico. California law prohibits shipping fresh, frozen, or canned abalone harvested in California to other states. Available canned, dried, fresh (in season), frozen whole in shell, or vacuum-packed meat.

CANNED ABALONE
Available in steaks and minced.

Pack:
Packed in water in various size cans; 1-lb (450-g) can is common.

Kitchen Yields
1-lb (450-g) can contains 13 to 14 oz (360 to 400 g) drained abalone, which yields 4 servings for appetizer or 2⅓ servings for main course.

Serving size:
3 oz (84 g) drained meat as appetizer; 6 oz (170 g) as main course.

DRIED ABALONE
Oriental item.

Pack:
By weight.

Kitchen Yields

Serving size:
1 oz (28 g).

FRESH ABALONE
Most abalone is imported from Mexico or from the Orient. Available in shell, shucked, and trimmed.

Pack:
By piece.

Sizes:
Shell sizes range from 11 in (270 mm) across for red abalone to about 3 to 5 in (70 to 120 mm) across for flat abalone.

Kitchen Yields

Serving size:
4 oz (112 g).

Pound thin and sauté quickly. Serve immediately. Abalone trim is used for soups.

Pack:
By weight.

FROZEN ABALONE
Harvested in Alaska or imported from Mexico.

Pack:
3-lb (1.35-kg) boxes. Other packs are available.

Sizes:
Twelve 4-oz (112-g) pieces. Other sizes are available.

Serving size:
4 oz (112 g) as appetizer or main course.
Pound thin and sauté quickly. Serve immediately.

ACKEE

Tropical fruit about the size of a large plum. NOTE: *The fruit is poisonous until ripe and has opened naturally, exposing the kernels.*

Season:
Year-round.

Pack:
By count.

Size:
About 4 oz (112 g) each fruit.

Kitchen Yields
Three double kernels to each fruit.

Serving size:
About eight double kernels as an appetizer garnish. Sauté quickly and serve hot.

AGAR-AGAR

Also called *Japanese gelatin*, it is a seaweed-based natural thickening agent used for thickening jams and ice cream. Normally sold in thin, brittle sticks or in powder.

Pack:
1-lb (450-g) packages.

Kitchen Yields
Thickening power is about five times greater than that of plain gelatin. It will set in room temperature and is not affected by acidity to the same extent as gelatin.

Agar Agar thickening power:
½ oz (14 g) for 20 cups or 5 qt (4.7 l);
1 oz (28 g) for 40 cups or 10 qt (9.4 l).

AGAR-AGAR CANDY

Formula
    1 oz (28 g) agar-agar
    3 lb (1.35 l) water
    2 lb, 8 oz (1.12 kg) sugar
    1 lb, 4 oz (560 g) corn syrup

Boil to 218°F (108°C), then add:

    1 lb, 4 oz (560 g) corn syrup

Cool to 120°F (50°C), then add:

    ½ tb granulated citric acid
    ¾ oz (0.022 l) liquid fruit acid
    fruit flavor to taste

Kitchen Yields
5 lb (2.2 kg) mix; about three hundred and twenty ¼-oz (7-g) candies.

ALFALFA SPROUTS

See Sprouts.

ALLIGATOR MEAT

Available frozen from Florida.

Pack:
By weight, normally 5-lb (2.25-kg) cartons.

Size:
Boneless tail pieces, about 4 to 6 oz (112 to 170 g) each.

Serving size:
4 oz (112 g).

Kitchen Yields
The tail pieces are best cut into small medallions of about 2 oz (60 g) each and pounded well.

Trimming waste:
About 5 percent.

ALMONDS

Almonds used in foodservice are normally purchased shelled. They are available with skin on and blanched (skin removed). The major varieties are: Nonpareil, Carmel, California and Mission.

CALIFORNIA

Size:
18 to 40 kernels per 1 oz (28 g).

    Whole, skin on
    Cross-cut, skin on
    Halves, skin on
    Splits, skin on
    Cube-cut, skin on
    Diced, skin on, available in two sizes
    Diced, buttered and roasted, skin on

CARMEL

Size:
18 to 40 kernels per 1 oz (28 g).

    Whole, skin on
    Blanched, fine dice
    Blanched, slivered in 2 sizes
    Diced, skin on
    Chopped pieces, skin on, available in three
        sizes

MISSION

Size:
20 to 40 kernels per 1 oz (28 g).

    Whole, skin on
    Whole and broken, skin on
    Pieces, skin on

Slices, skin on, in three sizes
Powder, all white

NONPAREIL

Size:
20 to 40 kernels per 1 oz (28 g).

Whole, skin on
Whole, blanched
Blanched, whole and broken
Blanched splits
Blanched sliced
Blanched slivers and diced, available in two
sizes

Pack:
Six 5-lb (2.25-kg) cans whole raw or blanched almonds.
Six 5-lb (2.25-kg) cans whole blanched or salted almonds.
Six 5-lb (2.25-kg) cans sliced raw almonds.
Six 5-lb (2.25-kg) cans sliced blanched almonds.
10- and 25-lb (4.5- and 11.25-kg) cartons of above varieties.
30-lb (13.5-kg) case of granulated, bleached or natural skin on almonds.

Kitchen Yields
1 cup chopped 4½ oz (126 g) = 130 almonds.
1 cup slivered 4 oz (112 g) = 115 almonds.
1 lb (450 g) in shell = 2 cups nutmeat.
1 lb (450 g) nutmeat = 3⅔ cups.

Calories:
1 cup chopped = 775 Calories.
1 cup slivered = 690 Calories.

ALMOND FILLING FOR BAKING

Formula
2 lb (900 g) almond paste
2 lb (900 g) sugar
2½ lb (1.12 kg) butter
1 qt (0.47 l) or about 20 whole eggs
Grated lemon peel to taste

Kitchen Yields
For Danish pastry, serving size is 1 oz (28 g) per piece; total formula yields 130 pieces.

For coffeecake, serving size is 8 oz (225 g) per ring; total formula yields 17 rings.

ALMOND PASTE
Sweet almond paste is called *marzipan* in German. It is available with either 60 percent unblanched almonds or with 60 percent blanched almonds. Almond paste made with blanched almonds is whiter than paste made with unblanched almonds.

Pack:
Six #10 cans are equivalent to 39 lb (17.5 kg). One #10 can is equivalent to 104 oz or 6½ lb (2.9 kg).

Kitchen Yields
Depending on use.

MARZIPAN PASTE FOR MODELING

Formula
One #10 can (104 oz) almond paste, warmed
1 lb (450 g) glucose, warmed
3 lb (1.35 kg) confectioners sugar

Kitchen Yields
11 lb (4.95 kg) paste.

SALTED ALMONDS

Pack:
200 each ½-oz (14-g) packets. Other packs are available.

AMARANTH

Spinach-like vegetable with dark green leaves, available year-round. The small seeds are also used as starch and have valuable protein, but low gluten content. Flour made from amaranth seeds must be blended with wheat flour for baking.

Pack:
By weight.

Kitchen Yields
1 cup amaranth and 3 cups water, simmered 25 minutes, yield 2½ cups cooked grain.

ANISE

Bulb-shaped vegetable with fine, bushy leaves. The flavor is slightly licorice. The vegetable is sometimes confused with the vegetable fennel, but fennel does not form a bulb. Available canned and fresh. *See also* Fennel.

CANNED ANISE

Pack:
Various packs are available. It is often marketed as fennel.

FRESH ANISE

Season:
Domestic anise is available fall to spring and is imported the rest of the year.

Pack:
40- to 50-lb (18- to 22.5-kg) boxes; most imports are in 10-kg (22-lb) boxes.

Count:
24 bunches to a box.

Size:
1¾ to 2 lb (780 to 900 g) with greens still attached. Imported anise is shipped trimmed.

Kitchen Yields
Average size of bulb with most greens removed is 10 oz (280 g).

ANNATTO (ACHIOTE)

See Mexican Foods.

APPLES

Available canned, dehydrated, fresh, and frozen.

APPLE CIDER

Cider is available in four forms: fresh, sweet apple cider (cloudy, with a limited shelf life); pasteurized apple cider (clear or slightly cloudy, with long shelf unopened; it is almost indistinguishable from apple juice); fermented sweet cider (may contain 2 to 3 percent alcohol); and hard cider (fully fermented alcoholic beverage that can be distilled into apple brandy).

Pack:
1-gal, ½-gal, or 1-qt (3.9-, 1.88-, or 0.94-l) bottles.

Kitchen Yields
Pasteurized apple cider is often substituted for apple juice.

Serving size:
Varies, depending on use, between 6 and 10 oz (0.17 to 0.3 l).

APPLE JUICE

Available aseptic pack, canned, in glass bottles, and as frozen concentrate.

Pack:
Juice, ready to serve, in the following sizes:

> Forty-eight 5½-oz (0.016-l) cans.
> Twenty-four 8-oz (0.23-l) aseptic pack.
> Twenty-four 10-oz (0.29-l) glass bottles.
> Twelve 46-oz (1.33-l) cans.
> Twelve 1-qt (0.94-l) glass bottles.
> Six 64-oz (1.9-l) bottles.
> Four 1-gal (3.8-l) glass or plastic bottles.

Kitchen Yields

Serving size:
Varies from 6 to 10 oz (0.17 to 0.3 l).

Pack:
Frozen juice concentrate, in the following sizes:

> Six 46-oz (1.33-l) cans.
> Twelve 32-oz (0.94-l) cans.

Kitchen Yields
Mix one part frozen juice with three parts water.

Serving size:
Varies from 6 to 10 oz (0.17 to 0.3 l). One 32-oz (0.94-l) can produces 1 gal (3.8 l) juice, which yields twenty-one 6 oz (0.17 l) servings.

CANNED APPLES

Available as pieces, rings, slices, and sauce. Apple sauce is available with varying sugar content.

APPLE PIECES

Pack and weight:
One #10 can contains 93 oz (2.6 kg), drained weight; thus, six #10 cans contain 34.8 lb (15.7 kg), drained weight.

APPLE SAUCE

Apple sauce is available sweetened and unsweetened, coarse and strained.

Pack and weight:
One #10 can contains 104 oz (2.91 kg), drained weight; thus, six #10 cans contain 39 lb (17.5 kg), drained weight.
One #303 can contains 15.5 oz (434 g), drained weight; thus, twenty-four #303 cans contain 23.2 lb (10.46 kg), drained weight.

Kitchen Yields

Serving size:
½ cup, or 4 oz (1.2 l). One #10 can yields 25 servings.

Calories:
½ cup, or 4 oz (1.2 l) unsweetened = 50 Calories.
½ cup, or 4 oz (1.2 l) sweetened = 101 Calories.

APPLE SLICES

Pack and weight:
One #10 can contains 96 oz (2.68 kg), drained weight.
Six #10 cans contain 36 lb (16.20 kg), drained weight.
One #2½ can contains 26 oz (728 g), drained weight.
Twenty-four #2½ cans contain 39 lb (17.5 kg), drained weight.
One #2 can contains 18 oz (504 g), drained weight.
Twenty-four #2 cans contain 27 lb (12.15 kg), drained weight.

BAKED APPLES

Pack and weight:
Six #10 cans contain 96 oz (2.68 kg).

Kitchen Yields
One can contains 20 medium size apples. Other counts are available.

SPICED APPLE RINGS

Pack:
Six #10 cans.

Kitchen Yields
One #10 can contains 85 to 90 rings. Other sizes are available.

WHOLE SPICED CRAB APPLES
See also Crab Apples.

Pack:
Six #10 cans.

Kitchen Yields
One #10 can contains 60 to 70 apples.

DEHYDRATED APPLES
Available as rings, wedges, and pie pieces.

Pack:
By weight. Various packs are available.

Kitchen Yields

Serving size:
½ cup. 1 lb (450 g) produces 4⅓ lb (1.9 kg) when cooked, and yields 14 servings.

FRESH APPLES
Apples are generally classified as eating apples, cooking apples, and all-purpose apples.

Season:
Apples are available year-round. Table A-1 lists recommended uses and seasons of popular apple varieties.

Pack:
Loose cartons of 38 to 42 lb (17.1 to 18.9 kg).
Tray pack cartons of 40 to 45 lb (18.0 to 20.2 kg).
Cell pack cartons of 37 to 43 lb (16.6 to 19.3 kg).
Bushels of 42 to 52 lb (18.9 to 23.4 kg).

Table A-1 Recommended Uses and Seasons of Fresh Apples

Variety	Flavor/Texture	Fresh Salads	Pie	Sauce	Baking	Freezing	Season
Cortland	Crisp/firm	Good	Good	Good	Very Good	Good	September to February
Golden Delicious	Sweet/semifirm	Excellent	Excellent	Good	Good	Good	Year-round
Granny Smith	Tart/crisp	Very good	Very good	Very good	Very good	Very good	November to July
Jonathan	Tart/tender	Very good	Very good	Very good	Poor	Very good	September to January
McIntosh	Aromatic/juicy	Excellent	Good	Good	Good	Good	October to April
Newton Pippin	Slightly tart/firm	Very good	Excellent	Excellent	Very good	Excellent	September to June
Red Delicious	Sweet/crisp	Excellent	Fair	Fair	Poor	Fair	Year-round
Rome Beauty	Slightly tart/firm	Good	Very good	Very good	Excellent	Very good	October to June
Winesap	Slightly tart/firm	Excellent	Good	Good	Good	Very good	October to July

Table A-2 Counts and Sizes of Fresh Apples

Cartons		Bushels	
Counts	Diameter	Counts	Diameter
72	3½ in (88.9 mm)		
88	3¼ in (82 mm)	90	3¼ to 3½ in (83 to 89 mm)
100	3⅛ in (80 mm)	100 to 110	2¾ to 3 in (70 to 76 mm)
112	3 in (76 mm)		
125	2⅞ in (73 mm)		
138	2¾ in (70 mm)	135 to 145	2¼ to 2¾ in (57 to 70 mm)
150	2⅝ in (67 mm)		
163	2½ in (63 mm)	185 to 195	2¼ to 2½ in (57 to 63 mm)
		250	2¼ in (57 mm)

Counts:
Tray Packs: 48, 56, 64, 72, 80, 88, 100, 113, 125, 138, 150, 163, 175, 198.
Cell Packs: 64, 80, 96, 100, 120, 140, 160, 200, 216.

Sizes:
Table A-2 lists apple sizes by diameter and count for cartons and bushels.

Common hotel or fancy foodservice sizes:
Baking apples, 48-, 56-, or 64-count tray pack.
Eating apples, 80- or 88-count tray pack.

Weights:
Four small, three medium, or two large apples weigh 1 lb (450 g).

Kitchen Yields
1 cup diced apple is equivalent to 1 medium apple; 3 cups diced apples is equivalent to 1 lb (450 g) apples.

Pie:
2½ lb (1.8 kg) yield one 9-in-diameter pie. 1 bushel apples yields about ten 9-in-diameter pies.

Sauce:
1 bushel apples makes 16 to 20 qt (15.0 to 18.8 l) apple sauce.

Calories:
One apple, medium, unpeeled, 5⅓ oz (150 g), 2¾ in-diameter = 90 Calories.
One apple, medium, unpeeled, 8 oz (225 g), 3¼ in-diameter = 135 Calories.

FROZEN APPLES

Peeled and sliced Delicious apples are available as Straight Pack and as Flavor Pack. "Flavor Pack" indicates that the apples are mixed with sugar in the ratio of seven parts apples to one part sugar (by weight).

Pack:
Straight Pack sliced apples come in 40-lb (18-kg) cans. Flavor Pack sliced apples come in 30-lb (13.6-kg) cans.

Kitchen Yields

Serving size:
For cooked apples, a dessert serving is ½ cup, or 4 oz (112 g). One 30-lb (13.6-kg) can Flavor Pack contains 100 servings.

Pie:
One 40-lb (18.1-kg) Straight Pack yields thirty-two 9-in (228-mm) diameter pies.

FROZEN BAKED APPLES

Frozen baked apples are available ready to heat.

Pack:
Four 6-lb (2.7-kg) boxes, for a total weight of 24 lb (10.8 kg).

Size:
3¾ in (95 mm) across. Other sizes are available.

Kitchen Yields

One 6-lb (2.7-kg) box contains 12 baked apples. One case yields 48 servings.

APRICOTS

Available canned, dried, fresh, and frozen. In addition, apricot glaze for baking and apricot nectar are often used in foodservice.

CANNED APRICOTS

Available in many can sizes and counts. The most common institutional sizes are shown in Table A-3. The product is available in halves or whole with pits, in light or heavy syrup.

Pack:
Six #10 cans.

Serving size:
½ cup.

Calories:
Halves in heavy syrup: ½ cup, or 4 oz (112 g) = 220 Calories.

DRIED APRICOTS

Apricot halves are normally purchased in foodservice. Pieces are available for baking. Apricots are

Table A-3 Sizes and Counts of Canned Apricots

Product	Syrup	Weight	Drained Weight	Count
Whole peeled	Light	108 oz (3.24 kg)	62 oz (1.73 kg)	45 to 55
Halves	Heavy	108 oz (3.24 kg)	62 oz (1.73 kg)	86 to 108
Halves	Heavy	108 oz (3.24 kg)	62 oz (1.73 kg)	108 to 130
Halves	Heavy	108 oz (3.24 kg)	64 oz (1.81 kg)	150 to 175
Halves	Light	106 oz (2.96 kg)	64 oz (1.81 kg)	86 to 130

available sulphured (to retain color) and unsulphured.

Pack:
Individual 25-lb (11.25-kg) bags; twenty-four 1-lb (450-g) boxes.

Sizes:
#1 Jumbo, 1⅜-in diameter, to #6 Standard, ¹³⁄₁₆-in diameter.

Kitchen Yields
1 lb (450 g) yields 5 cups cooked or 10 servings.
1 lb (450 g) contains 75 to 90 jumbo halves.
1 lb (450 g) contains 3 to 3¼ cups.
1 cup contains about 28 jumbo or 37 medium halves.

Serving size:
½ cup cooked fruit.

Calories:
Seven jumbo, uncooked = 85 Calories.
Six medium, uncooked = 56 Calories.

FRESH APRICOTS

Season:
June through August; imports are available during the rest of the year. Only tree-ripened fruit is of highest quality; since the ripened fruit does not ship well, most apricots on the market are not ripe.

Pack:
24-lb (10.8-kg) lugs; 12-lb (5.4-kg) tills; 6-lb (2.7-kg) baskets.

Counts and sizes:
The size is determined by the number of fruits, arranged in layers.
The count on the lowest layer is usually less than that of the top layers.

Counts:
6-lb (2.7-kg) baskets = 44 pieces 4 × 4
                      = 55 pieces 4 × 5
                      = 65 pieces 5 × 5.
24-lb (10.8-kg) lug = 176 pieces 4 × 4
                      = 220 pieces 4 × 5
                      = 260 pieces 5 × 5.

Sizes:
Extra Extra Jumbo: 6 per lb (450 g).
Extra Jumbo: 8 per lb (450 g).
Jumbo: 10 per lb (450 g).
Large: 12 per lb (450 g).
Medium: 14 per lb (450 g).

Kitchen Yields
8 to 10 large fruits yield 3 cups sliced.
3 large fruits yield 1 cup sliced.
1 lb (450 g) large fruits yield ⁵⁄₆ servings.

Serving size:
½ cup, sliced.

Calories:
Three large apricots, or 4 oz (112 g) = 55 Calories.

FROZEN APRICOTS
Available are apricot halves packed in sugar.

Pack:
Six 6½-lb (2.9-kg) cans; 25-lb (11.1-kg) cans; 30-lb (13.5-kg) cans.

Kitchen Yields

Serving size:
½ cup (0.12 l) cooked; one 30-lb (13.5-kg) can yields 100 servings.

Pie:
One 30-lb (13.5-kg) can yields eighteen 9-in-diameter pies.

APRICOT GLAZE
Baking glaze used for Danish and other products.

Pack:
Six #10 cans.

Kitchen Yields
One #10 can will glaze 300 large Danish pastries, brushed on.

APRICOT NECTAR
Sweetened apricot juice, available canned.

Pack:
Twelve 46-oz (1.33-l) cans; forty-eight 5½-oz (0.160-l) cans.

Kitchen Yields

Serving size:
5½ oz (0.160 l); one 46-oz (1.3-l) can yields 8 servings.

ARTICHOKES

Bulb or globe artichokes are available canned, fresh, and frozen.

CANNED ARTICHOKES

Available are bottoms, hearts, and pieces in brine.

Packs:
Bottoms: Twenty-four 14-oz (400-g) cans.
Hearts: Twenty-four 14-oz (400-g) cans; six #10 cans.
Pieces: Six #10 cans.
Other packs are available.

Counts:
Bottoms: One 14-oz (400-g) can may yield a count of 5 to 7, 6 to 9, or 8 to 10.
Hearts: One 14-oz (400-g) can may yield a count of 8 to 10 or 14 to 16; one #10 can may yield a count of 90 to 100 or 110 to 120.
Pieces: One #10 can may yield a count of 180 to 200.

Kitchen Yields

Serving sizes:
One filled bottom as garnish; four to five pieces (120-count) of hearts as appetizer. One #10 can of 120-count hearts yields 24 to 26 servings; thus, one case of #10 cans of 120-count hearts yields 150 servings.

FRESH ARTICHOKES

Fresh artichokes are purchased by weight and count.

Season:
November through March; June through October. Imports are available year-round.

Pack:
20- and 25-lb (9.0- and 11.35-kg) boxes.

Counts:
18, 24, 36, 48, and 60. Small loose artichokes without counts are available by weight. The count is applicable to both size boxes.

Sizes:

Small:
Less than 2 in (50 mm) across.

Medium:
36 size: 10 oz (280 g) each,
48 size: 8 oz (225 g) each.

Large:
18 size: 20 oz (560 g) each,
24 size: 15 oz (420 g) each.

Serving sizes:
Whole artichoke served as appetizer—18 or 24 size.
Bottom for stuffing—24 size, with 2½-in (63-mm) diameter when peeled and cleaned.

Calories:
One 24 size, plain = 31 Calories.

FROZEN ARTICHOKES

Available as hearts and quarters.

Pack:
Twelve 2-lb (0.90-kg) boxes.

Sizes:
Vary, there is no count.

Kitchen Yields
Product is fully cooked and there is no waste.

MARINATED ARTICHOKE HEARTS

Ready-to-serve product is available imported and from domestic producers.

Pack:
Six ½-gal (1.9-l) jars. Other packs are also available.

Count:
85 to 105 pieces.

Kitchen Yields

Serving size:
Appetizer portion is 4 to 5 pieces each. One ½-gal jar yields 20 to 22 portions; one case yields 120 portions.

ASIAN PEARS

See Ottahitia Apples.

ASPARAGUS

Available canned, fresh, and frozen.

CANNED ASPARAGUS

Available are green asparagus and white asparagus in stalks, cuts, and bottom cuts. Canned green asparagus has lost importance in foodservice, because fresh and frozen asparagus are readily available.

Inexpensive white asparagus is imported from the Orient. Jumbo-size white asparagus is imported from Europe and is considered a luxury item.

GREEN ASPARAGUS

Pack:
Twenty-four #303 cans; twenty-four #2 cans; six #10 cans.

Drained weight:
#303 can contains 9 to 10 oz (250 to 280 g).
#2 can contains 11½ to 13½ oz (322 to 378 g).
#10 can contains 60 to 64 oz (1.68 to 1.79 kg).

Serving size:
½ cup, about 4 oz (112 g) spears or pieces.

Kitchen Yields
One #303 can yields 2½ servings, drained weight.
One #2 can yields 3 servings, drained weight.
One #10 can yields 16 servings, drained weight.

INEXPENSIVE WHITE ASPARAGUS

Pack:
Six 64½-oz (1.80-kg) cans.

Counts:
40 to 60, 60 to 80, 80 to 100 count.

Kitchen Yields

Serving size:
As appetizer, 4 pieces of 40 or 60 count. Other serving sizes depend on operational needs. One can yields 12 to 15 servings.

FRESH ASPARAGUS

BABY ASPARAGUS
See Baby Vegetables.

GREEN ASPARAGUS
Green asparagus is very popular. The yield varies greatly, because the stem ends of the stalks get tougher as the season progresses. At the beginning of the season, almost the whole stems can be eaten; toward the end, about half must be discarded.

Season:
Peak is March to June, and again October to November. Green asparagus is available almost year-round. Some asparagus is imported.

Pack:
30-lb (13.5-kg) 12-bunch pyramid crates;
15-lb (6.75-kg) 6-bunch crates;
27-lb (12.1-kg) loose pack pyramid crates;
13½-lb (6-kg) loose pack half pyramid crates;
24- to 25-lb (10.8- to 11.25-kg) cartons.
Other packs are also available.
Bunches can weigh 1, 2, or 2½ lb (450, 900, or 1120 g).

Sizes:
The names indicating size vary according to growing regions. The most recognized names are Colossal, Jumbo, Large, Medium, Small, and Pencil (or Grass). Table A-4 lists sizes and counts of fresh asparagus.

Kitchen Yields

Serving sizes:
For appetizer portion:

Table A-4 Sizes and Counts of Fresh Green Asparagus

Grade or Name	# of Spears per lb (450 g)	# of Spears per Case
Colossal	7 or 8	30 lb (13.5 kg) = 225 to 235 15 lb (6.75 kg) = 110
Jumbo	8 to 9	30 lb (13.5 kg) = 260 12 lb (5.4 kg) = 100
Large	9 to 10	30 lb (13.5 kg) = 300 12 lb (5.4 kg) = 112
Medium	10 to 12	30 lb (13.5 kg) = 350 15 lb (6.75 kg) = 175
Small	12 to 14	30 lb (13.5 kg) = 390 15 lb (6.75 kg) = 190
Pencil or Grass	14 to 16	30 lb (13.5 kg) = 450 12 lb (5.4 kg) = 180
Grass	26 to 28	30 lb (13.5 kg) = 800

Jumbo or Large:
5 to 6 spears at beginning of season; 6 to 8 spears at end of season.
At beginning of season, one 30-lb (13.5-kg) case yields 50 servings; thus, one 15-lb (6.7-kg) half-case yields 25 servings.
At end of season, one 30-lb (13.5-kg) case yields 40 servings; thus, one 15-lb (6.7-kg) half-case yields 20 servings.

Medium or Small:
6 to 7 spears at beginning of season; 7 to 9 spears at end of season.
At beginning of season, one 30-lb (13.5-kg) case yields 45 servings; thus, one 15-lb (6.7-kg) half-case yields 22 servings.
At end of season, one 30-lb (13.5-kg) case yields 45 servings; thus, one 15-lb (6.7-kg) half-case yields 22 servings.

Grass:
12 spears per person, regardless of season.

Serving sizes:
For side order portion in both restaurant and banquet service:

Jumbo or Large:
2 spears, cut in half (4 pieces) at beginning of season, 3 spears at end of season.
At beginning of season, one 30-lb (13.5-kg) case yields 140 servings; thus, one 15-lb (6.7-kg) half-case yields 70 servings.
At end of season, one 30-lb (13.5-kg) case yields 90 servings; thus, one 15-lb (6.7-kg) half-case yields 45 servings.

Medium or Small:
2½ spears, cut in half (5 pieces), at beginning of season; 4 spears at end of season.
At beginning of season, one 30-lb (13.5-kg) case yields 150 servings; thus, one 15-lb (6.7-kg) half-case yields 75 servings.
At end of season, one 30-lb (13.5-kg) case yields 95 servings; thus, one 15-lb (6.7-kg) half-case yields 45 servings.

Grass:
4 to 5 pieces per serving.
At end of season, one 30-lb (13.5-kg) case yields 100 servings; thus, one 15-lb (6.7-kg) half-case yields 55 servings.

NOTE: The above quantities are approximate and depend on the amount of skin removed and the length of stalk discarded.

Calories:
4 medium spears, or 4 oz (112 g) = 20 Calories.

WHITE ASPARAGUS
White asparagus is a specialty item. Some supply is imported. Sizes and pack varies greatly. Very tiny white asparagus is also available. *See* Baby Vegetables.

FROZEN ASPARAGUS
Available as spears in various sizes and as cut pieces. Available as frozen block or IQF.

Pack:
Twelve 2½-lb (1.1-kg) boxes per 30-lb (13.5-kg) case. Bulk packs are also available.

Kitchen Yields
One 2½-lb (1.1-kg) box contains 51 jumbo spears, packed in one direction; 80 randomly packed

medium spears; or cuts and tips, about 1-in long, randomly packed—about 18 percent tips.

Serving sizes (as garnish):
¼ cup, or about 3 jumbo or 4 medium spears.

Jumbo spears:
One 2½-lb (1.1-kg) box yields 14 to 16 servings.

Medium spears:
One 2½-lb (1.1-kg) box yields 18 servings.

Pieces:
One 2½-lb (1.1-kg) box yields 12 servings.

Frozen asparagus equivalent to fresh asparagus:
2½ lb (1.1 kg) frozen = 5 to 5½ lb (2.2 to 2.4 kg) fresh asparagus, as purchased.

ASPIC

Clear meat or fish jelly. Can be made with ready-to-use aspic powder or from scratch.

BEEF ASPIC

Formula
    1 gal and 1 pint (4.2 l) cold beef stock
    2 lb (900 g) lean ground beef
    8 oz (225 g) mirepoix
    1 cup (0.23 l) canned stewed tomatoes
    1 tb peppercorns
    4 oz (112 g) plain gelatin

Kitchen Yields
1 gal (3.8 l) beef aspic.

FISH ASPIC

Formula
    1 gal (3.8 l) fish stock
    1 cup (0.23 l) very dry white wine
    8 oz (225 g) mirepoix without carrots
    1 tb peppercorns
    2 tb white vinegar
    4 oz (112 g) plain gelatin

Kitchen Yields
1 gal (3.8 l) fish aspic.

AVOCADOS

FRESH AVOCADOS
Domestically grown avocados are produced in two areas, California and Florida. Avocados are also imported from other countries.

Varieties:
The two principal varieties are Hass, with a dark green to black, rough and leathery skin (Alligator Pear), and Fuerte, with a thin, pliable skin. About 90 percent of production are the Hass variety. Avocado leaves have become available as a flavoring agent when steaming food.

For avocado oil, *see* Oils.

Season:
Hass avocados peak from May to November, Fuerte in fall and winter. California produces year-round, while Florida varieties are harvested from late June through February, peaking in October.

When ordering, specify ripe or green, though this is no guarantee that fruits will be perfectly ripe. Fruit will continue to ripen at kitchen temperature.

Avocados ripen at a temperature of around 70°F. They do not fully ripen on trees. Store ripe California avocados at 38 to 44°F, Florida avocados at 50 to 55°F. Some produce is ripened with ethylene gas.

Packs:
12½-lb (5.6-kg) flats with one single layer of fruit, mostly from Florida.
25-lb (11.35-kg) lugs with two layers of fruit, mostly from California.

Counts:
9, 12, 14, 16, 18, 20, 24, 30, and 35 fruits per flat. 18, 20, 24, 28, 32, 36, 40, 48, 60, 70, 84, and 96 fruits per lug.
Most common sizes used in hotels are 12-, 14-, 16-count flats. Larger avocados, some weighing 1 lb (450 g) or more, come to the market frequently. Table A-5 lists information on average sizes and yields per carton.

Kitchen Yields
One and one-half #36 avocados or one #14 avocado yield 1 cup pulp.

Table A-5 Avocado Sizes and Average Yields

Count Double Carton	Count Single Carton	Average Weight per Fruit	Average Fresh Pulp per Fruit	Average Fresh Pulp Yield per Double Carton	Average Fresh Pulp Yield per Single Carton
70	35	5¾ oz (165 g)	3½ oz (100 g)	15⅓ lb (6.9 kg)	7½ lb (3.4 kg)
60	30	6¾ oz (190 g)	3⅜ oz (112 g)	12⅓ lb (5.6 kg)	6¼ lb (2.8 kg)
48	24	8½ oz (240 g)	4½ oz (125 g)	13½ lb (6.1 kg)	6¾ lb (3.0 kg)
40	20	10½ oz (290 g)	5¼ oz (145 g)	13 lb (5.9 kg)	6½ lb (2.9 kg)
36		11 oz (312 g)	6½ oz (185 g)	14¾ lb (6.6 kg)	

Two #48 avocados or one #12 avocado yield 1 cup diced. Twenty to twenty-four #36 avocados *or* twenty-three to twenty-six #40 avocados *or* twenty-eight to thirty-two #48 avocados yield 1 gal pulp. Table A-6 lists pulp yields of Hass variety avocados.

Calories:
3½ oz (100 g) pulp = 177 Calories.
One-half avocado weighing 10½ oz (300 g) whole = 185 Calories.

FROZEN PROCESSED AVOCADO
Frozen processed avocado is available in the following forms:

> Plain
> Dip
> Sauce
> Guacamole
> Hot'n spicy guacamole
> Western-style guacamole

This product is normally frozen.

Packs:
Twelve 1-lb (450-g) cans; six #10 cans; one 25-lb (11.255-kg) tub; 100 individual 1-oz (28-g) guacamole packets; eight ½-gal (1.8-l) containers avocado sauce.

Kitchen Yields

Serving size:
2 oz (56 g) per sandwich or as topping, or 4 oz (112 g) dip per person. Therefore, one 1-lb (450-g) can yields 8 servings topping or 4 servings dip, and one #10 can weighing 104 oz (2.91 kg) yields 50 portions topping or 24 portions dip.

Calories:
Sauce weighing 2 oz (56 g) = 80 Calories.
Pulp weighing 2 oz (56 g) = 100 Calories.
Guacamole weighing 4 oz (112 g) = 240 Calories.

Table A-6 Pulp Yields of Hass Variety Avocados

Count per Carton	Weight per Fruit	Pulp Yield per Fruit	Pulp Yield per Carton
84	4½ oz (126 g)	3½ oz (100 g)	18¼ lb (8.2 kg)
50	6¾ oz (191 g)	5 oz (142 g)	18¾ lb (8.4 kg)
48	8½ oz (241 g)	6⅓ oz (178 g)	18¾ lb (8.4 kg)
40	10½ oz (298 g)	7⅝ oz (225 g)	19½ kg (8.7 kg)

B

BABY VEGETABLES

Many types of fresh baby vegetables are on the market.

BABY ARTICHOKES

Season:
March through May.

Pack:
By weight.

Kitchen Yields
Very little waste. Only the outside leaves are peeled off.

BABY WHITE ASPARAGUS

Season:
Available year-round.

Size:
200 pieces per 1 lb (450 g).

Pack:
4-lb (1.8-kg) carton.

Kitchen Yields
No waste; use as is.

BABY AVOCADOS
Also known as *cocktail avocados* or *cukes*.

Season:
Available year-round, but supply is spotty.

Pack:
By weight; 10-lb (4.5-kg) pack is common.

Size:
About 1 × 3 in (25 × 75 mm), oval-shaped.

Kitchen Yields
Fruit is seedless or has soft pit; it can be eaten whole.

BABY BEETS
Available in red and gold varieties.

Season:
Available year-round.

Pack:
Bunches; count varies.

Kitchen Yields
Discard large leaves and serve whole. Do not peel.

BABY BOK CHOY

Season:
Fall and winter.

Pack:
Purchase by weight.

Size:
1½ oz (40 g) each, but size can vary.

Kitchen Yields
Vegetable is edible as is. There is no waste.

BABY BRUSSELS SPROUTS

Season:
Fall and winter.

Pack:
By weight.

Kitchen Yields
Very little waste. Count varies greatly. About ten servings per 1 lb (450 g).

BABY CARROTS
Available are long, round, and white baby carrots. They are very sweet.

Season:
Available year-round.

Pack:
Twenty-four bunches per case.

Kitchen Yields
Eight to ten baby carrots per bunch. Some green top should be left on to increase yield and eye appeal. Peeling of vegetable is not necessary.

Serving size:
Three to four pieces; 24 bunches yields 60 servings. On average, 14 bunches produce 3 lb (1.35 kg)

cleaned, with most green trimmed off. 1 case contains 4½ to 5 lb (2 to 2.2 kg).

BABY CAULIFLOWER

Season:
Fall and winter.

Pack:
By weight.

Kitchen Yields
Use as is, little waste. Do not trim off greens.

BABY CORN

Small hybrid corn available white and yellow. It is fully grown when harvested.

Season:
Summer.

Pack:
By weight, usually 100 per case.

Kitchen Yields
Husk must be removed before cooking. Weight loss is about 15 percent.

BABY CORN, CANNED

See Canned Corn, under Corn.

BABY EGGPLANTS

Available purple and white. Shape may be round or elongated.

Pack:
By weight.

Kitchen Yields
Sizes vary greatly. Common size are five pieces per 1 lb (450 g). Whole vegetables can be used. Baby eggplants are sometimes bitter and should be soaked in salt water to remove bitterness.

BABY LEEKS

Season:
Available year-round.

Pack:
By weight.

Kitchen Yields
There is no waste. Common sizes are 10 to 16 pieces per 1 lb (450 g).

BABY RADISHES

Season:
Available year-round.

Pack:
Bunches; count varies.

Kitchen Yields
Vegetable can be very pungent. Serve raw as garnish.

BABY SPINACH

Tiny spinach leaves.

Season:
Available year-round.

Size:
About 1 to 2 in (25 to 50 mm) long.

Pack:
Fully cleaned in 8-oz (225-g) bags; with roots in 2- or 3-lb (900- or 1.3-kg) boxes.

Kitchen Yields
Fully cleaned product is very light and there is no waste. Baby spinach with roots must be trimmed and washed.

BABY SQUASH

Many varieties are available, some with their flowers still attached.

BABY PATTY PAN SQUASH

Season:
Summer.

Pack:
By weight.

Count:
36 to 39 pieces per 1 lb (450 g).

BABY SCALLOP SQUASH

BABY SCALLOP SQUASH

A cross between zucchini and scallop squash. Available in yellow and green. Not to be confused with ornamental squash.

Season:
From May to October.

Pack:
By weight.

Kitchen Yields
Whole vegetable can be used without cleaning waste. About 20 pieces per 1 lb (450 g).

BABY TOMATOES
Available in red and yellow, round or pear-shaped.

Season:
Available year-round. Peak is in summer.

Pack:
By weight or volume.

Kitchen Yields
About fifteen pieces per 1 pint (0.47 l), but sizes vary.

BABY TOMATOES, SWEET 100'S
Small, sweet tomatoes.

Pack:
Eight 1-pint (0.47-l) baskets.

BABY ZUCCHINI
Often sold with flowers still attached.

Season:
Available year-round; peak is in summer.

Pack:
By weight.

Kitchen Yields
Size varies greatly. Average count is 15 pieces per 1 lb (450 g).

BACALAO

See Smoked and Cured Fish, under Fish.

BACON

See Pork Products, cured and smoked.

BAGELS

Baked item of Jewish origin. There are two basic varieties:

> *Water bagels:* They have a crisp crust and chewy texture.
> *Egg bagels:* They have a softer texture.

Both varieties are sold in different flavors and with different seed or onion toppings.

Pack:
Available fresh and frozen, normally by the dozen.

Sizes:
Common size is 3 in (85 mm) in diameter.

Weight:
4 oz (112 g).
Miniature bagels for receptions are also available fresh and frozen.

Kitchen Yields

Serving size:
Bagels are often served with cream cheese. Calculate 2 oz (56 g) cream cheese per serving; thus, one 3-lb (1.35-kg) loaf of cream cheese yields 24 servings.

Calories:
One water bagel: 2 oz (56 g) = 165 Calories.
One egg bagel: 2 oz (56 g) = 165 Calories.

BAMBOO SHOOTS

Available canned, packed in water. Fresh bamboo shoots are occasionally available at ethnic markets. The canned product is marketed in slices and whole.

Pack:
Forty-eight 15-oz (425-g) cans; forty-eight 19-oz (540-g) cans; twenty-four #2½ cans; six #10 cans.

Kitchen Yields

One 15-oz (425-g) can contains 8½ oz (240 g), drained weight.

One 19-oz (540-g) can contains 10½ oz (300 g), drained weight.

One #2½ can contains 18 oz (500 g), drained weight.

One #10 can contains 65 oz (1.8 kg), drained weight.

One #2½ can yields about 3 cups sliced; and one #10 can yields about 11 cups sliced.

BANANAS

Available, dehydrated, fresh, and as processed pulp.

DEHYDRATED BANANAS

Available as toasted chips with various flavors. Serve as snacks.

Pack:
By weight.

Kitchen Yields
Used as snacks.

FRESH BANANAS

Bananas are shipped green and are ripened with ethylene gas. US#1 is normally purchased for food-service. There are many other varieties and sizes available in ethnic food markets. Organic bananas are not gassed.

Season:
Available year-round. Peak is in summer.

Pack:
40-lb (18-kg) cartons.

Sizes:
100 to 150 count. Average count is 115 bananas per carton. The 150-count is called *Petite*.

Kitchen Yields
1 lb (450 g) yields 12 oz (340 g) peeled.
One medium banana yields 1 cup sliced, or 4½ oz (126 g).

Calories:
One peeled medium banana weighing 4½ oz (126 g) = 100 Calories.

FINGER BANANAS (MANZANITA BANANAS)
Small bananas are often called *finger bananas*.

Season:
Available year-round. Peak is in summer.

Pack:
By weight.

Size:
1 hand = 12 to 14 oz (340 to 400 g).

Count:
10 to 12 bananas.

PROCESSED BANANAS
Available in polyester bags and cans.

Pack:
Six #10 cans, containing 4.8 gal (18.09 l); individual 5-gal (19-l) bags.

Kitchen Yields
One #10 can contains 13 cups (3.01 l) or 6½ lb (3.37 kg), or the pulp of 24 medium-sized bananas.
Six #10 cans contain 39 lb (17.5 kg), or the pulp of 144 medium-sized bananas.
One 5-gal (19-l) bag contains 40 lb (18 kg), or the pulp of 145 medium-sized bananas.

BARLEY

Dry barley is used in soups and stews.

Pack:
Twenty-four 1-lb (450-g) boxes. Larger packs are available, normally individual 25-lb (11.25-kg) bags.

Kitchen Yields
1 cup, uncooked, weighs 7 oz (200 g).
½ cup, uncooked, yields garnish for 1¼ gal (4.75 l) soup.

Calories:

1 cup, weighing 7 oz (225 g), uncooked = 700 Calories.

BASIL

See Herbs & Spices.

BAY LEAVES

See Herbs & Spices.

BEAN CURD

Bean curd, commonly called *tofu* (its Japanese name), is a soybean product with a custard-like consistency. It is available in many shapes, flavors, and grades of firmness. Firm tofu is also called *Chinese-style tofu*. It is most likely to be sold in moist squares of various sizes, stored in brine.

Pack:

Twelve 20-oz (560-g) packages.

Kitchen Yields

1 lb (450 g) firm tofu equals: 2¾ cups, cut in cubes; 2 cups, crumbled and mashed; or 1½ cups, squeezed and crumbled.

Calories:

4 oz (112 g) = 114 Calories.

BEANS

Beans are classified as immature and mature. Immature beans—for example, string beans, lima beans, and flageolet beans—are still green when harvested. Mature beans—for example, kidney beans and navy beans—are dry when harvested.

The listing includes canned, dehydrated, fresh, and frozen beans.

CANNED BEANS

FLAGEOLET BEANS

Available imported from Europe, they resemble small lima beans.

Pack:

Twenty-four 15-oz (420-g) cans.

Kitchen Yields

One 15-oz (420-g) can yields 4 servings.

GARBANZO BEANS

Also called *chick peas*. Garbanzos are often classified as peas. They are a popular component of salad bars and the main ingredient of the Middle Eastern dip hummus.

Pack:

Six #10 cans.

Serving size:

½ cup (0.12 l).

Kitchen Yields

One #10 can contains 72 oz (2.02 kg), drained weight, and yields 22 servings.

GREEN BEANS

The most suitable variety for canning is Blue Lake. Canned beans are available whole, cut across, and cut lengthwise. This cut is referred to as *French style*. Green bean purée is also available.

Pack:

Six #10 cans for most varieties. Twenty-four #303 cans for green bean purée.

Sizes:

Extra large, large, medium, and small for both whole and cut beans. French style beans are not graded by size.

Kitchen Yields

Green Beans:

Serving size:

½ cup (0.12 l). One #10 can, drained, weighs between 61 to 66 oz (1.70 to 1.84 kg), and yields 22 servings.

Green Bean Purée:

Serving size:

½ cup, or 4 oz (0.12 l). One #303 can yields 2 cups, or 4 servings.

Calories:
⅔ cup = 15 Calories.

KIDNEY BEANS
Red kidney beans are identified with Mexican dishes and chili con carne. They are also used in salads. Available are light red and dark red beans. A mixture of three beans as salad is also available. Pinto beans belong to the broad group of kidney beans.

Pack:
Six #10 cans. Other packs are available.

Kitchen Yields

Serving size:
½ cup, or 4 oz (0.12 l). One #10 can, drained, weighs about 80 oz (2.2 kg), and yields 19 servings. One case of #10 cans yields 115 servings.

Calories:
½ cup, or 4 oz (127 g) = 115 Calories.

LIMA BEANS

Pack:
Six #10 cans. Other packs are available.

Sizes:
Tiny, small, medium, and large.

Kitchen Yields

Serving size:
½ cup (0.12 l) cooked beans. One #10 can weighs 70 oz (2 kg), drained, and yields 22 servings.

Calories:
½ cup = 123 Calories.

NAVY BEANS
Available "baked," with meat (such as pork or frankfurters) or without meat. The flavor choices are molasses or tomato sauce. Plain navy beans, flavored only with salt, are also available.

Pack:
Six #10 cans. Other packs are available.

Kitchen Yields

Serving size:
½ cup (0.12 l) cooked beans. One #10 can yields 20 servings; thus, one case of #10 cans yields 120 servings.

Calories:
½ cup baked, with meat and sweet sauce = 192 Calories.
½ cup baked, with pork and tomato sauce = 155 Calories.

WAX BEANS
Available whole and cut.

Pack:
Six #10 cans.

Kitchen Yields

Serving size:
½ cup (0.12 l) cooked beans. 1 can contains 62 oz (1.73 kg), drained, and yields 22 servings. Thus, one case yields 230 servings.

Calories:
½ cup = 15 Calories.

DRIED BEANS

ADZUKI BEANS
Tiny, deep-red, cylindrical beans.

Pack:
Twenty-four 1-lb (450-g) boxes; individual 25-lb (11.25-kg) bags.

BLACK TURTLE BEANS
A staple in South America, often served together with rice. The popular black bean soup is made with black turtle beans.

Pack:
Twenty-four 1-lb (450-g) boxes; individual 25-lb (11.25-kg) bags.

Kitchen Yields
1 lb (450 g) dry measure equals 2⅓ cups (0.5 l).

Serving size:

½ cup (0.12 l) cooked beans. One lb (450 g) yields 10 servings.

Calories:

½ cup cooked beans = 95 Calories.

FAVA BEANS

Large, flat, light brown beans, good in salads and in stews.

Pack:

Twenty-four 1-lb (450-g) boxes; individual 25-lb (11.25-kg) bags.

Kitchen Yields

1 lb (450 g) dry measure equals 2 cups (0.5 l).

Serving size:

½ cup (0.12 l) cooked beans. 1 lb (450 g) yields 9 servings.

Calories:

½ cup cooked beans = 95 Calories.

FLAGEOLET BEANS

Pack:

Twenty-four 1-lb (450-g) boxes; individual 25-lb (11.25-kg) bags.

Kitchen Yields

Serving size:

½ cup (0.12 l) cooked beans. One cup, or 8 oz (225 g), dry is equivalent to 3 cups (0.7 l) cooked, and yields 6 servings. 1 lb (450 g) dry is equivalent to 6 cups (1.4 l) cooked, and yields 12 servings.

Calories:

½ cup cooked beans = 95 Calories.

GARBANZO BEANS

Also called *chick-peas*, *chi-chi beans*.

Pack:

Twenty-four 1-lb (450-g) boxes; individual 25-lb (11.25-kg) bags.

Kitchen Yields

Serving size:

½ cup (0.12 l) cooked beans. One cup, or 8 oz (225 g), dry is equivalent to 3 cups (0.7 l) cooked, and yields 6 servings. 1 lb (450 g) dry is equivalent to 6 cups (1.4 l) cooked, and yields 12 servings.

Calories:

½ cup cooked beans = 100 Calories.

GREAT NORTHERN BEANS

White beans.

Pack:

Twenty-four 1-lb (450-g) boxes; individual 25-lb (11.25-kg) bags.

KIDNEY BEANS

Popular in bean salads and in other dishes. In Mexican cooking, the beans are used as refried beans, called *frijoles refritos*. Pinto beans are also used for refried beans.

Pack:

Twenty-four 1-lb (450-g) boxes; individual 25-lb (11.25-kg) bags.

Kitchen Yields

Serving size:

½ cup (0.12 l) cooked beans. One cup, or 8 oz (225 g), dry is equivalent to 3 cups (0.7 l) cooked, and yields 6 servings. 1 lb (450 g) dry is equivalent to 6 cups (1.4 l) cooked, and yields 12 servings.

Calories:

½ cup cooked beans = 100 Calories.

NOTE: The calorie content of refried beans depends on the amount of fat used.

LIMA BEANS

White, kidney-shaped beans.

Sizes:

Baby lima beans and large lima beans.

Packs:

Twenty-four 1-lb (450-g) boxes; individual 25-lb (11.25-kg) bags.

Kitchen Yields

Serving size:
½ cup (0.12 l) cooked beans. One cup, or 8 oz (225 g), dry is equivalent to 3 cups (0.7 l) cooked, and yields 6 servings. 1 lb (450 g) dry is equivalent to 6 cups (1.4 l) cooked, and yields 12 servings.

Calories:
½ cup cooked beans = 95 Calories.

MUNG BEANS
A staple in China and India, mung beans are available whole, skinned, and split. They are also used as fresh bean sprouts; *see* Sprouts.

NAVY BEANS
Small white bean, often called *Boston bean*. The traditional bean for Boston baked beans.

Pack:
Twenty-four 1-lb (450-g) boxes; individual 25-lb (11.25-kg) bags.

Kitchen Yields

Serving size:
1 cup (0.23 l) baked beans with sauce. 1 cup, or 8 oz (225 g), dry yields 3 servings; thus, 1 lb (450 g) dry yields 6 servings.

Calories:
1 cup cooked, drained, plain = 216 Calories.
1 cup cooked, with pork and tomato sauce = 360 Calories.

PINTO BEANS
Related to the pink beans of Arizona and New Mexico. Pinto beans are also used in Mexican cooking for refried beans.

Pack:
Twenty-four 1-lb (450-g) boxes; individual 25-lb (11.25-kg) bags.

Kitchen Yields

Serving size:
½ cup (0.12 l) cooked beans. One cup, or 8 oz (225 g), dry is equivalent to 3 cups (0.7 l) cooked,

and yields 6 servings. 1 lb (450 g) dry is equivalent to 6 cups (1.4 l) cooked, and yields 12 servings.

Calories:
½ cup cooked beans = 95 Calories.

FRESH BEANS

FAVA BEANS

Season:
Summer and fall.

Pack:
By weight.

Kitchen Yields
Yield varies because quality can be very uneven. Buying fresh is not recommended.

GARBANZO BEANS
Also called *chick peas*.

Season:
Late summer and fall.

Pack:
Twelve 11-oz (312-g) bags, shelled.

Kitchen Yields
No cleaning waste.

GREEN BEANS
Fresh green beans are also called bush or snap beans. They get stale and dry rapidly. A good indication of freshness is if they snap when broken. Green beans no longer have strings.

Season:
Available year-round. Peaks are in summer and fall.

Pack:
26- to 31-lb (11.7- to 13.9-kg) bushel baskets or cartons.

Count:
Varies. Length of beans are no indication of quality.

Kitchen Yields

Serving size:
½ cup (0.12 l).

Trimming loss is about 10 percent. Therefore, 1 lb (450 g) yields 14½ oz (420 g) cleaned or approximately 2½ cups, cooked and cut; this is equivalent to 5 servings. Thus, one bushel weighing 30 lb (13.5 kg) yields 160 servings.

Calories:
½ cup, or 2¼ oz (62 g) = 14 Calories.

HARICOTS VERTS
French name for green beans. Very tiny beans, usually imported, are marketed under this name.

Pack:
9-lb (4-kg) case.

Kitchen Yields
When merchandise is fresh, there is little cleaning waste.

Serving size:
2 oz (112 g). One case yields 70 servings.

LIMA BEANS
Fresh lima beans are seldom used in foodservice.

Season:
July to December.

Pack:

Whole:
26- to 31-lb (11.7- to 13.9-kg) hampers. Other packs are available.

Shelled:
Twelve 11-oz (312-g) bags.

Kitchen Yields

Serving size:
½ cup (0.12 l) cooked beans. 1 lb (450 g) beans in pod produces 6 oz (170 g) shelled beans, and yields 2 servings. 20 lb (9.1 kg) beans in pod produce 7½ lb (3.3 kg) shelled beans, and yield 20 servings. 1 lb (450 g) shelled beans yields 5 servings; and 10 lb (4.5 kg) shelled beans yield 50 servings.

Calories:
½ cup = 85 Calories.

PINTO BEANS
Available already shelled.

Season:
July to December.

Pack:
Twelve 11-oz (312-g) bags.

Kitchen Yields

Serving size:
½ cup (0.12 l) cooked beans. 1 lb (450 g) yields 5 servings; and 10 lb (4.5 kg) yield 50 servings.

Calories:
½ cup = 85 Calories.

WAX BEANS

Season:
Year-round. Peak is in summer and fall.

Pack:
26- to 31-lb (11.7- to 13.9-kg) bushels.

Kitchen Yields

Serving size:
½ cup (0.12 l) cooked beans. 1 lb (450 g) beans as purchased produces 14 oz (400 g) cleaned; and 14 oz (400 g) cleaned produces 11¼ oz (320 g) cooked, which yields 2½ cups.
1 lb (450 g) as purchased yields 5 servings, and 1 bushel weighing 30 lb (13.5 kg) yields 150 portions.

Calories:
½ cup whole = 14 Calories.

FROZEN BEANS

BUTTER BEANS

Pack:
Twelve 3-lb (1.35-kg) boxes.

Kitchen Yields

Serving size:
½ cup cooked beans. One 3-lb (1.35-kg) box yields 13 servings, and one 36-lb (16.2-kg) case yields 150 servings.

Calories:
1 cup, or 4 oz (112 g) = 30 Calories.

GARBANZO BEANS

Pack:
Twelve 2½-lb (1.1-kg) boxes; twelve 3-lb (1.35-kg) boxes.

Kitchen Yields

Serving size:
½ cup (0.11 l) cooked beans.
One 2½-lb (1.1-kg) box yields 13 servings; one 3-lb (1.35-kg) box yields 15 servings.

GREEN BEANS
Blue Lake variety is preferred for frozen beans. Available forms include regular cut, French cut, and whole in various sizes. Most varieties are available frozen in block and IQF.

Pack:
Twelve 2½-lb (1.1-kg) boxes; individual 30-lb (13.5-kg) IQF loose packs.

Kitchen Yields

Serving size:
½ cup (0.12 l) cooked beans. One 2½-lb (1.1-kg) box yields 12 servings; and one 30-lb (13.5-kg) case yields 140 servings.

Calories:
½ cup = 15 Calories.

ITALIAN BEANS

Pack:
Twelve 2½-lb (1.1-kg) boxes.

Kitchen Yields
2½ lb (1.1 kg) frozen is equivalent to 3 lb (1.35 kg) fresh.

Serving size:
½ cup (0.12 l) cooked beans. One 2½-lb (1.1-kg) box yields 12 servings; thus, one 30-lb (13.5-kg) case yields 140 servings.

LIMA BEANS
Two varieties are marketed, baby and fordhook. Baby lima beans are small, have thin skins, and are bright green. Fordhook lima beans are large and plumper, with a thicker skin than Baby lima beans. They have about ⅕ fewer calories than Baby lima beans.

Pack:
Twelve 2½-lb (1.13-kg) boxes.

Kitchen Yields
2½ lb (1.1 kg) frozen lima beans is equivalent to 6½ lb (2.9 kg) fresh beans in pod.

Serving size:
½ cup (0.12 l) cooked Fordhook lima beans or ½ cup (0.12 l) baby lima beans.
One 2½-lb (1.35-kg) box Fordhook limas yields 13 servings; one 2½-lb (1.35-kg) box baby limas yields 12 servings.

Calories:
½ cup, or 3 oz (84 g) Fordhook, cooked, drained = 85 Calories.
½ cup, or 3⅛ oz (90 g) baby limas, cooked, drained = 90 Calories.

WAX BEANS (CUT)

Pack:
Twelve 2-lb (0.9-kg) boxes; twelve 2½-lb (1.1-kg) boxes.

Kitchen Yields

Serving size:
½ cup (0.12 l) cooked beans. One 2-lb (0.9-kg) box yields 10 servings; thus, one case yields 120 servings.
One 2½-lb (1.1-kg) box yields 13 servings; thus, one case yields 150 servings.

Calories:
½ cup = 15 Calories.

BEAN SPROUTS

See Sprouts.

BEAR

Available frozen hind legs and loins.

Average sizes:

Hind Legs:
8 to 10 lb (3.6 to 4.5 kg).

Loins:
6 to 7 lb (2.7 to 3.1 kg), bone in.

Kitchen Yields
Basically the same as well-done beef.

BEEF

Beef is graded by the USDA at request of the packer. The grades of interest to foodservice operators are: Prime, Choice, Good, Select, and Standard. Much ungraded beef reaches the market and is sold under brand names. The USDA grade is applied with a roller stamp and ungraded beef is sometimes referred to as "no roll beef."

Weight is one criteria of the grading process, and a number of cuts are available only in Prime or Choice in a specific weight range. Other grading criteria are marbling and configuration, which determines yield. There is demand for leaner beef, and the grading criteria concerning marbling is undergoing periodic revisions.

Most beef shipped is packed in Cryovac wrapping and boxed. Fresh beef is about 10 days old when it reaches the market. It can be used without additional aging. Some purveyors dry age strips and ribs on request.

Black Angus is a brand name for a special breed of cattle.

Limousin Beef is a race of large cattle imported from France and now bred in the U.S.; the meat is leaner than U.S. Choice, and is therefore not graded.

Kobe beef comes from pampered cattle raised on a special diet. Massage is used to distribute the fat evenly. A very tiny amount is imported and available from specialty purveyors. It is very expensive.

Besides a description of the various cuts, the following subentries include the *Meat Buyers Guide* (MBG) numbers for further identification.

LARGER CUTS OF BEEF

BLADE MEAT, MBG #109B
Also called *deckel meat* or *corner pieces*. This boneless cut is situated over the shoulder end of the primal rib and is removed when the rib is prepared for roasting.

Pack:
By weight.

Size:
2½ lb (1.1 kg).

Best uses:
Stew meat.

Kitchen Yields
Trimming loss of 5 percent.

BONES, MARROW
Marrow bones are from the round and are very hard. They are purchased primarily to extract the marrow. There is little flavor in the bones.

Pack:
By weight.

Kitchen Yields
50 lb (22.6 kg) bones yield 10 to 12 lb (4.5 to 5.4 lb) marrow; 50 lb (22.6 kg) bones make 10 gal (38 l) clear stock.

BONES, SHIN, AND BACK
The best bones for making stock are back bones or neck bones.

Pack:
By weight.

Kitchen Yields
50 lb (22.6 kg) bones make 5½ gal (20.9 l) brown stock; 50 lb (22.6 kg) bones make 3 gal (11.4 l) brown sauce.

BOTTOM ROUND, GOOSE NECK, MBG #170
Muscle inside the leg, called the *round*. This piece consists of the outside round and eye round. It also contains the heel muscle, which can only be used for stew. If this piece cannot be used, specify #170A.

Weight range:
18 to 29 lb (8.1 to 13 kg).

Best sizes:
26 to 29 lb (11.7 to 13 kg).

Best uses:
Roasted, stew, braised steaks.

Sample Kitchen Yields

Purchased weight:

Choice:
22 lb (9.9 kg).

Waste and trim:

Fat:
1 lb (450 g).

Usable trim:
3½ lb (1.5 kg).

Usable meat:
17½ lb (7.8 kg). One piece yields forty 6-oz (170-g) steaks for braising.

Roasted whole:
13½ lb (6 kg).

BOTTOM SIRLOIN BUTT, MBG #185
Tender muscle at the end of the short loin.

Weight range:
4 to 10 lb (1.8 to 4.5 kg).

Best weight:
8 lb (3.6 kg).

Best uses:
Roasted whole, steaks, cut in julienne and sautéed.

Sample Kitchen Yields

Purchased weight:

Choice:
8 lb (3.6 kg).

Waste and trim:

Fat:
8 oz (225 g).

Usable trim:
8 oz (225 g).

Usable meat:
7 lb (3.1 kg).

BRISKET, FRESH, MBG #120
This piece has the deckel meat already removed; however, it is still a rather wasteful piece.

Weight range:
6 to 12 lb (2.7 to 5.4 kg).

Best sizes:
10 to 12 lb (4.5 to 5.4 kg).

Best uses:
For boiling or braising. It is often corned.

Sample Kitchen Yields

Purchased weight:

Choice:
12 lb (5.4 kg).

Cooked weight:
8½ lb (3.8 kg).

Fat trim after cooking:
2¼ lb (1.0 kg).

Usable cooked meat:
6¼ lb (2.8 kg).

Serving size:
5 oz (140 g) for main course; a 12-lb (5.4-kg) piece, after cooking, yields 19 servings.

CHUCK ROLL, MBG #116A
Boneless, netted muscle from the inside of the shoulder. Tender and juicy meat for braising, can be fatty and fall apart after cooking Portion size hard to control, because muscle configuration is uneven.

Weight range:
13 to 25 lb (5.8 to 11.25 kg).

Best weight:
13 to 15 lb (5.8 to 6.7 kg).

Best uses:
Braise or roast.

Sample Kitchen Yields

Purchased weight:

Choice:
14 lb (6.3 kg).

Weight after braising:
9½ lb (2.9 kg).

Serving size:
4 oz (112 g). One manually-cut piece yields 32 servings.

CHUCK, BONELESS, SQUARE CUT, MBG #115

Boneless, whole shoulder. The shoulder clod, a large outside muscle weighing between 13 and 18 lb (5.8 to 8.1 kg), should be removed and used for braising If this piece is not needed, Chuck, MBG #116, should be specified. The remaining meat is best used as ground meat.

The fat content of ground meat should be approximately 20 percent of weight. It is best to weigh trimmings and lean before grinding. A fat-testing machine is inexpensive and easy to use.

Weight range:
55 to 90 lb (24.7 to 40.5 kg).

Best size:
65 to 85 lb (29.2 to 38.2 kg).

Best uses:
Ground meat, clod for roasting or braising.

Sample Kitchen Yields

Purchased weight:

Choice:
75 lb (33.8 kg).

Weight:
After clod has been removed, 59 lb (26.5 kg).

Waste and trim:
3 lb (1.35 kg).

Usable meat:
56 lb (25.2 kg) ground meat.

Serving size:
4 oz (112 g), with a total yield of 220 servings.

CLARIFICATION MEAT

When butchering is done in-house, the trimmings from tenderloins and other cuts can be used. They should be ground through the largest diameter plate of meat grinder. If meat for clarification is purchased, it should be as lean as possible. Shin meat is best for this purpose.

Kitchen Yields
Use 20 lb (9 kg) meat with 10 gal (38 l) stock to make 8 gal (30 l) consommé.

Formula for beef consommé is given under Soups.

DECKEL MEAT

See Blade Meat under this subheading.

EYE ROUND, MBG #171C

Evenly-shaped muscle inside the bottom round. Piece is often used for pot roast or for cutting braised steaks. The meat is rather dry.

Weight range:
3 to 6 lb (1.3 to 2.7 kg).

Best weight:
5 to 6 lb (2.2 to 2.7 kg).

Best uses:
Braised whole, braised steaks, or corned.

Sample Kitchen Yields

Purchased weight:

Choice:
6 lb (2.7 kg).

Waste and trim:

Fat:
6 oz (170 g).

Usable trim:
6 oz (170 g).

Usable meat:
5 lb 4 oz (2.25 kg).

Serving size:
4 oz (112 g) whole braised; thus, the total yield is 20 servings. If the round is cut into 6 oz (170 g) braising steaks, the total yield is 12 servings.

FILET TIPS
Also called *tails*, they are the pieces left when filet mignon is cut.

Pack:
By weight.

Weight range:
6 to 7 oz (170 to 200 g).

Best use:
Cut in strips or small slices and sauté quickly to order.

Sample Kitchen Yields
10 lb (4.5 kg) yield 9 lb (4 kg) usable meat.

Waste fat:
10 percent.

Serving size:
4 to 6 oz (112 to 170 g); 9 lb (4 kg) of usable meat provides 27 servings of 5 oz (140 g) each.

FLANK STEAKS, MBG #193
Skinned flat muscle from the belly.

Weight ranges:
1 to 1½ lb (0.4 to 0.6 kg);
2 to 2¾ lb (0.9 to 1.2 kg).

Best size:
2 to 2½ lb (0.9 to 1.2 kg).

Best use:
London broil.

Sample Kitchen Yields

Purchased weight:
2½ lb (1.2 kg).

Waste fat:
3 oz (80 g).

Usable meat:
2 lb 5 oz (1.1 kg).

Serving size:
5 oz (140 g) cooked meat. Thus, total yield of one piece is 5 servings.

GOOSENECK BOTTOM ROUND
See Bottom Round.

HAMBURGER MEAT, MBG #136
Fat content can be specified. Most common is 80 percent lean and 20 percent fat. The cut can be specified as well, and the buyer can select from various quality levels. Sirloin and chuck are considered best. Ground meat will oxidize and turn brown quickly after grinding.

Ground meat is available fresh and frozen. Frozen meat looses its juices after cooking.

Weight:
Normally 10-lb (4.5-kg) bags.

Kitchen Yields
Shrinkage varies according to fat content and to how well the meat is cooked. Average shrinkage is one-third by weight when meat is cooked to well-done stage.

Average size:
3 to 6 oz (85 to 170 g).

Typical size:
4 oz (112 g).
One 10-lb (4.5-kg) bag yields forty 4-oz (170-g) patties; thus, 50 lb (22.5 kg) yield two hundred 4-oz (170-g) patties.

Calories:
4 oz (112 g) patty, 80 percent lean = 324 Calories.

KNUCKLE, MBG #167
This tender piece is cut from the leg above the knee.

Weight range:
8 to 15 lb (3.6 to 6.7 kg).

Best size:
14 to 15 lb (6.3 to 6.7 kg).

Best uses:
Pot Roast, stew.

Sample Kitchen Yields

Purchased weight:

Choice:
10 lb (4.5 kg).

Waste and trim:

Fat:
1½ lb (670 g).

Usable trim:
8 oz (225 g).

Usable meat:
8 lb (3.6 kg).

Serving size:
4 oz (112 g) cooked. Thus, a knuckle braised whole yields 23 servings. For stew, the serving size is 4½ oz (127 g) cooked meat, and a knuckle yields 19 servings.

KNUCKLE, MBG #167A
Same piece as #167, but with fat trimmed off. It is referred to as *peeled knuckle.*

Weight range:
6 to 11 lb (2.7 to 4.9 kg).

Best size:
8 to 11 lb (3.6 to 4.9 kg).

Best uses:
Pot roast, stew, roasted whole, kebab, and tartar steak.

Kitchen Yields
Refer to knuckle, MBG #167.

OXTAILS
Make sure pieces are cut at the joints, not random cut with meat saw, because bone splinters will cook free and are a potential eating hazard.

Weight range:
1½ to 2 lb (0.6 to 0.9 kg).

Best size:
1½ to 2 lb (0.6 to 0.9 kg).

Best uses:
Stew and soup.

Sample Kitchen Yields

Purchased weight:
10 lb (4.5 kg).

Waste fat:
6 oz (170 g).

Usable meat:
For stewing, 7 lb 10 oz (3.3 kg); for soup, 3 lb (1.35 kg).

Serving size:
For stew, 10 oz (280 g) raw meat, or about 2 to 4 pieces, with a total yield of 12 servings. For soup, 5 lb (2.2 kg) of tail tips yield 1 gal (3.8 l) clear oxtail consommé.

RIB-EYE ROLL, MBG #112
This is the muscle part of the rib, boneless and completely trimmed.

Weight range:
5 to 12 lb (2.2 to 5.4 kg).

Best weight range:
8 to 10 lb (3.6 to 4.5 kg).

Best uses:
Roast whole or cut into rib-eye steaks.

Sample Kitchen Yields

Purchased weight:
9 lb (4 kg).

Cooked weight:
8 lb (3.6 kg).

Waste and trim:
¼ lb (112 g).

Serving size:
8 oz (225 g) servings, with a total yield of sixteen 8-oz (225-g) or fifteen 9-oz (255-g) steaks.

RIB, OVEN-PREPARED, MBG #107
Prime rib with short ribs and aitch bone removed, but with blade meat still attached.

Weight range:
17 to 28 lb (7.6 to 12.6 kg).

Best size:
20 to 22 lb (9 to 9.9 kg).

Best uses:
Prime rib and standing prime rib.

Sample Kitchen Yields
Oven-prepared rib, MBG #107, has the blade bone and the muscles above and below attached. Oven-ready rib, MBG #109, has the blade bone and muscles removed; these pieces weigh about 3 to 4 lb (1.3 to 1.8 kg). This is important to remember when comparing prices.

Purchased weight:
20 lb (9 kg).

Cooked weight:
16 lb (7.2 kg).

Waste and trim:
2½ lb (1.1 kg) after cooking.

Bones:
2¼ lb (1 kg).

Usable cooked meat:
11¼ lb (5 kg).

Serving size:
For à la carte, 10 oz (340 g) without bones; thus, one piece yields 16 total servings. Banquet serving size is 9 oz (255 g) cooked weight, medium and boneless. One piece yields 20 total servings. Buffet serving size is 6 oz (170 g) cooked weight, medium and boneless. One piece yields 30 total servings.

RIB, OVEN-READY, MBG #109
Prime rib with rib bones in, but aitch bone removed.

Weight range:
14 to 24 lb (6.3 to 9.9 kg).

Best sizes:
18 to 20 lb (8.1 to 9 kg) and 20 to 22 lb (9.9 kg).

Best uses:
Prime rib, standing prime rib.

Kitchen Yields
Yield depends on shrinkage during the roasting process. Normal roasting time is 3½ hours at 325°F. Low temperature roasting increases yield. *See* Rib, MBG #107, for yield information.

RIB, PRIMAL, MBG #103
Whole rib, with short ribs still attached. Few operators purchase the Primal Rib, MBG #103, because it is a heavy, unwieldy piece of meat.

Weight range:
24 to 40 lb (10.8 to 18 kg).

Best size:
33 to 40 lb (14.8 to 18 kg).

Best use:
Roast prime rib.

Kitchen Yields
One rib, MBG #103, weighing 38 lb (17.1 kg) yields one rib, MBG #109, weighing 22 lb (9.0 kg).

RIB, ROAST-READY AND BONELESS, MBG #110
This is a popular specification for banquet operations, because the meat needs little trim after roasting.

Weight range:
11 to 19 lb (4.9 to 8.5 kg).

Best weight:
13 to 16 lb (5.8 to 7.2 kg).

Best use:
Roasted whole.

Sample Kitchen Yields

Purchased weight:
16 lb (7.2 kg).

Cooked weight:
12 lb (5.4 kg).

Waste and trim:
1 lb (450 g) after cooking.

Usable cooked meat:
11 lb (4.9 kg).

Serving size:
For à la carte, 10 oz (340 g) cooked weight, medium; thus, one rib roast yields 16 total servings. Banquet serving size is 8½ oz (240 g)cooked weight, medium (outside cuts are counted as sold); one rib roast yields 20 total servings. Buffet serving size is 6 oz (170 g) cooked weight, medium; one rib roast yields 30 total servings.

ROUND, CHICAGO, MBG #158

Untrimmed Primal Round, with aitch bone and shin attached. This heavy piece needs considerable butchering before it can be used. Roasting time is about 6 hours at 325°F.

Weight range:
25 to 100 lb (26.5 to 45 kg).

Best weight:
80 to 95 lb (36 to 42.7 kg).

Sample Kitchen Yields

Purchased weight:

Choice:
80 lb (36 kg).

Waste and trim:

Fat:
8 lb (3.6 kg).

Usable scraps:
6 lb (2.7 kg).

Bones:
9 lb (4 kg).

Roasting weight:
57 lb (25.6 kg) with handle attached.

Serving size:
Roasted whole, this piece yields one-hundred and fifty 5-oz (140-g) servings on main-course buffet, when other items are served, or two-hundred 3½-oz (100-g) servings for cocktail reception, when other items are served.

ROUND, STEAMSHIP, MBG #160

Partially boneless round, with handle and shank bone removed.

Weight range:
47 to 80 lb (21.2 to 36 kg).

Best weight:
60 to 70 lb (27 to 31.5 kg).

Best use:
Roast whole as steamship round..

Kitchen Yields
Trimming waste before roasting is 5 percent, because the bone must be trimmed and some fat removed.

SHIN MEAT

Weight:
Purchase by weight.

Best uses:
Clarification for consommé, and as stew meat.

Kitchen Yields
When ordering, specify trimmed or untrimmed. When using for consommé, only the superfluous fat has to be removed.

Trimming loss:
For stew meat, 20 percent by weight; 50 lb (22.5 kg) as purchased yield 40 lb (18 kg) usable meat.

Serving size:
For stew, 4 oz cooked; thus, 40 lb (18 kg) meat yield 100 servings.

SHORT RIBS, THREE BONES, MBG #123

Weight:
1 lb (450 g) each.

Best use:
Boiling and braising.

Kitchen Yields
Ready to use; no further trim required.

Serving size:
One 11-oz (312-g) piece, cooked weight, depending on fatness of meat.

SIRLOIN BUTT, MBG #182

The boneless end piece of the loin, with some of the fat, flap piece, and connecting tissues removed. When split, it is separated into the Top Sirloin Butt, MBG #184, and the Bottom Sirloin Butt, MBG #185.

Weight range:
11 to 22 lb (4.9 to 9.9 kg).

Best weights:
18 to 22 lb (8.1 to 9.9 kg).

Best uses:
Steaks, split and roasted, cut in julienne and sautéed if meat is Choice grade and aged.

Kitchen Yields
It is best to purchase the piece split as Top Sirloin Butt, MBG #184, or Bottom Sirloin Butt, MBG #185.

STRIP LOIN, MBG #179
Short-cut strip loin, bone in.

Weight range:
10 to 20 lb (4.5 to 9 kg).

Best weight:
17 to 20 lb (7.6 to 9 kg).

Best uses:
Roast whole or cut into NY-cut shell steaks.

Kitchen Yields
When buying strip loin, the length of flank, which is basically worthless and must be trimmed off, determines usable yield. MBG #175 has a 4-in flank, MBG #177 has a 3-in flank, and #179 has the shortest—only 2-in flank—all measured at the sirloin end.
NOTE: Grade and age influence yield. Prime strips are fattier than Choice. Yield of Prime strips can be reduced by as much as 20 percent. Aged meat requires more trim, but weighs less on account of drying-out during aging.

STRIP LOIN, MBG #180
This is the MBG #179 loin, with bones removed.

Weight range:
8 to 15 lb (3.6 to 6.7 kg).

Best weight:
10 to 12 lb (4.5 to 5.4 kg).

Best uses:
Steaks and roasted whole..

Sample Kitchen Yields
When buying strip loin, the length of flank, which is basically worthless and must be trimmed off, determines usable yield. MBG #176 has a 4-in flank, MBG #178 has a 3-in flank, and MBG #180 has the shortest—only 2-in flank—all measured at the sirloin end.

Purchased weight:

Choice #180:
11 lb (5 kg).

Waste and trim:

Fat:
1 lb (450 g).

Usable scraps:
4 oz (112 g).

Usable meat:
9 lb 12 oz (4.3 kg).

Serving size:
Roasted, 6 oz (170 g) cooked meat, medium; thus, one piece yields 20 servings. Cut into 10-oz (280-g) steaks, one piece yields 12 servings (the nerve end piece is not used).
Note: Grade and age influence yield. Prime strips are fattier than Choice, and the yield might be reduced. Aged meat requires more trim, but weighs less on account of drying-out during aging.

TENDERLOIN, MBG #189
Often referred to as *filet*; it is the full tenderloin with all fat still attached.

Weight range:
5 to 8½ lb (2.2 to 3.8 kg).

Best size:
7 to 8½ lb (3.1 to 3.8 kg).

Best uses:
Roast tenderloin, chateaubriand, and filet mignon.

Sample Kitchen Yields

Purchased weight:
6½ lb (2.9 kg).

Waste and trim:

Fat:
1¾ lb (780 g).

Usable meat:

Defatted, side muscle on:
4¼ lb (2.25 kg).

Trimmed for roasting, side muscle on, head on:
¾ lb (1.7 kg).

Serving size:
Roasted whole, 4½ oz (126 g) cooked meat; one piece yields 8 to 9 servings. When the piece is cut into filet mignon, with side muscle on and head partly used, the following serving sizes and yields are obtained:

      6 oz (170 g) = 8 each,   7 oz (200 g) = 7 each,
      8 oz (225 g) = 6 each,   9 oz (255 g) = 5 each.

Usable tenderloin tips are 10 oz (280 g).

TENDERLOIN, MBG #190
Also referred to as *filet*. This piece is defatted (denuded), with silver skin, wedge fat, and side strip muscle still attached.

Weight range:
3 to 6 lb (1.3 to 2.7 kg).

Best size:
5½ to 6 lb (2.2 to 2.7 kg).

Best uses:
Roasting and filet mignon.

Kitchen Yields
Refer to MBG #189 for yields.

TENDERLOIN, SHORT, MBG #192
When tenderloin is removed from the short loin, it has no butt, also called *head*. The piece is normally sold with natural fat on.

Weight range:
2 to 5 lb (0.9 to 2.2 kg).

Best weight:
4 to 5 lb (1.8 to 2.2 kg).

Best use:
Filet mignon.

Kitchen Yields
The piece is awkward to use, because it renders only 3 to 4 servings of filet mignon; the rest consists of tenderloin tips and fat.

TONGUE, FRESH

Weights:
4 to 5 lb (1.8 to 2.2 kg).

Kitchen Yields

Serving size:
5 oz (140 g); 1 lb (450 g) as purchased produces 9 oz (255 g) cooked and trimmed; therefore, 4½ lb (2 kg) tongue produce 2 lb 9 oz (1.1 kg) cooked and trimmed, or 8 or 9 servings.

TOP ROUND, MBG #168
Also called *inside round*. It is a large muscle, available bone-in and boneless.

Weight range:
14 to 23 lb (6.3 to 10.3 kg).

Best weight:
21 to 23 lb (9.4 to 10.3 kg).

Best use:
Roast whole or split, pot roast, stew, and ground.

Sample Kitchen Yields
Specify boneless round. For roasting whole, purchase smaller rounds in the 15- to 18-lb (6.7- to 8.1-kg) range, or purchase 21- to 23-lb (9.4- to 10.3-kg) rounds, split and netted.

Purchased weight:
17 lb (7.6 kg) boneless.

Waste and trim:

Fat:
8 oz (225 g).

Scraps and trim:
12 oz (340 g).

Roasted weight:
12 lb 4 oz (3.5 kg).

Serving size:
For a sandwich, 4 oz (112 g); therefore, one round yields 46 servings.

TOP SIRLOIN BUTT, MBG #184

Weight range:
7 to 15 lb (3.1 to 6.7 kg).

Best weight:
12 to 15 lb (5.4 to 6.7 kg).

Best uses:
Steaks, roast, ground meat, cut in julienne and sautéed if meat is Choice grade and aged..

Sample Kitchen Yields

Purchased weight:

Choice:
20 lb (9 kg).

Waste and trim:

Fat:
4 lb (1.8 kg).

Usable scraps:
12 oz (225 g).

Usable meat:
15 lb 4 oz (6.9 kg).

POPULAR BEEF DISHES

BRACIOLE
Braciole are stuffed and braised Italian rouladen. The same cuts of meat can also be used for German beef rouladen.

Best cuts:
Bottom Round, MBG #170; or Top Round, MBG #168.

Best weight:

Bottom Round:
26 to 29 lb (11.7 to 13 kg).

Top Round:
21 to 23 lb (9.4 to 10.3 kg).

Eye Round:
5 to 7 lb (2.2 to 3.1 kg).

Kitchen Yields

Serving size:
5 oz (140 g) raw weight; cooked weight depends on weight of stuffing. For untrimmed Top Round, 22 lb (9.9 kg) yield 60 steaks. For Bottom Round, 27 lb (12.1 kg) yield 70 steaks. For Eye Round, 6 lb (2.7 kg) yield 16 steaks.
NOTE: Pieces must be pounded flat in order to achieve yield.

BRAISED STEAK
Best cuts:
Top Round, MBG #168; Bottom Round, MBG #170; Eye Round, MBG #171C.

Best weights:

Top Round:
21 to 23 lb (9.4 to 10.3 kg).

Bottom Round:
26 to 29 lb (11.7 to 13 kg).

Eye Round:
5 to 7 lb (2.2 to 3.1 kg).

Kitchen Yields

Serving size:
6 to 7 oz (170 to 200 g), raw; 4 to 5 oz (112 to 142 g) cooked. For untrimmed Top Round, 22 lb (9.9 kg) yield 40 steaks. For Bottom Round, 27 lb (12.1 kg) yield 50 steaks. For Eye Round, 6 lb (2.7 kg) yield 12 steaks.

Calories:
5 oz (140 g) cooked = 408 Calories.

BRISKET, BARBECUED

Purchase:
Fresh Brisket, MBG #120.

Best sizes:
10 to 12 lb (4.5 to 5.4 kg).

Kitchen Yields
11 lb (4.9 kg) brisket yields 4 lb (1.8 kg) cooked
and well-trimmed meat.

Serving size:
4 oz (112 g) cooked and lean; one brisket yields 16
servings.

Calories:
4 oz (112 g) cooked = 220 Calories.

BRISKET, BOILED

Purchase:
Fresh Brisket, MBG #120.

Best size:

11 to 14 lb (4.9 to 6.3 kg)

Kitchen Yields
1 lb (450 g) as purchased produces 9 oz cooked and
trimmed meat.

Serving size:
4 oz (140 g) cooked and lean; one 12-lb (5.4-kg)
brisket produces 6½ lb (3 kg) cooked and well-
trimmed meat, and yields 22 servings.

Calories:
4 oz (112 g) lean and fat = 326 Calories.

CHATEAUBRIAND

Large tenderloin steak, for two or more servings.
Roast tenderloin of beef is often referred to as
chateaubriand.

Best cut:
Tenderloin, fat on, MBG #189.

Kitchen Yields
Meat tastes better if some fat is left on during the
broiling and roasting process, and peeled away at
service. Normally, the head of the tenderloin is used
for chateaubriand.

Serving size:
10 oz (280 g) per person, including fat.

CHOPPED STEAK
Purchase the following cuts if meat is ground in-
house. (They are listed in order of preference.)

Boneless, Square-Cut Chuck, MBG #115:
65 to 85 lb (29.2 to 38.2 kg).

Top Sirloin Butt, MBG #184:
12 to 15 lb (5.4 to 6.7 kg).

Blade Meat, MBG #109B:
By weight.

Top Round, MBG #168:
14 to 15 lb (6.3 to 6.7 kg).

Corner Pieces:
Somewhat fatty, boneless pieces. Purchase by
weight.

Kitchen Yields

Serving size:
7 to 8 oz (200 to 225 g) raw weight. The following
weights and numbers of servings can be obtained
for these different cuts of beef:

Boneless, Untrimmed Chuck:
75 lb (33.8 kg) yield 140 chopped steaks.

Top Sirloin:
12 lb (5.4 kg) yield 25 chopped steaks.

Blade Meat:
40 lb (18 kg) yield 80 chopped steaks.

Top Round:
15 lb (6.7 kg) yield 30 chopped steaks.

Corner Pieces:
50 lb (22.5 kg) yield 100 chopped steaks.

KEBAB
Also spelled *kebob*. Kebab is also made with lamb.

Best cuts:
Tenderloin tips (pack by weight, 6 to 7 oz; 170 to
200 g); Top Sirloin Butt, MBG #184 (best weight
12 to 15 lb; 5.4 to 6.7 kg); Knuckle, MBG #167A
(best weight 8 to 11 lb; 3.6 to 4.9 kg); or Strip Loin,
MBG #180 (best weight 10 lb; 4.5 kg).

Kitchen Yields

Serving sizes:
5 oz (140 g) for main course; 1½ oz (42 g) for hors
d'oeuvres.

> For untrimmed Tenderloin Tips, 50 lb
> (22.5 kg) yield 130 main-course orders or
> 460 hors d'oeuvres.
> For untrimmed Top Sirloin Butt, 14 lb (6.3 kg)
> yield 35 main-course orders or 120 hors
> d'oeuvres.
> For untrimmed Knuckle, 10 lb (4.5 kg) yield 30
> main-course orders or 100 hors d'oeuvres.
> For Strip Loin, MBG #180, 10 lb (4.5 kg)
> yield 28 main-course orders or 90 hors
> d'oeuvres.

LONDON BROIL

Best cuts:
Flank Steaks, MBG #193 (purchase 2 to 2½ lb; 0.9
to 1.2 kg); Strip Loin, MBG #180 (purchase one
10-lb or 4.5-kg piece); Strip Loin, nerve-end cuts
(best weights are 22 to 24 oz; 625 to 680 g); Top
Sirloin Butt, MBG #184 (purchase 12 to 15 lb; 5.4
to 6.7 kg).

Kitchen Yields

Serving size:
5 oz (140 g) cooked medium rare.

> For flank steak, 2 lb (0.9 kg) yield 4 to 4½
> servings.
> For Strip Loin, MBA #180, 10 lb (4.5 kg)
> yield 20 servings when cut on machine for
> banquets.
> For Sirloin, nerve-end cut, 22 to 24 oz (625 to
> 680 g) yield 3½ servings.

For untrimmed Top Sirloin Butt, 14 lb (6.3 kg)
yield 25 to 26 servings.

Calories:
5 oz (140 g) Choice grade, cooked medium rare =
287 Calories.

NEW YORK-CUT SIRLOIN STEAK
Also called *strip steak* or *sirloin steak*.

Purchase:
Strip Loin, MBG #179, bone in—17 to 20 lb (7.6 to
9 kg) or 14 to 16 lb (6.3 to 7.2 kg)—or Strip Loin,
MBG #180, boneless—10 to 12 lb (4.5 to 5.4 kg).

Kitchen Yields

Serving sizes:
8 to 16 oz (225 to 450 g) for bone-in steak; 7 to
16 oz (200 to 450 g) for boneless steak.

> For Strip Loin, MBA #179, 15 lb (6.7 kg)
> yield 22 bone-in steaks of 10 oz (280 g)
> each, or 15 bone-in steaks of 14 oz (400 g)
> each, or 14 boneless steaks of 10 oz
> (280 g) each, or 9 boneless steaks of 14 oz
> (400 g) each.
> For Strip Loin, MBA #180, 10 lb (4.5 kg)
> yield 9 boneless steaks of 12 oz (340 g)
> each, or 12 boneless steaks of 8 oz (225 g)
> each.

POT ROAST

Best cuts and sizes:
Knuckle, MBG #167 (purchase 14 to 15 lb; 6.3 to
6.7 kg); Bottom Round, Goose Neck, MBG #170
(purchase 26 to 29 lb; 11.7 to 13 kg); Top Round,
MBG #168 (purchase 21 to 23 lb; 9.4 to 10.3 kg);
Chuck Roll, MBG #116A (purchase 13 to 15 lb; 5.8
to 6.7 kg); Eye Round, MBG #171C (purchase 5 to
6 lb; 2.2 to 2.7 kg).

Kitchen Yields
NOTE: Yield varies according to trim and fatness of
meat.

Serving size:
4 oz (112 g) cooked meat.

One 14-lb (6.3-kg) Knuckle yields 24 to 28 servings.

One 27-lb (12.1-kg) Bottom Round, Goose Neck yields 55 servings.

One 21-lb (9.4-kg) boneless Top Round, yields 40 to 45 servings.

One 15-lb (6.7-kg) netted Chuck Roll yields 35 servings.

One 6-lb (2.7-kg) Eye Round yields 16 to 18 servings.

Pot Roast Formula

10 lb (4.5 kg) meat
16 oz (450 g) mirepoix
2 cups (0.47 l) tomato puree
2 to 2¼ qt (1.9 to 2.1 l) cooking liquid
1 pint (0.47 l) dry red wine
4 oz (112 g) corn starch

Kitchen Yields

Serving size:
3 to 4 oz (84 to 112 g) cooked meat, plus 1½ to 2 oz (0.04 to 0.06 l) sauce. Therefore, 10 lb (4.5 kg) trimmed meat yield 30 servings.

Calories:
4 oz (112 g) meat, plus 1½ oz (0.04 l) gravy = 376 Calories.

PRIME RIB OF BEEF

Purchase:
Oven-ready Rib, MBG #109—18 to 20 lb (8.1 to 9 kg) or 20 to 22 lb (9.9 kg)—or boneless Roast-ready Rib, MBG #110—14 to 15 lb (6.3 to 6.7 kg). The Roast-ready Rib is a popular specification for banquet operations, because the meat needs little trim after roasting.

Kitchen Yields

Serving size:
10 oz (280 g) without bone.

One Oven-ready Rib, MBG #109, weighing 20 lb (9.9 kg) yields 20 banquet servings or 16 restaurant servings, if both outside cuts are sold.

One boneless Roast-ready Rib, MBG #110, weighing 14 lb (6.3 kg) yields 20 banquet servings or 30 buffet servings.

RIBS, BARBECUED

Best sizes:
1½ to 2 lb (0.6 to 0.9 kg).

Kitchen Yields
Shrinkage is 25 percent.

Serving size:
1 lb (450 g) cooked. 25 lb (11.25 kg) ribs yield 20 servings.

ROUND ROAST

Purchase:
Top Round, MBG #168—21 to 23 lb (9.4 to 10.3 kg).

Kitchen Yields

Serving sizes:
For cold sandwiches, 4 oz (112 g); for hot main course, 5 to 6 oz (142 to 170 g).
One 18-lb (8.1-kg) trimmed, oven-ready Top Round produces 14 lb (6.3 kg) roasted meat, medium rare. This yields 50 servings of cold sandwiches or 35 servings as hot main course.

Calories:
4 oz (112 g) lean meat = 180 Calories.

SIRLOIN ROAST

Purchase:
Loin, bone in, MBG #179—17 to 20 lb (7.6 to 9 kg) or 14 to 16 lb (6.3 to 7.2 kg)—or Strip Loin, MBG #180—10 to 12 lb (4.5 to 5.4 kg).

Kitchen Yields

Serving size:
For main course, 7 oz (200 g), consisting of 2 slices or 1 thick slice; for buffet, 3½ oz (100 g), consisting of 1 slice.

One Strip Loin, MBG #179, weighing 18 lb (8.1 kg) as purchased, yields 20 main-course servings of 2 slices each or 38 buffet servings.

One Strip Loin, MBG #179, weighing 16 lb (7.2 kg) as purchased, 18 main-course servings of 2 slices each or 34 buffet servings.

One Strip Loin, MBG #180, weighing 10 lb (4.5 kg) as purchased, yields 20 main-course servings of 2 slices each or 38 buffet servings.

TARTAR STEAK

Purchase:

Peeled Knuckle, MBG #167A, weighing 14 lb (6.3 kg); or Bottom Sirloin Ball Tip, MBG #185B, weighing 3 lb (1.35 kg); or Tenderloin, MBG #190A, weighing 4 lb (1.8 kg).

Kitchen Yields

Serving size:

6 oz (170 g) as main course, ½ oz (14 g) for each canapé, or 1½ oz (42 g) on buffets with other choices.

One peeled Knuckle, weighing 10 lb (4.5 kg), produces 7 lb (3.1 kg) clean meat. This yields 18 main-course servings, 220 canapés, or 75 buffet servings.

One Bottom Sirloin Ball Tip, weighing 3 lb (1.35 kg) produces 2½ lb (1.1 kg) clean meat. This yields 6½ main course servings, 80 canapés, or 60 buffet servings.

One Tenderloin, weighing 3 lb (1.35 kg), produces 2 lb 10 oz clean meat. This yields 7 main-course servings, 85 canapés, or 65 buffet servings.

TENDERLOIN ROAST

Purchase:

Tenderloin, with fat, MBG #189—7 to 8½ lb (3.1 to 3.8 kg)—or trimmed Tenderloin, MBG #190—5½ to 6 lb (2.2 to 2.7 kg).

Kitchen Yields

Serving size:

2 slices, or 5 oz (140 g) as main course; 1½ slices, or 3 oz (84 g) as buffet.

One Tenderloin, MBG #189, weighing 7½ lb (3.3 kg) as purchased, yields 8 main-course servings or 12 buffet servings.

One Tenderloin, MBG #190, weighing 5½ lb (2.2 kg) as purchased, yields 8 main-course servings or 12 buffet servings.

One trimmed, oven-ready Tenderloin, weighing 4 lb (1.8 kg), yields 8 main-course servings or 10 buffet servings.

PORTION CUTS OF BEEF

This list is a description of commonly available portion cuts. Additional cuts might be available locally. When ordering, specify frozen or fresh.

Pack:

Varies according to products. All items are sold by both count and weight.

BOTTOM ROUND STEAKS

Rather dry steaks, available in many sizes. Suitable for braising.

Sizes:

From 4 to 24 oz (85 to 680 g) in 2-oz (56-g) increments.

Kitchen Yields

Serving sizes:

4 oz (112 g) for buffets; 6 or 8 oz (170 or 225 g) for lunch; 8 or 10 oz (225 or 280 g) for dinner. Use the 24 oz (680 g) piece as Pot Roast; cut on bias to yield about 3 portions from each piece.

BRAISING STEAKS

Sizes:

4, 6, and 8 oz (112, 170, and 225 g).

Kitchen Yields

Serving sizes:

4 oz (84 g) for buffets; 6 or 8 oz (170 or 225 g) for main course.

CHOPPED STEAKS AND HAMBURGERS

Sizes:

From 1 to 10 oz (28 to 280 g).

Kitchen Yields

Serving sizes:
Varies according to operation.

CUBED STEAKS
Boneless steaks, mechanically tenderized for broiling.

Sizes:
3, 4, 6, and 8 oz (85, 112, 170, and 225 g).

Kitchen Yields
Inexpensive steaks to be cooked to order for sandwiches.

PORTERHOUSE STEAKS
Bone-in steak cut from the short loin. Basically the same as a T-bone steak, but with a larger tenderloin. Available with different trim.

Sizes:
From 10 to 24 oz (280 to 680 g) in 2-oz (56-g) increments.

Kitchen Yields
When ordering steaks, make sure to specify trim clearly.

Serving sizes:
12 to 16 oz (340 to 450 g) for one serving; 20 or 24 oz (568 or 680 g) for two servings.

RIB EYE STEAKS
Boneless steaks cut from the eye of the prime rib. Available with the tail (also called *lip*) left on, or as rib-eye roll steaks with lip removed. Suitable for broiling.

Sizes:
4, 6, 8, 10, and 12 oz (112, 170, 225, 280, and 340 g).

Kitchen Yields

Serving sizes:
6 or 8 oz (170 or 225 g) for lunch; 8, 10, or 12 oz (225, 280, or 340 g) for dinner.

RIB STEAKS, BONE IN
Trimmed steaks with bone in, cut from the prime rib. Suitable for broiling, and great for outdoor barbecues.

Sizes:
8, 10, 12, 14, 16, and 18 oz (225, 280, 340, 400, 450, and 510 g).

Kitchen Yields

Serving sizes:
8 or 10 oz (225 or 280 g) for lunch; 14 or 16 oz (400 or 450 g) for dinner.

STRIP LOIN STEAKS
Also called *sirloin steak* or *New York-cut steak*. Available bone in and bone removed. The length of flank left on steaks varies and should be clearly specified.

Bone-in Steaks:

Sizes:
6, 8, 10, 12, 14, 16, 18,and 20 oz (170, 225, 280, 340, 450, 511, and 568 g).

Kitchen Yields
Make sure the flank length is well specified when ordering. Intermediate size has about 3-in (75-mm) flank, when measured from the eye.

Serving sizes:
6 or 8 oz (170 or 225 g) for breakfast; 10 or 12 oz (280 or 340 g) for lunch; 14 or 16 oz (340 or 450 g) dinner; and 20 oz (568 g) for steak for two.

Boneless Steaks:

Sizes:
8, 10, 12, 14, 16, 18, 20, and 24 oz (225, 280, 340, 450, 511, 568, and 680 g).

Kitchen Yields
Make sure the flank length is well specified when ordering. Intermediate size has about 3-in (75-mm) flank, when measured from the eye.

Serving sizes:
8 oz (225 g) for breakfast; 10 or 12 oz (280 or 340 g) for lunch; 14 or 16 oz (340 or 450 g) dinner; and 20 and 24 oz (568 and 680 g) for steak for two.

Calories:
10 oz (280 g) strip loin steak, lean = 650 Calories.

TENDERLOIN STEAKS

A number of types of trim are available:

Fat on and side muscle on
Defatted with side muscle on
Silver skin on and side muscle removed
Both silver skin and side muscle removed

Sizes:
For most types of trim, 3 to 14 oz (85 to 400 g).

Kitchen Yields
Make sure trim and fat cover is clearly specified when ordering steaks.

Serving sizes:
3 or 4 oz (85 or 112 g) for breakfasts or buffet; 6 or 8 oz (170 or 225 g) for restaurant or banquet service; 10, 12, or 14 oz (280, 340, and 400 g) for steakhouse.

TOP ROUND STEAKS

Suitable for braising, such as Swiss steaks.

Sizes:
3, 4, 6, 8, 10, 12 oz (85, 112, 170, 225, 280, and 340 g).

Kitchen Yields

Serving sizes:
3 oz (84 g) for buffets; 4 oz (112 g) for buffets; 6 or 8 oz (170 or 225 g) for lunch; 8 or 10 oz (225 or 280 g) for dinner.

TOP SIRLOIN BUTT STEAKS

Juicy, tender steaks for broiling. Center cuts are more uniform in shape and have a better trim than end pieces.

Sizes:
4 to 24 oz (112 to 680 g), in 2-oz (56-g) increments.

Kitchen Yields

Serving sizes:
4 and 6 oz (112 to 170 g) for breakfast or lunch; 8 to 12 oz (225 to 340 g) for dinner.
When used as sliced steak, one 18-oz (500-g) piece yields 3 servings, and one 24-oz (680-g) piece yields 4½ servings.

SMOKED AND CURED BEEF PRODUCTS

BÜNDNERFLEISCH

Also called *viande de grison*. Air-dried beef, available imported or domestically produced. Use like prosciutto ham.

Weight:
5 lb (2.2 kg) average.

Kitchen Yields
The product is boneless and there is little waste.

Serving size:
1 oz (28 g). 5-lb (2.2-kg) piece yields 75 servings.

CHIPPED BEEF

Pack:
3 lb (1.35 kg), loose in boxes; 4, 5, and 6 oz (112, 140, and 170 g) in individual bags.

Kitchen Yields

Serving size:
4 oz (112 g).

Calories:
4 oz (112 g), without sauce = 232 Calories.

CORNED BEEF

Available canned, cooked, and raw. Many different cuts and trims are on the market.

BRISKET, COOKED
Fully-cooked briskets, with most fat removed. First-cut is a better trimmed piece.

Weight ranges:

Whole brisket:
5 to 8 lb (2.2 to 3.6 kg).

First-cut:
3 to 5 lb (1.3 to 2.2 kg).

Kitchen Yields
Whole cooked brisket has 5 percent trimming waste; first-cut brisket is fully trimmed and has minimal waste.

BRISKET, UNCOOKED, DELI TRIM AND FLAT-CUT
Some fat has been removed from deli trim briskets. Flat-cut briskets are split along the natural seam separating the two muscles in the brisket.

Weight ranges:

Deli trim:
8 to 13 lb (3.6 to 5.8 kg).

Flat-cut:
3 to 4½ lb (1.3 to 2 kg).

Kitchen Yields
Cooking loss about 40 percent and trimming loss about 5 percent. One 10-lb (4.5-kg) brisket yields 5½ lb (2.5 kg) cooked meat.

BRISKET UNCOOKED, REGULAR TRIM

Weight range:
12 to 14 lb (5.4 to 6.3 kg).

Kitchen Yields
Raw corned briskets are often delivered packed in brine, making it difficult to verify their real weight. The cooking and trimming losses are large.
1 lb (450 g) as purchased yields 7 oz (200 g) cooked, trimmed meat.

Serving size:
5 oz (140 g) as hot deli sandwich; 5 oz (140 g) as main course, served with cabbage.
One 13-lb (5.8-kg) brisket as purchased (drained but wet) produces 5½ lb (1.35 kg) lean, trimmed, cooked meat.
One brisket yields 16 servings for sandwiches or as main course.

Usable trimmings:
8 oz (225 g) from a 13-lb (5.8-kg) brisket, usable for hash.

CORNED BEEF, CANNED

Pack:
Six #10 cans, weighing 6 lb (2.7 kg) each. Other packs are available.

Calories:
4 oz (112 g) = 246 Calories.

CORNED BEEF HASH
Ground, cooked corned beef, mixed with diced cooked potatoes.

Pack:
Six #10 cans, weighing 6 lb (2.7 kg) each. Other packs are available.

Kitchen Yields

Serving size:
1¼ cup, or 9 oz (255 g), for restaurant size serving; ¾ cup, or 5½ oz (156 g), for buffet size serving. One #10 can yields 16 restaurant servings or 25 buffet servings.

Calories:
1 cup, or 7½ oz (213 g) = 387 Calories.

ROUNDS, ROASTED AND COOKED
Fully-cooked rounds are available fresh or frozen, normally shipped in vacuum bags.

Weight ranges:

Top rounds:
5 to 8 lb (2.2 to 3.6 kg).

Bottom round halves:
5 to 8 lb (2.2 to 3.6 kg).

Eye rounds:
4 to 7 lb (1.8 to 3.1 kg).
Portion packs are available in various sizes.

Kitchen Yields
There is little trimming waste, and the meat is ready for use.

Calories:
5 oz (140 g) = 300 Calories.

ROUNDS CORNED
Available bone in or boneless. Bottom rounds are more likely to be corned than top rounds.

Weight range:
35 to 45 lb (15.7 to 20.2 kg).

Kitchen Yields

Bone weight:
About 6 percent of weight.

Cooking loss:
35 percent is average.

Trimming loss:
5 percent of cooked weight.

GYROS
See Gyros.

PASTRAMI
Pastrami is cured, smoked beef that has been rolled in crushed coriander seeds. Genuine pastrami is made from the plate, but pastrami made from other beef cuts is also produced. Plate pastrami must be steamed before use. Most other cuts are fully cooked.

Weights:

Plate pieces:
2 to 4 lb (0.9 to 1.8 kg).

Round pieces:
2 to 6 lb (0.9 to 2.7 kg).
Other sizes are available.

Kitchen Yields

Cooking loss:
18 to 20 percent of weight for plate pastrami.

Trimming loss:
5 to 10 percent for plate pastrami; 5 percent for cooked round pastrami.

Serving size:
4½ oz (127 g) for sandwich.
3 lb (1.35 kg) plate pastrami as purchased produces 2 lb 8 oz (1.2 kg) cooked, and yields 8 servings for sandwiches. 5 lb (2.25 kg) cooked round pastrami yields 16 servings for sandwiches.

ROAST BEEF
Fully-cooked products are normally frozen. Many ready-to-eat products are poached in pouches with seasoning and caramel color. Oven-roasted products are roasted in pouches; some are dry roasted. Some products are identified by USDA Grades, normally Choice. Many different cuts are available. The most popular are:

> Bottom Round, no heel
> Eye Round
> Top Round, whole
> Top Round, split
> Prime Rib

Weight:
Varies, depending on cuts.

Kitchen Yields
The following facts should be taken into consideration when calculating yield:

Pouch weight:
2 oz (56 g).

Residual juices:
Up to 5 oz (140 g).

Trimming waste:
5 percent. Trim varies according to manufacturer.

Calories:
4 oz (112 g) lean roast round = 225 Calories.

SALAMI, BEEF

Sizes:
5 to 6 lb (2.2 to 2.7 kg).

Kitchen Yields
Trimming waste, end pieces, and wrapping accounts for 3 percent of purchased weight.

Serving size:
3 oz (80 g) for sandwiches. One 5½-lb (2.4-kg) salami yields 28 sandwiches.

Calories:
4 oz (112 g) = 180 Calories.

TONGUE, SMOKED, RAW

Size:
4 to 5 lb (1.8 to 2.2 kg).

Kitchen Yields

Cooking and trimming loss:
50 percent of weight. Therefore, 1 lb (450 g) as
purchased yields 8 oz (225 g) cooked and trimmed.

Serving size:
3 oz (84 g) for sandwich, so 5 lb (2.2 kg) yields 13
servings.

BEEF CONSOMMÉ

See Soups.

BEER

Keg Sizes:
1 barrel = 31 gal (112.8 l).
½ barrel (one standard keg) = 15½ gal (58.9 l).
½ barrel (one standard keg) = 165 bottles, 12 oz
(0.34 l).

Yields:
Table B-1 shows serving yields from a keg of beer,
based on type of glass and thickness of head.

Calories:
One 12-oz (0.34-l) bottle = 150 Calories.

BEER BATTER

Formula
  six 12-oz (0.34-l) cans beer
  3 cups (0.7 l) warm water
  ½ cup (0.17 l) oil
  8 cups (1.84 l) flour
  3 tb salt

Kitchen Yields
1 gal (3.8 l) beer batter.

BEETS

Available canned and fresh.

CANNED BEETS
Canned beets are available whole, diced, sliced, and
shoestring-style in various sizes.

Pack:
Six #10 cans.

Table B-1 Serving Yields for Beer (Glasses per Keg)

Type of Glass	Size	1-in Head (25 mm)	Number of Servings ¾-in Head (19.5 mm)	½-in Head (12.7 mm)
Pitcher	60 oz (1.7 l)	41		
	40 (1.1 l)	62		
Schooner	10 oz (0.29 l)	330	293	256
	12 oz (0.34 l)	256	214	198
Sham Pilsner	8 oz (0.23 l)	345	317	283
	10 oz (0.29 l)	264	248	233
	12 oz (0.34 l)	214	203	188
Footed Pilsner	10 oz (0.29 l)	248	233	220
	12 oz (0.34 l)	208	198	184
Stein	10 oz (0.29 l)	248	233	220
	14 oz (0.40 l)	170	165	158
Paper Cup	10 oz (0.29 l)	265	245	225
	12 oz (0.34 l)	245	220	205
	14 oz (0.40 l)	195	180	170

Kitchen Yields

Diced beets:

Serving size:
½ cup (0.12 l), and one #10 can yields 23 servings.

Sliced beets:

Serving size:
½ cup (0.12 l), and one #10 can yields 22 servings.

Whole beets:
One #10 can yields 250 to 300 tiny beets, 175 to 250 tiny beets, 174 to 125 small beets, 75 to 124 medium beets, or fewer than 74 large beets.

Counts:
Vary slightly from one packer to another.

Serving size:
4 to 5 small beets; thus, one #10 can yields 30 to 35 servings.

Calories:
½ cup whole, small (drained) = 30 Calories.
½ cup diced or sliced (drained) = 35 Calories.

FRESH BEETS
Sold with and without leaves.

Season:
Available year-round.

Pack:
25- and 50-lb (11.3- and 22.6-kg) bags, without leaves; 43- to 47-lb (19.3- to 21.1-kg) cartons of 24 bunches, with leaves still attached.

Count:
None established; sizes vary.

Kitchen Yields
1 lb (450 g) beets without leaves yields 12 oz (340 g) or 2 cups, cooked and sliced.

Calories:
½ cup diced or sliced (drained) = 35 Calories.
½ cup greens, leaves and stems, cooked (drained) = 20 Calories.

BELGIAN ENDIVE
Available canned and fresh.

CANNED BELGIAN ENDIVE

Pack:
Twenty-four 15-oz (426-g) cans.

Kitchen Yields

Serving size:
One piece, as hot vegetable.
One 15-oz (426-g) can yields 3 to 4 servings.

FRESH BELGIAN ENDIVE
Imported vegetable, most often used as salad, but can also be braised, grilled, or sautéed. Note that endive is also grown in California and is available white and purple. The domestic pack is the same as the import pack.

Season:
Fall until spring.

Pack:
10-lb (4.5-kg) boxes.

Count:
Varies, but approximately 50 pieces per box.

Kitchen Yields
Very little waste.

Serving size:
4 oz (112 g) for salad, cut up; thus, one box yields 40 servings.

BELL PEPPERS

See Sweet Peppers, under Peppers.

BIB LETTUCE

See Lettuce.

BISCUITS

Formula 1

1½ lb (675 g) bread flour
1½ lb (675 g) pastry flour
4 oz (112 g) baking powder
6 oz (170 g) sugar
8 oz (225 g) shortening
1 oz (28 g) salt
5 eggs
3 cups (0.7 l) milk

Kitchen Yields

Serving size:
1½ oz (42 g). The total mix yields 55 pieces.

Formula 2

4½ lb (2 kg) patent flour
8 oz (225 g) baking powder
8 oz (225 g) sugar
1½ lb (670 g) shortening
12 eggs
1 qt (0.47 l) milk

Kitchen Yields

Serving size:
1 oz (28 g). The total mix yields 90 pieces.

Calories:
One biscuit, 2-in (5-cm) in diameter, or 1 oz (28 g) = 105 Calories.

BITTER MELON

See Squash.

BLACKBERRIES

Available fresh. Domestic blackberries are also called *bushberries*.

Season:
Late spring to fall domestic production. Imports available in winter.

Pack:
Flats or trays with 12 half-pints (0.23 l).

Kitchen Yields

Count:
½ pint (0.23 l) contains 45 to 50 berries.

Serving size:
¾ cup (0.17 l) berries. One ½ pint yields 1½ servings for breakfast or dessert; thus, one flat yields 18 servings.
One ½ pint yields 3 servings as garnish with desserts and ice cream; thus one flat yields 36 servings.
There is no waste when merchandise is fresh.

Calories:
¾ cup berries, or 5 oz (140 g) = 65 Calories.

BLACK-EYED PEAS

See Peas.

BLACK MISSION FIG

See Figs.

BLACK RADISH

See Radishes.

BLINTZES

Thin pancake, baked on one side only and then filled with cottage cheese or fruit; served with sour cream and fruit sauce. Used in Jewish cooking.

Formula

2½ cups, or 14 oz (400 g) flour
10 eggs
1 qt + 1 cup (1.16 l) milk
¼ cup (0.06 l) oil

Kitchen Yields
Forty 6-in (150-mm) blintzes.

Formula for Cottage Cheese Filling

5 lb (2.2 kg) cottage cheese
8 egg yolks
1 lb (450 g) sugar
4 grated lemon rinds

Kitchen Yields
Filling for forty blintzes.

BLUEBERRIES

Available canned, fresh, and frozen.

CANNED BLUEBERRIES

Pack:
Six #10 cans; twenty-four #300 cans. Other packs
are available.

Kitchen Yields

Serving size:
½ cup fruit and juice. One #10 can yields 22 servings fruit and juice or 8 cups drained fruit.

FRESH BLUEBERRIES
Most blueberries sold on the commercial market
are cultivated. The juice of blueberries is white.
Huckleberries resemble blueberries, but have pur-
ple-colored juice.

Season:
June to September. Peak is in summer.

Pack:
Flats of twelve 1-pint (0.47-l) cartons; flats of eight
1-qt (0.94 l) cartons; 5-lb (2.25-kg) bulk cartons.

Kitchen Yields

1 pint yields 2 cups. There is basically no cleaning
waste.

Serving size:
½ cup (0.12 l). 1 pint yields 4 servings; one flat of
12 pints yields 48 servings; and one flat of 8 qt
yields 64 servings.
1 cup dry blueberries weighs 5½ oz (150 g).
For blueberry pie, 3½ cups, or 20 oz (560 g), blueberries fill one 9-in pie.
For blueberry muffins, add 3½ cups, 20 oz (560 g)
blueberries to 80 oz of batter. Yield is 48 muffins
formed by using a 2-oz (#16) scoop.

Calories:
½ cup blueberries = 35 Calories.

FROZEN BLUEBERRIES
Available IQF.

Pack:
Twelve 1-lb (450-g) polybags, for total of 12 lb
(5.4 kg); six 3-lb (1.4-kg) polybags, for a total of
18 lb (8.1 kg); individual 25-lb (11.25-kg) cans;
individual 30-lb (13.5-kg) cartons.

Kitchen Yields

Serving size:
½ cup (0.12 l). 1 lb (450 g) yields 3½ servings, and
one 25-lb (11.25-kg) can yields 90 servings.

BOAR

Wild boar meat is available from farm-raised animals.

Pack:

Fresh Ham, bone in:
8 to 12 lb (3.6 to 5.4 kg).

Loins:
10 lb (4.5 kg).

Kitchen Yields
Difficult to estimate, because fatness of meat varies
greatly.

BOILING ONIONS

See Onions.

BOK CHOY

See Chinese Foods.

BONIATO

See Sweet Potatoes & Yams.

BOTTLE SIZES

The following is a listing of champagne, liquor, and
wine bottle sizes.

Table B-2 Drink Yields for Liquors (per Bottle)

	Approximate Number of Drinks per Bottle					
Drink Size	Half-pint 8 oz (0.24 l)	Pint 16 oz (0.47 l)	Fifth 25.6 oz (0.75 l)	Quart 32 oz (0.94 l)	Liter 34.1 oz (1.0 l)	Half-gallon 64 oz (1.9 l)
⅞ oz (0.025 l)	9	18	30	37	40	150
1 oz (0.029 l)	8	16	25	32	34	64
1⅛ oz (0.033 l)	7	14	22	28	30	112
1¼ oz (0.036 l)	6½	13	20½	26	27	104
1½ oz (0.043 l)	5½	11	17	21½	23	87

Champagne Bottle Sizes:
> Split = 6.4 fl oz (0.187 l).
> Half-bottle = 12.8 fl oz (0.375 l).
> Fifth = 25.6 fl oz (0.75 l).
> Magnum = 2 fifths: 51.2 fl oz (1.5 l).
> Jeroboam = 4 fifths: 102.4 fl oz (3 l).
> Rehoboam = 6 fifths: 153.6 fl oz (4.5 l).
> Salmanazar = 12 fifths: 307 fl oz (9 l).
> Balthazar = 16 fifths: 409 fl oz (12 l).
> Nebuchadnezzar = 20 fifths: 512 fl oz (15 l).
> Sovereign = 34.6 fifths: 885.7 fl oz (26 l).

Liquor Bottle Sizes:
> Half-pint = 8 fl oz (0.23 l).
> Pint = 16 fl oz (0.47 l).
> Fifth = 25.6 fl oz (0.75 l).
> Quart = 32 fl oz (0.94 l).
> Liter = 34.1 fl oz (1.0 l).
> Half-gallon = 64 fl oz (1.9 l).

Wine Bottle Sizes:
> Half-bottle = 12.8 fl oz (0.37 l).
> Fifth = 25.6 fl oz (0.75 l).

Liter = 34.1 fl oz.
One-and-a-half liter = 51 fl oz.
Half-gallon = 64 fl oz (1.9 l).
Gallon = 128 fl oz (3.86 l).
Magnum = 2 fifths: 51.2 fl oz (1.5 l).
Double Magnum = 4 fifths: 102.4 fl oz (3 l).
Jeroboams = 6 fifths: 153.6 fl oz (4.5 l).
Imperial = 8 fifths: 204.8 fl oz (6 l).

The fifth, which contains 25.6 fl oz (0.75 l), is the most common wine bottle size.

Liquor Serving Yields:
Approximate number of drinks per bottle of liquor are listed in Table B-2.

Wine Serving Yields:
Approximate number of glasses per bottle of wine are listed in Table B-3.

Common Serving Sizes:
4 oz (0.12 l) for champagne and sparkling wine and for dessert wine (often sold in ½ bottles); 5 oz (0.15 l) for white wine; and 6 oz (0.17 l) for red wine.

Table B-3 Drink Yields for Wine (per Bottle)

	Approximate Number of Drinks per Bottle					
Serving Size	Half-bottle 12.8 oz (0.37 l)	Fifth 25.6 oz (0.75 l)	Liter 34.1 oz (1.0 l)	One-and-a-half liter 51 oz (1.5 l)	Half-gallon 64 oz (1.9 l)	Gallon 126 oz (3.86 l)
4 oz (0.12 l)	3	6	8	12	15	30
5 oz (0.14 l)	2	5	6	10	12	25
6 oz (0.17 l)	2	4	5½	8½	10½	21

Banquet Serving Sizes:
6 glasses per bottle for champagne toast; 2 bottles
of white wine for a table of 10 covers; 2 bottles of
red wine for a table of 10 covers.

BOYSENBERRY

Boysenberries are shaped like raspberries, but are
longer and slightly larger. The color is red.

Season:
Late summer.

Pack:
Flats of twelve ½-pint (0.23-l) containers.

Kitchen Yields

Serving size:
⅔ half-pint; thus, one flat yields 18 portions.
One ½-pint—8 fl oz (0.22 l)—weighs 5 oz (140 g).
Four ½-pints (0.9 l) weigh 1¼ lb (562 g).

Calories:
⅔ half-pint (0.1 l) berries = 55 Calories.

BRAZIL NUTS

Available shelled.

Pack:
By weight.

Kitchen Yields
1 lb (450 g) is equivalent to 3¼ cups (0.76 l).

Calories:
6 to 8 large kernels, weighing 1 oz (28 g) total =
185 Calories.

BREAD

Breads are available in countless varieties and
sizes. Listed are common sizes for commercial and
non-commercial loaves.

BREAD CRUMBS

Weights:
1 cup dry crumbs weighs 3½ oz (100 g).

1 cup soft white crumbs weighs 1⅝ oz (45 g).

Kitchen Yields
For soft white bread crumbs, 1 lb white bread, crust
removed, yields 7 cups (315 g); 5 lb white bread,
crust removed, yields 56 oz (1.6 kg).

Calories:
1 cup dry crumbs weighing 3½ oz (100 g) = 390
Calories.
1 cup soft crumbs weighing = 1⅝ oz (45 g) = 120
Calories.

BREAD DOUGH

BREADBASKET DOUGH
Baskets can also be made with noodle dough. *See*
Noodle Dough.

Formula
    2½ lb (1.1 kg) bread flour
    1 egg
    1 oz (28 g) shortening
    1 oz (28 g) oil
    1 pint = 16 oz (0.47 l) cold water

BREAD DOUGH FOR BASIC HARD ROLLS
This dough can also be used for decorative bread-
baskets.

Formula
    5 lb (2.25 kg) bread flour
    2 oz (56 g) salt
    2 oz (56 g) sugar
    2 oz (56 g) shortening
    2 oz (56 g) egg whites
    3 lb (1.4 kg) water
    3 oz (84 g) yeast

Baking Instructions:
Set oven to 400˚F (200˚C); steam for the first 10
minutes.

Kitchen Yields
1 lb (450 g) dough yields 1 dozen rolls; the total
mix yields 8½ dozen rolls or 3 French flutes.

Calories:
One 1¼ oz (35 g) roll = 110 Calories.

BREAD DOUGH SHRINKAGE

Shrinking loss of yeast dough in baking is approximately 11 percent.

Kitchen Yields

Shrinkage is 2 oz (57 g) for each 1 lb (450 g) of product; thus 18 oz (500 g) dough yields 1 lb (450 g) bread.

COCKTAIL LOAVES

Flavors:

Rye, pumpernickel, or marble.

Weights and counts:

8 oz (225 g) contains 30 to 32 slices.
12 oz (408 g) contains 42 slices.

COMMERCIAL SANDWICH LOAVES

Commercial loaves are available whole or sliced vertically or horizontally.

Flavors:

White, whole wheat, or square rye.

Sizes:

Commercial loaves are classified by the size of the slice, as detailed in Table B-4.

Thickness of slice:

Normal:
$8/16$ in (12.7 mm), or 32 slices.

Thin:
$7/16$ in (11 mm), or 34 slices.

Table B-4 Weights and Sizes of Commercial Bread Loaves

Size Number	Weight	Number of Normal Slices	Size of Slice
#2	2 lb (0.9 kg)	32	$3\frac{1}{2} \times 3\frac{1}{2}$ in (89 × 89 mm)
#3	3 lb (1.35 kg)	32	$3\frac{3}{4} \times 3\frac{3}{4}$ in (95 × 95 mm)
#4	4 lb (1.8 kg)	32	$4\frac{1}{4} \times 4\frac{1}{4}$ in (107 × 107 mm)

Extra thin:
$3/8$ in (10 mm), or 40 slices.

Bread is available sliced lengthwise for canapés or finger sandwiches. Length of such a loaf is 18 in (450 mm), and one loaf yields 11 to 12 slices.

NONCOMMERCIAL SANDWICH LOAVES

Flavors:

Raisin, rye, and white.

Sizes:

Table B-5 gives weight and slice information for noncommercial loaves.

Kitchen Yields of Commercial Bread Loaves

One loaf sliced vertically yields 48 finger sandwiches.

One loaf sliced horizontally yields 60 finger sandwiches.

One loaf sliced horizontally yields 420 canapés.

One horizontal slice yields 6 toast croustades; therefore, one 2-lb (900-g) loaf yields 156 toast croustades.

Weight:

One cup of fresh cubes of white bread weigh $1\frac{1}{8}$ oz (31 g). One #2 loaf yields 12 to 13 cups.

Table B-5 Weights and Sizes of Noncommercial Bread Loaves

Variety	Weight of Loaf	Number of Slices	Loaves per 100 Slices
Raisin Bread	1 lb (450 g)	18	$5\frac{3}{4}$
	2 lb (900 g)	36	3
Rye Bread	1 lb (450 g)	23	$4\frac{1}{2}$
	$1\frac{1}{2}$ lb (675 g)	28	$3\frac{3}{4}$
	2 lb (900 g)	33	3
White Bread	1 lb (450 g)	16	$6\frac{1}{4}$
	1 lb (450 g)	25 to 30	$3\frac{3}{4}$
	$1\frac{1}{4}$ lb (560 g)	19	$5\frac{1}{2}$
	$1\frac{1}{2}$ lb (675 g)	24	$4\frac{1}{4}$
	2 lb (900 g)	28	$3\frac{3}{4}$
	2 lb (900 g)	36	3

Calories:
#2 loaf, one slice = 75 Calories.
1 cup of white bread cubes, weighing 1⅛ oz (31 g) = 80 Calories.

BREADFRUIT

Large roundish fruit, belonging to the fig family. There are seedless and seeded breadfruit varieties. The unripe fruit has a slightly unpleasant aroma, which disappears when the fruit is ripe. Breadfruit should be roasted, rather than boiled or steamed.

Season:
May until February.

Pack:
By count.

Size:
Varies greatly, but normally 8 to 12 in (20 to 30 cm) long; best size is 3 to 3½ lb (1.3 to 1.5 kg) each.

Weight:
2 to 9 lb (1 to 4 kg).

Kitchen Yields

Best size:
3 to 3½ lb (1.3 to 1.5 kg).

Serving size:
⅙ breadfruit; one breadfruit yields 6 servings as vegetable garnish.

BRINE

Formula for Meat Brine
    14 oz (400 g) salt
    4 oz sugar (112 g)
    1½ oz (63 g) saltpeter
    2 oz (56 g) pickling spice
    1 gal (3.8 l) water

Formula for Fish
    2½ gal (11.4 l) water
    1 cup, or 8 oz (225 g), salt
    ¼ cup, or 2 oz (56 g), sugar

Soak thin fillets 30 minutes; soak thick pieces overnight. Air-dry in refrigerator before smoking.

BROCCOLI

Available fresh and frozen.

FRESH BROCCOLI

Broccoli is available in a broad range of packs. The stem length of the spears is crucial when calculating yield. For whole broccoli, the edible part is about 6 in down from the top, the rest is stem, which can be used in soups, purées, or in salads.

Season:
Available year-round, with no discernable peak months. Lower supply in summer.

Pack:
Table B-6 lists pack information for fresh broccoli.

Kitchen Yields

Serving size:
3½ oz (100 g) cleaned vegetable.
One 1¼-lb (560-g) bunch yields 13 oz (360 g) usable product, or about 4 servings; thus, 34 lb (15 kg), or 25 small bunches, as purchased, yields 22 lb (10 kg) cleaned vegetable, or 100 servings. Similarly, one 42-lb (19-kg) carton yields about 130 servings.

Calories:
One 3½-oz (100-g) serving, cooked = 30 Calories.
One cup, or 5½ oz (150 g), cooked = 45 Calories.

FROZEN BROCCOLI

Available as spears and as cut or chopped pieces in block or as IQF.

Pack:
Twelve 2½-lb (1.1-kg) boxes; one 30-lb (13.5-kg) case, loose. Other sizes are available.

Kitchen Yields

Serving size:
½ cup cooked spears or chopped pieces. One 2½-lb (1.1-kg) box yields 10 servings; one case yields 120 servings; and 10 boxes yields 100 servings.

Calories:
½ cup cooked = 22 Calories.

Table B-6 Pack Information for Fresh Broccoli

Pack and Weight	Number of Bunches	Weight per Bunch or Count	Size of Spears
Full carton 42 lb (19 kg)	18	2¼ to 2½ lb (1 to 1.10 kg)	8 to 9 in (200 to 230 mm)
Half-cartons 20 to 23 lb (9 to 10.3 kg)	14 to 18	1¼ to 1½ lb (560 to 675 g)	8 to 9 in (200 to 230 mm)
Carton spears 21 lb (9.45 kg)	loose pack	57	6 in (150 mm)
Carton spears 15 lb (7.75 kg)	loose pack	no count	3 to 4 in (75 to 100 mm)
Carton florets 9 lb (4.1 kg)	loose pack	no count	1 to 2¾ in (25 to 70 mm)
Carton buds 9 lb (4 kg)	three 3-lb bags	80 pieces per 1 lb (450 g) 720 pieces per case	
Carton buds 12 lb (5.4 kg)	four 3-lb bags	80 pieces per 1 lb (450 g) 960 pieces per case	
Carton buds 18 lb (8.1 kg)	six 3-lb bags	80 pieces per 1 lb (450 g) 1,440 pieces per case	

BROCAFLOWER

Cross between broccoli and cauliflower.

Pack:

Flat with 12 heads.

BROCCOLI RABE

Also called *rapini* or *broccoli rappe*. It is a leafy, bitter vegetable.

Season:

November to March.

Pack:

By weight or in bunches.

Kitchen Yields

Cleaning loss is about 20 percent by weight when the stem ends are discarded. Cooking loss is 30 per-cent. 1 lb (450 g) as purchased yields about 1½ cups (0.35 l) cooked.

Serving size:

½ cup (0.23 l).

BROWN RICE

See Rice.

BRUSSELS SPROUTS

Available fresh and frozen. Marinated (pickled sprouts) are available as delicatessen items.

FRESH BRUSSELS SPROUTS

Season:

Available year-round. Peak from August to March. Low supply from May to July. Brussels sprouts on the stems are specialty items.

Packs:
Twelve 1-pint (0.47-l) containers, weighing 12 oz (336 g) each, for a total of 9 lb (4.1 kg); twelve 10-oz (280-g) containers weighing 7½ lb (3.4 kg) total; individual 25-lb (11.15-kg) cartons, loose.

Kitchen Yields

Trimming waste:
By weight is about 20 to 25 percent.

Serving size:
½ cup (0.12 l), or 3 oz (84 g) cooked. 12 oz (340 g), or 1 pint (0.47 l), as purchased, produce 9 oz (255 g) ready-to-cook and yield 3 servings; thus, 10 oz (280 g) as purchased yield 2½ servings.

Counts:
Vary greatly.
1 pint (0.47 l) contains 25 to 30 pieces medium; and one 10-oz (280-g) container contains 20 to 25 pieces medium.

Calories:
½ cup cooked, drained = 38 Calories.

FROZEN BRUSSELS SPROUTS
Frozen brussels sprouts are graded by size.

Pack:
Twelve 2-lb (0.9-kg) packages; twelve 2½-lb (1.1-kg) packages; one 30-lb (13.6-kg) case, IQF.

Sizes:

Medium:
60 to 80 pieces per 1 lb (450 g).

Small:
100 or more pieces per 1 lb (450 g).

Kitchen Yields
3½ pints (1.17 l) fresh brussels sprouts are equivalent to 2 lb (0.9 kg) frozen brussels sprouts.

Serving size:
½ cup (0.12 l).
One 2½-lb (1.1-kg) package yields 13 servings; one 2-lb (0.9-kg) package yields 10 servings; one 30-lb (13.6-kg) case, IQF, yields 150 servings.

Calories:
½ cup, or 3½ oz (100 g), cooked, drained = 38 Calories.

BUFFALO

Most available cuts:

Prime Ribs:
18 to 24 lb (8.1 to 10.8 kg).

Rounds:
35 to 50 lb (15.7 to 22.5 kg).

Full Loins, bone in:
18 to 30 lb (8.1 to 13.5 kg).

Burgers:
8 oz (225 g) and 5 oz (140 g) sizes.

Kitchen Yields
Trim varies greatly between purveyors. Use beef yield information after trim has been confirmed. Note that meat is generally leaner than beef. Ribs and loins can be roasted, rounds should be braised. Buffalo burgers are leaner than most beef burgers.

BULGUR

Cracked wheatberry product that has been steamed, dried, and crushed into fine, medium, or coarse grind. It requires no further cooking after soaking in boiling water for about 30 minutes.

Kitchen Yields
Soak 1 cup (0.23 l) bulgar with 1½ cups (0.34 l) water. Drain and squeeze out excess moisture.

BURDOCK

See Japanese Foods.

BUTTER

Butter is made from pasteurized cream. It can be purchased salted and unsalted. USDA grades are AA (93 score), A (92 score), and B (90 score).

Grades lower than that are seldom purchased in foodservice. Scoring is based on flavor intensity, body, and color.

Butter is available pure, mixed with margarine, and whipped. Butter is best stored in the freezer. NOTE: Butter will change texture and flavor when mechanically manipulated (whipped or beaten).

Packs:

Solids:
1-lb (450-g) prints in a 36-lb (16.1-kg) case.

Reddies:
12- and 15-lb (5.4- and 6.7-kg) cases with varying counts; 30-lb (13.4 kg) cartons of six 5-lb (2.25-kg) cartons.

Quarters:
36-lb (16.2-kg) case with ¼-lb (112-g) sticks.

Cups:
8-lb (3.6-kg) case with ninety 1.4-oz (40-g) cups.

Tubs:
24-, 7-, and 5-lb (10.8-, 3.1-, and 2.2-kg) whipped tubs.

Bulk:
68-lb (30.6-kg), 64-lb (28.8-kg), 56-lb (25.2-kg), or 50-lb (22.5-kg) solid cubes, domestic or imported.

Butter pat counts:
1 lb (450 g) yields 60, 72, 90, and 108 pats. 90-count is the most common.

Butter chip weights:
60-count are ¼ oz (7.5 g) each.
72-count are ⅕ oz (5.6 g) each.
90-count are ⅙ oz (5.0 g) each.

1 lb (450 g) butter comprises 4 sticks or 2 cups;
1 lb (450 g) whipped butter comprises 6 sticks or 3 cups.
1 lb (450 g) butter is equivalent to ¾ cup, or 10 oz (340 g), melted, clear fat.
2 cups (0.47 l) melted, clear fat is equivalent to 2½ lb (1.1 kg) butter.

Calories:

Regular butter:
1 lb (453 g or 4 sticks) = 3,260 Calories.
1 stick (112 g or ½ cup) = 815 Calories.
1 tb (14 g or ⅛ stick) = 100 Calories.
Pat (1 in square; 90-count per 1 lb) = 35 Calories.

Whipped butter:
1 lb (453 g or 6 sticks) = 3,240 Calories.
1 stick (76 g or ½ cup) = 540 Calories.
1 tb (9 g or ⅛ stick) = 65 Calories.
Pat (120-count per 1 lb) = 25 Calories.

BUTTER, COMPOUND

Compound butter is flavored with herbs, spices, or extracts. The butter is added to sauces or finished dishes for flavor and shine. Most compound butters are made on premises. Lobster butter is made by slowly cooking lobster shells in butter. This can be done in the steam table. Cooked shells and carcasses can be used. The mixture should be strained after 5 hours, brought to a boil and chilled. The solidified butter on top can then be easily removed.

BUTTER COOKIES

See Cookies.

C

CABBAGE

Many varieties of cabbage are available.

BOK CHOY (CHINESE CABBAGE)
White vegetable in the cabbage family.

Season:
Available year-round.

Pack:

Half crate:
30 to 40 lb (13.6 to 18.1 kg).

Full crate:
65 to 70 lb (29.5 to 31.75 kg).

Size:
16 in (400 mm) long.

CELERY CABBAGE
Celery-like stalks.

Season:
Year-round.

Pack:
Sold by weight.

Half crate:
30 to 40 lb (13.6 to 18.1 kg).

Full crate:
65 to 70 lb (29.5 to 31.75 kg).

Size:
16 in (400 mm) long.

Kitchen Yields
Little cleaning waste and little shrinkage.

Calories:
1 cup, or 6 oz (170 g), cooked and drained, = 10 Calories.

GREEN CABBAGE
Cabbage is available whole, sliced, and as ready-to-use coleslaw mix. The most important varieties are Domestic and Danish. Domestic is a spring variety; Danish is a firm winter cabbage. Spring cabbage is greener and softer than winter cabbage.

Season:
Available year-round. Early cabbage from December to May. Domestic variety is available in spring; Danish variety in winter.

Pack:
40-, 50-, and 60-lb (18.1-, 22.6-, and 27.2-kg) cartons.

Sizes:

Early cabbage:
Small: under 1½ lb (0.6 kg).
Medium: 1½ to 3 lb (0.6 to 1.35 kg).
Large: over 3 lb (1.35 kg).

Domestic and Danish:
Small: under 2 lb (0.9 kg).
Medium: 2 to 5 lb (0.9 to 2.2 kg).
Large: over 5 lb (2.2 kg).
For sliced cabbage and ready-to-use coleslaw mix, pack is two 10-lb (4.5-kg) bags.

Kitchen Yields

Serving size:
For coleslaw as side order, 1 cup, or 2½ oz (70 g) raw cabbage; 1 lb (450 g) as purchased produces 12 oz (340 g) ready-to-cook shredded cabbage, so 10 lb (4.5 kg) as purchased yields 50 servings.
NOTE: Cabbage will shed liquid when mixed with dressing and will shrink when stored overnight. Serving size for cooked, chopped cabbage is ½ cup; 1 lb (450 g) as purchased yields 4 servings, so 10 lb (4.5 kg) as purchased yields 40 servings.

Calories:
1 cup, 2½ oz (70 g) raw, coarsely shredded = 20 Calories.
½ cup cooked, drained = 15 Calories.

RED CABBAGE
Available canned, whole, and as sliced red cabbage for adding to coleslaw.

CANNED RED CABBAGE

Pack:
Six #10 cans.

Kitchen Yields

Serving size:
½ cup; one #10 can yields 20 servings.

FRESH RED CABBAGE

Season:
Available year-round.

Pack:
40-, 50-, and 60-lb (18.1-, 22.6- and 27.2-kg) cartons. For coleslaw, sliced red cabbage is packed in four 5-lb (2.25-kg) bags.

Kitchen Yields
Same as for green cabbage.

Calories:
1 cup, or 2½ oz (70 g), raw, shredded = 20 Calories.

SAUERKRAUT
See Sauerkraut.

SAVOY CABBAGE
Curly, soft cabbage—edible only when cooked.

Season:
Late summer until spring.

Pack:
40, 50, and 60 lb (18.1, 22.6, and 27.2 kg).

Kitchen Yields
1 lb (450 g) as purchased produces 12 oz (340 g) shredded; 1 cup shredded weighs 2½ oz.

Serving size:
½ cup cooked; 1 lb (450 g) as purchased yields 6 servings.

Calories:
½ cup cooked, plain = 15 Calories.

CACTUS FRUIT (TUNA)

See Mexican Foods.

CACTUS LEAVES (NOPALES)

See Mexican Foods.

CAKE SCALING GUIDE

Refer to Table C-1 for information on scaling.

CALABASA (CUBAN SQUASH)

See Squash.

CALYMIRNA FIGS

See Figs.

CANTALOUPE

See Melons.

CAN SIZES

There are many different can sizes on the market. Table C-2 lists the most common can sizes found in institutional foodservice, plus their approximate sizes in fluid ounces and cups. Also listed are the number of cans per case. The weight of cans varies greatly, depending on their contents.

Table C-1 Cake Scaling Guide for Sponge Cakes

Size of Cake	Scaling Weight
6-in (150-mm) round	10 oz (280 g)
7-in (175-mm) round	14 oz (340 g)
8-in (200-mm) round	22 oz (600 g)
10-in (250-mm) round	28 oz (780 g)
12-in (300-mm) round	42 oz (1.17 kg)
14-in (350-mm) round	64 oz (1.8 kg)
18- × 24-in (450- × 600-mm) sheet	85 oz (2.3 kg)
8-in (200-mm) angel food cake	13 oz (365 g)

Table C-2 Can Names, Volumes, and Counts

Can Name	Volume in Fluid Ounces	Volume in Cups	Volume in Liters	Number per Case
#1 picnic	10½	1¼	0.308	24 or 48
#211 cylinder	12	1½	0.348	24, 36, or 48
#300	13½	1¾	0.391	24, 36, or 48
#303	15½	2	0.449	12, 24, or 36
#2	20	2½	0.580	12 or 24
#2½	28½	3½	0.826	12 or 24
#3	33½	4¼	0.971	12 or 24
#3 cylinder	46	5¾	1.334	12
#5	56	7	1.624	12
#10	103½	13	3.001	6
Gallon	126	16	3.812	6

TRANSPOSING CAN SIZES

To fill one #10 can, it will take approximately three #3 cans, five #2 cans, or two-and-one-quarter #3 cylinder cans.

NOTE: This table does not take count (number of pieces) into consideration.

Case equivalents:

Twenty-four #303 cans = Nineteen #2 cans.
Twenty-four #2 cans = Fourteen #3 cans.
Twenty-four #3 cans = Three #10 cans.
Twelve #10 cans = Thirty-six #3 cans.

CAPE GOOSEBERRY

The berry is enclosed in a papery pod, resembling a Chinese lantern. Fruit is light green or orange when ripe.

Season:
Winter.

Pack:
Sold by weight.

Size:
1½ to 2 in (45 to 50 mm) across.

Kitchen Yields
Use berry with pod as exotic garnish on fruit displays.

CAPERS

Capers are the buds of a shrub growing in the Mediterranean area. Imported, they are available pickled in vinegar or salted. Non Pareil is the pre-ferred variety. Caper berries, the mature fruits of the shrub, have been introduced as specialty items.

Pack:
Four 1-gal (3.8-l) jars. Other packs are available.

CARAMEL FOR DIPPING FRUITS

Formula
2 lb sugar (900 g)
10 oz glucose (270 g)
1½ cups water (0.33 l)

Boil to 310°F (160°C).

Kitchen Yields
Provides caramel for approximately 50 orange sections or 40 large strawberries.

CARDONI

Also spelled *cardoon*, this vegetable looks like celery, but is a member of the thistle family. It must be cooked before use.

Season:
Fall and winter.

Pack:
By weight.

Kitchen Yields

Trimming loss:
30 percent by weight.

CAROB

Also known as *St. John's bread*. Pods, normally available dried, contain twelve hard seeds. The pods are very hard when dried. The ground seeds are often used as a chocolate substitute.

Pack:
Pods and seeds are sold by weight, often in 10-lb (4.5-kg) cartons.

Size and count:
About 8 in (20 cm) long.

CARROTS

Available canned, fresh, and frozen.

CANNED CARROTS
Available whole, diced, sliced, and shoestring-style in various sizes; also available mixed with peas. Carrot purée is also available. Whole carrots are often imported.

Pack:

Domestic whole carrots:
Six #10 cans.

Imported whole carrots:
Six 5-lb 10-oz (3-kg) cans.

Diced or sliced carrots:
Six #10 cans.

Carrot purée:
Twenty-four #303 cans.

Kitchen Yields

DOMESTIC WHOLE CARROTS
One #10 can weighs 69 oz (1.9 kg), drained.

Counts:

Small:
180 to 225.

Tiny:
260 to 320.

Extra:
350 to 425.

IMPORTED WHOLE CARROTS
One can weighs 62 oz (1.7 kg), drained.

Counts:

Small:
180 to 220.

Tiny:
250 to 310.

Extra:
320 to 400.

Common foodservice size is 260- to 320-count.

Serving size:
2 oz (56 g), about 6 whole small carrots. One #10 can yields 30 servings; one case yields 180 servings; and four #10 cans yield 120 servings.

DICED OR SLICED CARROTS

Serving size:
½ cup diced or sliced carrots. One #10 can weighs 72 oz (2 kg), drained, and yields 25 servings.

CARROT PURÉE

Serving size:
½ cup. One #303 can weighs 15½ oz, contains 2 cups (0.47 l), and yields 4 servings.

Calories:
2 oz (56 g) whole, plain = 16 Calories.
Strained purée, 2 tb weighing 1 oz (28 g) = 10 Calories.

FRESH CARROTS
Fresh carrots are available with and without top greens. Carrots are also available peeled, shredded, cut in sticks, and turned and shaped in balls.

There are many carrot varieties. Important to foodservice operators are size and shape. Even-shaped carrots, regardless of size, are easier to peel and have less waste. The shapes can range from long and slender to round. Smaller carrots are more tender than large carrots.

Baby carrots can be either immature carrots of standard varieties, or more mature carrots of miniature varieties. Belgian carrots are a special variety of miniature carrots. The color of all carrots can range from light yellow to dark orange.

Carrots can be purchased with the green leaves on or off. Large carrots are seldom marketed with the greens on. Carrots store well. Fresh processed carrots are available grated and as sticks.

Season:
Available year-round. Peak is from late fall to spring.

Sizes:

Large or Jumbo:
1½ to 2½ in (53 to 88 mm) in diameter, and 7 to 12 in (188 to 304 mm) long.

Medium:
¾ to 1½ in (19 to 53 mm) in diameter, and 7 to 9 in (177 to 228 mm) long.

Pack:

Carrots without tops:
50-lb (22.6-kg) bags or boxes, and 1-, 2-, and 3-lb (0.45-, 0.9-, and 1.4-kg) bags.

Carrots with tops:
23- to 27-lb (10.3- to 12.1-kg) crate of 24 bunches.

Shredded carrots:
Four 5-lb (2.25-kg) bags.

Sticks, random pack:
Four 5-lb (2.25-kg) bags.

Sticks, precision pack:
Two 9-lb (4.1-kg) bags.

Kitchen Yields
1 lb (450 g) as purchased produces 14 oz (400 g) cleaned and peeled, and 12 oz (340 g) cooked.
1 lb (450 g) cello pack contains 10 to 12 thin carrots.
1 lb (450 g) cleaned carrots, grated, yields 3 cups (0.7 l).

Serving size:
½ cup shredded raw carrots; thus, 1 lb (450 g) as purchased yields 6 servings.
½ cup sliced, cooked carrots; thus 1 lb (450 g) as purchased yields 4 servings.

Calories:
One raw, whole carrot weighing 2½ oz (70 g) = 30 Calories.
One cup raw, grated carrots weighing 4 oz (112 g) = 45 Calories.
One cup cooked, drained carrots weighing 6 oz (170 g) = 55 Calories.

FROZEN CARROTS
Available whole, petite whole, diced, sliced, and shoestring-style in various sizes.

Pack:
Twelve 2-lb (0.9-kg) packages; individual 20-lb (9.1-kg) cartons.
Whole carrots are packed IQF.

Kitchen Yields
4 lb (1.8 kg) fresh carrots are equivalent to one 2-lb (0.9 kg) package frozen carrots.

Serving size:
½ cup (0.1 l); one 2-lb (0.9 kg) package yields 10 servings, and one case yields 120 servings.

Calories:
½ cup = 30 Calories.

CASINO BUTTER

For clams and other seafood.

Formula
½ cup (0.12 l) chopped garlic
½ cup (0.12 l) chopped shallots
2 cups (0.47 l) diced green pepper
2 cups (0.47 l) diced red pimentos

Sauté, cool, and mix with:

10 lb (4.5 kg) softened butter
salt and pepper to taste

Kitchen Yields
This formula produces 1½ gal (5.7 kg) casino butter; ½ gal (1.9 l) is enough casino butter for 150 little neck clams, so the total mix provides casino butter for 450 little neck clams.

CATSUP

See Tomatoes.

CATTAIL SHOOTS

Wetland plant with edible shoots.

Season:
March to May.

CAUL FAT

Net-like fat layer which keeps the intestines in place. Most caul sold to foodservice is from pigs. Caul is used to wrap pâtés, meat loaves, and other soft ground-meat products to provide moisture during the cooking process and to preserve the product shape.

Pack:
By weight.

Kitchen Yields
Caul is available fresh or frozen. It should be kept in ice water until use.

CAULIFLOWER

Available fresh and frozen. Marinated cauliflower is a delicatessen item.

FRESH CAULIFLOWER
Cauliflower is available as whole heads and cut into florets.

Season:
Year-round, with slightly larger supplies from October through January.

Pack and counts:

Whole heads:
16- to 23-lb (7.2- to 10.3-kg) cartons; 9, 12, or 16 heads per carton.

Florets:
6-lb (2.7-kg) cartons containing two 3-lb (1.35-kg) bags of florets; 12-lb (5.4-kg) cartons containing four 3-lb (1.35-kg) bags of florets.

Kitchen Yields

Serving size:
4 oz (112 g) raw. One head as purchased weighs about 2 to 2½ lb (0.9 to 1.1 kg). Smaller sizes are also available.
One 2½ lb (1.1 kg) head yields 21 oz (600 g) florets; thus, 1 lb (450 g) as purchased yields 8 oz (225 g) ready to cook, and 7 oz (200 g) cooked.
One large head yields 5 to 6 servings, so that a 21-lb (9-kg) carton with 9 heads yields 50 servings.

Calories:
4 oz (112 g) raw florets = 30 Calories.
½ cup cooked = 18 Calories.

FROZEN CAULIFLOWER
Available cut into small florets or as florets and pieces, about 1 to 2½ in (25 to 63 mm) long. Available in block and IQF.

Pack:
Twelve 2-lb (0.9-kg) packages in blocks and IQF bags; individual 30-lb (13.6-kg) boxes, IQF.

Kitchen Yields
2-lb (0.9-kg) package is equivalent to 5 to 6 lb (2.25 to 2.7 kg) fresh as purchased.

Serving size:
½ cup (0.1 l). One package yields 12 servings.

Calories:
½ cup = 18 Calories.

CAVIAR

Caviar is fish roe. The best is sturgeon roe, but other fish roe is also popular, including carp and trout caviar.

BELUGA STURGEON CAVIAR
Beluga is the largest species of sturgeon. Historically, almost all Beluga caviar is produced by Iran and Russia from fish caught in the Caspian Sea. Over-fishing and import restriction stimulated sturgeon production in other countries. Beluga sturgeon produces the largest eggs and is considered the most expensive caviar.

The word *malossol*, often found on caviar tins, means "lightly salted" in Russian. Caviar is available fresh and pasteurized.

Season:
Fresh and pasteurized caviar is available year-round.

Pack:
Caviar is imported in original tins, which are then repacked. Original 2-kg Tin (Russian pack) is equivalent to 4 lb 4 oz (2 kg). The Iranian pack is equivalent to 3 lb 14 oz (1.8 kg) because the original weight is in troy ounces. Other packs range upward from 1 oz (28.4 g). Smaller packs are often pasteurized.

Kitchen Yields
1 oz (28 g) is equivalent to 1½ level tb or 1 heaped tb.

Serving size:
1 oz (28 g) or more; this is sufficient to make 3 canapés. Therefore, 7 oz (200 g) yields 30 canapes. NOTE: Caviar should always be weighed before use to assure exact portion size.

LUMPFISH CAVIAR
Less expensive caviar; it is often dyed black. It is available black and red.

Pack:
Thirty-six 2-oz (56-g) jars; twenty-four 3½-oz (100-g) jars; twelve 7-oz (200-g) jars; twelve 12-oz (240-g) jars.
Use is same as for other caviar.

OSETRA STURGEON CAVIAR
Medium-size eggs from a species of medium-size sturgeon. Pack varies. Use is the same as with beluga caviar.

PRESSED CAVIAR
Imported sturgeon caviar of lesser quality, which has been pressed before shipment. The flavor is very concentrated and much acclaimed by connoisseurs. Not available pasteurized.

Pack:
By weight.

SALMON CAVIAR (KETA CAVIAR)
Available in various grades of quality and in various egg sizes, ranging in color from dark red to golden yellow.

Pack:
2-, 4-, 7-, and 12-oz (56-, 112-, 200-, and 240-g) jars, fresh or pasteurized. Other packs are available.

Kitchen Yields
1 oz (28 g) yields an average of 110 eggs.

SEVRUGA STURGEON CAVIAR
Roe of a small sturgeon, found in the United States and in some other countries. The eggs are small, but can be of excellent quality. Pack varies. Use is the same as with beluga caviar.

WHITEFISH CAVIAR

Domestic or imported caviar of small grain size.

Pack:
Jars of various sizes.

CELERIAC (KNOB CELERY)

Large, round root with white flesh. It can be used raw in salads or cooked as vegetable. Available canned or fresh, with or without green tops.

CANNED CELERIAC

Available imported in slices and cut as julienne.

Pack:
9-lb (4-kg) cans celeriac julienne. Other packs are available.

Kitchen Yields
One 9-lb (4-kg) can contains 4 lb 13 oz (2.1 kg), drained weight.

Serving size:
Varies.

FRESH CELERIAC

Season:
Fall and winter.

Pack:
½ bushel or in bunches.

Count:
Count varies because vegetable is sold with greens on or trimmed.

Size:
2½ to 4 in (63 to 100 mm) across.

Kitchen Yields
About 25 percent peeling waste after greens have been removed.

CELERY

Available canned, fresh, and frozen. Knob celery is called *celeriac. See* Celeriac.

CANNED CELERY

Canned celery is available as stalks or hearts.

Pack:
Twelve or twenty-four 28-oz (780-g) cans. Drained weight per can is 15 oz (420 g).

Kitchen Yields
One can yields 2½ to 3 portions; one case of 12 cans yields 30 portions; one case of 24 cans yields 60 to 68 portions.

FRESH CELERY

Available whole (trimmed), as hearts, sticks, and diced. Green celery of the Pascal variety is the most widely available variety on the market. There is no pronounced season. Celery is sized. Golden celery is yellowish-white, because it has been covered with soil during the growing process. It is a specialty item.

Packs:

Whole trimmed:
55- or 56-lb (24.7- or 25.2-kg) cartons or crates, with counts of 18, 24, 30, 36, and 48 pieces each.

Hearts:
25- to 28-lb (11.3- to 12.6-kg) cartons, with bag counts of 12, 18, or 24.

Sticks, cut and trimmed:
Four 5-lb (2.25-kg) bags.

Diced:
Four 5-lb (2.25-kg) bags.

Kitchen Yields

Serving size:
For raw celery, ½ cup (0.12 l) chopped or diced. 1 lb (450 g) as purchased produces 12 oz (340 g) ready to use, or 5 servings.
For cooked celery, ½ cup (0.12 l) diced. 1 lb (450 g) as purchased yields 4 servings.

Calories:
1 cup diced = 10 Calories.
1 stalk, 8 × 1½ in (200 × 38 mm), weighing 1½ oz (42 g) = 5 Calories.

Formula for Blue Cheese Stuffing for Celery
 10 lb (4.5 kg) blue cheese, crumbled
 5 lb (2.25 kg) cream cheese
 1 lb (0.4 kg) butter
 1 pint (0.47 l) heavy cream, whipped

Kitchen Yields
2 gal (7.6 l) stuffing.

FROZEN CELERY
Available diced.

Pack:
20-lb (9.1-kg) boxes celery.

Kitchen Yields
The same as cooked fresh celery. There is no waste.

CEREALS

DRY CEREALS
Many varieties are available. Most cereals are available both in self-serve bowls and regular boxes. Bulk packs are available for dispenser and kitchen use.

Pack:
Cases of 70 and 96 individual boxes each, with weight varying according to product; cases of 4 bags, with weight varying according to product. Corn flake crumbs for breading are packed in six 5-lb (2.25-kg) containers or in individual 30-lb (13.5-kg) cases.

Kitchen Yields

Milk per serving:
½ pint or 1 cup (0.23 l); therefore, 100 servings require 6 gal and 1 qt (23.5 l) milk.

Calories:
Vary according to product and serving size. Generally between 40 and 110 Calories per serving in individual box or bowl. Refer to label for information.

HOT CEREALS

CORN MEAL
Available coarse and fine ground. For polenta, *see* Polenta.

Pack:
1-lb (450-g) packages. Other packages are available.

Kitchen Yields
1 lb (450 g) dry equals 3 cups (0.7 l).

Serving size:
¾ cups (0.17 l).
1 cup (0.23 l) corn meal boiled with 1 qt (0.94 l) liquid yields 7 servings; 1 lb (450 g) yields 20 servings.

Calories:
¾ cup (0.17 l) cooked in water = 80 Calories.

CREAM OF WHEAT

Pack:
1-lb (450-g) packages.

Kitchen Yields
1 lb (450 g) dry measure equals 3 cups.

Serving sizes:
¾ cup (0.17 l). 2 cups cream of wheat boiled with 10 cups or 5 pints (2.3 l) water yield 15 servings; 1 lb (450 g) cream of wheat boiled with 15 cups water yields 23 servings.

Calories:
¾ cup (0.17 l) cereal, cooked in water = 100 Calories.

ROLLED OATS

Pack:
1-lb (450-g) packages.

Kitchen Yields
1 lb (450 g) dry measure equals 3 cups.

Serving sizes:
¾ cup (0.17 l). 2 cups oats boiled with 5 cups or 2½ pints (1.2 l) water yield 8 servings; 1 lb (450 g) oats boiled with 12½ cups or 6¼ pints (2.9 l) water yields 20 servings.

Calories:
¾ cup (0.17 l) oatmeal, cooked in water = 106 Calories.

CHAMPAGNE GRAPES

Tiny red gapes, grown especially to be used for garnish in small bunches. Sold in individual bunches and also in bulk. For other grape information, *see* Grapes.

Pack:
5-lb (2.2-kg) lugs.

Kitchen Yields

Serving size:
2-oz (56-g) bunches. One 5-lb (2.2-kg) lug yields 40 servings.

CHARD

See Swiss Chard.

CHAYOTE SQUASH

See Squash.

CHEESE

There are many varieties of cheeses and brands on the market. Following are descriptions of the most widely used and readily available cheese varieties.

AMERICAN PASTEURIZED PROCESS CHEESE

Available unsliced, sliced vertically, and sliced horizontally. Available yellow and white, regular and light (low-calorie) in both colors. Used for hot and cold sandwiches.

Pack:
Six 3-lb (1.35-kg) loaves; six 5-lb (2.2-kg) loaves; individual 10-lb (4.5-kg) loaves; four 5-lb (2.2-kg) loaves, with individual slices wrapped in plastic; four 5-lb (2.2-kg) loaves with ribbon-cut horizontal slices; individual 40-lb (18-kg) block.

Kitchen Yields

One 3-lb (1.35-kg) loaf yields 65 slices; and one 5-lb (2.2-kg) loaf yields 110 slices. 1 lb (450 g) pro-duces 5 cups (1.1 l) grated cheese. Average weight of one slice is ¾ oz (21 g).

Serving size:
3 oz (84 g), or 4 slices; therefore, one 3-lb (1.35-kg) loaf yields 16 servings, and one 5-lb (2.2-kg) loaf yields 17 servings.

Calories:

Regular cheese:
One ¾ oz (21 g) slice = 71 Calories.
1 oz (28 g) = 95 Calories.
3 oz (84 g) = 285 Calories.

Light cheese:
One ¾ oz (21 g) slice = 53 Calories.
1 oz (28 g) = 70 Calories.
3 oz (84 g) = 210 Calories.

AMERICAN PASTEURIZED PROCESS CHEESE SPREAD

Available with different flavorings ingredients, such as wine and herbs. Texture is smooth.

Pack:
1-lb (450-g) tubs. Other packs are available.

Needs ripening:
No.

Kitchen Yields

Serving size:
2 oz (56 g), as spread; one 1-lb (450 g) tub yields 8 servings.

Calories:
1 oz (28 g) = 82 Calories.
2 oz (56 g) = 164 Calories.

ASIAGO

Available in Mild, Semifirm, Medium, and Aged forms. Use for finger food, grating, or hot sandwiches.

Packs:
12-lb (5.4-kg) half moons; 22-lb (9.9-kg) daisies; 24-lb (10.8-kg) wheels.

Needs ripening:
No.

Kitchen Yields

Serving size:
2 oz (56 g).

BAKERS CHEESE
Cream cheese-type cheese used mostly in baking.

Packs:
3-lb (1.35- kg) loaves; 10-lb (4.5-kg) tubs.

Needs ripening:
No.

Kitchen Yields

Serving size:
Varies depending on recipe.

BEL PAESE
Rather soft, white cheese with wax coating. Available domestic and imported. Good cheese for cheese platters and banquets.

Pack:
Approximately 5-lb (2.2-kg) wheels.

Needs ripening:
No.

Kitchen Yields

Serving size:
3½ oz (100 g) restaurant portion; thus, one 5-lb (2.2-kg) wheel yields 20 servings, and one-third wheel yields 10 banquet servings.

BLUE CHEESE

BLEU DE BRESSE
One of many blue cheese varieties made in France. Crumbly, hard to cut. Nice cheese for cheese platters because it is small, has mild flavor, and is not smelly.

Pack:
8-oz (225-g) packages.

Needs ripening:
No.

Kitchen Yields

Serving size:
3 oz (112 g).

CRUMBLED BLUE
Domestic blue cheese in soft-textured, crumbled pieces. Used for dressing and stuffing.

Pack:
20-, 25-, and 50-lb (9-, 11.25-, and 22.5-kg) bags. Other packs are available.

Needs ripening:
No.

Kitchen Yields

Serving size:
1 oz (28 g) added to dressing.

Calories:
1 oz (28 g) = 100 Calories.

DANISH BLUE
Texture is semifirm to crumbly.

Pack:
One 5- to 5½-lb (2.2- to 2.5-kg) wheel; three 7½-lb (3.4-kg) wheels.

Needs ripening:
No.

Kitchen Yields

Serving size:
4 oz (112 g); one 5-lb (2.2-kg) wheel yields 19 servings.

Calories:
4 oz (112 g) = 400 Calories.

GORGONZOLA
See Gorgonzola as a primary subheading of Cheese.

INDIVIDUAL PACKAGED BLUE CHEESE
Available domestic and imported.

Weights:
From 1¼ oz (35 g) up.

Needs ripening:
No.

Serving size:
2 oz (56 g), as snack.

Calories:
2 oz (56 g) = 200 Calories.

ROQUEFORT
See Roquefort as a primary subheading of Cheese.

STILTON
See Stilton as a primary subheading of Cheese.

WISCONSIN BLUE
Texture is semifirm to crumbly.

Pack:
One 6-lb (2.7-kg) wheel.

Needs ripening:
No.

Kitchen Yields

Serving size:
4 oz (112 g); therefore, one 6-lb (2.7-kg) wheel yields 23 servings.

Calories:
4 oz (112 g) = 400 Calories.

BOURSIN
Delicate French cheese with high fat content. Available in a variety of flavors.

Pack:
5-oz (140-g) packages.

Texture:
Soft.

Needs ripening:
Yes.

BRICK
Texture is semisoft and waxy. Good cheese for cutting in cubes.

Packs:
5-, 10-, and 40-lb (2.2-, 4.5-, and 18-kg) blocks.

Needs ripening:
No.

Kitchen Yields

Serving size:
5 oz (140 g), for receptions; one 10-lb (4.5-kg) block yields 30 servings.

BRIE
One of the most popular soft dessert cheeses. Available domestically-made or imported from a number of countries. The cheese may be flavored, as with herbs, peppercorns, or other flavorings. Texture is firm when unripe, soft and runny when ripe. The fat content varies, about 60 percent is normal.

Packs:
8-oz (225-g), 2-lb (0.9-kg), 2.2-lb (1-kg), or 4.4-lb (2-kg) wheels.

Need ripening:
Yes.

Kitchen Yields

Serving size:
In restaurant, one-eighth of a 2.2-lb (1 kg) imported wheel, or 4⅓ oz (122 g); one-eighth of a 2-lb (0.9 kg) domestic wheel, or 4 oz (112 g).
In sandwich, one-twelfth of a wheel of domestic or imported wheel, or approximately 2½ oz (70 g).
For canapés, one 4.4-lb (2-kg) wheel yields cheese for 200 canapés.

Calories:
2½ oz (70 g) = 180 Calories.
NOTE: Calories vary according to fat content.

BUCHERON
Soft-textured French goat cheese.

Pack:
3¾-lb (1.6-kg) logs.

Needs ripening:
Little.

Kitchen Yields

Serving size:
2 oz (56 g); therefore, one 3¾-lb (1.6-kg) log yields 30 servings.

CAMEMBERT
Available domestic and imported. Texture is firm when unripe, soft and runny when ripe.

Pack:
8-oz (225-g) wheel. Individual packs are available in many sizes.

Needs ripening:
Yes.

Kitchen Yields

Serving size:
One 1⅓-oz (37-g) wedge; one 8-oz (225-g) wheel yields 6 wedges.

Calories:
One 1⅓-oz (37-g) wedge = 115 Calories.
2 oz (56 g) = 180 Calories.

CANTAL
Hard-textured French cheese. Good cheese for cheese boards.

Packs:
40- to 120-lb (18- to 54-kg) wheels.

Needs ripening:
No.

Kitchen Yields

Serving size:
3 oz (84 g), in restaurant; therefore, one 40-lb (18-kg) wheel yields 140 servings.

CHEDDAR
Firm-textured cheese, available sharp and mild from different states. Often covered with colored wax. Moisture content of cheese varies greatly depending on age and brand. This influences weights and slicing characteristics.

Packs:

Cylindrical, longhorn:
13 lb (5.8 kg).

Rectangular:
5, 10, and 40 lb (2.2, 4.5 and 18 kg).

Wheel:
12, 22, and 75 lb (5.4, 9.9 and 33.8 kg).

Needs ripening:
No.

Kitchen Yields

Serving size:
3 oz (84 g), in restaurant; 1½ oz (42 g) with apple pie.
1 cup shredded weighs 4 oz (112 g), on average.

Calories:
3 oz (84 g) = 345 Calories.
1- × 1- × 1-in cube weighing ⅝ oz (17 g) = 70 Calories.
1 cup shredded, weighing 4 oz (112 g) = 460 Calories.

CHEVRE
Soft-textured goat-milk cheese made domestically in various states; also available imported. Some imported cheeses are covered with a thin layer of ground cinders, which is edible. Cheese is available in different shapes, the most practical of which is the log shape.

Weights:
3 to 11 oz (85 to 320 g).

Needs ripening:
No.

Kitchen Yields

Serving size:
2 oz (56 g) for salads; one 11-oz (320-g) log yields 5 servings, or 16 slices for canapés.

COLBY
Type of cheddar cheese, sold in same sizes. Good for shredding.

Kitchen Yields
See Cheddar.

COLD-PACK CHEESE SPREADS
Spreads are available in a number of flavors. Soft, spreadable, versatile products for making canapés, dips, and sandwiches.

Packs:
5-lb (2.2-kg) tub; 10-lb (4.5-kg) tub; 30-lb (13.5-kg) tub.

Needs ripening:
No.

Kitchen Yields
Varies depending on use. There is no waste.

COTTAGE CHEESE
This soft-textured product is available creamed and in different-size curds. Fat content also varies.

Pack:
5-lb (2.2-kg) tubs. Many other sizes are available.

Needs ripening:
No.

Kitchen Yields

Serving size:
½ cup for fruit salad; 5 lb (2.2 kg) yield 19 servings.

Calories:

Creamed:
½ cup (112 g), 4 percent fat = 118 Calories.
                2 percent fat = 102 Calories.
                1 percent fat = 83 Calories.

Dry curd:
1 cup, or 5⅛ oz (145 g), ½ percent fat = 125 Calories.

COULOMMIERS
Soft-textured French cheese.

Pack:
1 lb (450 g), in wooden boxes.

Needs ripening:
Yes.

Kitchen Yields

Serving size:
2 oz (56 g); therefore, 1 lb (450 g) yields 8 servings.

CREAM CHEESE
Soft-textured cheese.

Pack:
1-oz (28-g) individual packs; 3-oz (84-g) individual packs; 8-oz (225-g) individual packs; 3-lb (1.35-kg) loaves; 18-lb (8.1-kg) cartons; 30-lb (13-kg) blocks.

Needs ripening:
No.

Kitchen Yields

Serving size:
2 oz (56 g) with smoked salmon.

Calories:
3 oz (84 g) = 300 Calories.
1 oz (28 g) = 100 Calories.

CREME FRAICHE
Texture is soft and creamy, like sour cream.

Pack:
Twelve 10-oz (225-g) container; 3-lb (1.35-kg) tubs; 5-lb (2.2-kg) tubs.

Needs ripening:
No.

Kitchen Yields

Serving size:
Varies according to recipe.

EDAM CHEESE
Ball- or round-shaped firm-textured cheese, most often covered with red or yellow wax. Attractive cheese for platters. Cheese can be hollowed out and filled with cubed cheese for display.

Weights:
Individual packs; 2 lb (0.9 kg); 4 lb (1.8 kg).

Needs ripening:
No.

Kitchen Yields

Serving size:
2 oz (56 g); thus, 4 lb (1.8 kg) yields 29 servings.

FETA

White cheese, made with goat or sheep milk, sometimes with cow milk. Popular in salads and in cooking. Cheese is slightly salty and has a slightly crumbly texture. The cheese is shipped in brine. There is no rind.

Pack:
8-lb (3.6-kg) tubs, net weight; 28-lb (12.6-kg) tubs, net weight.

Needs ripening:
No.

Kitchen Yields
There is little waste.

Serving size:
3 oz (84 g) for Greek Salad; thus, an 8-lb (3.6-kg) tub yields 40 servings.

FONTINA

Domestic and Italian import, with semisoft and buttery texture. Good cheese for cheese boards or for fruit baskets. Little smell.

Pack:
18-lb (8.1-kg) wheel.

Needs ripening:
No.

Kitchen Yields

Serving size:
2 oz (56 g); one wheel yields 140 servings.

GORGONZOLA

Blue cheese imported from Italy or made domestically. Texture is firm, but can be crumbly and hard to portion. Gorgonzola can be salty. It is wrapped in foil.

Pack:
4- to 7-lb (1.8- to 3.1-kg) wheels.

Needs ripening:
No.

Kitchen Yields
There is little waste.

Serving size:
4 oz (112 g) as dessert cheese.

GOUDA

Cheese that resembles Edam. Texture is firm to hard. Available imported and domestic. The domestic product is also available smoked. Good cheese for buffet displays. Baby Gouda is sometimes covered with red wax like Edam cheese.

Pack:

Imported:
Twelve 8-oz (225-g) Baby Gouda; 8-lb (3.6-kg) wheel.

Domestic:
Circular: 2-lb (0.9-kg) balls.
Rectangular: 5-lb (2.2-kg) loaf; 8-lb (3.6-kg) block.
Wheel: 11-lb (4.9-kg) wheel.

Needs ripening:
No.

Kitchen Yields

Serving size:
2 oz (56 g); 2 lb (0.9 kg) yields 14 servings.

GRAPE CHEESE

White, buttery cheese made in France. The outside is covered with the seeds and skins of black grapes. The rind should be served with the cheese, but is not intended to be eaten.

Weight:
4 lb (1.8 kg).

Needs ripening:
No.

Kitchen Yields

Serving size:
3 oz (84 g); thus, 4 lb (1.8 kg) yield 20 servings.

GRATED CHEESE

Grated cheese is available made from imported or domestic cheeses. It is often a blend of various cheeses, the most common varieties used are Parmesan and Romano, because they do not melt when exposed to heat.

Texture is dry. Fresh cheese should be kept refrigerated. It is best to get a number of samples from different purveyors and select the best suited for the operation. The least expensive cheese might not provide satisfactory yield and flavor.

Packs:
1 lb (450 g); 20 lb (9 kg), and larger.

Needs ripening:
No.

Kitchen Yields
1 cup is equivalent to 4 oz (112 g).
4 tb is equivalent to 1 oz (28 g).
1 tb is equivalent to 7 g.

Calories:
1 cup, or 4 oz (100 g) = 455 Calories.
1 oz (28 g) = 112 Calories.
1 tb (5 g) = 20 Calories.

GRUYÈRE

Version of Swiss cheese, originally made in the village of Gruyère in Switzerland. Texture is firm, with small holes. Available imported from Switzerland and France; also domestically made.

Packs:
40-lb (18-kg) wheel; 6-lb (2.7-kg) loaf.

Needs ripening:
No.

Kitchen Yields
When purchased in wedges with rind still attached, waste is about 5 percent.

LIEDERKRANZ

Soft-textured American cheese made originally in New York state.

Pack:
8-oz (225-g) packages.

Needs ripening:
Yes.

Kitchen Yields
There is no waste.

Serving size:
2 oz (56 g).

MASCARPONE

Soft-textured cream cheese of Italian origin, with very high fat content. Available imported from Italy and domestic. Use for Italian desserts.

Pack:
1.1 lb (1 kg) tubs.

Needs ripening:
No; use fresh.

Kitchen Yields
There is no waste.

MONTEREY JACK

Firm, cheddar-type cheese, often used in Mexican cooking,

Packs:

Cylindrical, longhorn:
13-lb (5.8-kg) blocks.

Rectangular:
5- and 10-lb (2.2- and 4.5-kg) prints.

Needs ripening:
No.

Kitchen Yields
Cheese has thin rind; there is little waste.

MOZZARELLA

CURED MOZZARELLA

Cheese mostly used for pizza, but also for sand-wiches.

Pack:

Rectangular:
5- to 6-lb (2.2- to 2.7-kg) loaves; 20-lb (9-kg) loaves; 40-lb (18-kg) blocks.

Sausage Shape:
12-lb (5.4-kg) packs.

Shredded:
Available in various packs.

Needs ripening:
No.

Kitchen Yields

Serving size:
For pizza, 1 lb (450 g) supplies cheese for one large pizza, and 10 to 12 oz (280 to 340 g) supplies cheese for one medium pizza. Therefore, one 30-lb (13.5-kg) box of mozzarella supplies cheese for 30 large or 40 medium pizzas.

Calories:

Whole Milk:
4 oz (112 g) = 360 Calories.
1 oz (28 g) = 90 Calories.

Part Skim Milk:
4 oz (112 g) = 320 Calories.
1 oz (28 g) = 80 Calories.

FRESH MOZZARELLA
Fresh mozzarella is a soft-textured cheese that is packed in brine. It is an excellent cheese to use for appetizers.

Pack:
3-lb (1.4-kg) tub containing one-hundred-forty-four ⅓-oz (9-g) ciliegine (small balls); 3-lb (1.4-kg) tub containing thirty-two 1½-oz (42-g) bocconcino (bite size); 3-lb (1.4-kg) tub containing twelve 4-oz (112-g) pieces; 6-lb (2.7-kg) tub containing six 16-oz (453-g) pieces.

Needs ripening:
No.

Kitchen Yields

Serving size:
⅓ oz (9 g) ciliegine for receptions; 4 oz (112 g) for appetizer.

MUENSTER CHEESE
Firm cheese, originally made in Alsace, France. Available imported and domestic. Muenster is a good cheese for sandwiches and slices well on machine. Rind is very thin and edible; do not remove it.

Packs:

Imported:
½ to 2 lb (0.22 to 0.9 kg).

Domestic:
Cylindrical longhorn: 10 to 11 lb (4.5 to 4.9 kg).
Rectangular: 5, 10 and 40 lb (2.2, 4.5, and 18 kg).
Wheel: 5 lb (2.2 kg).

Needs ripening:
No.

Kitchen Yields

Serving size:
3 oz (84 g), for sandwiches. One 5-lb (2.2-kg) loaf yields 25 servings.

PARMESAN
Italian cheese with a rather hard texture. It can be eaten as a dessert cheese, but mostly is used for grating. Parmesan is also made domestically. Available whole and grated.

Pack:

Whole wheels:
80-lb (36-kg) wheel; 40-lb (18-kg) half wheel; 20-lb (9-kg) quarter wheel; 10-lb (4.5-kg) eighth wheel.
Other sizes are available.

Grated:
5-lb (2.2-kg) bags; 1-lb (450-g) bags.

Needs ripening:
No.

Kitchen Yields
Parmesan cheese is hard to cut. When buying cheese for grating, buy already cut into chunks.

Serving size:
2 oz (56 g), as dessert cheese.

> 20-lb (9-kg) ¼ wheel produces 74 cups grated cheese.
> 1 cup grated cheese weighs 4 oz (112 g).
> 5½ tb grated cheese weighs 1 oz (28 g).
> 1 tb grated cheese weighs ⅕ oz (5 g).

PONT-L'EVEQUE
Soft-textured cheese imported from France.

Pack:
10-oz (225-g) square boxes.

Needs ripening:
Yes.

Kitchen Yields
There is no waste.

Serving size:
2 oz (56 g); thus, 10 oz (225 g) yields 5 servings. Good cheese for buffets and platters.

PORT DU SALUT
Firm to semifirm cheese with a thin rind.

Pack:
3½- to 4-lb (1.5- to 1.8-kg) wheels.

Needs ripening:
No.

Kitchen Yields
There is little waste.

Serving size:
1/16 wedge of one wheel—about 4 oz (112 g).

PROVOLONE
Firm and smooth-textured cheese. It is a good cheese to use for sandwiches and buffets. Easy to slice on machine.

Pack:

Rectangular:
20-, 40-, and 50-lb (9-, 18-, and 22.5-kg) blocks.

Round:
12-lb (5.4-kg) balls.

Sausage shape:
12-, 25-, and 50-lb (5.4-, 11.25-, and 22.5-kg) pieces.

Wheel:
6-lb (2.7-kg) half-moons.

Needs ripening:
No.

Kitchen Yields

Serving size:
3 oz (84 g), for sandwiches; 12 lb (5.4 kg) yields cheese for 60 sandwiches.

Calories:
3 oz (84 g) = 300 Calories.
1 oz (28 g) = 100 Calories.

REBLOCHON
Soft and buttery French cheese.

Pack:
1-lb (450-g) round loaves.

Needs ripening:
No.

Kitchen Yields

Serving size:
2 oz (56 g); 1 lb (450 g) yields 8 servings.

RICOTTA CHEESE
Soft cheese that resembles cottage cheese. Available made with skim milk or with whole milk. Excellent cheese for baking, or served with fruit salad.

Pack:
3-lb (1.35-kg) tubs; 5-lb (2.2-kg) tubs; 10-lb (4.5-kg) tubs; 20-lb (9-kg) boxes; 30-lb (13.5-kg) bags.

Needs ripening:
No; use as fresh as possible.

Kitchen Yields

Serving size:
Varies according to use.

Calories:

Whole milk:
1 cup, or 8½ oz (240 g) = 428 Calories.

Skim milk:
1 cup, or 8½ oz (240 g) = 340 Calories.

ROMANO
Hard cheese used for grating. Use like parmesan cheese.

Pack:
10 lb (4.5 kg).

Needs ripening:
No.

Kitchen Yields
1 cup grated weighs 4 oz (112 g).
5½ tb weighs 1 oz (28 g).
1 tb weighs ⅕ oz (5 g).

Calories:
4 oz (112 g) = 440 Calories.

ROQUEFORT
French blue cheese made with sheep milk. Roquefort has a crumbly texture and is hard to cut into portions. Cheese gives excellent flavor to dressing When the name *Roquefort dressing* is used on the menu, only genuine Roquefort cheese must be used. Cheese is wrapped in foil and there is no rind.

Packs:
5-lb (2.2-kg) wheel; 6-lb (2.7-kg) wheel. Individual packs are available.

Needs ripening:
No.

Kitchen Yields

Serving size:
1½ oz (42 g), for dressing; thus, one 5-lb (2.2-kg) wheel yields 50 servings.

SAINT PAULIN
Buttery cheese imported from France. It is easy to cut and is good to serve on cheese platters and buffets. The cheese has a thin rind.

Pack:
4-lb (1.8-kg) loaf.

Needs ripening:
No.

Kitchen Yields

Serving size:
3 oz (84 g); one 4-lb (1.8-kg) loaf yields 20 servings.

SAPSAGO
Hard cheese for grating made from cow milk in Switzerland and flavored with clover. It is used as a grating cheese.

STILTON
English blue cheese that is salty and hard to cut. Stilton is attractive on buffets.

Pack:
12-lb (5.4-kg) wheel; 14-lb (6.3-kg) wheel.

Needs ripening:
No.

Kitchen Yields
When Stilton is old, the yield is low, because crusty rind cannot be used.

Serving size:
2 oz (56 g); 12 lb (5.4 kg) yields 75 servings.

STRING CHEESE
A form of Mozzarella cheese available in sticks and twists. The texture is stringy. Individual portions are handy for cheese baskets.

Pack:
Sticks of 1 oz (28 g) each; twists of 6 to 10 oz (170 to 280 g) each.

Needs ripening:
No.

Kitchen Yields

SWISS CHEESE

DOMESTIC SWISS CHEESE
Domestic Swiss has a firm texture and slices well on machine.

Packs:

Loaves without rind:
4 × 4 in (101 × 101 mm), weighing 6 to 8 lb (2.7 to 3.6 kg); 4 × 8 in (101 × 202 mm), weighing 9 to 15 lb (4 to 6.7 kg); 90-, 100-, and 200-lb (40-, 45-, and 80-kg) blocks.

Wheels with rind:
175 lb (18.7 kg).

Baby Swiss:
3- to 5-lb (1.3- to 2.2-kg) wheels.

Needs ripening:
No.

Kitchen Yields
Cheese purchased in loaves has no rind and, therefore, very little waste. Cheese purchased in wheels has about 5 percent trimming waste.

Serving size:
3 oz (84 g) for sandwiches; thus, one 8-lb (3.6-kg) loaf, 4 × 4 in yields cheese for 40 sandwiches.

Calories:
3 oz (84 g) = 315 Calories.

IMPORTED SWISS CHEESE
A firm-textured cheese, genuine Swiss cheese is imported from the Emmenthal valley in Switzerland. In order to market the cheese, it is marked *Switzerland Swiss*. Swiss cheese is also imported from many countries, especially from Austria and Finland.

Packs:
Loaves without rinds, 4 × 7 in (101 × 175 mm), weighing 10 to 14 lb (4.5 to 6.3 kg).

Needs ripening:
No.

Kitchen Yields
When purchased as wedge with rind on, the waste is about 5 percent. Loaves have little cutting waste.

Serving size:
3 oz (84 g), for sandwiches; thus, one 10-lb (4.5-kg) loaf 4 × 4 in yields cheese for 50 sandwiches.

Calories:
3 oz (84 g) = 315 Calories.
1 oz (28 g) = 105 Calories.

CHEESE CAKE

Formula
Combine the following ingredients:

> 12 lb (5.4 kg) bakers cheese
> 3 lb (1.4 kg) cream cheese
> 7¾ lb (3.5 kg) sugar
> 3 lb (1.4 kg) softened butter
> 2¼ qt (2.1 l) egg yolks
> 1½ lb (675 g) patent flour
> 12 oz (340 g) corn starch
> 8½ qt (8 l) sour cream

In separate bowl whip:

> 2½ qt (2.1 l) egg whites
> 1½ lb (560 g) sugar

and fold into batter.

Kitchen Yields

Scale:
2 lb (900 g) for 8-in (200-mm) molds.
3 lb (1.35 kg) for 10-in (250-mm) molds.

Number of cheesecakes:
Twenty-three 8-in (200-mm) cakes.
Fifteen 10-in (250-mm) cakes.

CHERIMOYA

This fruit resembles a large, closed pinecone. It has large black seeds and a custard-like flesh.

Season:
November to May.

Pack:
By piece.

Size:
3½ to 5 in (7 to 12 cm) across.

Kitchen Yields
Use in fruit displays or make sorbet with fruit pulp.

Calories:
4 oz (112 g) edible fruit pulp = 130 Calories.

CHERRIES

SWEET CHERRIES
Sweet cherries are available candied, canned, fresh, frozen, and as processed maraschino cherries.

CANDIED CHERRIES
Used in baking.

Pack:
By weight.

CANNED CHERRIES
Available pitted and with pit. The two major varieties are Royal Ann, which is light colored, and Bing, which is dark colored. Available in various syrup densities. Bing cherries are less expensive than Royal Ann cherries.

Pack:
Six #10 cans, drained weight of 64 to 70 oz (1.8 to 2 kg); twenty-four #2½ cans, drained weight of 18 oz (504 g); twenty-four #2 cans, drained weight of 12½ oz (350 g). Other packs are available.

Counts:
Table C-3 identifies counts for various cherry sizes and can sizes.

Table C-3 Cherry Counts for Different Size Cans

	#2 Can	#2½ Can	#10 Can
Cherries	35 to 40	50 to 60	210 to 235
	36 to 39	65 to 70	240 to 260
	54 to 64	80 to 90	290 to 335
	64 to 75	90 to 103	335 to 390
	90 to 95	130 to 135	480 to 540

Kitchen Yields

Serving size:
½ cup fruit and some juice as dessert; so one #10 can yields 10 cups drained fruit or 22 servings.
2 oz (56 g) for dessert sauce; so one #10 can yields 30 servings.

Calories:
½ cup, fruit and juice, in medium syrup = 105 Calories.

FRESH CHERRIES
The principal varieties are as follows:

Bing:	Dark red, large, firm and juicy
Lambert:	Dark red, heart shape, slightly smaller than Bing
Vans:	Resemble Bings
Rainers:	Light colored, cream to golden
Black Republican:	Very dark, medium size
Royal Ann:	Light yellow with pink blush

Cherries do not continue to ripen once off the tree; they just decay.

Season:
May to July; imports available in winter.

Pack:
12-lb (5.4-kg) flats; 18-lb (8.2-kg) California lugs; 20-lb (9.1-kg) lugs.

Kitchen Yields

Count:
Depends on weather and on variety.
1 lb (450 g) Bing cherries ranges from 60 to 150 cherries; while 1 lb (450 g) other varieties ranges from 280 to 290 cherries.

Serving size:
½ cup (heaping) cherries, with pits and stems; 1 lb (450 g) yields about 3 cups or 5 servings. With pits in, 3½ oz (100 g) consists of 15 medium cherries or 10 to 12 large cherries.
1 qt (0.9 l) whole cherries yields 1 lb (450 g) pitted fruit.

Calories:
3½ oz (100 g) = 70 Calories.

FROZEN CHERRIES
Available pitted, IQF, and solid-pack vacuum pack.

Pack:
40-lb (18.14-kg) pack of pitted, IQF cherries; 37-lb (16.6-kg) vacuum pack, solid block.

Kitchen Yields
40 lb (18.14 kg) yield filling for twenty-four 9-in (225-mm) pies.

MARASCHINO CHERRIES
Preserved cherries, available red and green, with and without stem. Maraschino Cherries are always pitted.

Pack:
½-gal (1,8-l) jars; 1-gal (3.8-l) jars.

Count:
Table C-4 lists the count per gallon of maraschino cherries.

Table C-4 Maraschino Cherries per Gallon

Size	Whole with stems	Whole without stems
Medium	450	600
Large	350	500
Extra large	200	400

SOUR OR TART CHERRIES
Sour cherries are marketed primarily in canned and frozen forms or as pie filling. Dry cherries are available as specialty item. Principal varieties are Montmorency, Early Richmond, and English Morello.

CANNED SOUR CHERRIES
Available pitted and with pit. Packed in syrup or in water. Ready-to-use pie or Danish pastry fillings are also available.

Pack:
Six #10 cans; six #10 cans pie filling.

Kitchen Yields
One #10 can yields five 9-in (225-mm) pies.

Calories:
1 cup, or 8 oz (0.23 l) pitted, water-packed cherries = 105 Calories.

DRIED SOUR CHERRIES

Pack:
By weight.

Kitchen Yields
The product has become a specialty item with many uses.

FRESH SOUR CHERRIES
Specialty item; very little reaches the market fresh.

Season:
July.

Pack:
By weight.

Kitchen Yields
1 lb (450 g) is equivalent to 2½ cups (0.58 l).

FROZEN SOUR CHERRIES
Available pitted and mixed with sugar at a ratio of 5 lb (2.25 kg) sugar to 25 lb (11.2 kg) cherries. Used primarily in baking or in sauces.

Pack:
30-lb (13.5-kg) tins.

Kitchen Yields
One 30-lb (18.14-kg) can yields filling for eighteen 9-in (225-mm) pies.

CHESTNUTS

Available canned, dried, fresh, and candied (glazed).

CANNED CHESTNUTS

Available whole and as purée. Chestnut purée can be obtained in either sweetened or natural form.

Pack:

Whole chestnuts:
Twenty-four 15½-oz (440-g) cans; twelve 31-oz (880-g) cans.

Unsweetened purée:
Twenty-four 15½ oz (440 g) cans; twelve 31-oz (880-g) cans.

Sweetened purée:
Twenty-four 17-oz (482-g) cans.

Kitchen Yields
One 15½-oz (440-g) can yields 10 oz (283 g), drained weight; one 31-oz (880-g) can yields 20½ oz (580 g), drained weight.

DRIED CHESTNUTS

Available whole and as flour.

Pack:
25-lb (11.25-kg) bags.

Kitchen Yields
Dried whole chestnuts will double in weight, but not in volume after soaking and boiling.

FRESH CHESTNUTS

Old or improperly stored fresh chestnuts can be moldy or empty. Check before buying.

Season:
Winter.

Pack:
By weight.

Kitchen Yields
Peeling loss is about 50 percent of raw weight.

CANDIED (GLAZED) CHESTNUTS

Often called *marrons glacés*. These are whole, candied chestnuts. Use as candy or as garnish on desserts.

Pack:
5 oz (140 g) tin; 7¾ oz (225 g) tin; 14 oz (400 g) tin.

Kitchen Yields
One 5-oz (140-g) tin contains 7 glazed chestnuts; one 7¾-oz (225-g) tin contains 11 glazed chestnuts; one 14-oz (400-g) tin contains 20 glazed chestnuts.

CHICKEN

Major subheadings are Fresh Whole Chicken and Varieties, Fresh Chicken Parts, Frozen Chicken Parts, and Processed Chicken Products.

FRESH WHOLE CHICKEN AND VARIETIES

The yellow color of chicken is often achieved by mixing marigold petals in the feed before slaughter. Color is not necessarily an indication of quality.
NOTE: Whole chicken is sold with weight of gizzards included. Gizzards represent approximately 6 percent of weight.

Industry terms:

Dressed poultry:
Picked clean, head and feet still attached, not eviscerated.

Ready-to-cook poultry:
Picked clean and singed; head and feet removed; eviscerated.

BABY CHICKEN

Also called *squab chicken*, or *poussin* in French.

Pack:
By weight and by piece.

Sizes:

Bone in:
14 to 16 oz (400 to 450 g).

Boneless:
14 oz (400 g).

Kitchen Yields

Serving size:
1 bird.

BROILER
Available in a number of sizes.

Pack:
By weight and by piece, packed in ice.

Sizes:
2, 2¼, or 2½ lb (0.9, 1.0, or 1.12 kg). Common size is 2½ lb (1.12 kg).

Kitchen Yields

Serving size:
½ broiler per person.

CAPON
Capon is a castrated male bird. The meat is tender.

Pack:
By weight and by piece.

Sizes:
3 to 7 lb (1.3 to 3.1 kg).

Kitchen Yields

Serving size:
5 oz (140 g) boneless meat. One 5-lb (2.2-kg) capon weighs 3½ lb (1.5 kg) cooked and yields 2 lb 3½ oz (1 kg) cooked, boneless meat; this is equivalent to about 5 servings, in slices of white and dark meat, plus some leftover pieces for other uses.

CORNISH HEN
Young chicken from the Cornish chicken breed. Available boned or bone in.

Pack:
By weight and by piece.

Sizes:

Boned:
14 to 16 oz (400 to 450 g).

Bone in:
16 to 20 oz (450 to 570 g).

Kitchen Yields

Serving size:
1 bird, usually stuffed. When serving whole birds, purchase 14-oz (400-g) hens; when serving half-birds, purchase 20-oz (560-g) hens.

FOWL
Mature chicken, used for boiling.

Pack:
By weight and by the piece, packed in ice.

Sizes:
4½ to 5 lb (2 to 2.25 kg); 5 to 5½ lb (2.25 to 2.47 kg).

Kitchen Yields
5-lb (2.2-kg) bird yields 2 lb (0.9 kg) cooked meat.

FREE-RANGE CHICKEN
Free Range Chicken are birds not confined to cages. They are considered more flavorful than caged chickens. The flesh is often darker than that of caged birds.

Average size:
3 to 3½ lb (1.3 to 1.5 kg).

FRYER
Medium-size chicken.

Pack:
By weight and by piece.

Sizes:
2¾, 3, and 3½ lb (1.23, 1.35, or 1.5 kg).

ROASTER
Large chicken. The 3½-lb (1.5-kg) size is often cut into parts.

Pack:
By weight and piece.

Sizes:

3½, 4, or 4½ lb (1.56, 1.8. or 2.0 kg).

Kitchen Yields

Parts breakdown of one 3½-lb (1.56-kg) roaster, raw weights:

One 20-oz (568-g) double breast; two 8-oz (225-g) legs; 4-oz (112-g) neck and bones.

ROTISSERIE CHICKEN

Chicken prepared for spit roasting. This chicken is pumped with a saline solution to retain moisture during the roasting process. Chicken not pumped will shrink much. Available plain and with different flavors.

Sizes:

Average size is 3½ lb (1.5 kg).

Serving size:

Half or quarter chicken.

FRESH CHICKEN PARTS

BREAST

Available as single and as double breast. Single breast is available bone in and boned. Boned and skinless double breast is often marketed as *chicken cutlet*. The term *French-cut double breast* refers to a breast with wings and back removed.

Pack:

By weight and piece.

Sizes:

10-oz (283-g) single breast, bone in, skin on; 8-oz (225-g) single breast, boneless, skin on; 16- to 18-oz (450- to 504-g) French-cut double breast.

CUTLETS

Boneless and skinless breast, normally sold as double breast.

Pack:

By weight.

Sizes:

Pieces range from 4 to 14 oz (112 to 400 g).

Kitchen Yields

Specify size when ordering. Trimming waste is 5 percent or less, depending on how uniformly pieces must be cut. Trimming waste can be cooked and used in chicken salad or in other applications.

Serving size:

7 oz (200 g) for grilled main course; 6 oz (170 g) for breaded main course.

Cooking loss:

30 percent. Thus, 45 lb (20.2 kg) uncooked yields 31½ lb (14.1 kg) cooked.

GIZZARDS

Hearts and stomachs are available by weight.

LEGS

Pack:

By weight and by piece.

Sizes:

6, 8, and 10 oz (170, 225, and 280 g), bone in.

Kitchen Yields

Serving sizes:

8-oz (224-g) leg for broiling; 6-oz (168-g) leg for stuffing; 10-oz (280-g) leg for cutting into six tidbits.

LIVERS

Available by weight.

Pack:

5-lb (2.2-kg) tubs.

Formula for Chopped Chicken Liver

10 lb (4.5 kg) chicken livers, cleaned

4 lb (1.8 kg) peeled onions

3 lb (1.35 kg) chicken fat

24 hard-boiled eggs

Salt to taste

Sauté onions in chicken fat before grinding with broiled livers.

Kitchen Yields

Serving size:
6 oz (170 g) as appetizer; 3 oz (84 g) on buffet.
Total mix yields 17 lb (7.6 kg), which is equivalent
to 45 servings appetizer or 90 servings on buffet.

NECKS AND BACKS
Sold fresh or frozen, with little difference in quality. Used for sauces and stocks.

Pack:
Sold by weight—normally, 5-lb (2.25-kg) bags.

Kitchen Yields
10 lb (4.5 kg) bones produces 2 gal (7.6 l) chicken
stock, and 100 lb (45 kg) bones produces 20 gal
(76 l) chicken stock.
NOTE: Boil no longer than 1 hour.

FROZEN CHICKEN PARTS
Most frozen chicken parts are machine cut, with
bone in.

Parts with back bone:

Quarters:
8.7 oz (250 g); 60 pieces per pack.

Halves:
17.9 oz (508 g); 30 pieces per pack.

Pieces:
4 and 4½ oz (112 and 125 g); 96 or 108 pieces per
pack.

Segments:

Breast halves:
6.4 oz (180 g); 48 pieces per pack.

Thighs:
3.6 oz (102 g); 96 pieces per pack.

Drumsticks:
2.6 oz (74 g); 112 pieces per pack.

Whole legs:
6.5 oz (185 g); 50 pieces per pack.

Drumettes:
1.4 oz (40 g); 175 pieces per pack.

Wings:
2.5 oz (71 g); 96 pieces per pack.

PROCESSED CHICKEN PRODUCTS

CANNED CHICKEN STOCK
Chicken stock is the most frequently used canned
product in foodservice.

Sizes:
46 oz (1.3 l) cans.

FROZEN CHICKEN PRODUCTS
Numerous processed chicken products are on the
market. Some are fully cooked; others are ready to
cook.

Breaded boneless products:

Nuggets:
½ to 1¼ oz (14 to 35 g).

Patties:
2½ to 4 oz (70 to 112 g).

Breast filets:
3 oz (84 g).

Tenders:
1.2 oz (34 g).

Bone-in breaded segments:

Breast halves:
8 oz (225 g) and larger.

Drumsticks:
3.9 oz (110 g) and larger.

Thighs:
6.9 oz (196 g) and larger.

Wings:
3.3 oz (93 g) and larger.

Drumettes:
1.6 oz (45 g) and larger.

Breaded random pieces:
5 oz (140 g) per piece, average weight.

Other:

Nonbreaded, marinated, bone-in breasts:
4 and 6 oz (112 and 170 g), packed IQF, ready for broiling.

Cooked, boneless white meat:
One 10-lb (4.5-kg) bag, IQF.

Cooked, boneless white and dark meat:
One 10-lb (4.5-kg) bag, IQF.

SMOKED CHICKEN PRODUCTS
Available whole or in parts.

Pack:

Whole capon:
4 to 5 lb (1.8 to 2.2 kg) each.

Chicken:
1¾ to 2 lb (0.8 to 0.9 kg) each.

Rock Cornish:
18 to 21 oz (510 to 600 g) each.

Chicken breasts:
8 oz (225 g) average.

STUFFED BREASTS
Stuffed breasts are available with various stuffings. Some products are fully boneless; other have the wing bone still attached. Most products are pre-browned.

Packs:
Twenty-four 7- or 8-oz (200- or 225-g) breasts, bone in; twenty-four 6-oz (168-g) breast, boneless.

CHICK-PEAS (GARBANZOS)

See Beans.

CHILIES

See Mexican Foods.

CHILI POWDER

See Herbs and Spices.

CHILI SAUCE

A variety of tomato catsup. *See* Tomatoes.

CHINESE FOODS

ABALONE
See Abalone.

BAMBOO SHOOTS
See Bamboo Shoots.

BEAN CURD (TOFU)
See Bean Curd.

BEANS

FERMENTED BLACK BEANS

Pack:
Bottles, cans, or plastic bags.

Kitchen Yields
Use as a vegetable or as a condiment in sauces.

LONG BEANS

Season:
Year-round.

Pack:
Purchase by weight; often sold in bundles.

Size:
1 to 3 ft (30 to 90 cm).

Kitchen Yields
There is little waste.

BEAN SPROUTS
See Sprouts.

BECHE-DE-MER (DRIED)
Cucumber-shaped holothurian; also called *sea cucumber*.

Pack:
Dried only; available by weight.

Kitchen Yields

Size:
8 in (200 mm) long, Product will triple in size after soaking and cooking.

BIRD'S NEST
Available dried as clean whole and as bits. Clean whole nests are the most expensive kind. Soak and add to clear soups.

Pack:
6-oz (170-g) packages.

Kitchen Yields
1½ oz (42 g) yields 1 qt (0.47 l) soup.

BITTER MELON
See Squash.

BOK CHOY
See Cabbage.

CELERY CABBAGE
See Cabbage.

CELLOPHANE NOODLES
Transparent noodles made of mung bean flour.

Pack:
8-oz (225-g) packages.

Kitchen Yields
Boil about 10 minutes or fry raw. Noodles will expand.

Serving size:
3 oz (84 g) as base with meat.

CHINESE EGGPLANT
White outside and inside.

Season:
Available year-round.

Pack:
By weight.

Size:
6 to 8 in (150 to 200 mm) long.

CHINESE PARSLEY
See Cilantro under Herbs & Spices.

CHINESE TURNIP
Long white root resembling white radish. It has a strong taste and is used as a cooked vegetable. Also available salted and dried.

Season:
Available year-round.

Pack:
By weight.

Kitchen Yields

Size:
8 to 12 in (200 to 250 mm).

CUTTLEFISH (DRIED)
Dried small squid.

Pack:
By weight.

Size:
6 to 8 in (150 to 200 mm).

DUCK SAUCE
See Hoisin Sauce in this section.

EGGROLL WRAPPER

Pack:
1-lb (450-g) packages.

Size:
6-in (150-mm) square and round.

Kitchen Yields
1 package contains 14 wrappers. To seal wrapper properly, make a paste with water and flour.

GALANGAL

These aromatic roots are also called Siamese Ginger.

Pack:
Available dried in slices, fresh, and powdered.

Kitchen Yields
The dried root can be reconstituted by soaking it in water.

GARLIC CHIVES

Long chives with strong garlic smell.

Season:
Available year-round; peak is in spring.

Pack:
Sold in bunches of various sizes.

Size:
12 to 16 in (300 to 400 mm) long.

Kitchen Yields
Use the same as other chives.

GINGER

See Ginger Roots.

LILY ROOTS

Lotus root, available canned and fresh.

GREEN TEA

Kitchen Yields
1¾ oz (50 g) dry leaves yields 30 cups brewed tea.

HOISIN SAUCE

Often called *duck sauce*, it is a thick, slightly sweet sauce. It is used as a condiment.

Pack:
Cans or bottles.

JELLYFISH

Available dried—normally whole, but sometimes shredded.

Pack:
Individual jellyfish, sold by weight.

Size:
25 in (900 mm) square.

LEMON GRASS

A tropical grass resembling leeks. The lower white part is edible.

Pack:
Available dried, fresh, and powdered.

Kitchen Yields
The dried form can be reconstituted by soaking it in water.

LILY FLOWERS

Dried flower petals.

Pack:
By ounce, in cellophane bags.

LILY ROOT

See Lotus Root under this same general heading.

LITCHIS

See Lychees.

LONGANS

Fruit resembling litchis. Available pitted and dried, or canned.

LOTUS ROOT

Available fresh, canned, or dried.

Pack:
Fresh bulb sold by weight.
Dried root sold by weight.
Canned slices packed in water.

Size:
4 × 8 in (100 × 200 mm) fresh bulb.

LYCHEE NUTS

See Lychee.

100-YEAR-OLD EGG

Duck egg artificially aged by applying a black, salty crust. A number of varieties are available. Ready to eat.

Pack:
Sold individually or by dozen.

OYSTER SAUCE
Condiment sauce.

Pack:
Bottles and cans in various sizes.

OYSTERS (DRIED)
Available raw or cooked.

Pack:
1-lb (450-g) bags.

Kitchen Yields

Size:
About 2 in (50 mm) long. Soak raw dried oysters for 12 to 24 hours to remove sand.

RICE
Special high-gluten rice is grown under various brand names.

Pack:
50- and 100-lb (22.6- and 45.3-kg) cotton bags.

Kitchen Yields

Serving size:
½ cup cooked; 1.6 oz (45 g) raw. 10 lb (4.5 kg) yields 160 servings.

RICE NOODLES
These white noodles can be deep fried and will puff up and become crisp.

Pack:
By weight.

SCALLOPS (DRIED)

Pack:
By weight.

Size:
Pieces or shreds.

SESAME OIL
Yellow flavoring oil.

Pack:
Bottles in various sizes.

SHARK FINS (DRIED)
Dried cartilage from the fins of sharks. Also available canned.

Pack:
By weight.

Size:
Shaped like thin spaghetti. Length is indication of quality; best fins are 5 in (127 mm) long.

Kitchen Yields
1 oz (28 g) dried shark fin is sufficient for 1 qt (0.47 l) soup.

SHRIMP CHIPS
Popular snack items, available in many colors. Dried chips puff up when fried.

Pack:
By weight.

Kitchen Yields
Chips triple in size when fried.

SHRIMP (DRIED)
Small dried shrimp, available in various sizes. Very strong seafood smell.

Pack:
By weight, in bags.

Sizes:
½ to 2 in (12 to 50 mm) long.

SHRIMP PASTE
Thick paste used as condiment.

Pack:
8-oz (225-g) jars.

SOY SAUCE
See Soy Sauce.

TARO ROOT
Potato-like root used in Oriental and South American cooking.

Season:
Year-round.

Pack:
By weight.

Kitchen Yields
About 20 percent peeling loss.

TOFU
See Bean Curd.

WATER CHESTNUTS
See Water Chestnuts.

WINTER MELON
See Squash.

WONTON WRAPPERS
The traditional shape is square, but round wrappers are also available. The size and count varies.

Pack:
1-lb (450-g) package. Many other packs are available.

Kitchen Yields
1-lb (450-g) package contains 60 skins. NOTE: To seal wrapper properly, make a paste with water and flour.

CHOCOLATE

Chocolate is divided into bitter, sweet, and white chocolate. Couverture is a chocolate with high fat content; it is used for coating.

There are many varieties based on fat and sugar content, milk content, and country of origin.

BITTER CHOCOLATE

Pack:
5- and 10-lb (2.2- and 4.5-kg) blocks.

Calories:
1 oz (28 g) = 145 Calories.

SWEET CHOCOLATE

Pack:
5- and 10-lb (2.2- and 4.5-kg) blocks.

Calories:
1 oz (28 g) = 145 Calories.

Chocolate Mousse Formula 1
Boil together:

> 3 lb (1.35 kg) sugar
> 1 pint (0.47 l) water, heated to 235°F (155°C)

Blend in:

> 1½ qt (0.7 l) egg whites, whipped

Fold in:

> 6 lb (2.7 kg) sweet chocolate and 2 lb (0.9 kg) bitter chocolate, melted and stirred (tempered) until cooled to 86°F (30°C)

Again fold in:

> 3 qt (1.4 l) heavy cream, whipped

Kitchen Yields

Serving size:
5 oz (0.14 l). The total mix yields 120 servings.

Chocolate Mousse Formula 2:
Combine and boil together:

> 5 lb (2.25 kg) sugar
> 1 pint (0.47 l) water, heated to 235°F (155°C)

Cream, then add into sugar mixture:

> 2 qt (1.8 l), or 96 egg yolks
> 4 lb (1.8 kg) sweet butter

Blend in:

> 6 oz (170 g) unflavored gelatin dissolved in 1½ cup (0.35 l) water

Fold in:

> 3 qt (1.4 l) heavy cream, whipped
> 6 lb (2.7 kg) sweet chocolate and 2 lb (0.9 kg) bitter chocolate, melted and stirred (tempered) until cooled to 86°F (30°C)

Kitchen Yields

Serving size:
5 oz (0.14 l). The total mix yields 120 servings.

CILANTRO

See Herbs & Spices.

CLAMS

ATLANTIC HARD-SHELL CLAMS

Available canned, fresh in shell, shucked fresh, and shucked frozen. Also known under the name of *quahogs*, these clams are classified by size.

CHERRYSTONES

Cherrystones are medium-size clams, normally served raw on the half shell or baked. Available fresh (live) and frozen IQF on the half shell.

Season:
Available year-round. Scarce when inclement weather makes fishing difficult.

Pack:
Bushels or cartons.

Count:
275 to 300. On account of scarcity, size and count varies. Many operators purchase clams by the piece.

Kitchen Yields
Normal portion is 6 clams on the half shell. Therefore, 1 bushel yields 45 to 50 portions.

CHOWDER CLAMS

SHUCKED CHOWDER CLAMS
Available fresh-shucked with juice, either whole or chopped.

Pack:
1-gal (3.8-l) container.

Kitchen Yields
No waste.
1 gal (3.8 l) shucked clams provides clams for 5 gal (19 l) clam chowder.

Calories:
3 oz (84 g) raw clam meat = 65 Calories.

WHOLE CHOWDER CLAMS
Large clams, used for making chowder.

Season:
Available year-round. Scarce when winter is severe.

Pack:
Bushels or cartons.

Count:
150 to 175.

Kitchen Yields
1 bushel whole clams provides clams for 4 gal (15.2 l) clam chowder.

Calories:
3 oz (84 g) raw clam meat = 65 Calories.

LITTLE NECKS

Formula for butter sauce for Little Neck Clams Casino is given elsewhere, *see* Casino Butter.

Pack:
Bushels or cartons.

Count:
500 to 550.

Kitchen Yields

Serving size:
On the half shell, nine clams; therefore, 1 bushel yields 50 to 55 servings.

Calories:
3 oz (84 g) raw clam meat = 65 Calories.

ATLANTIC SOFT-SHELL CLAMS

Also called *steamer clams* or *piss clams*, they are steamed and served whole with clam broth and melted butter. The shells are soft and easily crushed. The clams are often sandy.

Season:
Available year-round, but scarcity develops during a strong winter.

Pack:
42- to 46-lb (18.9- to 20.7-kg) bushel baskets or cartons.

Sizes:
Small, medium, and large, but seldom graded. Medium-size clams are 2 to 4 in (50 to 100 mm) long.

Count:
550 to 600; count varies according to individual clam size.

Kitchen Yields
About 20 percent loss because of crushed clams is possible.

Serving size:
14 to 18 clams, weighing approximately 15 oz (420 g) total; 1 bushel yields 35 to 38 servings.

PACIFIC HARD-SHELL CLAMS

BUTTER CLAMS

Pack:
By weight, often 80-lb (36-kg) sacks.

Kitchen Yields
Clams are seldom sorted by size, although minimum sizes are established by state authorities.

LITTLE NECKS
Formula for butter sauce for Little Neck Clams Casino is given elsewhere, *see* Casino Butter.

Pack:
By weight, often in 80-lb (36-kg) sacks.

Kitchen Yields
Clams are seldom sorted by size, although minimum sizes are established by state authorities.

MANILA CLAMS
Small clams resembling scallops.

Pack:
By weight.

PISMO CLAMS
Large clam, used for making chowders.

Kitchen Yields
Clams are seldom sorted by size, although minimum sizes are established by state authorities.

GEODUCK CLAMS
Very large clam harvested along the Pacific Coast, especially in the Puget Sound. The meat is often breaded and fried or grilled. Geoduck clams are a popular selection in sushi bars. They are available canned, fresh, frozen, and smoked.

Pack:
By the piece.

Size:
3 lb (1.3 kg), on average.

Kitchen Yields
About 50 percent by weight, without shell.

PACIFIC SOFT-SHELL CLAMS

ATLANTIC SOFT SHELL CLAMS
This clam has been introduced along the Pacific coast from the Atlantic.

Pack:
By weight, often 50-lb (22.5-kg) sacks.

Kitchen Yields
Clams are seldom sorted by size, although minimum sizes are established by state authorities.

RAZOR CLAMS
This clam is normally minced for use in chowders.

Kitchen Yields

Size:
3½ to 4 in (87 to 100 mm) long.

PROCESSED CLAM PRODUCTS

CANNED CLAMS
The clams used for canning are called *skimmer clams*, also known as *beach clams*, *giant clams*, or *sea clams*. They are normally available chopped. Used for chowder and fritters.

Pack:
Twelve 5-lb (2.2-kg) cans; twelve 51-oz (1.4-kg) cans. Other packs are available.

Kitchen Yields
One 5-lb (2.2-kg) can yields 38 oz (1.1 kg) drained clams; one 51-oz (1.4-kg) can yields 24 oz (680 g) drained clams.

Calories:
3 oz (84 g) drained meat = 45 Calories.

CLAM JUICE
Available plain or mixed with tomato, called *clamato juice.*

Pack:
Twelve 46-oz (1.3-l) cans; twelve 16-oz, or 1-pint (0.47-l) bottles; twelve 8-oz, or ½-pint (0.23-l) bottles.

Kitchen Yields

Serving size:
4 oz (0.12 l).

FROZEN, BREADED SOFT-SHELL CLAMS

Pack:
Twelve 2-lb (0.9-kg) boxes.

Kitchen Yields

Serving size:
6 oz (170 g).

COCONUT

FRESH COCONUT
Available year-round, with peak supply during winter. Available green with outer fibrous husk intact or with husk peeled (referred to as bald).

Pack:
50-lb (22.5-kg) burlap bags, or loose by the piece.

Sizes:
Bald 24s; bald 30s; whole (with husk) 12s.

Weights:
Balds range from 26 to 33 oz (0.75 to 0.93 g).

Kitchen Yields
Balds have husk removed to expose the hard shell. Waste is about 50 percent of weight, depending on the amount of liquid left in nut.

Calories:
1 cup fresh, shredded coconut weighing 3 oz (84 g) = 280 Calories.

PROCESSED COCONUT PRODUCTS

CANNED COCONUT JUICE
Homogenized coconut liquid, with sugar added, is available for kitchen use and for bar drinks.

Pack:
Case of twenty-four 15-oz (0.43-l) cans; case of twelve 57.5-oz (1.66-l) cans; case of twenty-four 13-oz (0.37-l) bottles; case of twelve 32-oz (0.93-l) bottles.

Kitchen Yields
One 15-oz (0.43 l) can contains 1¾ cups. Use in dessert sauces, custards, curries, and in baking.

SHREDDED DRIED COCONUT
Available short, medium, and thin (angel hair). Dried coconut is usually sweetened, but shredded coconut without sugar is also available.

Pack:
10-, 25-, and 50-lb (4.5-, 11.3-, and 22.6-kg) bags; 1-lb (450-g) boxes.

Coconut Custard Cream Pie Formula
    5 qt (4.7 l) milk
    2 lb (0.9 kg) sugar
    30 whole eggs
    20 oz (568 g) shredded coconuts
    5 oz (140 g) melted butter
    Vanilla to taste

Kitchen Yields
Ten 9-in (225-mm) pies.
NOTE: Pie shells must be pre-baked.

COFFEE

Coffee is available as blends or from specific countries and specific regions. The year when the coffee was harvested and how long it was stored is not specified. The integrity and experience of the purveyor is the only guarantee for receiving consistent quality.

The customers' expectations of strength and flavor vary from region to region in the country.

Coffee companies adjust their products according to markets. The flavor differences depend on the bean blend, the degree of roasting, and also the fineness of the grind. All coffee is available whole or ground to different degrees of fineness. Different pieces of equipment require different grinds.

Coffee looses flavor as soon as it is roasted and even more when ground. It should be stored in a cool location in well-sealed containers. Coffee grinders in restaurants should be cleaned and the blades sharpened periodically. Dull blades will heat the coffee unnecessarily and dirty machines will impart stale flavor to the coffee. Reputable coffee companies will maintain the equipment, ensuring that it is sharp and scrupulously clean at all times.

DECAFFEINATED COFFEE

Available naturally or chemically decaffeinated. Nescafé and Sanka are trade names.

Packs:
Same as regular coffee. Sanka is available in single-serving packs.

Kitchen Yields
Same as regular coffee.

ESPRESSO COFFEE

Packs:
1-lb (450-g) bags, whole beans or ground. The grind for espresso is very fine.

Kitchen Yields

Serving size:
3-oz (0.09-l) cup; 1 lb (450 g) yields 30 to 35 cups.

FLAVORED COFFEES

Coffee flavored with natural and artificial agents has come on the market. The coffee beans are sprayed with flavoring agents during the final stage of the roasting process.

Packs:
Available by weight in many flavors.

Kitchen Yields
The same as other coffees.

INSTANT COFFEE

Packs:
4 trays of 100 single-service packets; 1,000-piece random pack.

REGULAR COFFEE
Ground coffee is available packed in vacuum-sealed packages, premeasured for use with specific equipment, and in 1-lb (450-g) bags.

Kitchen Yields

Serving size:
6 oz (0.17 l) and larger. Coffee mugs are often 12 oz (0.35 l).

Large urns water ratio:
Use 2½ gal (8.5 l) water with 1 lb (450 g) coffee. Yield is 2 gal (7.6 l) or 40 cups.
1 gal coffee yields 20 cups; thus, 5 lb (2.2 kg) coffee yields 200 servings.

Small coffee maker ratio:
Use 2 qts (1.8 l) or 8 to 10 cups water with 3 oz (57 g) coffee for weak coffee, 4 oz (84 g) coffee for strong coffee.

SPECIALTY COFFEES
Unblended coffees from around the world are available in different degrees of roast. The better coffees are Arabica varieties from countries such as Indonesia, Costa Rica, Colombia, and Brazil. Less desirable coffees are Robusta coffees grown in Africa.

BLUE MOUNTAIN COFFEE
Grown in Jamaica. Production is limited and the price is high.

KONA COFFEE
Grown in Hawaii. Production is limited and the price is high.

COLLARD GREENS

Available canned, fresh, and frozen.

CANNED COLLARD GREENS
Available chopped.

Pack:
Six #10 cans.

Kitchen Yields
One #10 can contains 62 oz (1.7 kg), drained weight.

Serving size:
½ cup drained vegetable. One #10 can yields 14 servings, so one case yields 84 servings.

Calories:
½ cup drained greens = 32 Calories.

FRESH COLLARD GREENS
Grown mainly in the southern states. There are four basic varieties:

> *Georgia:* Large, crumpled blue-green leaves.
> *Vates:* Thick, green leaves with short stems.
> *Morries Heading:* Broad, medium leaves with short stems.
> *Louisiana Sweet:* Large, thick leaves with short stems.

Season:
Available year-round. Peak supply is in winter, and low production occurs from June to August.

Pack:
By weight.

Kitchen Yields
1 lb (450 g) as purchased produces 11 oz (310 g) ready-to-cook.

Serving size:
½ cup; 1 lb (450 g) as purchased yields 3½ servings.

Calories:
½ cup cooked, drained leaves = 35 Calories.

FROZEN COLLARD GREENS
Available chopped.

Pack:
Twelve 3-lb (1.35-kg) boxes.

Kitchen Yields

Serving size:
½ cup. One 3-lb (1.35-kg) package yields 12 servings, so one case yields 144 servings.

Calories:
½ cup = 33 Calories.

CONCHES
Large tropical gastropod, normally sold shucked fresh, frozen raw, or frozen cooked.

Pack:
5-lb (2.25-kg) cartons.

Kitchen Yields
About 30 percent trimming waste from raw product. Cooked product also has some cleaning waste, unless purchased chopped.
3½ lb (1.5 kg) cleaned conch yields 3 gal (11.4 l) chowder.

COOKIES

BUTTER COOKIES
The weight of butter cookies varies greatly.

Formula
> 6½ lb (3 kg) butter
> 4½ lb (2 kg) sugar
> 1½ qt (0.7 l) heavy cream
> 4½ lb (2 kg) patent flour
> 4½ lb (2 kg) cake flour
> Salt, vanilla, and lemon to taste

Kitchen Yields

Serving size:
1 oz; yield from total mix is 350 pieces.

Average count:
1 lb (450 g) is equivalent to 25 cookies.
Banquet quantities are 1½ lb (675 g) for each table of ten.

BUTTER-AND-SHORTENING COOKIES
This is a basic cookie dough from which a multitude of varieties can be prepared.

Formula
> 3 lb (1.35 kg) butter
> 3 lb (1.35 kg) shortening

4½ lb (2 kg) sugar
1½ qt (0.7 l) heavy cream
4½ lb (2 kg) patent flour
5 lb (2.25 kg) cake flour
Salt, vanilla, and lemon flavor to taste

Kitchen Yields
The total mix yields 360 cookies of 1 oz (28 g)
each.

FROZEN COOKIE DOUGH
Frozen cookie dough is available from many manufacturers.

Pack:
Four 6-lb (2.7-kg) buckets.

Kitchen Yields
One 6-lb (2.7-kg) bucket yields ninety-six 1 oz
(28 g) cookies, uncooked.

CORIANDER

See Herbs & Spices.

CORN

Available fresh, canned, and frozen.

CANNED CORN
Available as cut corn, creamed corn, and whole baby
corn. Also available as vacuum-packed cut corn.

Pack:
Six #10 cans cut or creamed corn weighing 105 oz
(2.9 kg) each; six #10 cans whole baby corn weighing 103 oz (2.9 kg) each. Other packs are also
available.

Kitchen Yields
One #10 can cut corn contains 70 oz (2 kg), drained
weight; one #10 can whole baby corn contains
53 oz (1.5 kg), drained weight.

Serving size:
½ cup, or 3 oz (84 g) cut corn; thus, one #10 can
yields 20 servings, and one case cut corn yields 240
servings.

½ cup, or 4½ oz (127 g) creamed corn; thus, one
#10 can yields 22 servings, or one case yields 260
servings.
One #10 can yields 300 pieces whole baby corn, on
average, although count varies. Six pieces of whole
baby corn weigh 1 oz (28 g).

Calories:
½ cup cut corn, weighing 3 oz (84 g) = 65 Calories.
½ cup creamed corn = 60 Calories.
½ cup whole kernel, vacuum pack = 88 Calories.

FRESH CORN

CORN ON THE COB
There are many local varieties of corn on the market. In foodservice, the basic distinction is between
yellow and white sweet hybrid corn. A well-devel-
oped ear of corn has 12 to 14 even rows of kernels.
Corn will loose quality rapidly after picking,
although chilling helps to prevent flavor loss.

Season:
Year-round. Peak in Florida is from May to August,
and from July to September in other parts of the
country.

Pack:
45- to 50-lb (20.2- to 22.6-kg) cartons; 35-lb
(15.7-kg) bushel containing 42 to 48 ears.

Counts:
54, 60, and 66 ears per 50-lb (22.6-kg) carton.

Kitchen Yields

Serving size:
1 ear. Two 60-size ears yield 1 cup (0.29 l) fresh
corn kernels.

Calories:
One 5 × 1¾-in (127- × 45-mm) ear weighing 5 oz
(140 g) = 70 Calories.

FROZEN CORN
Available whole on the cob and shucked.

CORN ON THE COB
Available IQF fully cooked.

Packs:
30-lb (13.6-kg) cases or slightly smaller.

Counts:
48 whole or 96 half ears.

Kitchen Yields
Product is fully cooked and ready to use.

Calories:
One 5-in (127-mm) ear weighing 9 oz (255 g) = 120 Calories.

CORN KERNELS
Available cut or cream style; also available as suc-cotash.

Pack:

Cut Corn:
Twelve 2½-lb (1.1-kg) boxes; individual 20-lb (9.1-kg) cartons.

Cream-style Corn:
Twelve 4-lb (1.8-kg) boxes.

Kitchen Yields

Serving size:
For cut corn, ½ cup, or 3 oz (84 g); thus, one 2½-lb (1.1-kg) package yields 12 servings, and one case yields 150 servings. For creamed corn, ½ cup, or 4½ oz (127 g); thus, one 2½-lb (1.1-kg) package yields 14 servings, and one case yields 165 servings.

Calories:
½ cup cut corn, weighing 3 oz (84 g) = 65 Calories.
½ cup creamed corn, weighing 2½ oz (127 g) = 55 Calories.

CORN KERNELS MIXED WITH RED AND GREEN PEPPERS
Also called *succotash.*

Pack:
Twelve 2½-lb (1.1-kg) boxes.

Kitchen Yields

Serving size:
½ cup, or 3 oz (84 g). One 2½-lb (1.1-kg) package yields 12 servings, and one case yields 140 servings.

CORN BREAD

Formula
> 5 lb (2.2 kg) cornmeal
> 3 lb (1.3 kg) pastry flour
> ½ lb (225 g) sugar
> 4 oz (112 g) baking powder
> 4 oz (112 g) salt
> 3½ qt (3.31 l) milk
> 24 whole eggs
> 1½ lb (675 g) melted butter

Kitchen Yields
Two 18- × 24-in (450- × 600-mm) sheet pans, or 72 pieces, each 3 × 4 in (75 × 100 mm).

CORN HUSKS

See Mexican Foods.

CORNMEAL

See Cereals, under Hot Cereals.

CORN MUFFINS

Formula
> 1 lb (450 g) sugar
> ½ lb (225 g) butter
> 3 eggs
> 1½ pints (0.7 l) milk
> 1 lb (450 g) corn meal
> 1½ lb (680 g) cake flour
> 1 oz (28 g) salt
> 1½ oz (42 g) baking powder

Kitchen Yields

Size:
2 oz (56 g), or #16 scoop, of batter. The total mix yields 48 muffins.

CORNSTARCH

Pack:
1-lb (450-g) packages.

Kitchen Yields

Thickening power equivalent:
1 cup corn starch is equivalent to 2 cups flour.

COURGETTES

French and British term for zucchini. *See* Squash.

COUSCOUS

North African wheat product, consisting of small semolina kernels. Small, medium, and large kernels available. Most products are instant and need only mixing with boiling water.

Pack:
18-oz (500-g) boxes. Larger packs are available.

Kitchen Yields

Serving size:
½ cup (0.1 l). One cup dry measure is equivalent to 7 oz (200 g) raw and yields 3 cups cooked.

Couscous Formula
    1½ cup (250 g) couscous
    2⅛ cups (0.5 l) boiling water or stock
    2 oz (56 g) fat

Sauté couscous in fat; mix with boiling liquid; let stand 10 minutes; bake in oven, or steam 10 minutes.

Kitchen Yields
Formula yields 3¾ cups cooked or 7 servings.

CRAB APPLES

Crab apples are small ornamental apples, available fresh and canned.

Season:
Fall.

Kitchen Yield
Use as decoration.

CRAB MEAT SUBSTITUTES

Products based on Surimi (Japanese fish cakes) technology. They are available in many shapes resembling lobster tails, crab claws, and shrimp. The most popular products resemble king crab meat. Various brand names are used. Some products are shipped frozen; others are shipped refrigerated. The fish most widely used in making crab meat substitutes is pollock.

Pack:

Frozen:
Case of six 5-lb (2.25-kg) blocks IQF, consisting of 64 whole-leg, 5-in (127-mm) pieces; 384 bite-size, ¾ in (19 mm) pieces; or random chunks of ¼ to ½ in (6.3 to 12.7 mm).
Case of six 3-lb (1.4-kg) blocks IQF, consisting of 16 pieces per 1 lb imitation shrimp, 16 per box 3-oz (84-g) imitation lobster tails, 16 per box 2-oz (56-g) split legs.
Case of twelve 2.5-lb (1.1-kg) boxes, consisting of chunky leg and flaky body-style meat.

Refrigerated:
Case of twelve 8-oz (225-g) packages of whole leg meat, chunks (cut legs), or flakes.

Kitchen Yields

Serving size:
5 oz (140 g) random chunks for cocktail; therefore, one 5-lb (2.25-kg) box yields 16 servings.

Calories:
4 oz (112 g) imitation shrimp (4 pieces) = 118 Calories.
3 oz (84 g) imitation lobster tail (1 piece) = 80 Calories.

CRABS

ALASKAN KING CRAB
King crab is caught in the Bering Sea off Alaska. It is always marketed cooked and is available canned and frozen. The foodservice industry primarily uses frozen king crab meat. Only male crabs are processed, and they can weight up to 12 lb (5.4 kg).

Season:

Available year-round. The actual fishing season is from September to December. King crabs have population cycles and become very scarce in some years.

Pack:

Whole king crab:
Available for buffet displays. Sold by weight.

Merus leg meat:
Six 5-lb (2.25-kg) packages whole, unsplit leg meat.

Fancy meat:
Six 5-lb (2.25-kg) blocks, consisting of 25 to 35 percent merus leg meat, 20 to 25 percent broken leg and claw meat, 40 to 50 percent white shoulder meat, and 10 percent or less shreds.

Split legs:
Twelve 12-oz (340-g) bags.

Fancy legs and claws:
One 25-lb (11.25-kg) carton, layer-packed, with minimum leg length of 16 in (406 mm), minimum leg weight of 8 oz (225 g), 32 to 45 legs per carton, and 5 to 8 claws per carton.

Standard legs and claws:
One 20-lb (9-kg) carton, loose-packed, with minimum leg length of 16 in (406 mm), minimum leg weight of 7 oz (200 g), 24 to 36 legs per carton, and 8 to 12 claws per carton.

Crab claws with arms:
One 25-lb (11.25-kg) carton containing extra-large, large, or small claws. Extra-large claws come 35 to 50 per carton and weigh 8 to 10 oz (225 to 280 g) each. Large claws come 50 to 80 per carton and weigh 5 to 8 oz (140 to 225 g) each. Small claws come 75 to 125 per carton and weigh 3 to 5 oz (85 to 140 g) each.

Kitchen Yields

One 5-lb (2.25-kg) frozen block yields 4½ lb (2 kg), thawed and drained.

Serving size:

For crab meat cocktail, 4 oz (112 g); one 5-lb (2.25-kg) frozen block yields 18 servings.

For a main-course serving of crab meat in sauce, 6½ oz (180 g), two 5-lb (2.25-kg) blocks yield seafood for 2 gal seafood with sauce, or 44 servings.

Calories:

4 oz (112 g) edible meat = 114 Calories.

ALASKAN SNOW CRAB

Available frozen in blocks and cans, and canned. Foodservice uses mostly frozen products.

Pack:

Fancy snow crab meat:
Six 5-lb (2.25-kg) frozen blocks consisting of 45 percent red meat, 34 to 45 percent white meat, 10 to 20 percent shreds.

Tin-pack fancy crab meat:
Six 5-lb (2.25-kg) cans, frozen, consisting of 30 percent whole leg meat and 70 percent broken leg and shoulder meat.

Tin-pack whole leg meat:
Six 5-lb (2.25-kg) cans, frozen, consisting of 75 percent red meat and 25 percent white meat.

Cocktail claws:
Twelve 2-lb (0.9-kg) bags (available with shell removed above the pincers), in sizes of 7 to 12, 12 to 16, or 16 to 20 per 1 lb (450 g).

Kitchen Yields

One 5-lb (2.25-kg) frozen block yields 4½ lb (2 kg) thawed meat.

BLUE CRAB

The common crab found along the Eastern Seaboard from Maine to Texas. They are available live, frozen whole, and in pieces canned. When the crabs molt and the new shell is soft, they are marketed as soft-shell crabs.

BLUE CRAB MEAT

Lump crab meat is available in tins—fresh, frozen, or pasteurized. The size of the pieces is important when judging quality. The meat should be reasonable free of shell and should contain little roe. Cans should be opened as they are used, and the meat should not be handled. Good-quality crab meat should be wrapped in paper inside the can.

Size:
1-lb (450-g) tins.

Kitchen Yields
1-lb (450-g) tin yields 14 oz (390 g), drained meat.

Serving sizes:
For cocktail, 5 oz (140 g); one 1-lb (450-g) can yields 2½ to 3 servings. For salad, 7 oz (200 g); one 1-lb (450-g) can yields 2 servings.
NOTE: Crab meat is very perishable.

SOFT-SHELL CRAB
Blue crab caught after molting while the new shell is still soft. Soft-shell crabs are harvested in the Chesapeake Bay and along the Atlantic coast. They are available live and frozen. Fishing for molting crabs is prohibited on the Pacific coast.

Season:
April to July, depending on weather.

Pack:
Sold by dozen live, in flats lined with seaweed.

Sizes:

Hotel Prime:
3 to 3½ in (76 to 89 mm) across.

Large Medium:
3½ to 4 in (89 to 100 mm).

Prime:
4½ to 5 in (112 to 127 mm).

Large Prime:
5 to 5½ in (127 to 140 mm).

Jumbo
over 5½ in (140 mm).

Kitchen Yields
Soft-shell crabs are small when the season starts.

Serving size:
4 small crabs, 3 prime crabs, 2 large crabs as main course when sautéed or broiled; 1 large crab as main course when breaded and fried.

WHOLE BLUE CRAB
Whole blue crabs are marketed live or frozen.

Season:
May to August.

Pack:
By weight. Weight per piece varies.

DUNGENESS CRAB
Dungeness crabs are caught commercially from Alaska to southern California. Only male crabs of a specific size can be taken. Dungeness crabs are available fresh whole, frozen whole, and as picked crab meat frozen and canned.

Season:
From May to September in Alaska and the Pacific Northwest.

Pack:
Whole, with average weight of 2 to 2¼ lb (0.9 to 1 kg); clusters (half crabs); individual cut legs; cocktail claws; picked crab meat in 5-lb (2.25-kg) boxes.

Sizes:
22 to 24 lb (9.9 to 10.8 kg) per dozen, cooked whole.

Kitchen Yields
Varies depending on application.

Calories:
3½ oz (100 g) edible meat = 100 Calories.

OYSTER CRABS
Tiny crabs, normally dusted with flour, fried, and eaten. Available frozen.

Pack:
14-oz (400-g) tins.

Kitchen Yields
About 5 oz (140 g) per serving. Oyster crabs are often served combined with fried whitebaits.

RED CRAB
An underutilized species, this deep sea crab is caught off the coast of New England. Most of the harvest is canned.

Size:
1 to 2 lb (450 to 900 g) for whole crab.

STONE CRABS

Caught of the coast of Florida and normally shipped whole. Only the claws are eaten.

Pack:
Sold by weight or in bushels.

Kitchen Yields

Size:
About 3 whole, raw crabs per 1 lb (450 g).

CRANBERRIES

Available canned, fresh, and frozen.

CANNED CRANBERRY SAUCE

Available strained and whole, with different flavors added.

Pack:
Six #10 cans, for all varieties. Smaller packs are available.

Kitchen Yields

Serving size:
⅓ cup (0.23 l) average as garnish with turkey; one #10 can yields 36 restaurant servings and four #10 cans yield 100 banquet servings.

Calories:
⅓ cup (140 g) sweetened, strained sauce = 130 Calories.

FRESH CRANBERRIES

Season:
Late fall and winter.

Pack:
Twenty-four 1-lb (450-g) cello packs. Bulk packs are available.

Kitchen Yields
10 lb (4.5 kg) yields 10 qt (9.4 l) whole sauce or 7½ qt (7 l) strained sauce.

Cranberry Sauce Formula
    10 lb (4.5 kg) cranberries
    20 lb (9.4 kg) sugar
    5 qt (4.7 l) water

CRANBERRY JUICE

Available plain and mixed with other fruit juices.

Pack:
Forty-eight 6-fl-oz (0.20-l) bottles; twelve 1-qt (0.94-l) glass jars; four 1-gal (3.8-l) jugs.

Kitchen Yields

Serving size:
6 fl oz (0.17 l); therefore, 1 qt (0.94 l) yields 5 servings, and 1 gal (3.8 l) yields 21 servings.

Calories:
6 fl oz (0.17 l) sweetened juice = 123 Calories.

CRAYFISH

Available live, frozen whole, fresh tail meat, and frozen tail meat.

FRESH CRAYFISH TAILS

Available shelled, with fat on or washed. Shelf live is shorter with fat on.

Pack:
8-oz (225-g) or larger plastic bags.
Shelf live with fat on is about 2 weeks; shelf life washed is about 1 month.

Count:
None established.

FROZEN CRAYFISH TAILS

Available cooked and washed (with fat removed).

Pack:
8-oz (225-g), 16-oz (450-g), and other sizes of bags; IQF 8-oz to 15-lb (225-g to 6.8-kg) boxes. Shelf life for frozen crayfish tails is 12 months.

Kitchen Yields
There is no count. Approximate weight for tails broken out is ⅙ oz (5 g) each.

FROZEN WHOLE CRAYFISH

Available raw and cooked. Whole cooked crayfish are available flavored, such as with dill, Cajun, and others flavorings.

Pack:

For both cooked and raw frozen whole crayfish, 8⅞-oz, 17½-oz, and 35-oz (250-g, 500-g, and 1-kg) boxes.

LIVE CRAYFISH

Available live from Louisiana.

Season:

From early spring to early summer.

Pack:

Sold live by weight, often in 30-lb (13.6-kg) boxes.

Count:

1 lb (450 g) equals about 12 to 15 crayfish. Counts are not reliable.

Kitchen Yields

Size is about 1 oz (28 g) each.

Serving sizes:

35 to 40 whole crayfish per person when customers break out the meat themselves; 10 tails for appetizer with pasta; 25 tails for main course with pasta (plus 1 whole crayfish for decoration).

Do not buy any smaller size than 15 pieces per 1 lb (450 g). Crayfish suffocate easily. Make sure boxes are not filled too high and are kept refrigerated. Crayfish are freshwater animals, and should be kept wet.

SOFT-SHELL CRAYFISH

Pond-raised crayfish are harvested at the time of molting. Available fresh locally, and frozen.

FRESH

Season:

Harvested from December to July.

Pack:

By weight.

Sizes:

Jumbo Premium:
20 or more per 1 lb (450 g). Average weight is 23 g each.

Extra Large Premium:
20 to 25 per 1 lb (450 g). Average weight is 18 to 23 g each.

Large Premium:
25 to 30 per 1 lb (450 g). Average weight is 15 to 18 g each.

Medium Premium:
30 to 35 per 1 lb (450 g). Average weight is 13 to 15 g each.

Soft Fryers:
Miscellaneous sizes, including those with claws missing.

Kitchen Yields

Between 70 and 90 percent of the animal is usable, depending on the amount of processing.

FROZEN

Available stuffed and breaded, fully dressed, and ready to cook.

Season:

Available year-round.

Pack and sizes:

Giants:
3½ in (89 mm) long and more. A master carton contains eight 2-dozen trays.

Big daddies:
3 to 3½ in (76 to 89 mm). A master carton contains eight 3-dozen trays.

CREAM

Types considered under this heading are coffee or light cream, half-and-half, heavy cream, sour cream, and imitation (non-dairy) sour cream. Cream must contain at least 18 percent butterfat to be called cream.

Butterfat content of creams:
Coffee cream: 18 to 30 percent butterfat.
Half-and-half: 11½ percent butterfat.
Sour cream: 18 percent or more butterfat.
Whipping cream, light: 30 to 35 percent butterfat.
Whipping cream, heavy: 36 percent butterfat.

COFFEE OR LIGHT CREAM

Pack:
5-gal (19-l) containers for dispensers; one case of twenty-four 1-qt (0.95 l) containers, for a total of 6 gal (22.8 l); one case of forty-two 1-pint (0.47 l) containers, for a total of 5 gal 1 qt (19.7 l); 480 individual ⅜-oz (0.012 l) packs.

Kitchen Yields

Serving size:
⅜ to 1 oz (0.012 to 0.033 l) per person with coffee. 1 gal (3.8 l) yields 128 to 160 servings; 1 qt (0.94 l) yields 32 to 40 servings; 1 pint (0.47 l) yields 16 to 20 servings.

Calories:
1 cup = (0.23 l) light or coffee cream = 470 Calories.
1 tb (0.015 l) light or coffee cream = 30 Calories.

HEAVY OR WHIPPING CREAM

Pack:
One case of twelve 1-qt (0.47 l) containers, for a total of 3 gal (11.36 l); one case of forty-two ½-pint (0.23 l) containers for a total of 2⅝ gal (9.94 l).

Kitchen Yields
Cream doubles in volume when whipped.
1 cup (0.23 l) unwhipped cream yields 1 pint (0.47 l) whipped cream; 2 qt (1.9 l) unwhipped cream yields 1 gal (3.8 l) whipped cream.

Calories:
1 cup (0.23 l) as purchased = 820 Calories.

HALF-AND-HALF

Calories:
1 cup (0.23 l) half-and-half = 315 Calories.
1 tb (0.015 l) half-and-half = 20 Calories.

IMITATION SOUR CREAM
Imitation sour cream is a non-dairy product. The pack is the same as for sour cream.

Calories:
1 tb (12 g) imitation sour cream = 20 Calories.

SOUR CREAM

Pack:
5-qt (4.7-l) buckets. Other packs are available.

Kitchen Yields

Serving size:
3 oz (84 g), with baked potato; one 5-qt (4.7-l) bucket yields 50 servings.

Calories:
1 cup (0.23 l) sour cream = 495 Calories.
3 oz (84 g) sour cream = 180 Calories.

CREAM PUFF PASTE

See Pâte à Chou.

CRÊPES (THIN PANCAKES)

Formula
    2 lb (900 g) cake flour
    10 eggs
    1 qt (0.94 l) milk
    1 qt (0.94 l) light cream

Kitchen Yields
Fifty 4-in (100-mm) crêpes.

CROISSANTS

Frozen croissants are available baked and ready to bake.
Ready-to-bake are available filled and unfilled.

Sizes:

Plain:
1.3 oz (34 g) for bread baskets; 2.4 oz (68 g) for single servings; 3.5 oz (100 g) for entrées.

With sweet fillings:
2.8 to 3.9 oz (80 to 110 g).

With meat, cheese, or vegetable fillings:
5.3 oz (150 g).

CUCUMBERS

Cucumbers are classified as Slicing Cucumbers, Hothouse (also called Greenhouse or English) Cucumbers, and Pickling (or Kirby) Cucumbers. Hothouse Cucumbers have almost no seeds and are burpless. They are often grown hydroponically. Cucumbers are often shipped covered with wax, which is harmless.

HOTHOUSE CUCUMBERS

Hydroponically grown and virtually seedless.

Season:
Available year-round.

Pack:
By weight or by piece. Usually 12 cucumbers per case.

Average weight:
1 lb (450 g).

Kitchen Yields
For canapé bases, one cucumber yields 26 slices cut on a machine set at #30.

PICKLING (KIRBY) CUCUMBERS

Pack:
By weight.

Size:
4 oz (225 g) average.

SLICING CUCUMBERS

Season:
Available year-round, with peak in May and June.

Pack:
26- to 28-lb (11.7- to 12.6-kg) cartons with 24 cucumbers each; 30- to 32-lb (13.5- to 14.4-kg) cartons with 35 and 40 cucumbers each; 50- to 55-lb

(22.5- to 24.7-kg) cartons with 60, 70, 80, and 90 cucumbers each.

Kitchen Yields
1 lb (450 g) as purchased yields 15 oz (426 g) pared, or 1 lb (450 g) as purchased yields 11 oz (312 g) peeled with seeds removed.

Calories:
6 to 8 slices, with peel, weighing 1 oz (28 g) = 5 Calories.

CURRANTS

Currants are small berries growing in clusters on shrubs. There are three varieties: Black, Red, and White. Most currants are used in jellies or in syrups. Only small amounts of fresh currents reach the market.

Pack:
1 pint (0.47 l) or 1 qt (0.95 l).

Size:
About ½ in (1.3 cm) in diameter.

Kitchen Yields
The small clusters are often used as garnish.

Calories:
4 oz (112 g) = 45 Calories.

CUSTARD

CUSTARD SAUCE

Formula
    1 qt (0.95 l) milk
    1 tb corn starch
    6 oz (170 g) sugar
    7 egg yolks
    Flavoring to taste

Serving size:
2 oz (0.05 l) sauce for dessert; total mix yields 18 to 20 servings.

EGG CUSTARD

Custard for bread and butter pudding, creme brulée, and similar uses. Custard is very perishable and must be chilled as soon as prepared.

Formula

    1 qt (0.95 l) hot milk
    8 oz, or 1 cup (225 g), sugar
    7 to 8 whole eggs
    Flavor to taste

Serving size:

4½ oz (120 g); total mix yields 10 servings.

D

DAIKON

See Japanese Foods.

DAIRY PRODUCTS

See specific product names, such as Cream, Cheese, and Milk.

DANDELION GREENS

Used for salad when small or as a separate cooked vegetable. Leaves get bitter with size.

Season:
Available year-round, with peak supply during April and May.

Pack:
By weight; often packed in bunches.

Kitchen Yields
When used for salads, cleaning waste is about 20 percent When cooked as a vegetable, 1 lb (450 g) as purchased yields about 2½ to 3 cups (0.72 to 0.87 l) cooked.

Serving size:
As a vegetable, one ½ cup.

Calories:
1 cup, weighing 3¾ oz (105 g), cooked, drained greens = 35 Calories.

DANISH PASTRIES

Items considered under this general heading include dough, fillings, and whole pastries. *See also* Apricot Glaze, under Apricots, and Prune Paste.

DANISH PASTRY DOUGH

Formula
2 lb (0.9 kg) sugar
4 qt (3.8 l) milk
2 lb (0.9 kg) yeast
4 qt (3.8 l) whole eggs
4 lb (1.8 kg) butter
20 lb (9 kg) patent flour

4 lb (1.8 kg) cake flour
¼ cup (50 g) salt
Lemon flavor and nutmeg to taste

Make dough and let rest. The fold in:

12 lb (5.4 kg) sweet butter

Kitchen Yields

Miniature Danish:
Scale 1½ oz (40 g) each before filling. The total mix yields 50 dozen pieces of pastry.

Breakfast Danish for baskets:
Scale 2 oz (55 g) before filling. The total mix yields 37 dozen pieces of pastry.

Large Danish:
Scale 3½ oz (100 g) before filling. The total mix yields 22 dozen pieces of pastry.

DANISH PASTRY FILLINGS
Almond filling, *see* under Almonds.

CHEESE FILLING

Formula
16 lb (7.2 kg) bakers cheese
6 lb (2.7 kg) sugar
32 eggs
1 lb (450 g) cake flour
Lemon or vanilla flavor to taste

Serving size:
1½ oz (42 g) for regular pastry; the total mix yields 24 lb (10.8 kg) of filling for 260 pieces of pastry.

POPPY SEED FILLING

Formula
3 lb (1.36 kg) poppy seeds, ground
1 qt (0.94 l) milk
1½ lb (680 g) sugar
4 fl oz (0.12 l) honey

Bring to boil and add:

3 lb (1.36 kg) cake crumbs
3 eggs
Grated lemon peel to taste

Kitchen Yields
Total mix yields filling for 100 pieces of pastry.

STREUSEL FILLING

Formula
>   3 lb (1.35 kg) butter
>   3 lb (1.35 kg) sugar
>   6 lb (2.7 kg) flour
>   4 oz (112 g) cinnamon

Kitchen Yields
Total mix yields filling for 100 pieces of pastry.

DANISH PASTRY SUGAR ICING

Formula
>   5 lb (2.25 kg) icing sugar
>   8 fl oz (0.24 l) hot water
>   4 fl oz (0.12 l) corn syrup
>   1 egg white
>   Lemon flavor to taste

Kitchen Yields
Total mix yields sugar icing for 100 pieces of pastry.

Quantities needed for parties:
For breakfast parties, two 2-oz (56-g) pieces per person.

Calories:
1 round, commercial quality, 4¼-in (106-mm) piece, weighing 2⅓ oz (65 g) = 275 Calories.

DATES

The industry is centered in Indio, California. A number of varieties are grown. Medjool Dates are extra large dates. Dates are shipped fresh or dried, pitted or with pit in.

DRIED DATES

Types available:
Whole dates, pitted and un-pitted; pieces without pits; macerated dates (ground, chopped, and broken pieces); slab dates (ground, chopped, and broken pieces in slab form). Domestic and imported dates are available.

Pack:
15-lb (6.7-kg) cartons of whole pitted dates; 30-lb (13.4-kg) cartons of date pieces; 40-lb (18-kg) cartons of macerated dates; 50-lb (22.5-kg) cartons of slab dates.
Sizes and counts vary.

Kitchen Yields
1 lb (450 g) whole, dried dates with pits yields 2½ cups (0.5 l); 6¼ oz (177 g) whole, dried with pits yields 1 cup (0.23 l) chopped dates. 10 pitted dates weigh 3 oz (84 g).

Calories:
1 cup chopped dates, weighing 6¼ oz (177 g) = 490 Calories.

FRESH DATES
Fresh dates are available in the fall, but are seldom available nationally.

Season:
Fall.

Calories:
10 whole, pitted dates, weighing 2⅞ oz (80 g) = 220 Calories.
1 cup, or 6½ oz (180 g), chopped dates = 500 Calories.

DILL

See Herbs & Spices.

DOUGH

See entries for individual baked products, such as Biscuits, Bread, and Danish Pastry. For modeling dough, *see* Salt Dough.

DRESSING FORMULAS

COCKTAIL SAUCE

Formula
>   1 qt (0.94 l) tomato purée
>   One #10 can (3 l) chili sauce

One #10 can (3 l) catsup
1 pint (0.47 l) grated horseradish in vinegar
1 cup (0.23 l) lemon juice
1 fl oz (0.029 l) tabasco sauce
2 oz (56 g) salt
4 oz (112 g) sugar

Kitchen Yields
The total mix makes 2 gal (7.5 l) sauce.

Serving size:
2 oz (56 g). The total mix from the formula yields 125 servings.

FRENCH DRESSING

Formula
1 gal (3.8 l) oil
½ gal (1.9 l) cider vinegar
½ gal (1.9 l) wine vinegar
1 cup (0.23 l) prepared mustard
1 cup (0.23 l) dry mustard
1 cup (0.23 l) sugar
½ cup (0.12 l) crushed pepper corns
½ cup (0.12 l) salt

Kitchen Yields
Total mix yields 2 gal (7.6 l) dressing.

Serving size:
1 oz (28 g). The total mix yields 250 servings.

GREEN GODDESS DRESSING

Formula
1 gal (3.8 l) mayonnaise
½ gal (1.9 l) sour cream
1 qt (0.9 l) chopped parsley
1 qt (0.9 l) chopped, uncooked spinach
1 pint (0.47 l) chopped chives
One 28-oz (780-g) can anchovy fillets with oil
¼ cup chopped garlic
¼ cup lemon juice
1 cup (0.23 l) tarragon vinegar

Purée in food processor.

Kitchen Yields
Total mix yields 1¾ gal (6.6 l) dressing.

Serving size:
2 oz (56 g). The total mix yields 110 servings.

RUSSIAN DRESSING

Formula
3 qt (2.7 l) mayonnaise
1 qt + 1 cup (1.1 l) cocktail sauce, canned or prepared (see above recipe)
1 pint (0.47 l) cooked chopped eggs
1 cup (0.23 l) lemon juice

Kitchen Yields
Total mix yields 1 gal (3.8 l) dressing.

Serving size:
1½ oz (42 g). The total mix yields = 80 servings.

THOUSAND ISLAND DRESSING

Formula
1 gal (3.8 l) mayonnaise
½ gal (1.9 l) cocktail sauce
½ gal (1.9 l) whipped cream
1 qt (0.9 l) chopped dill pickle relish
1 qt (0.9 l) cooked, chopped beets, drained
1 cup (0.23 l) lemon juice

Kitchen Yields
Total mix yields 2½ gal (9.5 l) dressing.

VINAIGRETTE MARINADE

This marinade can be used for marinating cooked vegetables or mushrooms.

Formula
1 qt (0.9 l) dry white wine
1 pint (0.47 l) wine vinegar
2 qt (1.8 l) olive oil
1 tb chopped garlic
2 tb thyme
1 cup (0.23 l) lemon juice
1 cup (0.23 l) chopped onions
½ cup (0.12 l) prepared mustard
3 tb crushed pepper corns

Kitchen Yields
Total mix yields 1 gal (3.8 l) dressing.

DUCK

Duck is available fresh or frozen. *Duckling* is a term used for young duck. Virtually all ducks coming to the market are young and raised under controlled conditions.

FRESH OR FROZEN DUCKLING

Most ducklings are shipped frozen, but fresh ducklings are also available in some markets. The most common breeds are Barberie, Peking, and Mallard duckling. Various other breeds also reach the market.

BARBERIE DUCKLING

Bred from Muscovy stock, this duckling is often sold as breast only, to be grilled and served medium rare. Barberie ducklings are leaner than other breeds.

BARBERIE DUCKLING BREASTS

Pack:

Boned breast, (male):
Six 27- to 38-oz (0.766- to 1.07-kg) double breasts.

Boned breast, (female):
Twelve 19- to 23-oz (540- to 650-g) double breasts.

Kitchen Yields
Male (drake) double breasts yield 5 to 6 servings; female (hen) double breasts yield 2 servings. Duckling breasts are best served medium rare.

BARBERIE DUCKLING LEGS

Pack:
36 per case.

Sizes:
5- to 7-oz (140- to 200-g) hen legs; 10- to 12-oz (280- to 340-g) drake legs.

Kitchen Yields
One drake leg constitutes 1 main-course serving. One hen leg constitutes 1 appetizer serving.

WHOLE BARBERIE DUCKLING

Pack:
22- to 32-lb (9.9- to 12.8-kg) case of 4 drakes; 21- to 30-lb (9.45- to 13.5-kg) case of 6 hens.

Average sizes:

Drakes:
6 to 8 lb (3.6 kg).

Hens:
4 lb (1.8 kg).
Weights include gizzards, necks, and hearts.

Kitchen Yields

Servings:

Drake:
5 to 6 servings, using breast only.

Hen:
2 servings, using breast only.

MALLARD DUCKLING

Farm-raised gamy birds. Leaner than Peking ducklings.

Pack:
10 to 12 birds per carton.

Average sizes:
1¾ to 2¾ lb (0.8 to 1.2 kg).

Kitchen Yields
When serving half a duckling per person, purchase larger sizes.

PEKING DUCKLING

The prevalent domesticated variety of duck is the Peking duck. All ducklings, whether they are fresh or frozen, are shipped cleaned and eviscerated.

PECKING DUCKLING BREAST
Boneless duckling breasts.

Pack:
Twelve breasts per bag, 4 bags per master carton.

Sizes:
10 to 12 oz (280 to 340 g); 12 to 14 oz (340 to 400 g); 16 and 18 oz (450 to 500 g).

Kitchen Yields
The breasts are boneless. They should be served well-done.

Serving size:
One 12- to 14-oz (340- to 400-g) breast.

Calories:
12 oz (340 g) cooked breast = 960 Calories.

PEKING DUCKLING LEGS

Pack:
36 legs per case.

Size:
6 to 8 oz (170 to 225 g), bone in.

Kitchen Yields

Serving size:
2 legs per portion. Thus, one case yields 18 portions.

WHOLE PEKING DUCKLING
Available fresh or frozen. Long Island, New York was once a major producer of these ducklings.

Pack:
Six ducklings in various weight ranges.

Sizes:
4 to 4½ lb (1.8 to 2 kg); 4½ to 5 lb (2 to 2.2 kg); 5 to 6 lb (2.2 to 2.7 kg).

Kitchen Yields
Purchase at least 4½-lb (2-kg) size when serving one half duckling per person.
Purchase 6-lb (2.7-kg) size when serving one quarter duckling per person.

PROCESSED DUCKLING
Various processed duckling products are available.

BREADED DUCKLING STRIPS (FROZEN, RAW)
Lightly breaded with almonds.

Pack:
5-lb (2.25-kg) box.

Size:
1- to 1½-oz (28- to 42-g) strips.

Kitchen Yields
About 65 pieces per box. Use as hors d'oeuvres or as appetizer.

IQF DUCKLING MEAT
Boneless, uncooked leg meat.

Pack:
5-lb (2.2-kg) box.

Kitchen Yields

Serving size:
5 oz (140 g), stir-fried.

ROASTED DUCKLING HALF
Fully cooked product; available boneless and bone in.

Pack:
12 boneless halves; 10 bone-in halves.

Size:
11 to 13 oz (312 to 365 g), boneless; 14 oz (400 g), boneless, with sauce; 15 to 17 oz (426 to 480 g), bone in.

Kitchen Yields
Product is ready to use. There is no waste.

SKINLESS, MARINATED DUCKLING BREAST, (UNCOOKED)
Available plain or marinated in teriyaki, vinaigrette, or green peppercorns.

Pack and sizes:
Thirty-two 4-oz (112-g) portions per case; sixteen 6-oz (170-g) portions per case; sixteen 8-oz (225-g) portions per case.

Kitchen Yields

Serving sizes:
4 oz (112 g) as appetizer; 6-oz (170-g) or 8-oz (225-g) portions as main course.

SMOKED DUCK
Available whole or as breast meat.

Weights:

For whole duckling:
3½ to 5 lb (1.5 to 2.2 kg).

Weights for breasts:
8 to 12 oz (225 to 340 g).

DULSE

See Seaweed.

DUMPLINGS

BAKING POWDER DUMPLINGS

Formula
1 lb (450 g) cake flour
4 tsp baking powder
1 tsp salt
14 fl oz (0.4 l) milk

Kitchen Yields
Total mix yields ten 1-oz (56-g) dumplings.

E

EGGS

FRESH EGGS

Freshness, grade, and size are the important considerations when purchasing and using shell eggs. Eggs are graded by the USDA or by individual states. Almost all foodservice facilities use grade A eggs.

Pack:

One case contains 30 dozen (360) shell eggs; one-half case contains 15 dozen (180) shell eggs; one layer contains 2½ dozen (or 30) shell eggs.

Market sizes:

Table E-1 lists available sizes of fresh eggs, together with their unit weight.

Size conversions:

Table E-2 lists size substitutions for recipes that call for eggs.

Kitchen Yields

Serving sizes for scrambled eggs or omelettes:

Restaurant service:
3 eggs per person. 2 layers yield 20 servings; one-half case yields 60 servings; and one case yields 120 servings.

Banquet service:
2½ eggs per person. 2 layers yield 24 servings; one-half case yields 60 servings; one case yields 144 servings.

Table E-1 Sizes and Minimum Weights of Fresh Eggs

Size	Minimum Weight by Dozen	Minimum Weight per Case
Jumbo	30 oz (840 g)	56 lb (25.2 kg)
Extra large	27 oz (756 g)	50½ lb (22.7 kg)
Large	24 oz (672 g)	45 lb (20.2 kg)
Medium	21 oz (590 g)	39½ lb (17.8 kg)
Small	18 oz (504 g)	34 lb (15.3 kg)
Peewee	15 oz (420 g)	28 lb (12.6 kg)

Quantities:

For chopped, boiled eggs, 1 cup is equivalent to 4 large eggs.
For sliced eggs, 1 egg yields 6 slices.
For egg whites, volume will double when beaten.

Volume conversions:

Whole eggs:
1 cup = 8 fl oz (0.23 l) = 5 eggs.
1 pint = 16 fl oz (0.47 l) = 10 eggs.
1 qt = 32 fl oz (0.94 l) = 20 eggs.
1 gal = 126 fl oz (3.8 l) = 80 eggs (2⅔ layers).

Egg yolks:
1 cup = 8 fl oz (0.23 l) = 11 to 12 yolks.
1 pint = 16 fl oz (0.47 l) = 24 yolks (2 dozen).
1 qt = 32 fl oz 0.94 l) = 46 to 48 yolks (4 dozen).
1 gal = 126 fl oz(3.8 l) = 190 yolks (16 dozen).

Egg whites:
1 cup = 8 fl oz (0.23 l) = 7½ egg whites.
1 pint = 16 fl oz (0.47 l) = 15 egg whites.
1 qt = 32 fl oz (0.94 l) = 30 egg whites.
1 gal = 126 fl oz (3.8 l) = 120 egg whites (about 11 dozen).

Calories:

One raw 1¾-oz (50-g) large egg = 80 Calories.
One raw ⅝-oz (17-g) large egg yolk = 65 Calories.
One raw 1¹⁄₁₆-oz (33-g) large egg white = 15 Calories.
One hard-cooked 1¾-oz (50-g) large egg, = 80 Calories.
One large egg, fried in butter = 85 Calories.
Two large eggs, fried in butter = 170 Calories.
Three-large-egg plain omelette = 270 Calories.

Table E-2 Egg Size Substitution Chart

Jumbo	Extra Large	Medium	Small
2	2	2	3
5	6	7	8
10	12	13	15
21	24	27	28
44	50	56	62

FROZEN SHELLED EGGS

Available are whole eggs, yolks only, egg whites only, and whole eggs with extra yolks. Frozen egg yolks mixed with sugar are also available.

Pack:
30-lb (13.5-kg) can; 15-lb (6,750-g) can.

Weight conversions:
The following equivalencies exist for large eggs without sugar.

Whole eggs:
One 30-lb (13.5-kg) can = 300 eggs (25 dozen or 10 layers).
One 15-lb (6.75-kg) can = 150 eggs (12½ dozen or 5 layers).

Yolks only:
30-lb (13.5-g) = 675 yolks.
15-lb (6.75-g) = 338 yolks.

Egg whites only:
30-lb (13.5-kg) = 540 egg whites.
15-lb (6.75-kg) = 270 egg whites.

The following equivalencies exist for frozen egg yolks mixed with sugar.
30-lb (13.5-kg) can = 608 yolks and 3 lb (1.35 kg) sugar.
15-lb (6.75-kg) can = 304 yolks and 1.5 lb (675 g) sugar.
1 cup = 8 oz (0.23 l) = 10 yolks and ⅔ oz (22 g) sugar.

Table E-3 Conversion Amounts for Dehydrated Eggs, Water, and Fresh Eggs

Large eggs	Dried whole sifted	Water
6	3 oz (84 g): 1 cup	1 cup (0.23 l)
12	6 oz (170 g): 2 cups	2 cups (0.47 l)
24	12 oz (340 g): 1 qt	1 qt (0.94 l)
50	1 lb 9 oz (700 g): 2 qt & ⅓ cup	2 qt + ⅓ cup (1.95 l)
100	3 lb 3 oz (1.43 kg): 1 gal + ⅔ cups	1 gal + ⅔ cups (3.95 l)

OTHER EGG PRODUCTS

Eggs can be purchased hard boiled, dehydrated, and in various ready-to-use mixes. Table E-3 identifies conversion amounts for dehydrated eggs plus water and for fresh eggs.

SUBSTITUTES FOR EGG

Egg substitutes are commercial products made with egg whites and cholesterol-free additives. Products can be used for omelettes and scrambled eggs.

Pack:
Twelve 2-lb (0.9-kg) cartons; twenty-four 1-lb (450-g) cartons.

Kitchen Yields

Quantities:
¼ cup, or 2 oz (56 g) is equivalent to 1 egg.
1 cup, or 8 oz (225 g) is equivalent to 4 eggs.
1 pint, or 16 oz (450 g) is equivalent to 8 eggs.

Calories:
½ cup, or 4 oz (112 g) = 60 Calories.

EGGPLANTS

Eggplants are grown in many states and are always in good supply, because the seasons overlap in the various growing areas.

Season:
Available year-round.

Pack:
20- to 22-lb (9- to 9.9-kg) lugs containing 24 eggplants; 30- to 34-lb (13.5- to 15.3-kg) bushels containing 30 to 35 eggplants.

Weight:
About 15 oz (420 g) each.

Kitchen Yields
Size and shape are important for best yield. Best size is 3 in (76 mm) in diameter and 6 in (152 mm) long.
One eggplant produces 2 cups diced pieces or 22 cross slices, each ¼ in (6 mm) thick; 1 cup diced eggplant weighs 6 oz (170 g).

Calories:

4 oz (112 g) = 28 Calories.

ELDERBERRIES, ELDER BLOSSOMS

Shrub with clusters of fragrant blossoms, which mature into purple, rather acidic berries.

Season:

Blossoms in spring, berries in fall.

Kitchen Yields

Blossoms can be dipped in batter and deep fried. Berries make excellent stewed fruit, pie, and jelly, and can be fermented into wine.

ELEPHANT GARLIC

See Garlic.

ESCARGOTS

Available mostly canned and imported. Much is imported from Asia and is sometimes repacked in France. Large snails are of the Asian Achatina variety, and small snails are of the French Petit Gris variety. Petit Gris are cultivated in California. Clean, empty shells are sold separately.

Pack:

Giant:

4½-oz (127-g) packs with 12 snails each.
18-oz (500-g) packs with 60 snails each.

Extra Large:

4½-oz (127-g) packs with 18 each.
9-oz (255-g) packs with 36 each.
18-oz (500-g) packs with 72 each.

Very Large:

4½-oz (127-g) packs with 24 each.
9-oz (255-g) packs with 48 each.
18-oz (500-g) packs with 96 each.

Petit Gris:

7½-oz (213-g) packs with 36 each.

Extra Large Shells:

Two 864-piece packs = 1,728-piece case.

Very Large Shells:

Two 1,152-piece packs = 2,304-piece case.
Other packs are available.

F

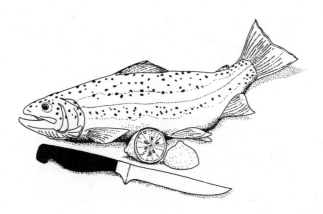

FENNEL

Fennel is often confused with cultivated anise, which forms a bulb. Some wild fennel reaches local markets. Fennel is also an herb.

Kitchen Yields

The stalks can be used as either a raw or cooked vegetable. Fennel seeds are used in baking and in flavoring stocks.

FIDDLEHEADS

The curly top of young ferns. Not all ferns are edible, and only the tops of ostrich ferns should be used. Available canned, fresh, and frozen.

CANNED FIDDLEHEADS

The supply is small and mostly appears in retail packs.

FRESH FIDDLEHEADS

Season:
Middle of April until June.

Pack:
By weight.

Kitchen Yields

There is basically no waste.

Serving size:
3 oz (85 g); 1 lb (450 g) as purchased yields 5 servings.

FROZEN FIDDLE HEADS

Only a small quantity in retail pack reaches the market. There is no waste.

FIGS

Figs are available canned, dried, and fresh.

CANNED FIGS

Available whole, whole split, and broken in syrup of various densities. Kadota is the most commonly used variety for canning.

Packs:
Six #10 cans; twenty-four #2½ cans; twenty-four #2 cans; twenty-four #303 cans.

Drained weights:
#10 can weighs 63 oz (1.8 kg); #2½ can weighs 18 oz (500 g); #2 can weighs 12½ oz (350 g); #303 can weighs 10 oz (285 g).

Counts:
#10 can yields 70 to 90 whole figs.

Kitchen Yields

Serving size:
Four fruits; thus, one #10 can yields 18 to 20 servings, and one case of #10 cans yields 110 servings.

Calories:
Four fruits, or 4¾ oz (130 g) with syrup = 100 Calories.

DRIED FIGS

A number of varieties are on the market. Adriatic, Calymirna, and Kadota figs are light to dark brown, Mission figs are dark purple to black. Figs are often imported for specific ethnic consumers.

Pack:
By weight.

Size:
Available whole, loose, and chopped for baking.

Count:
1 lb (450 g) is equivalent to 30 average-size figs.

Kitchen Yields

1 lb (450 g) dried figs produces 2¼ lb (1 kg) cooked figs.

FRESH FIGS

The important varieties are Calymirna, a green fig when ripe, and Black Mission. Fresh figs are highly perishable.

Season:
June to October.

Pack:
3¾-lb (1.7-kg) flats containing 30 figs each; 5-lb (2.25-kg) flats containing 56 figs each.

Weight:
1 oz (28 g) each and larger.

Kitchen Yields
Calymirna figs are often peeled for service. The peeling loss is about 20 percent.

Calories:
Three fresh fruits, weighing about 4 oz (112 g) = 130 Calories.

FILBERTS (HAZELNUTS)

Available shelled and in the shell. Filberts are almost always purchased shelled. They are available with skin on or peeled, whole or chopped. To peel filberts, dry roast the shelled nuts until skin becomes brittle and loose.

Although there is a botanical difference between filberts and hazelnuts, foodservice does not make a distinction.

Pack:
By weight.

Kitchen Yields
1 cup, or 4 oz (112 g) chopped requires 80 kernels. 1 lb (450 g) in shell yields 1⅓ cup whole nutmeats. 1 lb (450 g) whole nutmeats is equivalent to 3½ cups.

Calories:
1 cup, or 4 oz (112 g) = 730 Calories.

FILO

FILO SHEETS

Filo sheets (also spelled *phyllo sheets* or called *strudel leaves*) are shipped frozen and should be defrosted in the refrigerator for best results. Available as sheets and kataife (shredded dough).

Sizes:
Standard size is 14 × 8 in (355 × 100 mm); other widely available sizes are 12 × 17 in (304 × 430 mm) and 9 × 13 in (230 × 330 mm). Other sizes are available in bulk.

Thickness:
#4 (thinnest) to #10 (thickest). #6 or #7 are common thicknesses.

Pack:
Case of 12, 16, 24, or 30 packages, each weighing 16 oz (450 g).

Kitchen Yields
The number of filo sheets per package are approximate because some will break during handling.

Counts:

#4 (thinnest):
Twenty-six 12 × 17 in (300 × 430 mm) sheets.

#7 (medium):
Twenty-two 14 × 18 in (355 × 460 mm) sheets; eighteen 17 × 14 in (430 × 355 mm) sheets; twenty 12 × 17 in (300 × 430 mm) sheets.

#10 (thickest):
Eighteen 12 × 17 in (300 × 430 mm) sheets.

It is difficult to calculate a yield for kataife, because it is shredded fine dough, and its use varies.

FILO DOUGH (STRUDEL DOUGH)

Formula:
    1½ lb (0.675 g) high-gluten bread flour
    1½ oz (42 g) oil
    2 eggs
    1½ cups (0.35 l) warm water

Let rest 1 hour before stretching.

FISH

Fish are categorized as canned, fresh or frozen, and frozen or prepared products, and smoked or cured.

CANNED FISH

ANCHOVIES
Available packed in oil as flat fillets or as rolled fillets with caper in center. Also available salted. Anchovy paste is also available marketed in tubes. Practically all anchovy products are imported.

Pack:
Twenty-four 28-oz (780-g) cans of flat fillets; twenty-four 13-oz (365-g) cans of flat fillets; forty-eight 2-oz (56-g) cans of flat fillets; forty-eight 2-oz (56-g) cans of rolled fillets. Salt-packed anchovies are packed by weight.

Drained weight:
About 20 percent of a tin of anchovies is oil.

Kitchen Yields
Salt-packed anchovies can be rinsed and packed in oil. They can be used as a less expensive substitute for oil-packed anchovies. Anchovies packed in olive oil are more expensive than those than packed in other oils. Fillets are approximately the same size in all larger cans, and they are slightly smaller in the smaller cans.

GEFILTE FISH
Fish dumpling, normally made with carp. Available in jars, packed in its own jellied broth. For gefilte fish formula, *see* Frozen or Prepared Fish Products.

Pack:
Six 1-qt (0.94-l) jars.

Serving size:
Two pieces per person as appetizer.

Kitchen Yields
About 18 to 22 pieces per 1 qt (0.94 l).

HERRING
See Smoked and Cured Fish, under this general entry.

MACKEREL
Available whole or as fillet, smoked or plain, packed in oil.

Pack:
15-oz (420-g) cans. Other sizes are available.

Kitchen Yields
One 15-oz (420-g) can contains 12½ oz (350 g) mackerel, drained.

Serving size:
2 oz (56 g) as appetizer.

SALMON
Most canned salmon is produced in Alaska. There are five species of Alaskan salmon, each varying in color, texture, and cost. Most canned salmon is packed in brine. Some specialty packs of smoked or flavored salmon packed in oil are available, but they have little commercial distribution.

Varieties:

Red sockeye salmon:
Meat is deep red and firm; used in salads.

Pink salmon:
Pale color; less expensive than red sockeye.

King or chinook salmon:
Color ranges from deep red to white; meat is rich in oils and excellent for salads.

Coho or silver salmon:
Orange-red flesh; all-purpose use.

Chum or keta salmon:
Pale-colored, coarse-textured meat; this is the least expensive variety.

Packs:
Forty-eight 3¾-oz (106-g) cans; forty-eight 7¾-oz (225-g) cans; twenty-four 15½-oz (440-g) cans; six 4-lb (1.8-kg) cans.

Drained weights:
Good-quality salmon is solid-packed. Drained weights are about 10 percent less than net weights.

Kitchen Yields
For individual servings, use 3¾-oz (106-g) cans. For salads, use red sockeye salmon in the larger cans. One serving of salmon salad uses 4 oz (112 g) fish.

Calories:
3¾ oz (106 g) king salmon = 188 Calories.
          red sockeye = 161 Calories.
          coho or silver = 150 Calories.
          pink salmon = 130 Calories.
          chum or keta = 133 Calories.

SARDINES

Most products are packed in oil, but specialty packs such as sardines in tomato sauce or in mustard sauce are available. Distinction is made between skin-on sardines and skinless and boneless sardines. The bone structure is very soft, and all canned sardines can be completely eaten.

Much product is imported from Portugal and, to a lesser degree, from other countries. There is some domestic production. The quality of oil is important; better sardines are packed in olive oil. Brisling, also called *silt* or *small sardines*, are normally imported from Norway and are packed in oil.

Pack:

Twenty-four 15-oz (420-g) oval cans, usually packed in California; forty-eight 12-oz (340-g) cans, usually packed in Maine; one hundred 7-oz (200-g) cans; one hundred 3¾-oz (100-g) cans.

Drained weights:

One 15-oz (420-g) can weighs 11½ oz (326 g); one 12-oz (340-g) can weighs 10¾ oz (305 g).

Count:

Varies greatly. Brisling number about 8 fish per 3¾-oz (100-g) can.

Kitchen Yields

The size of fish varies greatly. Domestic products normally use larger fish. Portuguese sardines are considered to be of high quality.

Serving size:

2 oz (56 g) as appetizer or on sandwich. Serving size is most often determined by piece size.

Calories:

3¾ oz (100 g) canned, packed in oil, drained = 218 Calories.

TUNA

Available packed in oil or in water. The cans are labeled *light meat*, *dark meat*, or *mixed meat*. Canned tuna is manufactured from a number of different species. Albacore tuna has the lightest meat. Bonito is not considered tuna and cannot be labeled as such. Some canned tuna, mostly packed in water, is imported from Asia. High-quality tuna packed in olive oil is imported from Mediterranean countries.

Product varieties:

Prime Fillet—Solid Pack or Fancy Pack:
Meat from the loin; should be used for cold plates.

Chunk Style:
Mixture of pieces; up to 50 percent can be less than ½ in (12 mm) in size. Should be used for salads.

Flaked Tuna:
Mixture of small pieces. Can be used as salad, especially for sandwiches.

Grated Tuna:
Almost granular, but not pasty. Can be used as sandwich filling.

Pack:

Forty-eight 3½-oz (100-g) cans; forty-eight 6½- or 7-oz (184- or 200-g) cans; forty-eight 8-oz (225-g); twenty-four 9¼-oz (275-g) cans; twenty-four 13-oz (365-g) cans; twelve 42-oz (1.2-kg) cans; six 66½ oz (1.9-kg) cans.

Drained weights:

One 66½-oz (1.9-kg) can weighs 60 oz (1700 g); one 7-oz (200-g) can weighs 6 oz (185 g).

Kitchen Yields

For salads mixed with mayonnaise, buy tuna packed in water. For chunk tuna salad plate, use only tuna packed in oil.

Serving size:

3½-oz (100-g) can for single salad plate; 3 oz (85 g) for tuna salad sandwich, mixed with celery and mayonnaise. One 66½-oz (1.9-kg) can yields 20 servings for sandwiches.

Calories:

One 3½-oz (100-g) can tuna, packed in oil, drained = 170 Calories.
1 cup, or 7 oz (200 g) tuna salad made with celery and mayonnaise = 350 Calories.

FRESH OR FROZEN FISH

Fresh and frozen fish can be purchased with the following specifications:

Round: Not eviscerated; seldom marketed.
Drawn: Also called *gutted*; entrails removed.

Dressed: Scaled, eviscerated, with head and fins removed.
Steaks: Cut cross-sectionally across fish's spine, including bones and skin.
Fillets: Meat cut away lengthwise from fish's spine.

Both fresh or frozen fillets are marketed with skin on or with skin removed. Sometimes, some bones are still attached. When comparing prices, buyer should inquire how fillets are dressed.

ANCHOVIES
Small quantities of fresh anchovies are available. The fish spoil very rapidly, with a shelf life of less than 48 hours.

Season:
Available year-round.

Pack:
By weight.

Count:
Varies; often 12 to 18 fish per 1 lb (450 g).

Kitchen Yields
The whole fish is used, usually butterflied with the center bone removed.

BASS

BLACK SEA BASS
Harvested along the Atlantic coast.

Season:
Available year-round, with peak in spring.

Average size:
1½ lb (680 g).

Kitchen Yields
Purchase in fillets because spines are very sharp. Waste is about 50 percent.

STRIPED BASS
Nearly extinct on the Atlantic coast and protected by a complete ban on commercial fishing, this once very popular fish is presently not available wild. Farm-raised striped bass has come onto the market to fill the void.

Season:
Available year-round, with peaks in late fall and early spring.

Sizes:
1 to 1¼ lb (450 to 560 g) dressed, farm-raised; 6 to 8 lb (2.7 to 3.6 kg); 8 to 10 lb (3.6 to 4.5 kg).

Kitchen Yields
Purchase whole fish to be assured of freshness. Served filleted for appetizer and main course; whole poached bass may be used as buffet centerpiece.

Serving size:
For appetizer, 3 oz (85 g); for main course, 7 oz (196 g).

Waste:
About 40 percent. From drawn fish.

Best size:
For filleting purchase 6- to 8-lb (2.7- to 3.6-kg) whole fish. One 7-lb (3.2-kg) fish yields 4 lb (1.8 kg) fillet, and 4-lb (1.8-kg) fillet yields 20 appetizer servings or 8 main-course servings. For buffet service, purchase 8- to 10-lb (3.6- to 4.5-kg) whole fish. One such fish yields 35 servings when served with other items.

WHITE BASS
Also called *corvina*, the fish is not a true bass. Available whole and as fillets.

Season:
Summer.

Average size:
10 lb (4.5 kg).

Kitchen Yields
Fine eating fish resembling weakfish. Purchase fillets.

BLUEFISH
Popular and abundant Atlantic coast commercial and sport fish. Available whole and in fillets. Large fish can be oily and tough.

Season:
Summer.

Average size:
2 lb (0.9 kg) and larger.

Kitchen Yields
2- to 2½-lb (0.9- to 1.1-kg) dressed fish yields four 8-oz (224-g) servings.

Calories:
8 oz (225 g), baked with ½ oz (12 g) butter = 360 Calories.

BLOWFISH
Also called *chicken of the seas*, this fish is harvested in the Atlantic.

Season:
Summer.

Average sizes:
Skinned tail pieces, 4 to 8 oz (112 to 225 g).

Kitchen Yields
Purchase skinned tail pieces only. Cook whole.

BONITO
This member of the mackerel family resembles tuna. Most of the catch is canned. Fresh fish should be soaked in brine and acidulated water to lessen the strong taste.

BRILL
Also called *barbue*, it is an imported flat fish resembling flounder. Sometimes imported whole.

Pack:
10-kg (22.2-lb) crates.

Average size:
Varies; normally 2 to 4 lb (0.9 to 1.8 kg).

BUTTERFISH
Small, thin fish of little commercial distribution. Available on the Atlantic coast.

Season:
Summer.

Average sizes:
From 4 to 12 oz (112 to 340 g).

Kitchen Yields
Use whole fish for pan-frying.

CARP
Bony freshwater fish with little commercial importance in the United States. Used in making gefilte fish, a Jewish fish dumpling popular in central Europe. Large fish can taste muddy.

Season:
Winter and early spring.

Average sizes:
3 to 5 lb (1.4 to 2.25 kg).

Kitchen Yields
Red-fleshed fish, very bony, with large head and large belly cavity. Some species have scales; others do not. Purchase scaled and in fillet.

Waste factor:
Purchased whole, 60 percent; purchased in fillets, 20 percent.

CATFISH
Freshwater fish, although there is also a sea catfish that lives in the ocean. The most popular commercial species is the channel catfish. Most production is farmed in southern states. Catfish is normally sold in fillets.

Average sizes:
For whole fish, 15 to 20 lb (6.8 to 9.1 kg).

Pack:
IQF fillets with and without nuggets (small flank under head): 3 to 5 oz (85 to 140 g); 5 to 7 oz (140 to 200 g); 7 to 9 oz (200 to 225 g); 9 to 11 oz (225 to 311 g). IQF fillet strips, nuggets, and steaks are also available in various sizes.

Kitchen Yields

Serving size:
5 to 7 oz (140 to 200 g) breaded; 7 to 9 oz (200 to 225 g) blackened.

COD
Popular fish, without scales, harvested in both the Atlantic and the Pacific Oceans. Atlantic and Pacific

Cod are closely related species and little difference in made on the market. Most cod is processed into fish products and frozen fillets. Immature cod are called *scrod*. *See* Scrod. For black cod, *see* Sablefish.

Season:
Available year-round. Peak occurs from March to September.

Average sizes:
Up to 20 lb (9.1 kg).

Trade sizes:

Scrod:
1½ to 2 lb (675 to 900 g).
2 to 4 lb (0.9 to 1.8 kg).

Market:
2½ to 8 lb (1.13 to 3.6 kg).

Large:
8 to 20 lb (3.6 to 9 kg).

Frozen fillets:
4, 5, 6, 7, and 8 oz (112, 141, 170, 200, and 225 g).

Kitchen Yields
About 50 percent waste, when whole fish is cut in fillets. Fresh cod fillets, with skin still on, are available in some markets. Skin should be left on for broiling. When buying frozen fillets, make sure they are IQF or layer-packed.

Serving sizes:
5-oz (140-g) fillet in institutions; 7-oz (200-g) fillet in restaurants.
5-lb (2.25-kg) market cod yields 2½-lb (1.1-kg) fillet, and 2½-lb (1.1-kg) fillet yields 6 servings.

COD CHEEKS
New England specialty, available frozen.

Pack:
By weight.

Size:
Little nuggets about 1 oz (28.4 g) each.

Kitchen Yields
No waste; use as sold.

COD TONGUES
New England specialty, available frozen.

Pack:
By weight.

Size:
Varies; about 1½ to 2 oz (42 to 56 g).

SALTED COD
See Bacalao, under Smoked or Cured Fish.

SCROD
See Scrod under this same heading.

CROAKER
Small Atlantic coast pan fish.

Season:
March to October.

Average sizes:
½ to 2 lb (225 to 900 g).

Kitchen Yields
Purchase 2-lb (900-g) fish for fillets. One fish yields 2 servings.

CUSK
Also known as *deep-sea whitefish*, it is a deep-water flatfish, harvested along the New England coast. The fish has a white, delicate flesh.

Season:
February to July.

Average sizes:

Scrod:
1½ to 3 lb (0.675 to 1.4 kg).

Medium:
3 to 7 lb (1.3 to 3.1 kg).

Large:
7 to 15 lb (3.2 to 6.8 kg).

Jumbo:
15 lb (6.8 kg) and larger.

Kitchen Yields
About 60 percent waste when cut into fillets.

DAB (PLAICE)
Flatfish, found in both the Atlantic and the Pacific Oceans.

Season:
Available year-round.

Average sizes:
Small: Under 2 lb (0.9 kg).
Large: 2 lb (0.9 kg) and larger.

Kitchen Yields
Fish is used mostly for pan-frying whole.

Serving size:
1-lb (450-g) whole fish per person.

DOLPHIN
See Mahi Mahi, under this same heading.

EEL
Elongated, snakelike fatty fish that lives in both freshwater and saltwater. Most production is smoked.

Season:
Available year-round. Peak is in November and December.

Average size:
From 3 lb (1.4 kg) up, with head and skin removed.

Kitchen Yields
When eel is cut for fillets, the waste is only 15 percent.

BABY EEL
Baby eel is a specialty of Spain and is available frozen year-round. The tiny fish are fried in olive oil and eaten whole.

Season:
Early spring, for fresh baby eel.

Kitchen Yields
Use whole; there is no waste.

ENGLISH OR DOVER SOLE
Imported flatfish of excellent quality, available fresh or frozen. It is normally imported whole, with skin, head, and fins still attached. Flatfish of lesser quality are harvested under the name *Dover sole* in the Pacific. NOTE: The English sole found in fine restaurants on the East Coast is an imported fish and not directly related to the English sole marketed on the West Coast.

Average sizes:
10 to 12 oz (280 to 340 g); 12 to 16 oz (340 to 450 g); 16 to 20 oz (450 to 570 g); 20 to 24 oz (570 to 680 g); 24 to 28 oz (680 to 780 g); 28 oz (780 g) and larger.

Pack:
Fresh fish: 25-lb (11.25-kg) cases.
Frozen fish: 50-lb (22.5-kg) cases.

Kitchen Yields
Fish is normally served whole, one fish per serving. Some operations feature the 23-oz (650-g) fish for 2 servings. Fish gives best yield when filleted after cooking.

Waste:
About 30 percent, when head, fins, and skin are removed.

Best size:
For restaurant use, 19 oz (532 g) or larger. If fish is filleted raw, buy very large fish. Yields is very low, approximately 30 percent.

ESCOLAR
Available in fillets. Excellent fish for grilling.

FLOUNDER
Both winter flounder and summer flounder (also called *fluke*) belong to the large family of flatfish. There are a number of distinct subspecies, marketed under many local names. The fish is found on both the Atlantic and the Pacific Coasts, and the following varieties are often found:

> *Atlantic Coast:* Blackback or winter flounder (also called *lemon sole*); fluke or summer flounder, yellowtail flounder.
> *Pacific Coast:* Rex, petrale sole, English sole, Dover sole, sand sole, and rock sole.

The name *sole* is often used interchangeably with *flounder*. Most fish is purchased as fresh or frozen fillets under the name *fillet of sole*. There are noticeable differences in texture and flavor between the different species, but the market often does not indicate which species is used. There is much confusion regarding names. Large amounts of fillet of sole are imported.

Season:
Available year-round, but larger supply in summer.

Average sizes:
Whole fish: ½ to 6 lb (0.225 to 2.7 kg).
Fillets: 3 oz (85 g) and larger.

Kitchen Yields

Best sizes:
For pan-frying, use ¾- to 1-lb (337- to 450-g) whole fish. For filleting, buy 5- to 6-lb (2.25- to 2.7-kg) whole fish.

Boning yield:
When fillets are cut, waste from gutted fish is 50 percent.

GAR
See Needlefish, under this same heading.

GROUPER
Grouper belong to the large family of sea bass. Grouper of various species are found in the Atlantic Ocean from Brazil to Virginia.

Season:
Available year-round. Peak is from April to December.

Average sizes:
5 to 15 lb (2.25 to 6.8 kg); 2 to 3 feet (0.2 to 0.9 meter) long.

HADDOCK
Scaleless bottom fish found in the North Atlantic Ocean. Although most of the catch is filleted and frozen, a large volume is processed into frozen fish sticks and related products. Haddock and cod are related but distinct species; however, the names are often used interchangeably.

Season:
Available year-round.

Average size:
For whole fish, 1½ to 6 lb (0.6 to 2.7 kg).

Pack:
For IQF fillets, 5-lb (2.2-kg) cartons.

Fillet sizes:
6, 8, or 10 oz (170, 225, or 280 g).

Kitchen Yields

Serving sizes:
6 to 7 oz (170 to 200 g) for broiling; 4 to 5 oz (112 to 140 g) for frying.

Waste:
About 45 percent when fish is cut into fillets and skin is left on.

Best size:
For whole fish, 5 to 6 lb (2.2 to 2.7 kg). One 5½-lb (2.5-kg) whole fish yields 2 lb 7 oz (1.1 kg) fillet, which provides 6 servings for broiling or 8 serving for frying.

Calories:
6 oz breaded haddock, fried = 280 Calories.

HAKE
Cod-like bottom fish harvested in both the Atlantic and the Pacific Oceans. Most production is processed. The meat is white and lean.

Season:
June to September.

Sizes:
From ½ to 6 lb (225 to 2.7 kg).

Kitchen Yields
Buy fresh fillets only.

HALIBUT
Large flatfish found in both the Atlantic and Pacific Oceans. Halibut is graded according to size.

Season:
Available year-round. Peak is from March to August.

Average sizes:

Chicken:
5 to 10 lb (2.25 to 4.5 kg).

Medium:
10 to 60 lb (4.5 to 27 kg).

Large:
60 to 80 lb (27 to 36 kg).

Whales:
80 lb (36 kg) and larger.

Boneless fillets are called *fletches* and are available fresh or frozen, in many sizes. Steaks are normally sold bone in, with skin on, under the following trade names:

> *Full moon:* crosscut.
> *Half moon:* half cross cut.
> *Loin cut:* almost boneless cut.
> *Regular cut:* cut from full moon cut.
> *Roast:* tail cut, has most bones per weight of any cut.

Pack:
For steaks, 5-, 10-, and 15-lb (2.25-, 4.5-, and 6.8-kg) cartons.

Steak sizes:
4 to 6 oz (112 to 170 g); 6 to 8 oz (170 to 225 g); 8 to 10 oz (225 to 285 g).

Kitchen Yields
Whole halibut is shipped dressed and with head removed.

Waste factor:
For fresh fish, 40 percent when fish is cut into fillets and skin is removed. For frozen fish, 50 percent, because fish is glazed with ice.

Calories:
7-oz (200-g) fletch = 200 Calories.

HERRING
Herring is a small fish abundant in both the Atlantic and the Pacific Oceans. Fresh herring is seldom marketed; most is canned or pickled. Herring roe is a delicacy in Japan and is exported fresh from Washington State during a limited season.

JOHN DORY
Also called *Saint Pierre. See* St. Peter Fish, under this same heading.

KEY WEST YELLOW GROUPER
Florida fish.

Season:
Available year-round.

Size:
1.5-lb (670-g) whole fish; 7-oz (196-g) fillets.

LOTTE
French name for monkfish. *See* Monkfish, under this same heading.

MACKEREL
The species are related to tuna and are found along both the Atlantic and the Pacific coasts. Three commercial varieties are commercially important: Spanish mackerel (the smallest of the three), Boston mackerel, and King mackerel (the largest).

Season:
Spanish mackerel is available year-round; Boston mackerel is available from early summer to December; King mackerel is available from November to March.

Market sizes:

Spanish mackerel:
1½ to 4 lb (0.675 to 1.8 kg).

Boston mackerel:
½ to 2½ lb (0.225 to 1.1 kg).

King mackerel:
5 to 30 lb (2.25 to 13.6 kg).

Kitchen Yields
About 50 percent waste when cut into fillets.

Serving size:
One 1¼-lb (560-g) fish yields 2 servings for broiling or sautéing.

MAHI MAHI
Also known as *dolphin*, this fish is not related to the sea mammal of the same name. Most is harvested in the Pacific and sold under the name *Hawaiian Mahi Mahi*. Available fresh or frozen.

Season:
Available year-round.

Sizes:
Up to 50 lb (22.5 kg).

Pack:
Sold whole or as fillet, with skin on.

Kitchen Yields
Fish must be skinned. Waste is about 10 percent by weight if fish is purchased as fillet.

MONKFISH

Also called *angler fish*, and often placed on elegant menus under the French name *lotte*. Harvested in the Atlantic.

Season:
Available year-round.

Average sizes:
1- to 2-lb (450- to 900-g) fillets.

Kitchen Yields
Trimming waste when fillets are purchased is 10 percent.

Serving size:
6 oz (170 g), 2 pieces per serving, as main course; thus 2 lb (900 g) yield 5 servings.

MULLET

Popular fish in the southern states, harvested in the Atlantic and off the southern California coast. Available as whole fresh fish and as fresh and frozen fillets.

Season:
Available year-round. Peak is in September.

Average sizes:

Small:
1 to 2 lb (450 to 900 g).

Medium:
2 to 3 lb (0.9 to 1.35 kg).

Large:
Over 3 lb (1.35 kg).

Kitchen Yields
About 50 percent waste when fish is cut into fillets. Purchase fillets when possible. Fillets have some bones left in.

NEEDLEFISH

Also called *needle fish*. This fish lives in the temperate and tropical oceans. It has an elongated snout resembling an alligator. Good eating fish, but seldom found on the market. The bones can have a slightly green tint.

Average size:
Up to 10 ft (3 m) long.

OCEAN PERCH

Atlantic ocean food fish, available mostly in fillets. Imported frozen fillets are available. Fish is small.

Average sizes:
From ½ to 2 lb (220 to 900 g).

Season:
Early summer.

Kitchen Yields
Purchase fillets, which can weigh 3 oz (85 g) or more. Good buy for buffets and inexpensive meals.

ORANGE ROUGHY

Fish with firm, white flesh, imported as fillets from the subantarctic waters around New Zealand.

Pack:

Frozen fillets:
22-lb (10-kg) box.

Fresh fillets:
35-lb (15.7-kg) box.

Sizes:
2 to 4 oz (60 to 115 g); 6 to 8 oz (170 to 225 g); 6 to 8 oz (170 to 225 g); 8 oz (225 g) and larger.

Kitchen Yields
Use as is, there is no waste.

Calories:
6 oz (170 g) = 270 Calories.

PIKE (NORTHERN PIKE OR MUSKELLUNGE)
Fine freshwater fish, but of little commercial importance.

Season:
Summer.

Average sizes:
1 to 2 lb (450 to 900 g).

Kitchen Yields
Fish has scales and is bony. Pike is excellent in fish mousse. Buy fillets.

PLAICE
See Dab, under this same heading.

POLLOCK
Harvested off the coast of Alaska and in the Atlantic, pollock is also known as Boston bluefish or Alaska snow cod. The fish resembles Haddock in taste and texture, with meatier and firmer flesh. It represents the single largest edible fish harvest in the world by volume. Pollock is used for surimi.

Season:
Available year-round. Peak is in late fall.

Average sizes:

Alaskan pollack:
1 lb (450 g), 16 in (406 mm).

Atlantic pollack:
4 to 12 lb (1.8 to 5.4 kg), 2 to 3 ft (0.6 to 0.9 m).

Pack:

Alaskan pollack:
3- to 10-oz (85- to 280-g) frozen fillets.

Calories:
3½ oz (100 g) = 78 Calories.

POMPANO
Very delicate fish harvested on the Florida coast. Some imports are available. Marketed whole, as fresh fillets, and as frozen fillets.

Season:
Available year-round. Peak is from March to May.

Average sizes:
Whole, from 1½ to 4 lb (0.68 to 1.8 kg). Fillets, from 6 oz to 1¾ lb (170 to 800 g).

Kitchen Yields
Fish is expensive.

Best size:
For cutting fillets, 1¾ lb (800 g). One 1¾-lb (800-g) fish yields two 6-oz (170-g) fillets.

RED SNAPPER
Popular fish harvested in the Gulf of Mexico and in other tropical waters. Available whole or in fillets, fresh or frozen. Frozen fillets are often imported.

Season:
Available year-round. Peak is in summer.

Average sizes:

Whole small:
Under 2 lb (900 g).

Whole medium:
2 to 5 lb (0.9 to 2.25 kg).

Whole large:
5 to 8 lb (2.25 to 3.6 kg) and larger.

Fillets:
3½ oz (100 g) and larger.

Kitchen Yields
About 55 percent waste, because head is very large.

Serving size:
For broiling with skin on, 6 oz (170 g). One 1¾-lb (790-g) whole fish yields 2 servings.
Buy 6- to 8-lb (2.7- to 3.6-kg) fish for cutting fillets. One 7-lb (3.2-kg) fish yields 3-lb 3-oz (1.5-kg) fillets, which provides 8 servings. Larger fish give slightly better yields, but they can be dry and tough.

ROCKFISH
Found along the Pacific coast in many varieties. Mostly available as fresh or frozen fillets. The most important commercial varieties are:

Orange rockfish: Up to 30 in (760 mm) long.
Yellow eye rockfish: Up to 26 in (660 mm) long.
Bocaccio: Up to 40 in (1 meter) long.
Red rockfish: This fish resembles red snapper and is often sold as such, although not related to the genuine red snapper of the Atlantic. Up to 3 ft (900 mm) long.

Kitchen Yields
Buy 3- to 4-lb (1.4- to 1.8-kg) fillets.

SABLEFISH
Also known under the names of *butterfish* or *black cod*, but not related to the Atlantic cod. Sablefish is found along the Pacific Coast from Alaska to California. A large amount of sablefish is smoked. It is considered kosher because it has scales. It is available fresh or frozen, whole or dressed, and in fillets and steaks.

Average sizes:
Dressed, 3 to 5 lb (1.5 to 2.25 kg), 30 in (0.76 m) long.

Season:
Late summer and fall.

Calories:
3½ oz (100 g) = 192 Calories.

ST. PETER FISH
Cultivated fish, originally cultivated in the Sea of Galilee. It is available whole and in fillets.

SALMON
Most fresh salmon comes from Alaska and the Pacific Northwest. Canada is a big producer of Atlantic salmon, but most of its production is smoked. Because salmon are successfully raised in ponds, it is now available year-round. Fresh pond-raised salmon are imported from Norway and other countries. Chile has been become a big producer.

Alaskan salmon species:

King or chinook salmon: Fish with high oil content and (usually) very red flesh. Often smoked. White king salmon has pale flesh and is often kippered. Size is up to 20 lb (9.1 kg).
Sockeye or red salmon: Fish with very red flesh. Excellent for broiling. Weight ranges from 4 to 12 lb (1.8 to 5.4 kg).
Silver or coho salmon: Fish with orange-red flesh, often smoked. Size about 6 lb (2.7 kg).
Pink salmon: Most abundant Alaska salmon; often sold whole, but most production is canned. Average weight is about 2 to 3 lb (0.9 to 1.4 kg).
Chum or keta salmon: Lightest in color and leanest salmon. Most production is canned. Weight ranges from 4 to 13 lb (1.8 to 5.9 kg).
Mini salmon: Hatchery-raised fish; normally sold frozen, boneless, with head on.

Season:
Farm-raised salmon is available year-round, but there are distinct seasons for fresh wild salmon:

King or chinook salmon: October to April.
Sockeye salmon: June to August.
Silver or coho salmon: July to October.
Pink salmon: July to September.
Chum or keta salmon: July to October.
Atlantic salmon: June to September.

Pack:

Whole salmon:
Headless, dressed, 6 to 8 lb (2.7 to 3.6 kg).
Headless, dressed, 8 to 10 lb (3.6 to 4.5 kg).
Other sizes are available.

Fillets:
Boneless, skin on, imported from Norway; 22- to 26-lb (10- to 12-kg) cartons consisting of ten 2½-lb (1.1-kg) sides.

Loins:
Skinless, boneless pieces, individually wrapped, imported from Norway; sizes vary.

Steaks:
Cross-cut, with bone in and skin on; 8 oz (225 g) each. Other sizes are available.

Mini salmon:
8- to 10-oz (225- to 280-g) fish, boneless, with head and tail on, packed 10 fish per 5-lb (2.2-kg) box; six boxes make up a 30-lb (13.5-kg) master carton.

Kitchen Yields

Waste:
About 20 percent when fish is purchased head on; about 10 percent waste when fish is purchased headless.
One 7-lb (3.1-kg) fish, head on, produces 5½ lb (2.4 kg) fillets, skin on. One 10-lb (4.5-kg) fish, head off, produces 9 lb (4 kg) fillets, skin on.

Serving sizes:
5 to 7 oz (140 to 200 g) for boneless fillet, with skin on for broiling; 7 oz (200 g) for boneless fillet to be eaten cold, with skin removed after poaching; 5 oz (140 g) for boneless fillet to be poached and served with a sauce.

Calories:
All figures are for 5-oz (140-g) boneless fillet:

> King or chinook = 270 Calories.
> Sockeye = 230 Calories.
> Silver or coho = 190 Calories.
> Pink = 172 Calories.
> Chum or Keta = 171 Calories.

SALMON TROUT (LAKE TROUT)
Freshwater fish, with pale pink to grey flesh. Harvested in the Great Lakes.

Season:
Peak is in summer. Small catch is available in winter.

Trade sizes:
2 to 4 lb (0.9 to 1.8 kg); 4 to 8 lb (1.8 to 3.6 kg).

Kitchen Yields
Delicate fish; buy whole and cut into fillets. Waste is about 50 percent. Leave skin on for broiling or pan frying; remove skin for poaching.

SARDINES
Maine sardines belong to the herring family. Relatively little is sold fresh; most is canned.

Average size:
3 to 4 in (76 to 100 mm) long; 6 to 9 pieces per 1 lb (450 g).

Season:
Winter.

Kitchen Yields

Serving size:
4 pieces with bones removed, fried whole.

SCROD
Immature cod, haddock, or pollack.

Season:
Available year-round. Peak is in late fall and winter.

Average sizes:

Boston scrod:
New York market: 1½ to 2 lb (675 to 900 g).
Boston market: 2 to 4 lb (0.9 to 1.8 kg).

SEA BASS
See Bass, under this same heading.

SEA TROUT
Also called *weakfish*. Harvested along the coast of the Gulf states. Lean and delicate fish, it spoils rapidly.

Season:
Available year-round.

Average size:
1 to 5 lb (0.45 to 2.2 kg).

Kitchen Yields
Purchase fillets.

SHAD
Fatty fish remotely related to the herring, shad is found on both the Atlantic and Pacific coasts. The fish returns to spawn in the freshwater streams where they were hatched. Both shad fillets and roe are marketed. Shad have an erratic bone structure which is difficult to remove, and for this reason shad is marketed as boneless fillets. The fillets are sold as two fillets wrapped in paper. Roe is marketed by the pair.

Season:
Early spring until mid-June, depending on weather.

Average sizes:

Shad fillets, individual:
8 to 10 oz (225 to 285 g) each.

Shad fillets, pairs:
16 to 20 oz (450 to 570 g).

Roe pairs:
6 to 8 oz (170 to 225 g); 8 to 10 oz (225 to 280 g);
12 to 14 oz (340 to 400 g).

Kitchen Yields
The customer is normally given a choice of ordering shad fillet only, shad and roe, or roe only.

Serving sizes:

Shad fillet only:
7 to 8 oz (200 to 225 g).

Shad and roe:
5 oz (140 g) shad, 4 oz (112 g) roe.

Roe only:
8 to 10 oz (225 to 280 g) per pair.
One pair shad fillets yields approximately 4 servings when served with roe; one pair roe yields 2 portions when served with fillets, or one portion when served alone.

SHARK
There are many different species, and only few reach the commercial market. The fish is harvested in both the Atlantic and the Pacific Oceans. Mako shark is a well-recognized food fish.

Season:
Available year-round.

Average size:
Varies greatly.

Kitchen Yields
Shark skin is very tough and leathery and must be removed before cooking. Bones are very soft. Purchase fillets only.

SKATE
Also called *ray*, this fish renders excellent meat. The wings only are used.

Season:
Available year-round.

Average sizes:
16 to 30 oz (450 to 840 g). The pieces are sold skinned, but the thin, secondary skin and bone should be removed before preparation.

Kitchen Yields
Purchase ready to cook. One 30-oz (840-g) wing yields 20 oz (560 g) boneless fillet.

SMELTS
Small fish, related to salmon that are capable of living in both freshwater and saltwater. Smelts are harvested in the Atlantic Ocean, the Pacific Ocean, and in many lakes, including the Great Lakes.

Season:
Late winter and early spring.

Average sizes:
1½ to 1¾ oz (40 to 50 g), 7 to 8 in (177 to 200 mm) long.

Kitchen Yields
1 lb (450 g) smelts yields 8 to 11 pieces, and 1 serving, fried, consists of 4 to 5 pieces.

SOLE
Flatfish, considered the best eating fish. Sole is found on both the Atlantic and the Pacific Coast. The names *sole* and *flounder* are often used interchangeably, but they cover a number of distinct but closely related species. *See also* Flounder under this same heading. Most production is sold as fresh or frozen fillets. Much is imported. Domestically harvested species include the following:

> *Atlantic sole species:* Grey sole and lemon sole, also called *winter flounder* or *blackback* when less than 3½ lb (1.5 kg).
> *Pacific sole species:* Petrale sole, brill sole and English sole. (often called *lemon sole*, but it is a different species from the Atlantic lemon sole).

Season:
Available year-round.

Average sizes:

Whole fish:
1 to 6 lb (0.45 to 2.7 kg).

Fillets:
6 to 8 oz (170 to 225 g); 8 to 10 oz (225 to 280 g).

Kitchen Yields
About 50 percent waste when fish is cut into bone-less fillets.

Serving size:
For poaching, 7 oz (200 g).
Buy 5- to 6-lb (2.25- to 2.7-kg) fish for cutting into fillets. One 5½-lb (2.5-kg) whole fish produces 2 lb 14 oz (1.35 kg) fillets, which yields 6 to 7 portions.

STRAWBERRY GROUPER
Fish with firm meat. Available in fillets.

STURGEON
Harvested in both the Atlantic and Pacific Oceans, the fish lives in saltwater and spawns in freshwater rivers. Lake sturgeon lives in freshwater. Sturgeon is known primarily as the producer of caviar and as an excellent smoked fish.

Much sturgeon is frozen and imported from caviar-producing countries and from Canada for smoking. Sturgeon species are distinguished in the caviar trade, but little distinction is made when purchasing sturgeon meat. Sturgeon has no bones, only soft cartilage, but skin is tough and must be removed. The spine marrow is called *vesiga*, and can be used in fish soups and coulibiac.

Season:
Spring and summer.

Average size:
From 5 to 500 lb (2.25 to 225 kg).

Kitchen Yields

Waste:
About 30 percent when buying whole fish.

Best size:
Buy 8- to 10-lb (3.6- to 4.5-kg) fish with head removed or 8 to 10-lb (3.6- to 4.5-kg) sturgeon saddle.

SWORDFISH
Large fish found in warm waters in both the Atlantic and the Pacific Oceans. Available fresh in pieces and frozen in steaks.

Season:
June to October; imports available year-round.

Average sizes:
From 100 to 200 lb (45 to 90 kg).

Pack:
Sold by weight, bone in, skin on.

Kitchen Yields
Purchase by weight and cut in kitchen. Specify center cut, with no belly flap. Skin is usually left on. Tail pieces have high ratio of bones to meat. Flap pieces left on cut can reduce yield by as much as 25 percent. Heavy pieces give better yield. Frozen swordfish steaks are usually dry.

Serving size:
3 oz (85 g) for appetizer; 8 oz (225 g) for thick steak.
One 20-lb (9-kg) center cut, with no belly flaps yields 17 lb (6.3 kg) usable meat.

TILEFISH
Atlantic coast fish with firm flesh and good flavor.

Season:
Summer.

Average sizes:
2 to 6 lb (0.9 to 2.6 kg).

Kitchen Yields
Purchase fillets. Best size is 1½ lb (675 g).

TROUT

FRESH WATER TROUT
The best-known species is the rainbow trout. Most commercial production is hatchery-grown. Fresh

trout are available in many states. The whole fish is always sold gutted, with head and tail attached. It is also available boned and as fillets. Live trout are available in selected markets. The fish can be kept alive in a fish tank. It needs clean, fresh water with sufficient oxygen.

Season:
Available year-round. Peak is in summer. Frozen trout are readily available at all times.

Average sizes:
From 5 oz (140 g) up.

Kitchen Yields

Serving size:
For stuffed trout as appetizer, 5 oz (140 g). For main course, single service, 7- to 9-oz (200- to 255-g) or 9- to 11-oz (255- to 312-g) whole fish. For main course, double service, 20 oz (570 g) whole fish.

Waste:
For filleting, 45 percent.
For filleting, buy 28-oz (780-g) or larger fish.

LAKE TROUT
See Salmon Trout under this same heading.

SEA TROUT
See Weakfish, under this same heading.

TUNA
Fresh tuna has become widely accepted as a fresh-food fish in fine restaurants. It is often cooked rare, like a steak. Fresh tuna is one of the most important fish varieties used in sushi bars. The flesh of all species is dark but lightens after cooking. Four species are available:

> *Albacore.* Fish with light-colored flesh. Weights range from 10 to 60 lb (4.6 to 27.2 kg).
> *Yellowfin.* Fish with light-colored flesh. Weights range from 40 to 100 lb (18.1 to 45 kg).
> *Bluefin.* Also called *horse mackerel.* Weights range from 15 to 80 lb (6.7 to 36 kg).

> *Skipjack.* The smallest of the four tuna species. Weights range from 4 to 24 lb (1.8 to 10.8 kg).

Bonito is a member of the mackerel family and is not classified as genuine tuna. It is very similar in taste and flesh to tuna. It is found along the Atlantic coast. Weights range from 5 to 12 lb (2.25 to 5.4 kg).

Season:
Fresh tuna is available year-round, but supply peaks in summer.

Kitchen Yields
Fillets are generally the best buy. Make sure to specify loin fillets. Tuna should be undercooked, and consequently the portion size is small.

Serving size:
5 oz (140 g).

TURBOT
Turbot, imported from Europe, is an elegant flatfish, not to be confused with the lower-quality Pacific turbot. The fish is available frozen, but occasionally freshly flown in for the luxury market. Available whole.

Pack:
22.2- to 26.6-lb (10- to 12-kg) cases.

Sizes:
With head on, 6 to 9 lb (2.7 to 4 kg), 9 to 12 lb (4 to 5.4 kg), 12 to 15 lb (5.4 to 6.7 kg), 15 lb (6.7 kg) and larger.

Kitchen Yields
The fish is normally sold eviscerated, with head on. It has a very large head and heavy bones. Best size to buy is 9- to 12-lb (4- to 5.4-kg) fish.

Waste:
When turbot is cut into steaks, with skin on and bone in, 40 percent; when it is cut into boneless fillets, with skin off, 60 percent.
One 10-lb (4.5-kg) fish yields 4 lb (1.8 kg) fillets.

WEAKFISH
Also called *grey sea trout.* Harvested off the Atlantic coast. Good eating fish.

Season:
Summer.

Average sizes:
1 to 3 lb (0.45 to 1.4 kg).

Kitchen Yields
Purchase largest whole fish available, and cut fillets. There is about 45 percent waste.

WHITEBAITS
Tiny fish that are dusted with flour and fried. Available fresh or frozen IQF or in block.

Pack:
By weight.

Kitchen Yields
Serve whole. About 10 to 15 percent loss occurs as a result of sorting out impurities.

WHITEFISH
A freshwater fish harvested mainly from the Great Lakes. Cisco and lake herring are related.

WHITING
Inexpensive fish with limited application in the hospitality industry. Harvested off the coast of New England.

Season:
Summer.

Average size:
1 to 4 lb (0.45 to 1.8 kg).

WHITE STURGEON
Farmed fish from California with firm meat.

WOLFISH
A fish that feeds on crustaceans and has a firm texture and sweet flavor. Available in fillets.

FROZEN AND PREPARED FISH PRODUCTS
There are numerous ready-to-cook fish products on the market. This section mentions a few of these products. Size and pack of product vary from manufacturer to manufacturer.

BLACKENED CATFISH
Fully-seasoned ready-to-bake blackened catfish is available.

Pack:
10-lb (4.5-kg) cartons.

Size:
6- or 8-oz (170- or 225-g) fillets.

Count:
Twenty-seven 6-oz (170-g) fillets; twenty 8-oz (225-g) fillets.

COD PRODUCTS
Many products, either plain or breaded, are on the market.

Sizes:
3 to 6 oz (85 to 170 g).

Pack:
Varies.

FISH MOUSSE

Formula
> 8 lb (3.6 kg) solid fish, such as halibut, sole, pike, or salmon
> 20 egg whites, or 2½ cups (0.6 l)
> 3½ qt (3.1 l) heavy cream (36 percent butterfat)
> Salt and pepper to taste

Fish should be fresh. If frozen fish is used, the amount of egg whites should be increased. It is advisable to mix frozen fish with about 30 percent fresh scallops, in order to improve the binding of the mixture.

Kitchen Yields
The total mix yields 50 appetizer servings or 40 main-course servings.

FISH STICKS
Fish portions, usually made of cod, haddock, or pollack. Available breaded or batter-dipped, raw or precooked, in different shapes and sizes. Fish sticks contain at least 60 percent fish, by weight.

Pack:
Varies.

Sizes:
1½ to 5 oz (43 to 140 g).

Kitchen Yields
There is no waste.

Serving size:
Approximately 4 to 6 oz (112 to 170 g).

Calories:
4 oz (112 g) = 200 Calories.

GEFILTE FISH
For canned gefilte fish, *see* Canned Fish.

Formula
    2 lb (0.9 kg) whitefish fillets, skinless
    2 lb (0.9 kg) carp fillets, skinless
    2 lb (0.9 kg) pike fillets, skinless
    6 eggs
    1 cup matzo meal
    3 tb salt
    1 tb sugar
    1 tb ground white pepper
    1 cup chopped onion
    Fish stock (made with fish bones, sliced car-
       rots, sliced onions, salt, pepper, and allspice)

Kitchen Yields
The total mix yields fifty 2-oz (56-g) pieces, raw weight.

STUFFED FLOUNDER
Available with many varieties of stuffing and in many sizes.

Sizes:
6 to 10 oz (170 to 280 g).

Pack:
Varies.

SMOKED OR CURED FISH
Smoked fish is shipped freshly smoked, frozen, dried, or canned.

BACALAO
Also called *salt cod* or *stock fish*, it is salted and air-dried fish, sold split or in fillets. Most is imported from Europe or Canada. Available with skin on and off.

Pack:
Sold by weight.

Kitchen Yields
Soak overnight. Size will roughly double in volume.

Serving size:
3 oz (85 g) dried product.

BLOATERS
Fat herring, salted and smoked.

CHUBS
Smoked small whitefish.

Average sizes:

Whole fish:
4 to 6 oz (112 to 170 g).

FINNAN HADDIE
Smoked haddock, available in fillets fresh or frozen. Some product is only cured and colored, but not smoked, and has inferior flavor.

Pack:
By weight. Often sold in 15-lb (6.8-kg) cases.

Kitchen Yields
Poach in milk/water mixture to reduce saltiness.

Serving size:
4 oz (112 g) for breakfast; 6 oz (170 g) for luncheon dishes.

Trimming waste:
About 5 percent or less.

GRAVELAX
Swedish pickled salmon, made most often on premises.

Pickling Formula
    1 cup salt
    1 cup sugar
    ¼ cup crushed juniper berries
    ¼ cup crushed peppercorns
    2 cups coarsely chopped dill (including stems)

Kitchen Yields
The mixture produced by the formula is sufficient to pickle two 4-lb (1.8-kg) fillets, with skin on.

Serving size:
For appetizer, 2½ oz (70 g); thus, one side (skin-on fillet) yields 20 to 22 appetizer servings. For buffet, 1 oz (28 g); thus, one side yields 40 to 50 servings.

HERRING SPECIALTIES
There are many varieties of cured, smoked, and preserved herring specialties on the market, including the following:

Bismark herring: Marinated fillets, available in plain marinade and in sour cream.

Bratherring: Herring fillets or the whole fish dipped in flour, fried, pickled, and canned.

Bückling: Smoked whole herring.

Digby chick: Smoked fillets.

Matjes herring: Marinated fillets from young herrings.

Fresh matjes herring: Available in June, this Dutch specialty herring is lightly cured in brine, and then is shipped by air in boneless fillets ready to eat.

Kippered herring: Butterflied smoked herring, served grilled, usually with scrambled eggs. When customer demand is low, purchase canned product.

Rollmops: Herring fillet rolls filled with onions, pickle, and sauerkraut, marinated in vinegar and spices.

Herring in sour cream: Available in fillets and bite size. Specify boneless pieces.

Schmaltz herring: Fat, skinless marinated herring pieces.

Sill: Swedish name for various herring specialties.

Sprat: Small herring that can be smoked or pickled.

Pack:
Varies. Most products are packed in 1-qt (0.94-l) or 1-gal (3.8-l) glass jars or plastic buckets.

Sizes and counts:
Vary greatly, according to product.

LOX
Cured salmon from large, fatty fish. The name *lox* is sometimes used erroneously for smoked salmon. Sold sliced or whole. Sliced lox is often frozen or canned.

Pack:
Four 3-lb (1.4-kg) trays of sliced fish.

Sizes:
About ½ oz (14 g) per slice.

Kitchen Yields
When lox is purchased sliced, there is no waste. When purchased whole, yield is the same as for smoked salmon, if the fatty belly part is used.

Serving size:
For buffet service, with scrambled eggs and bagels, 3 slices per serving, totaling 1½ oz (40 g).

SMOKED EEL
Available whole, with head on or off. Skin is normally left on. Skinless fillets are also available canned.

Sizes:
3 lb (1.35 kg) and larger.

Kitchen Yields
Buy the 4- to 5-lb (1.8- to 2.2-kg) size. Larger eels are fatty.

Waste:
About 25 percent when fish is purchased with head on.

SMOKED MACKEREL
Smoked mackerel is available whole, in fillets, and canned.

Pack:
Varies.

Sizes:

Whole Mackerel:
8 to 10 oz (225 to 280 g).

Mackerel Fillets:
4 to 5 oz (112 to 140 g), 2 fillets per pack.

Kitchen Yields
Serve as is.

SMOKED SABLEFISH
Fatty Pacific fish with small scales. The fish is considered kosher. Sold cured, smoked, and sprinkled with paprika.

Pack:
By weight.

Size:
Best size is 2- to 3-lb (0.9- to 1.4-kg) fillets.

Kitchen Yields
Little waste; skin only must be discarded. About 5 percent trimming waste.

Serving size:
2 oz (56 g).

SMOKED SALMON
Smoked salmon is available in many sizes, quality levels, and packs. It is available whole, skin on, and pre-sliced with and without skin. Some products are imported.

Average sizes:

Canadian nova, sides:
3½ lb (1.5 kg).

Canadian nova, pre-sliced:
2 to 3 lb (0.9 to 1.35 kg).

Gaspe nova, sides:
4 to 6 lb (1.8 to 2.7 kg).

Irish salmon, sides:
3 to 3½ lb (1.3 to 1.5 kg).

Norwegian salmon, pre-sliced:
3 lb (1.35 kg), 2.2 lb (1 kg).

Pacific nova, sides, headless:
4 to 10 lb (1.8 to 4.5 kg).

Scotch salmon, sides, headless:
2¼ to 3 lb (1 to 1.35 kg).

Scotch salmon, pre-sliced:
1½ lb (675 g).

Kitchen Yields
Trimming waste from whole sides is about 15 percent. Skin weight is about 5 percent, not included in the preceding waste estimate. Usable scraps such as end pieces account for 5 percent after slicing.

Serving size:
3 oz (85 g) for appetizer; 2 oz (56 g) for buffet; ⅓ oz (10 g) each for canapés. One side weighing 8 lb (3.6 kg), as purchased, yields 30 appetizer servings, 45 buffet servings, or 260 pieces for canapés. Larger sides have better yield than do smaller sides.

SMOKED SHAD
Boneless smoked shad is a spring specialty.

Pack:
By weight. Fillet size is about 8 oz (225 g).

Kitchen Yields

Serving size:
4 oz (112 g).

SMOKED STURGEON
This elegant fish is considered kosher.

Pack:
By weight. Average weight is 3 to 5 lb (1.4 to 2.2 kg).

Kitchen Yields
Order #1, center cut. The pieces should be without cartilage. Skin is often left on. Some pieces have belly flap left on, reducing the yield. Trimming waste is about 10 percent. Slice on machine; smoked sturgeon is not available pre-sliced.

Serving size:
3 oz (85 g) for appetizer; thus, one 4-lb (1.8-kg) piece yields 18 appetizer servings.

SMOKED TROUT

Available whole, with head on, and in boneless fillets. Product is sometimes frozen.

Pack:

Sold by piece. Two 2-oz (56-g) fillets: Tray pack is available.

Sizes:

Whole fish:
6 to 8 oz (170 to 220 g);
8 to 10 oz (220 to 280 g).

Kitchen Yields

Serving size:

½ trout, for appetizer.

SMOKED WHITEFISH

Available whole, head on. The fish is considered kosher. Available as hot-smoked and cold-smoked. Cold-smoked fish is firmer than hot-smoked fish.

Pack:

By weight.

Size:

1½ to 2½ lb (0.67 to 1.12 kg). Other sizes are available.

Kitchen Yields

Fish must be boned, with head and skin removed. Waste is about 50 percent.

Serving size:

6 oz (168 g), cleaned for salad plate, as main course; one 2-lb (0.9-kg) fish yields 2½ servings.

SPRATS

Small smoked herring, sold whole as a specialty item.

STOCKFISH

Salted and wind-dried cod fillets. The name is German and refers to the the "stock" (stick) on which the fish is dried. Sold by weight. For yields, *see* Bacalao.

FLOUR

Wheat flour is classified as hard wheat flour and soft wheat flour.

Hard wheat flours:
    Strong flour: Also called high-gluten flour. A flour used for hard rolls and pizza.
    Patent flour: Also called bread flour. A general-use flour used for rolls and breads.
    First clear and second clear: Flours with darker color and high gluten content, often used in making rye bread.
    Bran flour: A flour used for muffins.
    Whole wheat flour: A flour used for breads.

Soft wheat flours:
    Cake, pastry, and cookie flours: Flours used for cakes, pies, and cookies.

Rye flour:
    This flour has a low gluten content and must be mixed with wheat flour for bread making. It is available in different grades.

Kitchen Yields

Table F-1 identifies unsifted and sifted weights for different volumes of flour. The chart is based on bread flour; cake flour is slightly lighter.

FLOWERS

Many varieties of edible flowers come onto the market.

ACACIA BLOSSOMS

Dip acacia blossoms in batter and fry as dessert.

Table F-1 Converting Flour Volume to Weight

Volume	Weight Unsifted	Weight Sifted
1 cup	6 oz (170 g)	4¼ oz (120 g)
1 pint	12 oz (340 g)	10 oz (285 g)
1 qt	1½ lb (675 g)	1 lb 2 oz (510 g)
1 gal	6 lb (2.7 kg)	4½ lb (2 kg)

Season:
Spring.

BORAGE
Tiny blue stars that taste like cucumbers.

Season:
Available year-round.

Pack:
100, 300, and 600 blooms.

CALENDULA
Large full cushion of petals in yellow or orange. Use whole or sprinkle the petals.

Season:
Available year-round.

Pack:
100, 300, and 600 blooms.

CHAMOMILE
Fresh or dried blossoms and leaves are used as tea.

Season:
Available year-round.

CHRYSANTHEMUM
Use chrysanthemums in hot dishes as garnish, or in salads.

Season:
Fall.

CLOVER
Clover blossoms can be used in salads, teas, and compound butters.

Season:
Summer.

DAISY
Daisy flowers can be used to flavor wine.

Season:
Summer.

DANDELION
Dandelion blossoms and leaves are used in wine and salad.

Season:
Spring and summer.

ELDER
Dip elder blossoms in batter and fry as dessert.

Season:
Spring.

FUCHSIA
Frilly blooms in pinks, whites and blues. Flowers keep well. Use as a garnish.

Season:
Available year-round.

Pack:
100, 300, and 600 blooms.

JASMINE
Flower essence used with desserts.

Season:
Spring and summer.

LILAC
Used for candied flowers and water ice.

Season:
Spring.

MARIGOLD
Flower petals used as a flavoring agent in meat dishes and desserts.

Season:
Available year-round.

NASTURTIUM
Bright red, yellow, and orange flowers with peppery taste.

Season:
Spring.

Pack:
100, 300, and 600 blooms.

ORANGE
Orange flowers may be used in ice cream and other desserts.

Season:
Available year-round.

ORCHIDS

Wanda orchids are used in salads, desserts, and as a drink garnish.

Season:
Available year-round.

PANSY

Large round blooms in beautiful colors. Used as a garnish.

Pack:
100, 300, and 600 blooms.

RACIAL (JELLY OKRA)

This flower is use to make jelly.

Season:
Spring and summer.

ROSES

Flower petals are used for jelly, as candied dessert, or in flavored water. Rose fruit, called *rose hips*, are used for jelly and tea.

Season:
Spring and summer.

SQUASH

Squash flowers can be put in salads and used to make fritters.

Season:
Available year-round.

TIGER LILY

Used fresh and dried in Oriental cooking.

Season:
Spring.

VIOLETS

Violets are used in making candied petals, flavored water, water ice, and syrup.

Season:
Spring.

WOODRUFF

Used to flavor for wine or tea.

Season:
Spring.

ZUCCHINI

Season:
Zucchini blossoms can be used to make fritters or can be stuffed.

Season:
Available year-round.

FOIE GRAS

Fatty goose or duckling liver. Available canned, fresh, and frozen in many varieties and levels of quality.

CANNED FOIE GRAS

There are a number of products on the market with distinct quality and price differences. Some products must be refrigerated for storage; all must be refrigerated for service. The following terminology is most often used to describe the products:

> *Terrine:* Whole liver poached in a ceramic container and studded with truffles. Available in the decorated container that the product was cooked in, or canned. Terrines are considered top-of-the-line products.
>
> *Whole liver:* Canned whole liver in natural shape, without truffle center.
>
> *Block:* Whole liver with truffle center, mostly in tunnel-shaped cans.
>
> *Parfait:* Puréed liver, often with truffle center. Mostly in tunnel-shaped cans.
>
> *Pâté:* Large chunks of liver baked in crust and filled with aspic jelly. The name pâté is also used often for products without crust.
>
> *Purée or mousse:* Liver product to which binders such as eggs and gelatin have been added.
>
> *Roulade:* Purée or mousse packed in a cylindrical can, often with truffle center.

Liver pâté: Canned liver product made of pork and other livers, to which a small percentage of foie gras has been added.

Pack:

Terrine:
Packed in ceramic containers, with net weight of 7 oz (200 g), 3.8 oz (105 g), 3.5 oz (100 g), 2.25 oz (67 g), or 1.5 oz (43 oz).

Whole liver:
1 lb 12 oz, or 28 oz (780 g), net.

Block:
Packed in tunnel-shaped can, weighing 10⅞ oz (309 g) or 7⅜ oz (209 g), net. Large slice, 15 oz (420 g) or 5 oz (140 g), net.

Purée:
10⅞ oz (309 g), net.

Roulade:
Packed in tall, cylindrical tin, 11¼ oz (320 g), net.

Liver pâté:
34½ oz (980 g), 14 oz (400 g), or 7 oz (200 g), net.

Kitchen Yields

Serving size:
Individual-serving terrine is 1½ oz (43 g) or 2.25 oz (67 g). For block foie gras, one 15-oz (420-g) can yields 20 to 22 large slices, and one 5-oz (140-g) can yields 6 to 7 large slices.

FRESH FOIE GAS
Domestic foie gras of excellent quality is produced in a number of states and is available shipped by air. Imported livers, precooked and cryovac-packed, with a shelf life of 3 to 4 weeks, are available around Christmas. The size and weight of fresh livers determines their grade. The largest livers are the best.

Season:
Fall and winter.

Pack and grades:

Domestic livers:
Grade A = 14 to 22 oz (400 to 625 g).

Grade B = 11 to 13 oz (312 to 365 g).
Grade C = 7 to 10 oz (200 to 285 g).

Imported livers:
9 to 10 oz (256 to 285 g), precooked.

Kitchen Yields
Use the largest livers for slicing and cooking to order, or for making terrines. Livers should always be cooked pink. Use the smaller livers and any liver trimmings for making pâtés.

Serving size:
3 oz (85 g) raw, or 2 slices, as appetizer; one 18-oz (512-g) liver yields 4 to 5 portions, with some usable trimmings left over.

FROZEN FOIE GAS
Liver freezes well for short-term storage, and some "fresh livers" are shipped frozen to prevent spoilage. Pâtés and other prepared products do not freeze well.

FRAISE DES BOIS

French name for wild strawberries.

FROGS

Usually only the legs are sold, although Oriental markets sell the whole frogs live. Legs are sold fresh or frozen, fully cleaned, normally in pairs. Some shippers do not trim spine close to legs, thereby inflating weight and reducing yield. Most product is imported, and quality varies greatly.

Sizes:
6 to 8 pairs per 1 lb (450 g); 8 to 10 pairs per 1 lb (450 g); 10 to 12 pairs per 1 lb (450 g).

Kitchen Yields
Large frog legs can be tough and dry.

Serving size:
For dinner, 1 lb (450 g) untrimmed yields 2 servings. For receptions, buy the 12 pieces per 1 lb size.

FRYING BATTER

Formula

> 1 cup flour
> 1 tb oil
> 1 tsp salt
> 1 can (12 oz) beer

Let batter rest 3 hours at kitchen temperature before use.

Kitchen Yields

Yield depends on size of product to be fried.

G

GALAX LEAVES

Round, tough leaves about 2½ in (63 mm) across, green or reddish brown, used for garnishing fruits. Order from florist.

Pack:
Bunches of 24 leaves each.

Kitchen Yields
Leaves will keep well when refrigerated.

GAME

Refer to name of particular species.

GARBANZOS

See Beans.

GARLIC

Available dehydrated, fresh, and processed chopped.

DEHYDRATED GARLIC
Dehydrated ground garlic is available both plain and mixed with salt.

Pack:
By weight.

Kitchen Yields
1 tb dehydrated is equivalent to 1 tb minced fresh garlic; ¼ cup (0.06 l) is equivalent to 4 tb minced fresh garlic.

FRESH GARLIC
Several varieties of garlic are widely available.

DOMESTIC GARLIC
Common white garlic, available domestic and imported. Domestic production starts July in California. Gilroy is a California community famous for growing garlic.

Season:
Available year-round.

Pack:
By weight.

Kitchen Yields
Peeling waste is about 12 percent.

ELEPHANT GARLIC
Large garlic with milder flavor than ordinary garlic. Can be served raw or cooked as vegetable.

Season:
May to December.

Pack:
By weight.

Size:
8 to 16 oz (225 to 450 g) each.

Kitchen Yields
There is little waste.

ITALIAN GARLIC
Slightly pink garlic with strong flavor and smaller cloves.

Pack:
By weight.

Kitchen Yields
About 15 percent waste.

TAHITI GARLIC
Large garlic with good yield.

Size:
Bulbs 2 to 3 in (50 to 75 mm) in diameter.

PROCESSED CHOPPED GARLIC
Processed garlic is available peeled and chopped, often packed in oil, with preservatives added.

Pack:
Case of twelve 1-qt (0.9-l) jars. Smaller packs are also available.

Kitchen Yields
1 tb minced is equivalent to 4 to 5 cloves; ¼ cup (0.07 l) is equivalent to 18 cloves, average size.

PROCESSED WHOLE GARLIC

Whole peeled garlic is available from most produce purveyors. It should be kept dry and refrigerated.

Kitchen Yield
There is no waste.

GEFILTE FISH

See Fish.

GELATIN

FLAVORED GELATIN

Meat- and fruit-flavored gelatin is available under different brand names, granulated or in powder. Follow package directions.

UNFLAVORED GELATIN

Available granulated and in sheets.

Pack:

Granulated:
By weight, normally in 1-lb (450-g) containers; envelopes of ¼ oz (7 g) each.

Sheets:
Packages of 500 g (17½ oz), often imported.

Kitchen Yields

Weight and volume:
1 cup weighs 5½ oz (154 g), and 1 pint weighs 11 oz (308 g).

Thickening power:
    1 oz (28 g) thickens 2 qt (1.8 l) plain liquid.
    2 oz (56 g) thickens 1 gal (3.7 l) plain liquid.
    1 cup, or 5½ oz (154 g) thickens 2¾ gal
       (10.3 l) plain liquid.

The thickening power of gelatin is influenced by acidity. More gelatin must be used when the liquid is acidic. In hot weather, the amount of gelatin should be increased by about 25 percent. It is always advisable to make a small sample to check the firmness of the resulting product.

Calories:
1 oz (28 g) dry gelatin = 100 Calories.

GINGER POWDER

Aromatic spice used in baking.

Pack:
1-lb (450-g) cans.

GINGER ROOT

Brown fibrous root, used in Oriental cooking, as flavoring in baking, and in beverages. Available year-round.

Pack:
5-, 10-, or 30-lb (2.25-, 4.4-, or 13.6-kg) cartons. Average size varies.

Kitchen Yields
Peeling loss is about 20 percent.

Calories:
3½ oz (100 g) = 49 Calories.

GNOCCHI

There are three basic gnocchi varieties: the Northern Italian gnocchi is made with potato dough; the Roman variety is made with semolina; and the Swiss variety, often called *gnocchi parisienne*, is made with cream puff paste. The best known variety is made with potatoes. The product can be made fresh or purchased frozen.

POTATO GNOCCHI

Formula
    5 lb (2.25 kg) peeled russet potatoes, raw
    1 lb 12 oz (0.78 kg) bread flour
    4 whole eggs
    1 cup, or 6 oz (170 g) grated parmesan cheese
    1 tsp salt
    ¼ tsp nutmeg

Boil potatoes, then drain well. Mash while still hot. Add all ingredients when potatoes have cooled.

Kitchen Yields
The total mix yields about 350 pieces, weighing
⅓ oz (9 g) each.

Serving size:
12 pieces, or 4 oz (123 g), per portion as appetizer;
8 pieces, or 2½ oz (85 g), per portion as garnish
with main course.

FROZEN POTATO GNOCCHI

Pack:
Twenty 1-lb (450-g) packages.

Kitchen Yields
One 1-lb (450-g) package yields about 50 pieces.

Serving size:
12 pieces, or 4 oz (123 g), per portion as appetizer;
8 pieces, or 2½ oz (85 g), per portion as garnish
with main course.

ROMAN GNOCCHI

Formula
2½ qt (2.37 l) milk
2 oz (56 g) butter
1 lb (450 g) semolina (coarse cream of wheat)
4 egg yolks
½ cup, or 3 oz (84 g) grated cheese
Salt, pepper, and nutmeg to taste

Boil milk and butter, add semolina, stir well, and
cook covered for 15 minutes. Cool, add cheese, egg
yolks, and season to taste. Spread a 1-in thick layer
on oiled baking sheets, cover and cool. When cold,
cut into pieces, sprinkle with butter and cheese, and
bake.

Kitchen Yield
30 side orders.

SWISS GNOCCHI
Also called *gnocchi parisienne*, these gnocchi are
made with cream puff paste.

Formula
1 qt (0.94 l) water
½ cup (0.12 l) oil
1 qt (0.94 l) flour

12 eggs
Salt and pepper to taste

Make cream puff paste, then shape small dumplings
with pastry bag directly into simmering water.
Simmer, then cool the gnocchi in cold water. To
serve, bake the gnocchi with grated cheese and
cream sauce.

Kitchen Yield
25 appetizer servings.

GOAT

Available in ethnic markets.

Size:
Carcasses range from 30 to 60 lb (13.5 to 27 kg).

Kitchen Yields
Goat is generally less fatty than lamb. Use lamb
cuts and yields as guidelines. Best size is 30 to
40 lb (13.5 to 18 kg).

GOOSE

Available fresh and frozen.

Pack:
Four birds each.

Sizes:
8 to 10 lb (3.6 to 4.5 kg); 10 to 12 lb (4.5 to 5.4 kg);
12 to 14 lb (5.4 to 6.3 kg); 14 lb (6.3 kg) and larger.

Kitchen Yields

Best size:
10 lb (4.5 kg), which yields 6 servings.

SMOKED GOOSE
Available whole or as breasts only.

Pack:

Breasts:
2 lb (0.9 kg), on average.

Whole birds:
7 to 9 lb (3.1 to 4 kg).

Kitchen Yields

Purchase breasts only for best yield. Weight of fatty skin, if removed, is 20 percent of purchased weight.

Serving size:

3 oz (85 g) as appetizer.

GOOSE LIVER

See Foie Gras.

GOOSEBERRIES

Available canned, fresh, and frozen. Fruit is green or red; berries are sometimes slightly fuzzy and often tart.

CANNED GOOSEBERRIES

Usually imported. Packed in light syrup or water.

Pack:

Twelve 12½-oz (350-g) cans; six #10 cans.

Kitchen Yields

Drained weights:

One 12½-oz (350-g) can contains 9 oz (250 g) berries; one #10 can contains 75 oz (2.1 kg) berries.

FRESH GOOSEBERRIES

Season:

Summer.

Pack:

1-pint (0.47-l) containers. Other packs are available.

Size:

About 1 in (2.5 cm) across.

Kitchen Yields

Serving size:

½ cup (0.23 l); thus, 1 pint (0.47 l) yields 4 servings.

Calories:

4 oz (112 g) = 35 Calories.

FROZEN GOOSEBERRIES

Pack:

30 lb (13.5 kg), IQF.

GOURDS

Ornamental gourds are sold by weight or by the piece.

GRANITE (WATER ICE)

Formula

>   6 qt (5.6 l) water
>   6 lb (2.7 kg) sugar
>   1 cup (0.23 l) lemon juice
>   1 qt (0.9 l) dry fruit brandy

Kitchen Yields

Total mix yields 2 gal (7.6 l).

NOTE: Water can be flavored with fruit, herbs, or replaced with juice. The sugar quantity should be adjusted as necessary.

GRAPEFRUIT

GRAPEFRUIT JUICE

Available canned, freshly squeezed, and as frozen concentrate. Canned juice is available sweetened and unsweetened.

CANNED GRAPEFRUIT JUICE

Pack:

Twelve 46-oz (1.35-l) cans; forty-eight 6-oz (0.17-l) cans.

Kitchen Yields

Serving size:

6 fl oz (0.17 l); therefore, one 46-oz (1.35-l) can yields 7½ servings.

Calories:

Unsweetened, 6 fl oz (0.17 l) = 75 Calories.
Sweetened, 6 fl oz (0.17 l) = 101 Calories.

FRESH GRAPEFRUIT JUICE

Pack:
Twelve 1-qt (0.94-l) containers.

Kitchen Yields

Serving size:
6 fl oz (0.17); therefore, one 1-qt (0.94-l) container yields 5⅓ servings.

Calories:
6 fl oz (0.17 l) = 66 Calories.

FROZEN CONCENTRATED GRAPEFRUIT JUICE

Pack:
Six 46-oz (1.3-l) cans.

Kitchen Yields
Dilute 1 part concentrate with 3 parts water.

Serving size:
6 fl oz (0.17 l). One 46-oz (1.3-l) can yields 23 servings.

GRAPEFRUIT SECTIONS
Available canned and fresh in jars. The market distinguishes between cold-peeled and hot-peeled sections. The cold-peeled sections are considered superior.

CANNED GRAPEFRUIT SECTIONS

Pack:
Twelve #3 cylinder cans; twenty-four, thirty-six, or forty-eight #300 cans.

Kitchen Yields

Serving size:
½ cup, or 4½ oz (130 g); thus, one #300 can yields 3 servings, one #3 cylinder can yields 10 servings with syrup or 4 cups drained fruit.

FRESH GRAPEFRUIT SECTIONS

Pack:
Four 1-gal (3.8-l) jars.

Kitchen Yields

Serving size:
½ cup, 4½ oz (130 g); thus, one 1-gal (3.8-l) jar yields 22 servings with juice.

Calories:
½ cup (130 g) sections in light syrup = 90 Calories.

WHOLE FRESH GRAPEFRUIT
The main varieties are March Seedless White and Ruby, which has pinkish flesh. Duncan grapefruit has the most seeds. Florida and Texas grapefruits are generally juicier than California and Arizona fruits. The Indian River region in Florida and Rio Grande Valley in Texas are known for producing quality grapefruits. Grapefruits are picked when ripe and do not ripen any further once off the tree.

Season:
Available year-round. Winter grapefruit comes from Florida, California, and Texas. Summer fruit is from Arizona and California. Red Grapefruit is in season from October to May.

Packs and counts:

California and Arizona:
38- to 42-lb (17.1 to 18.9-kg) cartons, or ⁷⁄₁₀ bushel, with 23, 27, 32, 36, 40, 48, 56, or 64 fruits each.

Florida:
40- to 50-lb (18.1- to 22.7-kg) cartons, or ⅘ bushel, with 23, 27, 32, 36, 40, 48, 56, or 64 fruits each.

Texas:
38- to 42-lb (17.7- to 18.9-kg) cartons, or ⁷⁄₁₀ bushel, 18, 23, 27, 32, 36, 40, 48, 56, 76, or 84 fruits each.

Sizes:
#27 = 4¹¹⁄₁₆ in (118 mm) in diameter.
#32 = 4½ in (112 mm) in diameter.
#36 = 4¼ in (107 mm) in diameter.
#40 = 4¹⁄₁₆ in (103 mm) in diameter.
#48 = 3⅞ in (98 mm) in diameter.

Kitchen Yields
One fruit contains 10 to 12 sections. One medium-size raw fruit weighing about 1 lb 1 oz (475 g)

yields 8½ oz (240 g) sections or ⅔ cup (0.15 l) juice. One and a half medium-size fruits yield 1 cup diced fruit.

Common hotel size is #23.

Calories:

For a medium-size (3¾ in in diameter) raw fruit weighing about 1 lb 1 oz (475 g):

½ fruit, 8½ oz (237 g), pink or red = 50 Calories.
½ fruit, 8½ oz (237 g), white = 45 Calories.

GRAPES

Available canned and fresh.

CANNED GRAPES

Available in light and heavy syrup.

Pack:

Six #10 cans; twenty-four #2½ cans.

Kitchen Yields

One #10 can contains 8 cups (1.8 l) drained fruit.
One #2½ can contains 2 cups (0.47 l) drained fruit.

Serving size:

½ cup, or 4½ oz (130 g).

FRESH GRAPES

Domestic table grapes are available year-round, supplemented by imports. However, all varieties have distinct seasons. Grapes are distinguished by whether they are seedless or seeded and by color (red and green). The shades of color vary widely and can range from light green to purple and dark blue, regardless of whether seedless or seeded. The trade distinguishes between green and colored grapes. Table G-1 lists varieties of domestic table grapes, their characteristics, and their seasons. For foodservice use, seedless grapes are preferred. Both red and green grapes can be seedless.

Imported seedless grapes are available in winter and spring.

Pack:

23-lb (10.3-kg) lugs; 17-lb (7.6-kg) boxes; 12-lb (5.4-kg) boxes.

Sizes:

Preportioned bunches are available in weights of 2, 3, 4, and 8 oz (56, 85, 112, and 225 g).

Table G-1 Varieties and Seasons of Domestic Table Grapes

Variety	Characteristics	Season
Almeria	seeded, green	October through February
Calmeria	seeded, green	October through February
Cardinal	seeded, red	mid-May to mid-August
Concord	seeded, dark blue	September to November
Emperor	seeded, red	September through March
Exotic	seeded, red	June through August
Flame Seedless	seedless, red	mid-June through September
Golden Muscat	green	September to December
Italia	seeded, green	August through September
Perlette	seedless, green	mid-May to mid-July
Queen	seeded, red	August and September
Ribier	seeded, red	August through mid-February
Ruby	seedless, red	mid-August through January
Thompson Seedless	seedless, green	June to November
Tokay	seeded, red	July through November

Kitchen Yields

Serving size:
½ cup, or 3 oz (85 g).
The size of different varieties of grapes varies greatly. Typically, there are 35 to 45 grapes in one cup.

Seedless grapes:
1 lb (450 g) as purchased yields 15 oz (420 g) stemmed grapes. 1 cup weighs 5¾ oz (160 g). One 20-lb (9-kg) lug of grapes yields 50 cups or 12½ qt (11.6 l) stemmed grapes or 100 servings.

Grapes with seeds:
1 lb (450 g) as purchased yields 14½ oz (400 g) stemmed grapes. 1 cup weighs 6 oz (170 g). One 23-lb (10.3-kg) lug yields 55 cups stemmed grapes or 13¾ qts (12.3 l) or 110 servings.

Calories:

Seedless:
½ cup, or 3 oz (85 g) = 53 Calories.

Seeded:
½ cup, or 3 oz (85 g) = 51 Calories.

GRAPE JUICE
Available canned, in glass bottles, or frozen.

CANNED GRAPE JUICE

Pack:
Twelve 24-oz (0.7-l) cans.

Kitchen Yields

Serving size:
6 oz (0.17 l); thus, one 24-oz (0.7-l) can yields 4 servings.

Calories:
6 oz (0.17 l), canned or bottled = 164 Calories.

FROZEN CONCENTRATED GRAPE JUICE

Pack:
Six 42-oz (1.2-l) cans.

Kitchen Yields
Combine 1 part concentrate with 3 parts water.

Serving size:
6 oz (0.17 l); thus, one 42-oz (1.2-l) can yields 5½ qt (4.9 l) juice, or 28 servings.

GRAPE LEAVES
Grape leaves for stuffing are available imported and also from California. They are used for making Dolmas. The leaves are packed in brine and should be soaked in cold water before use to remove the saltiness.

Pack:
16-oz (450-g) jars, net weight.

Kitchen Yields
40 leaves per 16-oz (450-g) jar.

GRENADINE

A thick, sweet syrup, originally made from the juice of pomegranates or sometimes of red currants. Most grenadine today is made from sugar syrup and citric acid. It is used as a drink ingredient or with desserts.

Pack:
25-oz (0.75-l) bottles.

GRIDDLE CAKES (PANCAKES)

Available as dry mix, ready-to-use batter, and can also be made from scratch.

Formula
    18 lb (8.1 kg) cake flour
    3 gal (11.4 l) milk
    1 gal (3.8 l) or 80 whole eggs
    4 lb (1.8 kg) sugar
    1 lb (450 g) baking powder
    5 lb (2.25 kg) melted shortening

Kitchen Yields
The total mix yields 5 gal (19 l) batter.

Serving size:
Three cakes, 5 in (127 mm) across, which use 5 oz (140 g) batter. The total mix yields 186 pieces, or 62 servings.

GRIDDLE CAKE DRY MIX

Griddle cake (pancake) mix is available in many flavors.

Packs:
Six 5-lb (2.25-kg) bags; individual 50-lb (22.5-kg) bags.

Kitchen Yield
Follow package directions. Some brands can be used to make both pancakes and waffles.

GRIDDLE CAKE READY-TO-USE BATTER

Ready to use.

Pack:
Twelve 1-qt (0.47-l) cartons.

GRITS

See Hominy.

GUAVA

This pear-shaped tropical fruit is available fresh. Ripe fruit gives off a wonderful aroma.

Season:
Spring and summer. Small supplies are available year-round.

Pack:
10-lb (4.5-kg) cartons.

Count:
30 to 32 pieces per carton.

Size:
4½ in (11 cm) long.

Weight:
2⅓ to 2½ oz (65 to 70 g).

Calories:
4 oz (112 g) usable flesh = 70 Calories.

GUINEA HEN

Available fresh and frozen. Normally sold whole. Called *pintades* in French.

Average size:
2¼ to 2½ lb (1 to 1.1 kg).

Kitchen Yields
One bird yields 2 servings.

GYROS

Chopped meat cone of Middle-Eastern origin, cooked on a revolving vertical spit and served (usually) on pita bread. Available made with lamb or beef.

Sizes:
10, 20, and 30 lb (4.5, 9, and 13.5 kg).

Pack:
Four 10-lb (4.5-kg) cones; two 20-lb (9-kg) cones; individual 30-lb (13.5-kg) cones.

Kitchen Yields

Serving size:
3½ oz (100 g) cooked meat; therefore, one 10 lb (4.5 kg) cone yields 30 servings.

H

HAMBURGER PATTIES

See Chopped Steaks and Hamburger, under Beef.

HAMS

See Smoked and Cured Pork Products, under Pork.

HARE

Available fresh and frozen. Hare has dark meat, unlike rabbit, which has light meat. Sold skinned or with skin on.

Season:
Fall and winter.

Average size:
4 lb (1.8 kg), skinned and eviscerated.

Kitchen Yields

Serving size:
One leg or one whole loin. One hare thus yields 3 servings (legs or loin). There is approximately 8 oz (225 g) of shoulder and rack meat that can be used for pâté or other dishes.

HARICOTS VERTS

Tiny string beans. *See* Beans.

HAZELNUTS

See Filberts.

HEARTS OF PALM

Available canned.

Pack:
Twenty-four 28-oz (780-g) cans, with drained weight of 17¼ oz (490 g) each; twenty-four 14-oz (400-g) cans, with drained weight of 7 oz (200 g) each.

Kitchen Yields
One large can yields 8 to 9 stalks; one small can yields 5 to 6 stalks.

Serving size:
2 stalks, for salad.

HERBS & SPICES

Most herbs are available fresh year-round, also fresh chopped, frozen, and dried. Dried herbs are often sold whole or ground. Ground herbs lose flavor faster than whole herbs.

ACHIOTE
See Mexican Foods.

ALLSPICE
Tropical berries sold dried. The flavor resembles cloves, cinnamon, and nutmeg.

ANGELICA
Also called *wild parsnip*. The seeds are used in the manufacture of liquors. The fleshy leaves are candied and used as cake decoration on gingerbread.

BASIL (SWEET BASIL)
There are a number of basil varieties on the market. This annual plant is in the mint family.

Season:
Summer.

Pack:
Bunches and by weight. Sold on stems. Fresh basil wilts quickly.

Kitchen Yields
1 cup plugged leaves weighs 2 oz (60 g).

BAY LEAVES (MONTEREY LAUREL)
Available dried and fresh. Bay leaves grown in California and Oregon are called *Oregon myrtle* and are stronger than other bay leaves.

Kitchen Yields
Dried bay leaves are more pungent than fresh. Use with caution.

BORAGE
Annual plant with fuzzy leaves. The leaves can be used in salads when young; the flowers are sometimes candied.

CARAWAY
Available as dried seeds. The roots can be eaten, but are seldom marketed. Seeds are often used in rye bread and in German dishes. The seeds should be chopped because they can lodge between the teeth. Caraway oil and seeds are used to flavor liquors.

CARDAMOM
Tropical seeds used in baking and as coffee flavoring in Arabic countries.

CELERY
The dried seeds and leaves are used. *See also* Celery.

CHAMOMILE
Annual plant with yellow flowers. The flowers are dried and used as tea.

CHERVIL
Annual plant with tiny, delicate leaves. Used in mild sauces.

CHILI POWDER
Spice mixture consisting of ground chili, garlic, oregano, and salt. Available in different degrees of heat.

Pack:
By weight.

Kitchen Yields
2 cups weigh 9½ oz (260 g).

CHIVES
Available dried and fresh. Garlic chives are long, fresh chives with flat leaves and are available in Oriental markets.

DRIED CHIVES
Pack:
Various packs are available.

FRESH CHIVES
Available year-round as cut or as live potted plants.

Pack:
Bunches in various sizes.

Kitchen Yields
Size of bunches varies greatly; they are smallest in early spring. 3½ average bunches yield 1½ cups, or 2 oz (56 g) cut.

FROZEN CHIVES
Pack:
4 oz (112 g).

CILANTRO
Also known as *Chinese* or *Mexican parsley*, cilantro constitutes the leaves of the coriander plant.

Season:
Available year-round.

Pack:
By weight or by 30-bunch crates.

CINNAMON/CASSIA
Bark from two related trees, available in sticks (quills) or ground. Although there is a flavor difference between cinnamon and cassia, a distinction is seldom made. Cinnamon oil is used in baking.

Pack:
By weight.

CORIANDER
Coriander seeds are used for pickling meat and fish. Pastrami is rolled in crushed coriander seeds. The leaves are known as cilantro.

CLOVES
The dried flower bud of a tropical tree; its flavor is aromatic and sweet. Available whole or ground. Cloves are used in ham dishes, in beverages, and in baking.

CURRY LEAVES
Available fresh and dried. The leaves are no substitute for curry powder. It is often used in Indian dishes.

CURRY POWDER

Spice mixture available by weight or as paste. Also called *masala*. The composition of the blend varies by geographic region and can range from very hot (sharp) to mild. Masala paste consists of oil, spices, and ground lentils.

Pack:

Curry powder by weight; paste in 10-oz (280-g) jars.

DILL

The leaves are available fresh and dried, while the seeds are available dried only. The leaves are often used in Scandinavian dishes.

GINGER

See Ginger Powder and Ginger Root.

JUNIPER BERRIES

Dried juniper berries are used in game dishes. They are also a major flavoring agent in gin.

LEMON BALM (MELISSA)

The fresh and dried leaves are used in drinks and fruit salads.

Season:

Summer.

LEMON GRASS

Tropical plant with long leaves, available fresh and dried.

LEMON VERBENA

The leaves have a strong lemon smell and can be used in salads and dressings. Available fresh in summer and dried.

LOVAGE

Called *Liebstöckel* in German. Its leaves are used in soups.

MARJORAM

Plant in the mint family and closely related to oregano. Marjoram is more delicate than oregano. Available fresh or dried.

NUTMEG AND MACE

The seed of a tropical tree. The outside fibrous coating of the seed is dried and becomes mace, the inside nut is nutmeg. Mace is always sold ground; nutmeg is available whole and ground. The whole nut has better flavor, but is difficult to grind.

OREGANO

Available fresh and dried, it is the herb typically used in pizza and other Italian dishes.

PARSLEY

FRESH PARSLEY

There are 2 types of parsley, *curly leaf* and *Italian*. Curly leaf parsley is mostly used for garnishing; Italian parsley is used for flavoring.

Season:

Available year-round.

Pack:

Sold by bunches. Size of bunches varies.

Kitchen Yields

Average weight of bunch is 2 oz (56 g).

PEPPER

The dried berries of a tropical vine. The berries are black when dried. The black outer shell is black pepper which, when ground away, exposes the lighter inner kernel, which is white pepper. Pepper will lose its flavor quickly and should be ground when needed. Black pepper is slightly more pungent than white pepper.

POPPY SEEDS

Black or slate-blue seeds. Available whole or ground. Whole poppy seeds are used in baking and in dressings; ground poppy seeds can be boiled with milk and sugar for danish pastry filling.

ROSE HIPS, ROSE PETALS

The fruit of the rose is used dried or fresh in tea or in making jam. The rose petals are available candied for cake decoration. Rose water is a fragrant liquid and is used in Middle Eastern dishes.

ROSEMARY

Perennial shrub requiring a mild climate. The pine-needle-shaped leaves are available fresh or dried. It is often used in lamb and beef dishes or in conjunction with tomatoes.

SAFFRON

Genuine saffron is imported from Spain. Imitation saffron is available from Mexico.

Pack:

By weight. Various packs from 1 oz (28 g) to 1 lb (450 g).

Kitchen Yields

Whole saffron is better than ground saffron. Allow flower stigmas to steep in liquid to get better flavor extraction.

Kitchen Yields

⅛ oz (3.5 g) saffron flavors 3 gal (11.4 l) stock.

SAGE

The leaves are available fresh and dried.

SAVORY

There are two varieties of savory. Summer savory is an annual and winter savory is a perennial. Summer savory is available fresh and has a delicate flavor. Dried savory is mostly winter savory, which has a less delicate flavor. Used with beans and meat.

SESAME SEEDS

The seeds are available dried and can be beige or black in color. The seeds are used in baking, in desserts, and in hors d'oeuvres. A paste made with sesame seeds is called *tahina* (*tahini*) paste and is used in Middle-Eastern cooking.

SORREL (SOUR GRASS)

Season:

Spring and summer.

Pack:

By weight, usually 20-lb (9.1-kg) crates.

Kitchen Yields

For vegetable dishes, remove stems, and boil leaves in their own juices. They will shrink and become brown on account of their acidity.

1 lb (450 g) as purchased will season 1 qt (0.94 l) soup.

STAR ANISE

Dried fruits of a tropical tree in the magnolia family. The star-shaped fruit is used in Chinese cooking.

TARRAGON

There are two varieties, French and Russian tarragon. Only the French tarragon is suitable for cooking. The slender leaves are available fresh and dried.

THYME

An herb with many varieties. The most important ones are common thyme, lemon thyme, and caraway thyme. This herb is used in stocks and in meat dishes.

TURMERIC

Root vegetable resembling ginger. The ground root is used as spice. It is yellow and sometimes erroneously called *saffron*. Turmeric is an important ingredient in curry powder.

Pack:

By weight.

Size:

Roots are 3 to 5 in (12 to 20 cm) long.

VANILLA

See Vanilla.

WOODRUFF

Called *Waldmeister* in German, the leaves of this leafy spring plant are used primarily to flavor wine drinks. Available fresh in spring.

HOMINY

Available canned and dried.

CANNED HOMINY

Yellow hominy and white hominy are both available fully cooked.

Pack:
Six #10 cans.

Kitchen Yields

Serving size:
1 cup, or 8 oz (225 g), for breakfast. One #10 can contains 75 oz (2.1 kg), drained weight, and yields 7 servings. One case yields 42 servings.

Calories:
1 cup, or 8 oz (225 g) = 120 Calories.

DRY HOMINY GRITS

Pack:
By weight.

Kitchen Yields

1 lb (450 g) dry is equivalent to 2¾ cups (0.64 l) and yields 50 cups cooked cereal.

Calories:
1 cup cooked, weighing 8 oz (225 g) = 120 Calories.

HONEY

Pack:
Jars in various sizes, or portion pack.

Calories:
1 tb (21 g) = 65 Calories.

HORSERADISH

Available whole and fresh, or grated and preserved with vinegar. Most operators use horseradish that has already been grated. Grated horseradish is available plain or mixed with beet juice.

FRESH HORSERADISH

Brown root with white flesh, pungent and hot. Used raw, grated, and mixed with vinegar as a condiment.

Season:
Available year-round.

Pack:
By weight.

Kitchen Yields
Peeling waste about 20 percent. Keep peeled roots in ice water to avoid discoloration.

GRATED HORSERADISH

Available plain or flavored with red beet juice.

Pack:
1-qt (0.94-l) jars.

Kitchen Yields
Varies. About 3 oz (85 g) per serving.

HOTCAKES

See Griddle Cakes.

HOT PEPPERS

See Chiles, under Mexican Foods.

HUCKLEBERRY

European variety of blueberry, seldom available commercially. The juice of huckleberries is dark purple.

Season:
Midsummer to late summer.

Calories:
4 oz (112 g) = 60 Calories.

I AND J

ICE

The production and storage capacity of ice machines is rated in pounds.

Ice cube weights:

1 cubic ft (0.28 cubic m) ice cubes weighs 35 lb (16 kg); 1 lb (450 g) cubes will ice 3 to 4 water glasses.

ICE FOR CARVING

Standard size block:

Weight:
300 lb (135 kg).

Size:
40 × 20 × 10 in (100 × 50 × 25 cm).
Other sizes are available.

Melting speed:

1½ in (38 mm) per hour at room temperature.

ICE CREAM AND SHERBETS

Quality is measured in terms of butterfat content, weight (overrun), and flavor. Butterfat content is measured in percentages, based on weight:

14 to 16 percent: High quality
16 to 18 percent: Deluxe quality
12 percent: Minimum for vanilla ice cream
10 percent: Minimum for ice cream with added solids, such as chocolate or nuts

Overrun is the amount of expansion in volume that occurs during the freezing process. Some overrun is normal, but it can be increased by whipping air into the product. Ice cream with high overrun is weak in flavor, light, and has a limited shelf life. The volume will be reduced when this ice cream is processed in the kitchen. The amount of overrun is reflected in percentages in relation to volume: 100 percent overrun means that the product doubled during the freezing process.

100 percent: High
80 percent: Normal
50 percent: High-quality product

Sherbets are frozen desserts made with milk and flavorings. There is no minimum butterfat content and sherbets are labeled low-calorie or low-fat.

Pack:

2½-gal (9.5-l) tubs; 3-gal (11.4-l) tubs. The 3-gal size is standard in many locations.

Weight:

Weight is an important quality indicator. Ice cream should be weighed occasionally when received to ensure that quality standards are met.

1 gal (3.8 l) = 4½ lb (2 kg) minimum weight
1 gal (3.8 l) = 6 lb (2.7 kg) best-quality ice cream with 50 percent overrun
2½-gal (9.5-l) tub = 11¼ lb (5 kg) minimum weight
2½-gal (9.5-l) tub = 15 lb (6.75 kg) high-quality ice cream
3-gal (11.4-l) tub = 13½ lb (6 kg) minimum weight
3-gal (11.4-l) tub = 18 lb (8.1 kg) high-quality ice cream

Kitchen Yields

Scoops are classified by the number of scoops per 1 qt (0.94 l). For instance, there are twelve #12 scoops in 1 qt ice cream. Measurements are approximate, since they depend on how well the portions are dipped, and on the overrun of the product. High-overrun ice cream shrinks during storage. Portion weight depends on the overrun. One #8 scoop of high-quality ice cream weighs about 3½ oz. Other scoop sizes are listed under a separate entry; *see* Scoop Sizes.

Ice cream rings are often used for banquets. The serving size is 3.2 fl oz (0.09 l), so 1 qt (0.94 l) provides ice cream for 10 covers.

Calories:

3½ oz (100 g), with 11 percent butterfat = 200 Calories.
3½ oz (100 g), with 16 percent butterfat = 236 Calories.

ICES

See Granite (Water Ice).

ICING

See Royal Icing.

IQF

Abbreviation for *individually quick frozen*. IQF products are frozen loose, and therefore are easier to use than products frozen in solid blocks. To pre-vent freezer burn, the products are sprayed with water during the freezing process; this is called *glazing* in the trade.

Kitchen Yields

About 10 to 15 percent lower yield per unit weight, on account of glazing, compared to block-frozen products. The weight loss varies greatly depending on the product.

J

JALAPEÑO PEPPERS

See Chiles, under Mexican Foods.

JAPANESE FOODS

ASAKUSA NORI

Also called *lavar*, asakusa nori is a seaweed, available fresh and as thin, dried sheets. Lack of uniform color is an indication of good quality.

Season:
For fresh nori, late summer and fall.

Pack:
Varies.

Size:
6 × 10 in (150 × 250 mm).

DAIKON

Long, white Oriental radish with flavor resembling ordinary radish. It is eaten raw or cooked as a condiment or as a vegetable.

Season:
Available year-round.

Pack:
Purchase by weight. Average weight is about 2 lb (0.9 kg). Sold often with leaves on—3 radishes to a bunch, 12 bunches to a case.

Size:
1 to 1½ lb (0.45 to 0.67 kg).

Kitchen Yields

Calories:
¼ cup or 1½ oz (42 g) shredded = 25 Calories.

EDA MAME

Fresh soybeans, most often sold still in their pods.

Season:
Late spring through summer.

Pack:
Sold by weight or in bunches.

Calories:
1¼ cups cooked and shelled = 200 Calories.

GOBO

Called *burdock* in English, a root vegetable common in most parts of Europe. The tender roots are peeled and cooked. They resemble salsify.

Season:
August to December.

Size:
10 to 16 oz (228 to 450 g).

JAPANESE EGGPLANT
Small, purple eggplant.

Season:
Available in spring.

Pack:
By weight and by piece.

Size:
4 to 5 oz (112 to 140 g) each.

JAPANESE MUSHROOMS
See Mushrooms.

KANTEN
See Agar-agar.

KATSUO BUSHI
Flakes of dried bonito—the main ingredient for making dashi, the basic stock.

Pack:
2.8- and 5.2-oz (100- and 150-g) bags.

Kitchen Yields
⅔ cups flakes yield 1½ qt (0.7 l) stock.

Calories:
¼ cup dry flakes = 25 Calories.

KOMBU
Kelp, normally sold dry. Used in making stocks and added to other dishes.

MIRIN
Sweet rice wine.

Pack:
1 l (2 qt 2½ oz).

MISO
Bean paste, available fresh in three basic flavors:

> *Aka:* red, pungent

> *Chu:* gold-colored, mild
> *Shiro:* white, almost sweet

Pack:
Purchase by weight.

OCHA
Green tea.

OKOME
Short-grain rice, grown for Japanese cooking. The variety is called California Rose, Blue Rose, or Calrose rice. Grown mostly in California, available under various brand names, this rice is used for sushi and as side dish.

Pack:
1-, 5-, 10-, 25-, and 50-lb (0.45-, 2.25-, 4.5-, 11.3-, and 22.6-kg) bags.

Kitchen Yields

Serving size:
½ cup cooked, equivalent to 1.6 oz (45 g) raw; 10 lb (4.5 kg) yields 100 portions.

Calories:
½ cup cooked = 90 Calories.

SAKE
Alcoholic beverage made from fermented rice; usually served warm.

Calories:
1 cup (0.23 l) = 200 Calories.

SHISO LEAVES
The pungent green or purple perilla leaf, used as a garnish or a sushi wrap. The flavor is strong and distinctive. It is usually used raw, seldom in marinades and almost never cooked, because it turns black and bitter when heated.

WAKAME
Seaweed, available fresh or pickled in salt.

WASABI
Powdered green horseradish. Mixed with cold water to a mustard-like consistency.

JELLY OKRA

See Racial, under Flowers.

JERUSALEM ARTICHOKE

See Sunchoke.

JICAMA (MEXICAN POTATO)

Available fresh, the jicama is a white tuber resembling a large turnip. It can be used raw in salads, or steamed, fried, or boiled. The tuber peels easily and there is little waste.

Season:
September to June.

Pack:
Sold by weight.

Average weight:
6 to 8 oz (170 to 225 g).

Kitchen Yields
About 25 percent peeling loss.

JUJUBE

Yellowish, olive-shaped fruit with one single stone. Available fresh.

Season:
Late summer until spring.

Kitchen Yields

Size:
1 to 2 in (2.5 to 5 cm) long.

Weight:
1½ to 3 oz (70 to 85 g).

K

KALE

Available canned, fresh, and frozen.

CANNED KALE

Available chopped.

Pack:
Six #10 cans.

Drained weight:
One #10 can weighs 62 oz (1.7 kg), drained.

Kitchen Yields

Serving size:
½ cup, or 4 oz (112 g). One #10 can yields 15 servings; one case yields 90 servings.

Calories:
1 cup, or 4 oz (112 g) = 40 Calories.

FRESH KALE

Scotch Kale and Blue Kale are important varieties that have curly leaves. Smooth-leaf varieties are also available, especially in the spring. Kale can be purchased whole in bunches or stripped. It is often shipped iced.

Season:
December to April.

Pack:
18- to 25-lb (8.1- to 11.25-kg) bushels.

Kitchen Yields
Yields are very difficult to estimate on account of the amount of stripping. Waste is about 30 percent by weight.

Calories:
½ cup, or 4 oz (112 g), cooked and drained = 45 Calories.

FROZEN KALE

Available chopped.

Pack:
Twelve 2-lb (0.9-kg) boxes.

Serving size:
½ cup, or 4 oz (112 g).

Kitchen Yields
There is little shrinkage since the product is already cooked.

Serving size:
¾ cup, or 4 oz (112 g); thus, one box yields 8 servings, and one case yields 96 servings.

Calories:
½ cup, or 4 oz (112 g) = 40 Calories.

KASHA

Cracked buckwheat; used as cereal in Jewish and Russian cooking.

Pack:
Twenty-four 1-lb (450-g) packages. Larger packs are available.

Kitchen Yields
1 lb (450 g) kasha yields 2¼ cups dry.

Serving size:
⅔ (0.15 l) cup; 1 lb (450 g) yields 12 servings.

Formula
> 1 lb (450 g) kasha
> 2 whole eggs, mixed dry into kasha
> ½ cup shortening
> 4 cups water or stock

KELP

See Seaweed.

KIRBY CUCUMBERS

Pickling-size cucumbers. *See* Cucumbers.

Season:
Summer until early winter.

Pack:
Purchase by weight.

Size:
About 4 oz (112 g) and smaller.

KIWI FRUITS

Also called *Chinese gooseberry*, it is a green fruit with thin, fuzzy skin. The fruit is ripe when it gives slightly under light pressure. To make a kiwi fruit ripen quickly, store it at room temperature in a plastic bag together with apples or bananas. The fruit stores well for several weeks at 33°F.

Season:

California kiwi:
October until May.

Imported Kiwi:
Available year-round.

Pack:
7-lb (3.15-kg) flats; 20-lb (9-kg) cartons.

Sizes:
Counts of 25, 28, 30, 33, 36, 39, 42, and 45 in 7-lb (3.15 kg) flats.

Weight range:
1 to 4 oz (28 to 112 g).

Kitchen Yields

Average weight:
2½ to 3 oz (70 to 85 g) per fruit. One 2½-oz (70-g) fruit yields 5 to 6 slices. 2½ fruits, diced large, yield 1 cup, or 6 oz (170 g). One #39 flat yields 16 cups, or 96 oz (2.7 kg) diced fruit.

Calories:
4 oz (112 g) = 39 Calories.

KOHLRABI

Also called *cabbage turnip*, this vegetable has a swollen stem that grows above ground. It is available with green or purple skin. Kohlrabi should not be larger than 2 in (50 mm) across, because larger kohlrabi are often woody and cannot be used.

Season:
May to November, with peaks in July and August.

Pack:
By weight or by bunches. When purchasing by weight, ascertain whether the leaves are trimmed off.

Kitchen Yields
Waste is at least 40 percent after trimming leaves.

KUMQUATS

Small citrus fruits resembling oranges.

FRESH KUMQUATS

Season:
Fall and winter.

Pack:
10-lb (4.5-kg) cartons.

Kitchen Yields
Use as is; there is no waste.

PRESERVED KUMQUATS
Preserved in light or heavy syrup.

Pack:
Four 1-gal (3.8-l) jars.

Kitchen Yields
Use as is; there is no waste.

L

LADLE SIZES

Table L-1 lists common ladle sizes and their equivalents in cups, quarts, and liters.

LAMB KEBAB

See Shish Kebab, under Lamb Dishes and Yields.

LAMB AND MUTTON

Lamb generally comes from animals less than one year old. Mutton comes from animals over one year old, but should not be older than two years. The term *yearling* is used for animals one year old. The term *spring lamb* indicates that the animal was born in spring of the same year. It is generally from a 3-month-old animal, but can be marketed as late as October of their year of birth.

LARGER CUTS OF DOMESTIC LAMB AND MUTTON

The American Lamb Council is recommending changes in some of the specifications listed under this heading, in order to make the cuts easier to use. The new specifications are listed at the end of this general entry.

To make product identification easier, *Meat Buyers Guide* (MBG) numbers have been used when practical.

Table L-1 Ladle Sizes and Equivalents

Size	Fraction of 1 cup	Number per 1 qt	Number per 1 l
1 oz	⅛	32	34
2 oz	¼	16	17
2⅔ oz	⅓	12	13
4 oz	½	8	8.6
6 oz	¾	5⅓	5.7
8 oz	1	4	4.3

BABY LAMB
Often sold whole, with the pelt on.

Weight range:
20 to 40 lb (9 to 18 kg).

Best size:
26 to 30 lb (11.7 to 13.5 kg).

Kitchen Yields
The carcass is divided into legs, boneless shoulders, racks, and backs. The parts are very small, and normally slices from various parts are combined to produce a single serving. Meat should be cooked until lightly pink.

Serving size:
5 oz (140 g). One 28-lb (12.6-kg) lamb, pelt on, yields 22 servings.

BACK, MBG #236
Whole back, with rack and loin still attached.

Weights:

Lamb:
8 to 15 lb (3.6 to 6.7 kg).

Mutton:
11 to 26 lb (4.9 to 11.7 kg).

Kitchen Yields
Good buffet piece when roasted whole.

Best size :
15 lb (6.7 kg) for lamb; 20 lb (9 kg) for mutton.

Servings:
One 15-lb (6.7-kg) lamb back yields 25 buffet servings; one 20-lb (9-kg) mutton back yields 30 buffet servings.

BREAST, MBG #209A
Cut includes plate and brisket. Best use is to cut this piece on meat saw for stew or use as barbecue ribs.

Weights:

Lamb:
3 to 8 lb (1.3 to 3.6 kg).

Mutton:
4 to 10 lb (1.8 to 4.5 kg).

Kitchen Yields
Meat is very fatty.

Serving size:
12 oz (336 g), raw weight.

CHUCK, MBG #206
Whole chuck, with bone in.

Weight ranges:

Lamb:
11 to 14 lb (4.9 to 6.3 kg).
14 to 19 lb (6.3 to 8.5 kg).
19 to 23 lb (8.5 to 10.3 kg).

Mutton:
19 to 26 lb (8.5 to 11.7 kg).
26 to 33 lb (11.7 to 14.8 kg).
33 to 40 lb (14.8 to 18 kg).

Kitchen Yields
Chuck can be fatty. Use for stew or make into bone-less roast. Boneless roast is fatty and will not slice well.

LAMB:

Best weight:
18 lb (8.1 kg). Boned and trimmed, this yields 10 lb (4.5 kg).

Serving size:
For stew, 8 oz (225 g) raw meat, which yields 5 oz (140 g) cooked stew; thus, 10 lb (4.5 kg) meat yields 20 servings. For roast, 7 oz (200 g) raw meat, which yields 5 oz (140 g) cooked roast. Chuck, boned and tied, yields one 6-lb (2.7-kg) roast, or 3 lb (1.35 kg) stew meat. One 6-lb (2.7-kg) tied roast yields 12 servings.
NOTE: Not all chuck meat is suitable for roasting.

Shrinkage loss:
For stew cooked medium well, 35 percent; for roast, 25 percent.

MUTTON:

Best weight:
24 lb (10.8 kg). Boned and trimmed, this yields 14 lb (6.3 kg).

Serving size:
For stew, 8 oz (225 g) raw meat, which yields 5 oz (140 g) cooked meat; thus, 14 lb (6.3 kg) stew meat yields 28 servings. For roast, 7¼ oz (203 g) raw meat, which yields 5 oz (140 g) cooked meat; thus, 10 lb (4.5 kg) tied meat yields 22 servings.

Shrinking loss:
For stew, 35 percent; for roast, 28 percent.
NOTE: Not all chuck meat is not suitable for roast-ing. About 3 lb (1.35 kg) meat should be used as stew meat.

Calories:
5 oz (140 g) cooked roast = 575 Calories.

HOTEL-SIZE EIGHT-RIB RACK, MBG #204

Weight ranges:

Lamb:
3 to 5 lb (1.3 to 2.2 kg).
5 to 6 lb (2.2 to 2.7 kg).
6 to 8 lb (2.7 to 3.6 kg).

Mutton:
6 to 8 lb (2.7 to 3.6 kg).
8 to 10 (3.6 to 4.5 kg).
10 to 14 lb (4.5 to 6.3 kg).

Best size:
6 to 8 lb (2.7 to 3.6 kg).

Kitchen Yields

LAMB:

Best size:
Whole. 7 lb (3.1 kg).

Trimmed size:
Two racks, frenched, 2 lb (0.9 kg) each.

Serving size:

For roast rack, two 8½ oz (300 g) pieces, cooked, with bone. Half a rack yields 3 servings; one whole rack yields 6 servings; and ten racks yields 60 servings. For rib chops, serving size is one 9-oz (250-g) piece or two 4½-oz (125-g) pieces. Half a rack yields 3 servings; one whole rack yields 6 servings; and ten racks yield 60 servings.

Calories:

Lean and fat boneless meat, 3½ oz (100 g) = 365 Calories.

MUTTON:

Best size:

Whole. 10 lb (4.5 kg).

Trimmed sizes:

Two racks, frenched, 3 lb 5 oz (1.5 kg) each.

Serving size:

For roast rack, two 4½-oz (128-g) pieces cooked, each with bone. Half a rack yields 4 servings; one whole rack yields 8 servings; and ten racks yield 80 servings.

For rib chops, serving size is one 12-oz (336-g) piece with two bones. Half a rack yields 4 chops; one rack yields 8 chops; ten racks yield 80 chops.

LEGS, MBG #233

The weights listed are for pairs, bone in.

Sizes:

Lamb:
11 to 14 lb (4.9 to 6.3 kg).
14 to 19 lb (6.3 to 8.5 kg).
19 to 23 lb (8.5 to 10.3 kg).
23 to 27 lb (10.3 to 12.1 kg).

Mutton:
19 to 26 lb (8.5 to 11.7 kg).
26 to 33 lb (11.7 to 14.6 kg).
33 to 40 lb (14.6 to 18 kg).
40 to 46 lb (18 to 20.7 kg).

Kitchen Yields

LAMB:

Best size:

Pair:
18 lb (8.1 kg).

Single leg:
9 lb (4 kg).

Serving size:

For roast, 6 oz (170 g). One 7½ (3.3-kg) oven-ready single leg, bone in, yields 8 to 10 servings sliced, with bone in. One 6¼-lb (2.8-kg) boneless and tied roast yields 12 machine-sliced servings.

Shrinkage loss:

20 percent.

MUTTON:

Best size:

Pair:
22 lb (9.9 kg).

Single leg:
11 lb (4.9 kg).

Serving size:

For roast, 6 oz (170 g). One 9-lb (4-kg) oven-ready single leg, bone in, yields 12 to 14 servings, sliced, with bone in. One 8-lb (3.6-kg) roast, boneless and tied, yields 18 machine sliced servings.

Calories:

4 oz (112 g) roast, cooked = 320 Calories.

LOIN, MBG #231

Full loin, with kidneys, kidney fat, and flanks attached.

Sizes:

Lamb:
5 to 6 lb (2.2 to 2.7 kg).
6 to 8 lb (2.7 to 3.6 kg).
8 to 10 lb (3.6 to 4.5 kg).
10 to 12 lb (4.5 to 5.4 kg).

Mutton:
8 to 11 lb (3.6 to 4.8 kg).
11 to 14 lb (4.8 to 6.3 kg).
14 to 17 lb (6.3 to 7.6 kg).
17 to 20 lb (7.6 to 9 kg).

Best size:
8 to 10 lb (3.6 to 4.5 kg) for lamb; 8 to 11 lb (3.5 to 4.9 kg) for mutton.

Kitchen Yields

LAMB:

Best size:
10 lb (4.5 kg).

Serving size:
For roast boneless loin, 5 oz (140 g), cooked. Two boned, trimmed, and rolled halves weigh 2½ lb (1.1 kg), so one half weighs 20 oz (568 g). One half yields 3 servings, and one full loin yields 6 servings. For boneless chops, serving size is two 3¼ oz (92 g) pieces. Two halves, boned, trimmed, and rolled, weigh 2½ lb (1.1 kg); and one loin (two halves) yields 12 pieces or 6 servings. For bone-in loin chops, serving size is one 7-oz (200-g) piece; one loin (two halves) yields 8 chops.

Shrinking loss:
20 percent.

MUTTON:

Best size:
12 lb (5.4 kg).

Serving size:
For roast boneless loin, 5½ oz (156 g), cooked. One loin (two halves), boned and trimmed, weighs 3 lb (1.35 kg) and yields 7 servings.

Shrinkage loss:
20 percent.

SHANKS, MBG #210
For braising, whole.

Weights:
1 to 2.5 lb (0.4 to 1.1 kg).

Kitchen Yields

Best size:
1 lb (450 g).

Serving size:
One shank.

NEW SPECIFICATIONS FOR DOMESTIC LAMB AND MUTTON
The American Lamb Council is recommending a change to new specifications and cuts to make lamb more "user-friendly."

BONELESS SADDLE

Sizes:
1½ to 2 lb (675 to 900 g).

Kitchen Yields

Serving size:
5 oz (140 g); one loin yields 4 servings.

BONELESS SARATOGA ROLL
Chuck roll; can be fatty.

Sizes:
1½ to 2 lb (675 to 900 g).

Kitchen Yields

Serving size:
For roast, 6 oz (170 g); one piece yields 4 servings.

BONELESS SIRLOIN

Sizes:
2 to 3 lb (0.9 to 1.35 kg).

Kitchen Yields
Roast whole or cut into medallions.

Serving size:
5 oz (140 g) for cooked roast; one 3-lb (1.35-kg) piece yields 8 servings of roast.
6 oz (168 g), as medallions (2 pieces per serving); one 3-lb (1.35-kg) piece yields 7 servings of medallions.

BONELESS SHOULDER ROLL

Sizes:
4 to 6 lb (1.8 to 2.7 kg).

Kitchen Yields

Serving size:
6 oz (170 g) roasted; one 5-lb (2.2-kg) piece yields
9 servings of roast.

DENVER RIB
Whole ribs, trimmed.

Sizes:
12 oz (340 g).

Kitchen Yields

Serving size:
One rib.

DOUBLE BONELESS LOIN

Weight:
3½ to 4½ lb (1.5 to 2 kg).

Pack:
Two loins per box, totaling 7 to 9 lb (3.1 to 4 kg).

Kitchen Yields

Servings size:
For roast, cooked, 5 oz (140 g). One 4-lb (1.8-kg)
piece yields 11 servings of roast. For loin cut into
chops, serving size is 6 oz (170 g) raw weight, and
one 4-lb (1.8-kg) piece yields 10 chops.

DOUBLE BONELESS LOIN CHOP
Loin with the tenderloin removed.

Size:
6 oz (170 g) raw weight.

Kitchen Yields

Serving size:
6 oz (170 g), or one chop per serving.

FRENCH RACK

Sizes:
1¾ to 2¼ lb (0.8 to 1 kg) each, split.

Pack:
Six racks per box, totaling 10½ to 13½ lb (4.7 to
6 kg).

Kitchen Yields
One rack yields 3 servings.

STEAMSHIP LEG
Sirloin removed, aitch bone removed, and shank
attached.

Sizes:
6 to 8 lb (2.7 to 3.6 kg).

Kitchen Yields

Serving size:
6 oz (170 g), cooked. One 7-lb (3.1-kg) leg yields 7
to 8 servings.

TENDERLOIN
All fat removed, but silver skin left on.

Sizes:
4 to 5 oz (112 to 140 g).

Pack:
5 lb (2.2 kg) per box.

Kitchen Yields

Serving size:
1 piece; one box contains 16 to 18 pieces.

POPULAR LAMB DISHES

BONE-IN LOIN CHOP

Kitchen Yields

Serving size:
One 7-oz (200-g) piece. One Loin, MBG #231,
10 lb (4.5 kg), yields 8 chops; one half loin yield 4
chops.

BONELESS LOIN CHOP

Kitchen Yields

Serving size:
Two 3¼ oz (92 g) pieces. One loin (two halves) yields 12 pieces. To obtain 50 servings, purchase nine Loin, MBG #231, weighing 10 lb (4.5 kg) each.

BONELESS ROAST LOIN

Kitchen Yields

Serving size:
5 oz (140 g), cooked. One half loin yields 3 servings; thus, one loin yields 6 servings. To obtain 50 servings, purchase nine Loin, MBG #231, weighing 10 lb (4.5 kg) each.

LAMB STEW

Kitchen Yields

Serving size:
8 oz (225 g) raw meat or 5 oz (140 g) cooked stew. To obtain 50 servings, purchase two and one-half 18-lb (8.1-kg) pieces of Chuck, MBG #206, or 25 lb (11.25 kg) stew meat.

MOUSSAKA

Kitchen Yields

Serving size:
4 oz (112 g) ground lamb. To obtain 50 servings, purchase two 18-lb (8.1-kg) pieces of Chuck, MBG #206.

RIB CHOPS

Serving sizes:
One 9-oz (250-g) piece or two 4½-oz (125-g) pieces. To obtain 50 servings, purchase ten 7-lb (3.1-kg) Hotel-size, Eight-rib Racks, MBG #204. For small chops for receptions, serving size is one 3½-oz (100-g) chop. To obtain 100 chops, purchase seven 5-lb (2.2-kg) Hotel-size, Eight-rib Racks, MBG #204.

ROAST LEG OF LAMB

Serving size:
5 oz (140 g) cooked meat. To obtain 50 servings, purchase two 18-lb (8.1-kg) pairs of Legs, MBG #233, machine-sliced, or five 9-lb (4-kg) single legs, sliced on bone, or three 7- to 8-lb (3.1- to 3.6-kg) boneless Legs, MBG #234A.

SHISH KEBAB

Serving size:
6 oz (168 g), raw. To obtain 50 servings, purchase two 18-lb (8.1-kg) pairs of Legs, MBG #233, or fifty 6.2-oz (176-g) pieces of New Zealand boneless short loin.

Pack:
4 pieces per vacuum pack; 20 pieces per box; 80 pieces per carton.

PORTION-CONTROLLED LAMB

LOIN CHOPS

Cut across the loin. All bones are left attached; only the skin is removed.

Sizes:
4 to 10 oz (112 to 280 g), in increments of 1 oz (28 g).

Kitchen Yields

The flank attached is normally 3 in (75 mm) long. Since the bones are left attached, the edible meat portion is smaller than in boneless chops cut in the kitchen.

Serving size:
Varies. Two 6-oz (170-g) chops are an average dinner portion.

RIB CHOPS

Available regular and frenched, with the end of the rib bone exposed. The chops are cut across the rack. Bones are still attached, the blade bone and surrounding muscle are removed.

Sizes:

Regular chops:
3 to 10 oz (85 to 280 g), in increments of 1 oz (28 g).

Frenched chops:
3 to 8 oz (85 to 225 g), in increments of 1 oz (28 g).

Kitchen Yields
Since the feather bone and aitch bone are still attached, the chops are difficult to eat.

Serving size:
Varies. Two 6-oz (170-g) chops is an average dinner portion.

SHOULDER CHOPS
Cut across the blade and arm.

Sizes:
4 to 8 oz (112 to 225 g), in increments of 1 oz (28 g).

Kitchen Yields
These chops are bony and fatty. Braise with vegetables.

Serving size:
Varies. Two 6-oz (170-g) chops is an average dinner portion.

STEW MEAT

Pack:
By weight.

Kitchen Yields
Stew meat is cut from different muscles, and its degree of tenderness varies. Shrinkage is about 35 to 40 percent.

Serving size:
9 oz (250 g) raw meat or 5½ oz (156 g) cooked meat; 10 lb (4.5 kg) yields 18 servings.

SPECIFICATIONS FOR NEW ZEALAND LAMB
New Zealand lamb is generally half the size of domestic lamb. It is best purchased fully trimmed and ready for use.

BONE-IN RACKS

Weight:
6 to 7 oz (176 to 200 g).

Pack:
Two pieces per vacuum pack; five vacuum packs per box; four boxes per carton.

Kitchen Yields

Serving size:
One piece per person.

BONELESS SHORT LOIN

Weight:
6.2 oz (176 g).

Pack:
Four pieces per vacuum pack; five vacuum packs per box; four boxes per carton.

Kitchen Yields

Serving size:
One piece per person, roasted whole or used as shish kebab.

BONELESS STEW MEAT

Pack:
10-lb (4.5-kg) boxes, 40-lb (18-kg) cartons.

Kitchen Yields

Serving size:
8 oz (225 g). One box yields 20 servings.

LOIN CHOPS
Bone-in loin chops.

Weight:
3 to 3¼ oz (76 to 92 g).

Pack:
48 to 52 pieces per 10-lb (4.5-kg) box.

Kitchen Yields

Serving size:
Three pieces as main course.

SHANKS

Weight:
9.2 oz (260 g).

Pack:
Twenty pieces per box; four boxes per master carton.

Kitchen Yields

Serving size:
Two shanks; therefore, one box yields 10 servings.

LATKES (POTATO PANCAKES)

Available frozen or can be made fresh.

FRESH LATKES

Formula
    10 lb (4.5 kg) peeled russet potatoes, raw
    3 lb (0.9 kg) peeled onion
    10 eggs
    1 cup (0.23 l) matzo meal
    1 cup (0.23 l) flour
    1 tb salt

NOTE: Make sure potatoes and onions are well drained after grinding

Kitchen Yields

Serving size:
3 oz (85 g) per piece: 2 pieces for reception, or 3 pieces as garnish with meat.
The total mixture yields 100 pieces.

FROZEN LATKES

Pack:
Varies.

LEEKS

Leeks are vegetables with large flat leaves and white stems. The white part is primarily used in cooking, and it should extend at least 3 to 4 in (7.6 to 10 cm) from the roots.

Pack:
24- to 30-lb (11- to 13.6-kg) crates.

Size:
The white stem should be at least ¾ in (1.9 cm) in diameter, but not larger than 1¼ in (3 cm), because the centers of large leeks are often woody.

Count:
12 bunches to a crate.

Kitchen Yields
There are about 12 to 25 leeks to a bunch, but sizes vary greatly. For this reason, leeks should be purchased by weight. If only the white part is used, trimming loss is about 50 percent. Leeks are woody in early spring, and the core cannot be used. This can reduce the usable yield by an additional 50 percent.

LEMON BALM (MELISSA)

See Herbs & Spices.

LEMONS

Season:
Available year-round, peak is in May, June, and July.

Pack:
37- to 40-lb (16.6- to 18-kg) cartons.

Sizes:
Counts of 63, 75, 95, 115, 140, 165, 200, and 235. The most common sizes are counts of 115 to 165.

Kitchen Yields
When buying for juice, the lowest price per pound is the best buy, because the yield per pound is approximately the same regardless of price.
Eight medium lemons yield 1 cup juice; and four #165 lemons weigh 1 lb (450 g).
One case #165 lemons yields 300 halves, 660 quarter wedges, and 990 sixth wedges.
One lemon yields 7 to 10 slices when sliced on a machine. A lemon crown is half a lemon with six points. Lemon tulips are made by cutting crowns into thirds.

10 large lemons yield 1¾ oz (50 g) grated lemon rind.

Calories:
1 cup = 60 Calories.

LEMON JUICE
Available in bottles.

Pack:
Twenty-four 10-oz (0.29-l) bottles; twelve 1-qt (0.94-l) bottles.

Kitchen Yields
1 qt (0.47 l) is equivalent to the juice of 32 fresh lemons.

LETTUCE

Lettuce can be distinguished as head lettuce and loose leaf lettuce. Many varieties are on the market, and new varieties are being developed. Baby lettuce, with one head used as one serving, is becoming popular. Some lettuce is grown hydroponically and is shipped with the roots still attached. This increases the keeping quality.

Season:
Lettuce is available year-round, because growing seasons overlap; but price, quality, and variety can vary greatly, depending on weather.

BIBB
This small lettuce, related to Boston Lettuce, has soft leaves and a firm head. Available with green or slightly red leaves. Kentucky Bibb Limestone lettuce has firm, crisp heads and is considered a delicacy.

Pack:
Baskets containing 18 to 22 heads.

Kitchen Yields
When heads are firm, serving size is one-half head.

BOSTON (BUTTERHEAD)
Also called *butterhead lettuce*. There are a number of varieties available, which range from lettuce with firm heads and crisp yet tender leaves, to rather loose-headed lettuce.

Pack:
Cartons containing 24 heads.

Kitchen Yields
Heads are larger than Bibb lettuce, but less firm.

Serving size:
Half a head.

Calories:
One 8-oz (224-g) head, cleaned = 25 Calories.

CHICORY (ENDIVE)
Also referred to as *endive*, this slightly bitter lettuce has a loose head with curly, edge-indented leaves that can be dark green at the edges and almost white at the center.

Season:
Summer.

Pack:
35- to 40-lb (15.7- to 18-kg) cartons with 24 heads each; 18-lb (8.1-kg) cartons with 12 to 18 heads each.

Kitchen Yields

Waste:
About 30 percent.

Calories:
1 cup, or 2 oz (56 g), cut = 10 Calories.

CORN SALAD
See Mache, under this same heading.

COS
See Romaine, under this same heading.

ENDIVE
See Chicory under this same heading, for the domestic variety; *see* Belgium Endive for the imported form.

ESCAROLE
Closely related to curly endive or chicory. It has a looser head and broader, less ruffled leaves. The lettuce should be crisp.

Season:
Year-round, with peak in December.

Pack:
35- to 40-lb (15.7- to 18-kg) cartons with 24 heads each; 18-lb (8.1-kg) cartons with 12 to 18 heads each.

Kitchen Yields

Waste:
About 45 percent.

Calories:
1 cup, or 2 oz (56 g), cut = 10 Calories.

FRISÉE
Curly chicory. *See* Chicory, under this same heading.

GREEN OAK LEAF
Baby lettuce with lobed green leaves. Sharper flavored than Red Oak Leaf lettuce.

Season:
Summer.

Pack:
Individual pack.

Kitchen Yields

Serving size:
1 head.

LEAF LETTUCE
Also called *garden lettuce*, this is a leafy variety that does not form a head.

Season:
Available year-round, peak is in summer.

Pack:
6-lb (2.7-kg) baskets.

Kitchen Yields

Waste:
40 percent.

Calories:
1 cup, or 2 oz (56 g), cut = 10 Calories.

LAMB'S LETTUCE
Also called *corn salad. See* Mache.

LOLLO BIONDO
Ruffled, crinkly baby leaf lettuce with white tips. Mostly grown hydroponically.

Pack:
Individual packs.

Kitchen Yields
There is no waste.

LOLLO ROSA
Ruffled, crinkly baby leaf lettuce with rosy tips. Mostly grown hydroponically.

Pack:
Individual packs.

Kitchen Yields
There is no waste.

MACHE
Also known as *corn salad* or *lamb's lettuce,* Mache is a delicate, teaspoon-shaped salad.

Pack:
11-lb (5-kg) cases.
Hydroponically-grown Mache is shipped in 8-oz (225-g) plastic trays.

Kitchen Yields
Mache is very light. It wilts quickly once dressing is applied.

Serving size:
1½ oz (42 g); 8 oz (225 g) hydroponically-grown with roots yields 4½ oz (125 g) salad.

ICEBERG
Firm head lettuce that keeps well under refrigeration.

Season:
Available year-round, but weather might influence supply and quality.
Types of trim available include chopped; shredded; whole, cored and trimmed; and whole, uncut.

CHOPPED OR SHREDDED

Pack:
20-lb (9-kg) cartons, consisting of either four 5-lb (2.25-kg) clear poly bags or two 10-lb (4.5-kg) clear poly bags.

Kitchen Yields
One 20-lb (9-kg) carton yields 160 small tossed salads of 1 cup or 2 oz (56 g), or 80 large tossed salads of 2 cups or 4 oz (112 g).

WHOLE, CORED AND TRIMMED

Pack:
30 lb (13.5 kg), with 24 or 30 heads packed in poly bags of 6 heads each.

Kitchen Yields
Same as from whole, uncut.

WHOLE, UNCUT

Pack:
50-lb (22.5-kg) cartons.

Sizes:
24 heads per carton; cartons with 30 or 18 heads are also available.

Weight:
Average head, with outer leaves trimmed, weighs 1¾ lb (790 g).

Kitchen Yields
One 24-head carton yields 120 4-oz (112-g) wedges or 120 to 144 large leaves, or 240 small tossed salads of 1 cup or 2 oz (56 g), 120 large tossed salads of 2 cups or 4 oz (112 g), 15 gal (57 l) torn or shredded lettuce, or 10 gal (38 l) lettuce chunks.

Calories:
1 cup, or 2 oz (56 g), chopped = 5 Calories.
One 5-oz (140-g) wedge = 20 Calories.

PERELLA
Red and green baby lettuce.

Pack:
Grown hydroponically.

Kitchen Yields
Basically no waste, because the lettuce is grit-free.

RADICCHIO
Red leaf lettuce of the chicory family. *See* Radicchio.

RED OAK LEAF
Baby lettuce with deeply-cut, finely-divided leaves that have burgundy centers. About 8 leaves per head.

RED ROMAINE
Also called *Rouge d'Hiver*, this is a red-tipped baby Romaine lettuce.

Pack:
Grown hydroponically.

Kitchen Yields
Basically no waste, because the product is delivered clean and grit-free.

ROMAINE (COS)
Loaf-shape head lettuce with broad, white-stemmed leaves.

Season:
Available year-round.

Pack:
40-lb (18-kg) cartons with 24 heads; 18-lb (8.1-kg) cartons with 12 to 18 heads.

Kitchen Yields

Waste:
45 percent cleaning loss.

Calories:
1 cup, or 2 oz (56 g), chopped = 10 Calories.

TREVISE
Red lettuce that is hothouse-grown.

Pack:
11-lb (5-kg) case.

LILY ROOT

See Lotus Root, under Chinese Foods.

LIMES

Limes are available fresh and as juice.

FRESH LIMES

There are two varieties: acid limes and sweet limes. Almost all limes sold commercially are classified as acid limes. The Florida Key West lime is the only sweet lime variety of some commercial importance.

ACID LIMES

Persian lime, produced in Florida and the Caribbean Islands, is the most important variety.

Season:
Available year-round. Peak is in spring.

Pack:
Flats with 63 and 72 fruits each. Most common hotel size is 63 count.

Kitchen Yields

Normally, limes are cut in quarters for garnish; thus, one 63-count flat yields 250 pieces.
1 lb (450 g) fruit yields ¾ cup (0.17 l) juice.

Calories:
1 cup (0.23 l) juice = 65 Calories.

KEY WEST SWEET LIMES

Yellow, thin-skinned limes with a pleasant taste. No longer grown commercially in Key West, some supply comes from the Caribbean Islands and Mexico. Some bottled Key West lime juice is available.

Season:
August and September.

Key West Lime Pie Formula

One 14 oz (0.4 l) can sweetened condensed milk
4 egg yolks
½ cup (0.12 l) Key West lime juice
4 egg whites
4 oz (112 g) sugar
One 9-in pre-baked pie crust

Blend eggs and milk well, and stir in only lime juice. Fill pie crust. Make meringue with egg whites and sugar; brown meringue.

Kitchen Yields

One 9-in (228-mm) pie yields 8 portions.

LIME JUICE

Available unsweetened and sweet.

Pack:
Twelve 12-fl-oz (0.35-l) bottles; twelve 25-fl-oz (0.75-l) bottles.

Kitchen Yields

Use unsweetened juice as if it were fresh juice.

Calories:
1 cup (0.23 l) unsweetened juice = 65 Calories.

LINGONBERRIES

Variety of cranberries found in Europe. Smaller than the American cranberry, and are tart and acidic. Whortleberry is a related species found wild in North America.

Pack:
Twelve 14-oz (400-g) cans; six #10 cans. Other packs are available.

Serving size:
1½ oz (42 g) as condiment.

Kitchen Yields

One #10 can yields 60 servings.

LIQUID MEASUREMENTS

	Cups	Fluid Ounces	Liters
1 tsp		⅙	0.005
3 tsp	1 tb	½	0.015
4 tb	½	2	0.060
8 tb	½	4	0.120
16 tb	1	8	0.240
1 pint	2	16	0.480
1 qt	4	32	0.960
1 gal	16	128	3.800

LITCHIS

See Lychee.

LITER

Metric volume measure. One liter contains 100 centiliters (cl) or 1000 milliliters (ml).

1 l = 33.8 fl oz or 1 qt 2 fl oz
750 ml = 24 fl oz
½ l = 17 fl oz or 1 pint + 1 fl oz
½ l = 8.5 fl oz or 1 cup + ½ fl oz

LO BOK (CHINESE RADISH)

Chinese radish similar to daikon.

LOBSTER

Available canned, fresh (live), and frozen.

CANNED ATLANTIC LOBSTER MEAT

Available packed in brine; often shipped frozen.

Pack:
12-oz (340-g) cans.

Kitchen Yields
Typical pack contains 2 small tails, plus shredded meat.

Drained weight:
9 oz (250 g).

FRESH LOBSTER

ATLANTIC LOBSTER

Also called *Maine lobster*, this crustacean is trapped in the waters off New England and the eastern coast of Canada. Large numbers of freshly caught lobster are shipped live—some by air—anywhere in the world. Raw lobster, whole or split, are available frozen. Lobster farming is successful in some places.

Tomalley is the green liver, a delicacy that becomes pasty when cooked. *Coral* is the undeveloped egg mass, which turns solid and red when cooked. It, too, is considered a delicacy.

Season:
Available year-round. Peak is in summer.

Pack:
Purchased by piece and weight.

Sizes:

Culls:
1 lb (450 g) and under; animals are live but damaged, normally with one claw missing.

Chicken:
1 lb (450 g).

Regular:
1½ lb (675 g).
1¾ to 2 lb (0.78 to 0.9 kg).
2 to 2½ lb (0.9 to 1.1 kg).
2½ to 3¼ lb (1.1 to 1.6 kg).
Over 3½ lb (1.6 kg).

Lobster Meat:
Fresh shelled lobster meat is available by weight, normally sold in 1-gal (3.8-l) cans, weighing 8 lb (3.6 kg) net.

Kitchen Yields
The yield depends much on freshness, because live lobsters, when stored, sustain themselves by using their own body juices.
One 1-lb (450-g) lobster weighs approximately 14 oz (400 g) when cooked. The shelled meat weighs 3½ to 4 oz (100 to 112 g).
Five 1-lb (450-g) lobsters yield 1¼ lb (560 g) shelled meat.

Serving size:

Shelled meat:
3½ oz (100 g) as appetizer.
6 oz (170 g) as main course with sauce.
5 oz (140 g) for buffet service, hot.
4½ oz (130 g) for salad.

Half lobster:
1½-lb (O.67-kg) size, split, as cold appetizer.
2-lb (0.9-kg) size, split, as cold main course.

Whole lobster:
2½ lb (1.1 kg) is a popular restaurant weight.

Calories:
3½ oz (100 g) = 100 Calories.

SPINY LOBSTER(ROCK LOBSTER)

A clawless lobster related to crabs and shrimp, it is harvested in both tropical and temperate to cold waters. Spiny lobster is available in Florida live, but is seldom shipped whole out of state.

Season:
December to May.

Sizes:
2 to 5 lb (0.9 to 2.25 kg).

Kitchen Yields
Known under the name *langouste* in Europe, the spiny lobster makes an attractive buffet centerpiece. It is sold as lobster in Caribbean resorts and in South America.

FROZEN LOBSTER TAILS

These come from the tails of spiny lobsters. Most product is imported. Available as cold-water lobster tails and as warm-water lobster tails. Cold-water tails are better than warm-water tails.

Pack:
Five 10-lb (4.5-kg) boxes.

Sizes:
5 to 6 oz (140 to 170 g); 8 to 10 oz (225 to 285 g). Other sizes are available.

Kitchen Yields
Lobster tails are frozen ready to use. Best use is broiled to order. When meat is boiled, it tends to be dry.

Serving sizes:
Two 5- to 6-oz (140- to 170-g) tails as main course; one 8-oz (225-g) tail with Surf and Turf.

Calories:
4½ oz (127 g) meat from 8-oz (225-g) tail = 130 Calories.

LOGANBERRY

Berries resembling blackberries in shape and raspberries in color, but not directly related to either plant. They are very tart unless picked ripe.

Season:
Summer.

Pack:
Flats of twelve ½-pint (0.23-l) containers.

Kitchen Yields
Used primarily for jams and jelly.

Calories:
4 oz (112 g) = 29 Calories.

LOGANS

Fruit resembling lychees. Available pitted and dried, or canned.

LOQUAT

Also know as *Japanese plum*. Seedy fruit, yellow to orange, with white to pink flesh.

Season:
Spring.

Pack:
10-lb (4.5-kg) cartons.

Size:
About 3 in (76 mm) long.

LYCHEES

Available canned, dehydrated, and fresh.

CANNED LYCHEES

Pack:
Twenty-four #2 cans. Other packs are available.

Kitchen Yields

Drained weight:
12½ oz (350 g); approximately 35 to 40 pieces.

Serving size:
½ cup (0.12 l), with syrup. One #2 can yields 5 servings.

DRIED LYCHEES (LYCHEE NUTS)

Lychee nuts, used in oriental cooking, are dried lychee fruits. The whole fruit is dried, and it separates from its shell. As it shrivels around the seed, it acquires a different flavor. The shell becomes paper-thin and brittle. Neither the shell nor the seed are edible.

Pack:

By weight.

Kitchen Yields

Count:

1 lb (450 g) contain about 70 to 80 pieces; 1 oz (28 g) equals 4 to 5 pieces.

FRESH LYCHEES

Lychee fruits are grown in Florida and are usually of a red variety. Imports may be green, yellow, or pink. The flesh is white and perfumed. Shelf life is limited, but the fruits can and freeze very well.

Season:

June until late July.

Pack:

By weight. Normally, the whole fruit cluster—including the tip of the branch—is shipped.

Size:

About 1 in (25 mm) in diameter and 1½ in (38 mm) in length. The pit is not edible, but it slips off easily, and is about ¾ in (19 mm) long.

Kitchen Yields

Ten fruits yield 4 oz (112 g) fresh pulp.

Calories:

Ten fruits = 66 Calories.

M

MACADAMIA NUTS

This soft, round nut is available shelled and in the shell.

Pack:
5-lb (2.25-kg) carton, shelled. Other packs are available. Macadamia nuts are most commonly packed in jars.

Kitchen Yields
Nuts are normally purchased shelled.

MACAROONS

Formula for Almond Macaroons
    10 lb (4.5 kg) almond paste
    8 lb (3.6 kg) sugar
    3 lb (1.35 kg) 6X sugar
    2 qt (0.94 l) egg whites

Dress on kraft paper to bake. Moisten back of paper to remove macaroons.

Kitchen Yields

Serving size:
1 oz (28 g). The total mix yields 380 pieces.

MACHE

See Lettuce.

MANDARIN ORANGES

Available are canned sections and fresh.

CANNED MANDARIN SECTIONS
Available packed in light or heavy syrup.

Pack:
Six #10 cans.

Drained weight:
74 oz (2 kg).

Kitchen Yields
Use as garnish.

FRESH MANDARIN ORANGES
The term *mandarin orange* is a generic name applied to a number of orange varieties, such as Clementines, Kings, Satsumas, Tangerines, and Temple oranges.

Season:
November to March.

Pack:
Packed in cartons. Weight varies.

Count:
Varies.

MANGOES

Mangoes are available canned, dehydrated, and fresh.

CANNED MANGO
Imported product, normally packed in heavy syrup.

Pack:
Twenty-four #2 cans; twenty-four #2½ cans.

Drained weight:
One #2 can equals 10 oz (280 g). One #2½ can equals 17 oz (478 g).

Kitchen Yields

Serving size:
½ cup (0.14 l), with syrup. One #2 can yields 5 servings; one #2½ can yields 7 servings.

DRIED MANGO
Called *amchooor* in India, this is raw mango that has been dried and ground. The powder is acidic and is used as a spice. Candied dry mango strips are also available.

Pack:
By weight.

FRESH MANGO
Kidney-shaped fruit with large pit and fibrous flesh. Mangos vary greatly in size. Much production is used in the manufacture of chutney. The fruit is green when unripe, yellow and soft when ripe.

Season:
May to September. Peak is in August, with imports available year-round.

Pack:
10- to 12-lb (4.5- to 5.4-kg) cartons.

Counts:
8, 9, 10, 12, 14, 15, 16, 18, 20, 24, 28, or 30.

Weight:
For 15 or 16 size, 10 to 12 oz (280 to 340 g) each.

Kitchen Yields
Very difficult to get good yield. Pits are hard to remove, and sometimes the fruit's flesh is woody and stringy.
One 12-oz (340-g) fruit yields ¾ cup, or 4½ oz (130 g) flesh.

MANZANITA BANANAS

See Bananas.

MARGARINE

Margarine is available salted, sweet, whipped, and mixed with butter. Specialty margarine for baking (puff pastry) is also available.

Pack:

Prints:
Thirty 1-lb (45-g) boxes. Prints are often divided into four 4-oz (112-g) sticks.

Bulk:
50-lb (22.5-kg) boxes.

Whipped:
Six 4-lb (1.8-kg) tubs.

Pats:
Same counts as for butter.

Kitchen Yields
Basically the same as for butter. For whipped margarine, 1 lb (450 g) is equivalent to 6 sticks. 1 lb (450 g) yields 12 oz, or 1½ cups, melted clear fat.

Calories:
Regular margarine, 1 stick, or ½ cup (112 g) = 815 Calories.
Regular margarine, 1 tb, or ⅛ stick (14 g) = 100 Calories.
Regular margarine, 1 pat, 90-count (5 g) = 35 Calories.
Soft spread, 8-oz (112-g) container = 1,635 Calories.
Whipped margarine, ½ cup (76 g) = 545 Calories.
Whipped margarine, 1 tb, or ⅛ stick (9 g) = 70 Calories.

MARRONS GLACES

See Chestnuts.

MARZIPAN

See Almonds.

MAYONNAISE

Mayonnaise is available commercially as regular and as light (or low-calorie) mayonnaise, or it can be made fresh.

COMMERCIAL MAYONNAISE

Pack:
Four 1-gal (3.8-l) jars. Other packs are available.

Kitchen Yields
Proportions of main ingredient and mayonnaise in salads:

> 10 lb (4.5 kg) cooked meat, chicken, or seafood
> 3 lb (1.35 kg) diced celery
> 1 qt (0.94 l) mayonnaise

NOTE: Celery should be heat sterilized.

Calories:
Regular mayonnaise, 1 oz (28 g), or 2 tb = 200 Calories.
Light mayonnaise, 1 oz (28 g), or 2 tb = 90 Calories.

HOME-MADE MAYONNAISE

Formula

120 egg yolks or 5 pints (2.35 l) egg yolks
1¼ cup (280 g) salt
1 cup (200 g) dry mustard
5 gal (19 l) oil
1 qt (0.94 l) warm water
3 cups (0.70 l) vinegar

NOTE: It is recommended to use only pasteurized eggs for mayonnaise.

Kitchen Yields
The total mix yields 6 gal (22.2 l).

MEATBALLS

Formula

10 lb (4.5 kg) ground meat
1 lb (450 g) stale rolls, soaked
1 lb (450 g) onions
2 tb chopped garlic
6 eggs
1 bunch parsley
Spices

Kitchen Yields
The total mix yields 75 meatballs of 2½ oz (70 g) each, using a #12 scoop, and these yield 25 servings spaghetti and meatballs. Alternatively, the formula produces 200 meatballs of 1 oz (28 g) each, using a #30 scoop, for hors d'oeuvres.

MEAT LOAF

A cheaper grade of beef is often used for meat loaf. *See* Hamburger Meat, under Beef for meat information.

Formula

10 lb (4.5 kg) ground meat
1 lb (450 g) stale rolls, soaked
1 lb (450 g) onions
2 tb chopped garlic
6 eggs
1 bunch parsley
Spices

Kitchen Yields
Four 3-lb (1.35-kg) loaves.

Serving sizes:

4 oz (112 g) cooked, in 2 slices. One loaf yields 20 slices or 10 servings; therefore, four 3-lb (1.35-kg) loaves yield 40 servings.

MELONS

Melons available in most parts of the country are listed. Small specialty melons are occasionally imported from Europe and Israel.

CANARY MELON
Also called *Juan canary melon*.

Season:
Summer.

Pack:
26- to 27-lb (11.7- to 12.1-kg) cases, containing 6, 7, 8, or 10 melons;
29- to 30-lb (13- to 13.5-kg) cartons, containing 4, 5, or 6 melons.

Weight range:
From 2¼ to 4½ lb (1 to 2 kg).

CANTALOUPE

Cantaloupe melons belong to the broad group of muskmelons. They are widely available, and well-sized. Much of the market supply is domestically grown, and there are imports in off-season. Some small muskmelons are imported from Europe as specialty items.

Season:
Available year-round. Peak is in June to August.

Packs and counts:
75- to 85-lb (33.8- to 38.2-kg) standard crates of 18, 23, 27, 36, or 45 melons.
53- to 55-lb (23.8- to 24.7-kg) ⅔ crates of 12, 13, 18, 24, or 30 melons.
38- to 41-lb (17.1- to 18.4-kg) half-crates of 12, 15, or 18 melons.

Sizes:
45- or 36-counts in 85-lb (38.2-kg) crates are the most common sizes.

Kitchen Yields
One 45-size melon yields twenty-five ⅞-in (22-mm) melon balls, or four wedges. 100 melon balls weigh 2¼ lb (1 kg).

Serving size:

Breakfast:
Half a 45-size melon.

Main course:
Half a 36-size melon.

CASABA MELON
Late-variety melon with soft, white, and juicy flesh. Because the melon is normally vine-ripened, it is very sweet.

Season:
Fall and early winter.

Packs and counts:
26- to 27-lb (11.7- to 12.1-kg) cases of 6, 7, or 8 melons.
29- to 30-lb (13- to 13.5-kg) cartons of 4, 5, or 6 melons.

Weight range:
4 to 6 lb (1.8 to 2.7 kg).

Kitchen Yields
4 servings from small melons; 6 servings from large melons.

CHRISTMAS MELON
See Santa Claus Melon, under this same heading.

CRANSHAW MELON
Also spelled *crenshaw.* This dependable melon stores well and has a rich, sweet flavor. The flesh is bright salmon color.

Season:
Summer, fall, and winter.

Packs and counts:
26- to 27-lb (11.7- to 12.1-kg) cases of 6, 7, or 8 melons.
29- to 30-lb (13- to 13.5-kg) cartons of 4, 5, or 6 melons.

Weight range:
4 to 6 lb (1.8 to 2.7 kg).

Kitchen Yields
4 servings from small melons; 6 servings from large melons.

HAND MELON
Sweet, juicy, and expensive melon cultivated at the Hand farm in Greenwich, New York. The season is very short, and the melons are only shipped at the peak of ripeness. The melon is a muskmelon, and is identified by a red hand decal.

Season:
August.

Pack:
40-lb (22.5-kg) cartons.

Count:
16 melons.

Average weight:
3 lb (1.35 kg) or less.

Kitchen Yields

Serving size:
⅓ melon for appetizer or dessert.

HONEYDEW MELON
Large melon with flesh that is light green, sweet, and delicate.

Season:
July to October for domestic products; winter to spring for imports.

Packs and counts:
26- to 27-lb (11.7- to 12.1-kg) cases of 6, 7, or 8 melons.
29- to 30-lb (13- to 13.5-kg) cartons of 4, 5, or 6 melons.

Weight range:
4 to 6 lb (1.8 to 2.7 kg).

Kitchen Yields

Serving size:
Quarter of a 6- or 8-size melon; sixth of a 5-size melon.
One 5-size melon yields 35 melon balls; 100 melon balls weigh 2¼ lb (1 kg).

Calories:
8 oz (224 g) = 55 Calories.

PERSIAN MELON

Season:
Summer and fall.

Pack:
Six melons per half-crate.

Size:
Average 7 lb (3.1 kg).

SANTA CLAUS MELON

Also called *Christmas melon*, this fruit resembles watermelon, with a light green, mottled rind and green flesh.

Season:
Late summer. Peak is in winter.

Packs and counts:
26- to 27-lb (11.7- to 12.1-kg) cases of 6, 7, or 8 melons.
29- to 30-lb (13- to 13.5-kg) cartons of 4, 5, or 6 melons.

Weight range:
4 to 6 lb (1.8 to 2.7 kg).

Kitchen Yields
4 servings from small melons; 6 servings from large melons.

SPANISH MELON

This melon is hard-skinned with a green to deep-yellow exterior and sweet, orange-colored flesh.

Season:
Winter.

Packs and counts:
26- to 27-lb (11.7- to 12.1-kg) cases of 6, 7, or 8 melons.
29- to 30-lb (13- to 13.5-kg) cartons of 4, 5, or 6 melons.

Weight range:
4 to 6 lb (1.8 to 2.7 kg).

Kitchen Yields
4 servings from small melons; 6 servings from large melons.

WATERMELON

Very large melon. Also available is a smaller, seedless variety.

Season:
Mid-April to mid-December. Peak is in late summer.

Pack:
70- to 85-lb (31.5- to 36-kg) cartons.

Count:
2, 3, 4, or 5 melons.

Weight ranges:
15 to 40 lb (6.7 to 18.0 kg). Larger sizes are available.

Kitchen Yields
For buffet display, purchase 30-lb (13.5-kg) melons. One 22-lb (9.9-kg) melon yields 22 cups bite-size pieces.

Serving size:
One 32-lb (14.4-kg) melon yields 16 large portions.

Calories:
2-lb (0.9-kg) slice = 110 Calories.

MERINGUE

Formula
  1 lb (450 g) egg whites
  2 lb (900 g) sugar

Kitchen Yields
The total mix yields 50 individual shells for dessert.

MEXICAN FOODS

The components for assembling Mexican dishes are available canned, dried, fresh, or frozen. Complete prepared Mexican dishes are also available frozen.

ACHIOTE (ANNATTO)

Very hard, reddish/yellowish seeds from the tropical annatto tree. They are used as a dyeing and flavoring agent. Available also in paste form. Sauté in oil to release the flavor, then discard the seeds.

Pack:

By weight.

Kitchen Yields

Use according to taste.

CHILES

Available canned, dried, and fresh. As a general rule, fresh chiles impart more flavor than do dried chiles. Normally, the seeds are hotter than the flesh.

CANNED CHILES

CALIFORNIA CHILES

Also called *Anaheim chile*. Normally moss-green, but also available red. Available whole, diced, or in strips.

Kitchen Yields

Sweet to slightly hot. California chiles are canned already peeled. Remove seeds before use.

CASCABEL CHILES

Small, rather peppery chiles.

CHIPOTLE CHILES

Jalapeño chile that has been ripened, dried, and smoked. This reddish-brown chile is canned in either vinegar or adobo sauce.

GREEN CHILES

Green chiles are available diced, in strips, and whole in cans.

Pack:

Diced:
Twelve or twenty-four #2½ cans weighing 29 oz (820 g), containing about 3½ cups (0.82 l).
Six #10 cans, containing 13 cups (3 l); individual 5-gal (19-l) cans.

Strips:
Twelve or twenty-four #2½ cans weighing 29 oz (820 g), containing about 3½ cups (0.82 l).
Six #10 cans, containing 13 cups (3 l).

Whole:
Twelve or twenty-four #2½ cans weighing 29 oz (820 g), containing about 3½ cups (0.82 l).

JALAPEÑOS

Like green chiles, jalapeños are available diced, in slices, and whole. They may be slightly hot to very hot.

Pack:

Diced:
Twelve or twenty-four #2½ cans weighing 29 oz (820 g), containing about 3½ cups (0.82 l).
Six #10 cans, containing 13 cups (3 l).

Sliced
Six #10 cans, containing 13 cups (3 l).

Whole:
Twelve or twenty-four #2½ cans weighing 29 oz (820 g), containing about 3½ cups (0.82 l).
Six #10 cans, containing 13 cups (3 l).

PIMENTOS

Mild red chiles that are peeled before canning. Pimentos are available whole and diced.

Pack:

Twenty-four #2½ cans, weighing 28½ oz (0.825 l); twelve 14-oz (400-g) cans.

DRIED CHILES

ANCHO

Dried poblano chiles with dark, reddish-brown color. Widely used in Mexican cooking.

Kitchen Yields
Relatively mild. Soak in water or vinegar and use shredded or ground in sauces.

PASILLA
Long, thin, dark brown to black chile. It is usually toasted and ground.

Kitchen Yields
Medium hot.

FRESH CHILES

ANCHO
Resembles a bell pepper and turns red when mature. Often called *poblano* on the market.

Size:
About 4 to 5 in (100 to 127 mm) long.

Kitchen Yields
Mildly peppery.

CALIFORNIA CHILES
Also called *Anaheim chiles*, it is about 5 to 8 in (127 to 203 mm) long, and dark green.

Season:
Available year-round. Peak is in summer and fall.

FRESNO CHILES
Bright green to reddish-orange when ripe. Often referred to as "hot peppers."

Size:
About 2 in (50 mm) long.

Kitchen Yields
Mildly hot to very hot.

JALAPEÑOS
Dark green, about 2½ in (63 mm) long.

Kitchen Yields
Very hot.

POBLANOS
Large green pepper that resembles a deflated bell pepper and is used for stuffing.

Kitchen Yields
Most varieties are relatively mild. Skin and seeds are removed before stuffing.

SERRANOS
Small green chile about 3 in (76 mm) long.

Kitchen Yields
Flesh is very hot, and seeds are dynamite. Base ingredient for Salsa Cruda.

CHEESE SAUCE FOR NACHOS

Pack:
Six #10 cans, each weighing 106 oz (3 kg).

Kitchen Yields

Serving size:
2 oz (56 g), for topping. Therefore, one #10 can yields 50 servings.

Calories:
2 oz (56 g) = 95 Calories.

CHORIZOS
Fatty pork sausages, available mild or hot.

Pack:
By weight.

Kitchen Yields
30 to 40 percent shrinkage, depending on brand.

CILANTRO
See Herbs & Spices.

CORN HUSKS
Available dry, corn husks are used for making tamales.

Pack:
By weight.

Kitchen Yields
1 lb (450 g) yields 40 leaves for medium-size tamales.

ENCHILADA SAUCE
Red sauce made of mild chile pulp, tomatoes, onions, and other ingredients. Available canned.

Pack:
Six #10 cans.

Kitchen Yields

Serving size:
½ cup (0.23 l) with main course. One #10 can yields 24 servings.

FAJITA SEASONING

Seasoning mix consisting of chile, cumin, garlic, salt, and peppers.

Pack:
By weight.

GUYABATE

Firm, sweet guava paste, usually served with cheese as a dessert.

Pack:
3¼ lb (1.5 kg) block. Other sizes are available.

Kitchen Yields

Serving size:
2 oz (56 g). One 3¼ lb (1.5 kg) block yields 25 servings.

HUITLACOCHE

Also called *corn smut* or *Mexican truffle*, it is a black fungus that grows inside corn kernels while still on the stalk. The pieces can be as large as a quarter, but smaller pieces are common. It is available fresh or frozen from a domestic producer in Florida.

Pack:
By weight.

Kitchen Yields
1 lb (450 g) is equivalent to 4 cups (0.94 l).

JICAMA

See Jicama (Mexican Potato).

MASA HARINA

Trade name for specially-treated corn flour. It is also known as *tamale flour* and as *corn tortilla flour*.

Pack:
5-lb (2.25-kg) bags.

Kitchen Yields
Use according to instructions on bag.

MOLE

Seasoning that contains chocolate and chiles; available as a paste or as a powder. Available as mild and hot mole. For average tastes, mild mole is recommended.

Kitchen Yields
Use according to instructions on bag.

NOPALES (CACTUS LEAVES)

Nopales, or cactus leaves, are broad green pads with thorns. The flavor is mild. They can be eaten raw in salads or cooked as vegetables.

Season:
February to November.

Pack:
By weight, or in trays with twelve 8-oz (225-g) leaves.

Sizes:
Each leaf weighs about 3 to 8 oz (85 to 225 g).

Kitchen Yields
Nopales are shipped with the thorns removed. There is still about 15 percent cleaning loss.

REFRIED BEANS

Called *frijoles refritos* in Spanish, they are most often made with pinto beans. Refried beans are available canned or dehydrated, ready to use, or they can be home-made.

CANNED REFRIED BEANS

Pack:
Six #10 cans.

Kitchen Yields

Serving size:
¾ cup (0.17 l). One #10 can yields 13 cups (2.8 l) or 16 servings.

HOME-MADE REFRIED BEANS

Formula
    1 lb (450 g) pinto beans or red kidney beans
    5 cups (1.17 l) water
    1 cup, or 6 oz (170 g) diced onions
    ½ cup, or 4 oz, bacon drippings

Kitchen Yields
The total mix yields 5½ cups (1.3 l).

DEHYDRATED (INSTANT) REFRIED BEANS
The product is ready to use when mixed with hot water. Follow directions on bag.

Pack:
5-lb (2.25-kg) bags.

SALSA
Hot sauce made of jalapeño chiles, onions, and tomatoes. Available red and green, in mild, medium, and hot spiciness levels.

Pack:
Available in cans and bottles of various sizes.

Kitchen Yields

Serving size:
Varies according to individual tastes.

TACO SAUCE
Sauce made of tomatoes, vegetables, and chiles. Available hot and mild.

Pack:
Six #10 cans, containing 12 cups (2.8 l) sauce each; five hundred ⅓-oz (9-g) individual packets.

Kitchen Yields

Serving size:
Varies according to taste.

TACO SHELLS
Ready-to-fill shells that resemble crispy corn tortillas.

Pack:
200 shells per case.

Weight:
½ oz (14 g) each.

Kitchen Yields

Serving size:
1 shell per person as snack; 2 shells per person as main course.

TAMALES
Corn husks stuffed with corn masa dough. They can be sweet or meat-filled.

Tamale Dough Formula
    1½ lb (0.9 kg) lard
    4½ lb (2 kg) masa harina
    6 tb salt
    2 qt (1.9 l) warm water or chicken broth

Kitchen Yields
The total mix yields 4 qt (3.7 l) tamale dough, which—when shaped, filled, and cooked—yields 85 pieces weighing 1½ oz (42 g) each.

TOMATILLO
Also called *tomate verde*. Sour green tomato with a parchment-like covering. Available fresh and canned.

Pack:
36-lb (16.2-kg) flats.

TORTILLAS
Available as corn tortillas and as flour tortillas, in various sizes.

Corn Tortilla Formula
    6 cups, or 2¼ lb (1.0 kg), masa harina
    4½ cups (1.0 l) warm water

Kitchen Yields
The total mix yields thirty-six 2-oz (56-g) tortillas.

TUNAS (CACTUS FRUIT)
Prickly pears are the fruits from a cactus bearing the same name. The Mexican word for them is *tunas*. The spines are sharp, but most have been removed by the time the fruit reaches the market.

Season:
September to December, and March to May.

Pack:
By weight.

Size:
2½ to 4 in (7 to 10 cm) long.

Kitchen Yields
Two large fruits yield 1 cup (0.23 l) purée.

Calories:
4 oz (112 g) edible flesh = 65 Calories.

MILK & MILK PRODUCTS

Cream is discussed in greater detail under its own alphabetical entry; *see* Cream.

MILK
Available condensed, evaporated, dehydrated, and fresh.

> *Buttermilk:* At least 8¼ percent nonfat milk-solids
> *Condensed milk:* 8½ percent butterfat content, 28 percent milk-solids, 45 percent sugar
> *Evaporated milk:* Not less than 7.9 percent butterfat content, 25 percent milk-solids
> *Dried milk, nonfat:* 1¼ percent fat content
> *Dried milk, whole:* 26 percent butterfat content
> *Fresh milk, skim:* Less than 3¼ percent butterfat content
> *Fresh milk, fat-free:* Less than 0.1 percent butterfat content
> *Fresh milk, whole:* 8¼ percent milk-solids, 3¼ percent butterfat content

CONDENSED AND EVAPORATED MILK
Types include concentrated milk, condensed milk, and evaporated milk.

CONCENTRATED MILK
Canned milk product made by evaporation, without sugar added.

Pack:
6-oz (0.17-l) cans; six #10 cans (3 l) cans. Other packs are available.

Kitchen Yields
One #10 can + 14 cups water yields 7 qt (6.5 l) whole milk.

CONDENSED MILK
Evaporated, sweetened milk that has a higher milk-solids and fat content than evaporated milk. Sugar content is equivalent to 19 to 20 lb (8.5 to 9 kg) sugar for every 100 lb (45 kg) fresh milk.

Pack:
6 oz (0.17 l) cans; six #10 (3-l) cans. Other packs are available.

Kitchen Yields
To reconstitute condensed milk, mix 2 parts condensed milk with 3 parts water.
One 6-fl-oz (0.17-l) can mixed with 9-fl-oz (0.27-l) water yields 15 fl oz (0.44 l) reconstituted milk.

EVAPORATED MILK
Available sweetened and unsweetened.

Pack:
Six #10 cans. Other sizes are available.

Kitchen Yields
One #10 can is equivalent to 14 cups.
1 cup evaporated milk + 1 cup water yields 2 cups (0.47 l) milk. One #10 can + 14 cups water yields 7 qts (6.6 l) milk.

Calories:
1 cup (0.23 l), unsweetened, diluted = 170 Calories.
1 cup (0.23 l), unsweetened, not diluted = 340 Calories.
1 cup (0.23 l), sweetened, not diluted = 980 Calories.

DEHYDRATED MILK
Available as dry crystal milk, dry malted milk, dry nonfat milk, and dry whole milk.

DRY CRYSTAL MILK

Pack:
By weight.

Kitchen Yields

1 lb (450 g) is equivalent to 6½ cups dry milk; 1½ cups weighs 3¾ oz (106 g).

3¾ oz (106 g) dry milk + ¾ cup water (0.88 l) yields 1 qt (0.94 l) milk.

DRY MALTED MILK

Dry malted milk is whole dried milk, with 55 to 60 percent malt extract added before drying. Extra-strength malted milk has double the normal amount of malt extract.

DRY NONFAT MILK

Pack:

By weight.

Kitchen Yields

1 lb (450 g) is equivalent to 3¼ cups dry milk; ¾ cup weighs ¾ oz (106 g).

¾ oz (106 g) dry milk + ¾ cup (0.18 l) water yields 1 qt (0.94 l) milk.

DRY WHOLE MILK

Pack:

By weight.

Kitchen Yields

1 lb (450 g) is equivalent to 3½ cups dry milk; 1 cup weighs 4½ oz (126 g).

4½ oz (126 g) dry milk + 3½ cups (0.82 l) water yield 1 qt (0.94 l) milk.

FRESH MILK AND MILK PRODUCTS

Milk in foodservice is packed in cartons or in plastic jars. Cartons are prevalent. Milk not requiring refrigeration is available.

Pack:

5-gal (19-l) containers for dispensers; one case of twenty-four 1-qt (0.95-l) containers, totaling 6 gal (22.8 l); one case of forty-two 1-pint (0.47-l) containers, totaling 5 gal 1 qt (19.7 l); one case of seventy-two ½-pint (0.23-l) containers, totaling 4½ gal (17.1 l).

Fat contents:

Nonfat milk: Less than 0.1 percent butterfat.

Skim milk: Less than 3½ percent butterfat content.

Whole milk: At least 3½ percent.

BUTTERMILK

Calories:

1 cup (0.23 l) = 100 Calories.

CHOCOLATE MILK

Calories:

1 cup (0.23 l), regular = 210 Calories.

1 cup (0.23 l), low-fat, 2 percent = 180 Calories.

1 cup (0.23 l), low-fat, 1 percent = 160 Calories.

HALF AND HALF

See Half and Half, under Cream.

LOW-FAT MILK

Calories:

1 cup (0.23 l), 2 percent fat = 120 Calories.

1 cup (0.23 l), 1 percent fat = 100 Calories.

Calories:

1 cup (0.23 l) = 85 Calories.

WHOLE MILK

Calories:

1 cup (0.23 l) = 155 Calories.

CASE MILK CONVERSION CHART

1 case of 24 quarts (0.95 l) = 96 half-pints (0.24 l) = 6 gal (22.8 l)

1 case of 42 pints (0.47 l) = 21 quarts = 5 gal 1 qt (19.7 l)

1 case of 72 half-pints (0.23 l) = 18 quarts = 4½ gal (17.1 l)

MIREPOIX

Mixed vegetables used for flavoring stewed meats, sauces, and gravies.

Formula

50 percent onions, coarse cut

25 percent carrots, coarse cut

25 percent celery, coarse cut

Crushed peppercorns and bay leaves (optional)
Herbs (optional)

MIRLITON SQUASH

See Chayote, under Squash.

MOUSSE

BASIC COLD MOUSSE

Made with either meat, fish, or shellfish.

Formula

    5 lb (2.25 kg) cooked meat, fish, or shellfish
    1 qt (0.94 l) cold cream sauce or mayonnaise
    6 cups (1.4 l) aspic jelly with the same flavor
        as the main ingredient
    6 cups (1.4 l) heavy cream, whipped

Kitchen Yields

Serving size:
For appetizer, 3 oz (85 g). The total mix yields 65 servings.

BASIC COLD SWEET MOUSSE

Formula

    2 gal (7.6 l) milk
    48 egg yolks
    12 oz (340 g) gelatin
    1½ lb (675 g) corn starch
    3 lb (1.35 kg) sugar
    1 qt (0.94) suitable concentrated fruit flavor
    48 egg whites
    1½ lb (675 g) sugar
    2 gal (7.6 l) heavy cream

Make pastry cream with first six ingredients. Beat separately and fold in egg whites and heavy cream.

Kitchen Yields

Serving size:
¾ cup (0.17 l). The total mix yields 6 gal (22.8 l) or 125 servings.

CHOCOLATE MOUSSE

See Chocolate.

HOT FISH MOUSSE

See Frozen or Prepared Fish Products, under Fish.

FROZEN SWEET MOUSSE

Formula

    32 egg yolks
    1 qt (0.94 l) sugar syrup*
    1 qt (0.94 l) heavy cream
    8 oz (0.23 l) liquor or other concentrated flavor

*To make the sugar syrup, boil 4 lb (1.8 kg) white sugar with 5 cups (1.1 l) water for 10 minutes.

Kitchen Yields
The total mix yields 1 gal (3.8 l).

MUFFINS

Muffins can be prepared from scratch, from mix, or from ready-to-use batter. Muffin batter is normally scooped into molds.

Scoop chart:
#8 scoop holds 4 oz (112 g) batter.
#10 scoop holds 3.2 oz (90 g) batter.
#12 scoop holds 3 oz (85 g) batter.
#24 scoop holds 1½ oz (45 g) batter.

DRY MUFFIN MIX

Pack:
Six 5-lb (2.2-kg) bags.

Kitchen Yields
For 3.2-oz (90-g) portion of batter, use #10 scoop; the yield is 240 muffins per case.
For 1½-oz (45-g) portion of batter, use #24 scoop; the yield is 480 muffins per case.
Yields vary slightly according to type of muffin.

READY-TO-USE FROZEN MUFFIN BATTER

Packs:
Four 5-lb (2.25-kg) buckets; four 8-lb (3.6-kg) containers.

Kitchen Yields
For 3-oz (85-g) portion of batter, one 8-lb (3.6-kg) container yields 42 muffins.

For 4-oz (112-g) portion of batter, one 8-lb (3.6-kg) container yields 32 muffins.

Yields vary slightly according to type of muffin.

MUSHROOMS

This section is divided into two parts: Cultivated Mushrooms and Wild Mushrooms.

CULTIVATED MUSHROOMS

Cultivated mushrooms are available canned, dehydrated, fresh, and to a small extent frozen. A large variety of cultivated mushrooms are available fresh. Some "wild" varieties reaching the markets are actually cultivated.

CANNED CULTIVATED MUSHROOMS

CHAMPIGNONS OR COMMON MUSHROOMS
Available as whole buttons, in slices, and as stems and pieces. Some products are imported.

Pack:
Twenty-four #303 cans; twenty-four #2 cans; twenty-four 16-oz (450-g) cans; six #10 cans. Many other packs are available.

Sizes:
#1 tiny: ½- to ⅝-in (12- to 15-mm) diameter.
#2 small: ⅝- to ⅞-in (15- to 22-mm) diameter.
#3 medium: ⅞- to 1⅛-in (22- to 28-mm) diameter.
#4 large: 1⅛- to 1⅜-in (28- to 34-mm) diameter.
#5 extra large: 1⅜-in (34-mm) diameter and larger.

Kitchen Yields

Drained weights:
#303 can: 10 oz (280 g).
#2 can: 12 oz (340 g).
#10 can: 68 oz (1.9 kg).

Counts:
For buttons, one 16-oz (450-g) can contains 10 to 15, 15 to 20, 20 to 25, 25 to 35, or 35 to 45.

DEHYDRATED CULTIVATED MUSHROOMS

Dried mushrooms are very light. It takes about 10 lb (4.5 kg) fresh mushrooms to get 1 lb (450 g) dried

mushrooms. In some varieties, the flavor is much intensified, much stronger than in the fresh variety. NOTE: Dehydrated mushrooms are often sandy. After cooking, they should be lifted out of the liquid and the cooking stock decanted to keep the sand collected at the bottom and out of the food.

CHAMPIGNONS OR COMMON MUSHROOMS
Rather flavorless, these dehydrated mushrooms are seldom used because fresh and canned mushrooms are readily available.

Pack:
By weight.

Kitchen Yields
4 oz (112 g) dehydrated mushrooms is equivalent to one 2½-lb (1.1-kg) basket fresh mushrooms.

BLACK CHANTERELLES (TRUMPETS OF DEATH)
Dried black chanterelles are a little more successful than dried regular chanterelles.

Kitchen Yields
5 oz (140 g) dried is equivalent to 2 lb (900 g) fresh mushrooms.

SHIITAKE
Dried shiitake mushrooms are seldom used in Western cooking.

WOOD EARS
Oriental mushroom, popular in Chinese cooking.

Pack:
By weight.

FRESH CULTIVATED MUSHROOMS

CHAMPIGNONS OR COMMON MUSHROOMS
Marketed as white, off-white, and brown mushrooms, the most common variety is white. Champignon mushrooms are sized by the number of mushrooms per 1 lb (450 g). Mushrooms are perishable and store best refrigerated and in darkness.

Season:
Available year-round; low season is middle of summer.

Pack:
3-, 5-, and 10-lb (1.4-, 2.25-, and 4.5-kg) cartons; individual 2- to 2½-lb (0.9- to 1.12-kg) baskets. The basket is being phased out in many markets.

Sizes:
Table M-1 lists champignon diameters and number per pound for champignons of different sizes. Medium-size mushrooms are often marketed as "Silver Dollar" size. Nonselect mushrooms are also on the market, usable for chopping or slicing.

Kitchen Yields
1 lb (450 g) yields 1 qt whole, raw; 5 cups sliced, raw; 6 cups chopped, raw. 1 lb (450 g) yields 2 cups sliced cooked, or 2 cups diced cooked.

Waste:
About 5 percent.

Calories:
1 lb (450 g) raw = 120 Calories.
1 cup raw, chopped 2½ oz (70 g) = 20 Calories.

CORALS
Corals look like hens-of-the-woods. They are golden tinged with a white at the base of the florets. However, these mushrooms do not taste as good as the hen-of-the-woods; some, especially the cultivated ones, can be bitter. These are are often used only for displays.

Season:
Summer.

Pack:
Sold by weight.

CRAB MUSHROOMS
Crab mushrooms look like a lady's powder puff. They look much better than they taste, however.

They have an unpleasantly bitter taste and, though safe to eat, are not recommended as a food item.

CREMINI
Cremini mushrooms are the forerunners of today's common cultivated mushrooms. They are more like the ones our grandparents would have known in America. Shelf life is about 1 week.

Season:
Available year-round.

Pack:
Sold by weight, often in 5- to 6-lb (2.25- to 2.7-kg) boxes.

ENOKI
Enoki mushrooms look like enlarged pins. They have a long, skinny stem, about 3 or 4 in (76 to 100 mm) in length, and a tiny round head or cap. They have almost no taste, but they look great and are common decorations in Japanese cuisine.

Season:
Available year-round.

Pack:
10-, 16-, or 32-oz (280-, 450- and 900-g) packages.

Kitchen Yields
There is some trimming loss. Enokis are usually purchased in small quantities.

HEN-OF-THE-WOODS (CAULIFLOWER)
Hen-of-the-woods are uncommon but delicious mushrooms. They resemble the head of a cauliflower, with a brownish-grey tinge.

Season:
Late summer.

Table M-1 Champignon Diameters and Numbers per Pound

	Small	Medium	Large	Extra Large
Diameter	¾ to 1¼ in (1.9 to 3.1 cm)	1¼ to 1¾ in (3.1 to 4.5 cm)	1¾ to 3 in (4.5 to 7.6 cm)	3 in and up (7.6 cm and up)
Numbers per 1 lb (450 g)	30 to 40	18 to 20	12 to 14	7 to 10

Pack:
3-lb (1.35-kg) flats, or individual by weight.

Kitchen Yields

Although expensive to purchase, there is no trimming loss. They should be served cut into florets, but it is impressive to show one whole.

PLEUROTES (OYSTER MUSHROOMS)

Pleurotes are grown in straw or sawdust. Look for non-leggy mushrooms with short stalks. Four key varieties are in commercial cultivation—some are grown domestically, and others are imported.

American Golden Pleurotes

Also known as *golden trumpets*, because of their shape and color, these mushrooms are from an Italian strain. The American varieties come trimmed, with or without the stalk. The American pleurotes are usually not as large as the Italian ones. As they become larger, they exude more spores, making them difficult for pickers because of allergic reactions.

Pack:
3- or 5-lb (1.4- to 2.25-kg) boxes.

American White Pleurotes

Pack:
1-lb (450-g) boxes.

Italian Golden Pleurotes

Imported yellowish to white mushrooms.

Pack:
3-, 4-, or 5-kg (6-lb 9-oz, 8-lb 12-oz or 11-lb) wooden flats.

Italian White Pleurotes

Also known as *white trumpets*, these imported mushrooms are very difficult to grow and are usually quite small in size. The white pleurotes have a short shelf life. They are well curved and look attractive. The mushrooms are shipped untrimmed.

Pack:
1-lb (450-g) boxes.

PORTOBELLO OR ROMAN MUSHROOMS

Actually the same mushroom species as cremini, but left to mature longer in the field. As they mature, they become flatter and their flavor intensifies. When cooking with them, it is advisable to use an acid such as lemon juice, to avoid having these mushrooms turn very dark.

Season:
Available year-round.

Pack:
Sold by weight, often in 5-lb (2.25-kg) boxes.

Kitchen Yields

About 6 large mushrooms weigh 1 lb (450 g).

SHIITAKE

Shiitake mushrooms are the most commonly cultivated mushrooms in the world. American production is expected to grow in the next 20 years, because of the influences of Oriental cuisines, and also because shiitake mushrooms taste delicious. The commercially-cultivated shiitake mushrooms taste better than those found in the wild. Shiitake mushrooms are marketed in two basic varieties: indoor-grown and outdoor-grown. The outdoor grown mushrooms are usually denser, woodier, and heavier. Fresh shiitakes have a long shelf life.

Grades:
There are two grades of both indoor- and outdoor-grown shiitakes:

Grade A:
Uniform in size with clear, neatly structured gills.

Grade B:
Larger and non-conforming in shape and size.

Packs:
3-, 5-, 7-, and 10-lb (1.35-, 2.25-, 3.1-, and 4.5-kg) flats.

Kitchen Yields

Use grade A for presenting the cap whole. The stems can be cut julienne style.
Use grade B for cutting up, or select the large caps for grilling.

WOOD EARS

Wood ears are most often sold dried, but some are also sold fresh. When reconstituted or fresh, they have a slick, slippery feel and an al dente texture.

FROZEN MUSHROOMS

Whole white mushrooms and mushroom caps (champignon) are available frozen IQF.

Pack:
Eight 2½-lb (1.12-kg) bags in master carton; individual 20-lb (9-kg) and 40-lb (18-kg) cartons.

Kitchen Yield
There is no waste.

WILD MUSHROOMS

Available canned, fresh, and in some instances frozen.

CANNED WILD MUSHROOMS

CHANTERELLES

Canned chanterelles are mostly imported, but the mushrooms are often from United States and canned in Europe. Their flavor is briny.

Pack:
Twenty-four 1-lb 13-oz (830-g) cans, with a drained weight of 14.1 oz (400 g) each; thirty-six 14⁶⁄₁₀-oz (415-g) cans, with a drained weight of 6⁷⁄₁₀ oz (190 g) each.

Kitchen Yields
Mushrooms are fully cooked and there is no additional shrinkage.

MORELS

Canned morels are available, but have little commercial importance because dehydrated and fresh morels are readily available.

PORCINI

Pack:
Twelve 22-oz (625-g) cans.

Drained weight:
16 oz (450 g).

STRAW MUSHROOMS

Mushroom popular in Oriental cooking. Packed in water.

Pack:
Thirty-six 1-lb (450-g) cans with a net weight of 15 oz (420 g) each.

Drained weight:
8 oz (225 g).

TRUFFLES

Canned truffles are available in cans and in jars. Truffles in jars are considered better quality than canned truffles. *See* Truffle Oil, under Oil. Preserved truffles are available as:

> Whole brushed truffle
> Peeled truffle
> Truffle peelings
> Truffle pieces
> Truffle juice
> Truffle paste
> Truffle powder
> Truffle butter
> Truffle oil

Pack:
1- to 8-oz (28- to 225-g) tins or jars.

Kitchen Yields
Truffles are very expensive. They dry out quickly when not covered with liquid. A good preservative is fortified wine. For economical truffle sauce, use one 8-oz (225-g) can truffle peelings for ½ gal (1.8 l) sauce, which yields 50 servings.

DEHYDRATED WILD MUSHROOMS

CHANTERELLES

Available dried, but the they tend to be a little tough.

Pack:
By weight.

Kitchen Yields
5 oz (140 g) dried is equivalent to 2 lb (900 g) fresh mushrooms.

MORELS

Morels are available imported and domestic. Little product comes from Europe; the majority is imported from India and Kashmir. The smoky smell of Indian morels is caused by drying the mushrooms over cow dung.

Domestic morels are normally mixed white and black varieties, but only professionals will notice the difference. Some are picked after forest fires; these morels have weak walls and are muddy. Better-quality morels are picked in clear-cut areas.

Pack:

Sold by weight. 3-lb (1.35-kg) bags are common.

Kitchen Yields

Dried morels have more intense flavor than fresh morels, so the high price is justified. The price of dried morels should be around 7 to 8 times the price of fresh.

PORCINI

One of the finest dried mushrooms, with strong flavor. The best quality is imported from Italy. Many different quality levels are on the market. Smaller mushrooms have a stronger flavor than larger ones.

Pack:

By weight.

Size:

Some packers market very large mushrooms, which can be tough.

Kitchen Yields

Since flavor level varies greatly, it is best to make a sample with a small amount. Dried porcini should be soaked and then simmered for about ½ hour in the same water they were soaked in. The water will carry the flavor. In some cases, the mushrooms are discarded.

FRESH WILD MUSHROOMS

A large quantity of wild mushrooms are picked in the United States and some are exported. Some of these mushrooms are processed abroad and re-imported canned or dried.

The location where the mushrooms are grown is the most important quality factor. The Midwest and eastern states grow the best-tasting mushrooms. Nova Scotia also produces excellent wild mushrooms. However, the Pacific Northwest is the most prolific producer.

Professional mushroom pickers are very fastidious, and some put every mushroom in separate bags to avoid infestation by worms, especially when picking porcini.

Wild mushrooms are inspected a number of times before shipping and are very safe. There has never been a reported case of mushroom poisoning attributed to commercially-picked wild mushrooms.

CHANTERELLES

Available domestic and imported. American chanterelles are related to the French girolles, but are not exactly the same species. Fresh chanterelles should be dry when picked, because they are susceptible to worm infestation. They should smell like apricots.

Season:

From May until late fall. The season beings in May in Morocco, North Africa; in July and August in Pennsylvania, followed by Nantucket and Nova Scotia; and in late August in California, Oregon, Washington, and Canada.

Pack:

By weight.

Size:

There is no count. Early chanterelles are small, and weigh between ¼ to ½ oz (7 to 14 g) each. Small chanterelles have a better flavor than later-picked mushrooms. Late mushrooms can be as large as 1 lb (450 g).

Kitchen Yields

To preserve chanterelles, sauté quickly and freeze. There is little shrinkage.

CORALS

Available spring and fall in small quantities.

GOAT'S BEARD

This rare mushroom looks like a goat's beard.

Season:
Fall.

HEDGEHOG MUSHROOMS
The caps are beige to orange in color, and the underside is white.

Season:
Winter and very early spring.

HEN-OF-THE-WOODS (CAULIFLOWER)
This excellent mushroom, perhaps the best of all, is very rare and expensive. They are delicious raw. Only domestic wild hens-of-the-woods are available.

Season:
Spring and fall.

Pack:
By weight.

HON SHIMEJI MUSHROOMS

Season:
Summer.

Pack:
By weight.

LOBSTER MUSHROOMS
Orange to red in color.

Season:
July and August.

Pack:
By weight.

MORELS
Nearly all fresh morels available in U.S. markets are domestic. The United States exports large quantities to Europe for canning. They are sometimes reimported to America. Cultivation of morels is not yet possible.

Morels, like all mushrooms, are underground plants; the visible "hat" is the fruit. Morels picked in the U.S. are normally not as sandy as their imported counterparts. There are over 22 varieties of morels found in the United States, but basically only black and white morels are of commercial importance. White morels are of superior quality, because they are lighter and more delicate than black morels. The best come from Michigan and Wisconsin. White morels are rarer than black morels, but not necessarily more expensive.

Season:
End of March until end of June in the northern hemisphere. Morels are also now coming from the southern hemisphere.

Pack:
By weight. When morels are shipped they generate heat, which can reach up to 100°F. Heated morels develop an ammonia smell and should not be accepted. Morels are not graded by size. A packer might pick large morels at request for a premium price.

False morels, called *snow morels*, reach the market occasionally. They are less expensive than real morels, but should never be used. Although not toxic, they will cause stomach cramps and indigestion if eaten in large quantities. Many cookbooks recommend that *all* morels should be blanched.

Kitchen Yields
Morels do not shrink much. Large morels are often stuffed.

PIEDS DE MOUTON
Called *lamb's feet mushrooms*, they look like chanterelles but have more gills, which come off in cooking and make the product look muddy.

Season:
November and December.

Size:
Small, about 1¼ in (32 mm) across.

Pack:
By weight.

PORCINI
They are considered the best-flavored wild species of mushrooms other than truffles. The German name is *Steinpilze*, the French name is *cèpes*. There are many species, but only two of these—Boletus edulis and Boletus miraculus—should be used.

Season:
Imports from Europe during summer and early fall. There are two domestic seasons: a short season in spring and a longer season in fall.

Pack:
By weight.

Size:
Size is no indication of quality. The large mushrooms are as tasty as small mushrooms. The large caps can be up to 15 in (380 mm) across and are used for grilling, and the whole mushroom can weigh as much as 3 lb (1.3 kg), while small ones are as tight as a baby's fist.

Kitchen Yields
Place of origin does not influence quality. The whole mushroom can be used. Porcinis are very perishable and subject to infestation. To preserve, sauté and freeze. There is some shrinkage, especially when sautéing porcinis. Very large caps have dark brown gills, which are often mushy and should be removed. Infestation by snails can also be a problem, and sometimes the trim loss exceeds 20 percent.

PUFF BALLS
Not commonly available, although not rare in the wild.

Season:
Late spring to fall.

Size:
About ½ lb (450 g) each, up to 3 lb (1.35 kg).

STRAW MUSHROOMS
Seldom available fresh. They are slimy and very perishable.

TRUFFLES
Fresh truffles are available domestic and imported. By far the majority (and those of the best quality) are imported. Two varieties of domestic truffles come to the market. They are different in size and smell from the imported varieties. Like imported truffles, they are available black and white, the white being more plentiful and slightly cheaper than the black. Most come from the Pacific Coast, especially from Oregon. Some domestic truffles have a camphor smell, which is not acceptable.

Imported truffles come mostly from France and Italy. They are available black and white, the black variety being slightly more abundant than the white. The flavor is carried in the volatile oils, and is easily imparted to other foods. Truffles can be flash-frozen successfully.

Seasons:

Black Truffles:
November to December.

White Truffles:
October to December.

Summer Truffles:
Black truffles with less flavor than winter truffles are imported from France and Italy from May until November. They are much less expensive than winter truffles.

Pack:
Sold by weight.

Size:
Varies from 1 to 4 oz (28 to 112 g).

Kitchen Yields
Truffles are very expensive, and maximum use must be made of the product to realize a return. Since truffles impart their flavor easily to other foods, they can be stored for a short time, such as one week, in oil or sherry wine. Truffles should be sliced thin and to order. White truffles are excellent grated raw, to order, over pasta dishes.

WINE CAPS
Lavender-colored caps with gills.

Season:
Spring and fall.

YELLOW FOOT CHANTERELLE
They are very different from other chanterelles. Because they are very light and tiny, they look like miniature yellow carnations.

Season:
Spring and fall.

Size:
1 oz (28 g) comprises 20 to 30 mushrooms.

FROZEN WILD MUSHROOMS

CHANTERELLES
Available in Europe, but seldom imported.

Pack:
1-kg (35-oz) bags.

PORCINI
Commercially flash-frozen whole and sliced mushrooms are available, mostly imported from Europe. The quality is good.

Pack:
1-kg (35-oz) bags.

TRUFFLES
Frozen truffles are imported from Europe, but the supply is small.

MUSSELS

Available canned, fresh, and frozen. Fresh mussels are sold cultivated and wild. Cultivated mussels are free of grit and can be very large.

CANNED MUSSELS
Available smoked and plain.

Pack:
Varies.

FRESH MUSSELS

Season:
Available year-round.

Pack:
Normally sold by weight.

Counts:

Small:
11 to 14 pieces per 1 lb (450 g).

Medium:
8 to 11 pieces per 1 lb (450 g).

Large:
5 to 8 pieces per 1 lb (450 g).

Extra Large:
3 to 5 pieces per 1 lb (450 g).

Serving sizes:
1 lb (450 g), for any size, for steamed mussels. The best size for receptions is medium.

FROZEN MUSSELS
Available shucked meat only IQF and on the half-shell.

Pack:
Varies.

MUSTARD GREENS

Available canned, fresh, and frozen.

CANNED MUSTARD GREENS

CHOPPED MUSTARD GREENS.

Pack:
Six #10 cans.

Kitchen Yields

Serving size:
½ cup (0.15 l). One #10 can yields 60 oz (1.7 kg), drained weight, or 20 servings; one case yields 120 servings.

Calories:
½ cup (0.15 l) = 20 Calories.

FRESH MUSTARD GREENS
Mustard greens are grown extensively in the South, but supplies also come from other states.

Season:
Winter.

Pack:
By weight.

Kitchen Yields
1 lb (450 g) raw yields 2 cups cooked.

Calories:
½ cup = 20 Calories.

FROZEN MUSTARD GREENS

Pack:
Twelve 2½-lb (1.1-kg) packages. Other packs are available.

Kitchen Yields

Serving size:
½ cup (0.15 l). One case yields 120 servings.

Calories:
½ cup (0.15 l) = 20 Calories.

MUTTON

See Lamb.

N and O

NASTURTIUMS

Annual plant with pleasant flowers. The leaves are bitter and can be used as a salad ingredient. The buds are sometimes pickled as a caper substitute.

NECTARINES

Juicy fruit closely related to peaches. Each fruit has one large pit. Freestone varieties should be purchased for foodservice. There is large domestic production, and imports are available in the off-season.

Season:
May to September, with peak in July and August.

Pack:
19- to 23-lb (8.5- to 10.3-kg) two-layer lugs, with 48, 56, 64, 72, 80, and 84; 25- and 35-lb (11.25- and 15.7-kg) loose-fill cartons.

Kitchen Yields
One medium (64-size) nectarine weighs 5 oz (140 g). Three medium fruits weigh 1 lb (450 g) and yield 2 cups (0.47 l) sliced, 1¾ cups (0.4 l) diced, or 1½ cups (0.34 l) puréed. One 22-lb (9.9-kg) case yields 2¾ gal (10.4 l) sliced.

Calories:
1 cup sliced fruit = 75 Calories.

NOODLE DOUGH

This dough can also be used for making baskets and other ornamental pieces.

Formula
5 lb (2.2 kg) bread flour
16 eggs
½ cup water
1 oz (28 g) oil

Kitchen Yields
The total mix produces 7 lb (3.1 kg) raw fresh noodles.

Serving size:

Main course:
3½ oz (98 g) raw, one cup (0.23 l) cooked. The total mix yields 32 main-course servings.

Garnish:
1½ oz (42 g), ⅓ cup cooked. The total mix yields 74 servings.

NOPALES (CACTUS LEAVES)

See Mexican Foods.

O

OCTOPUS

Available fresh and frozen.

Season:
Available year-round.

Average sizes:
From 3 lb (1.3 kg) and up.

Kitchen Yields
Most octopus is shipped frozen in 5-lb (2.2-kg) boxes. There is no waste because only the legs are shipped.

OILS

Cooking oils are extracted from the seeds, pods, and fruits of such items as corn, cottonseed, olives, peanuts, soybean, and other vegetable products. Cooking oils are manufactured to taste relatively bland and to be used for specific purposes, such as frying, salad-making, or all-purpose applications. Blended oils with an olive oil content of 25 percent or more are available.

Flavoring oils are made with the goal of retaining as much of their characteristic flavor as possible. They are used more for flavoring than for large volume cooking because they might be too expensive or because the flavor is too strong for general use. Flavoring oils are made from the seeds or pits of avocado, mustard, poppy, sesame, sunflower, and others. Some of these oils are used for dietary reasons. Flavoring oils are also made by steeping or cooking herbs and other ingredients in oil. Some chefs make their own flavoring oils.

Pack:
Packs range from 1-qt (0.94-1) bottles to 5-gal (19-l) containers. Common kitchen sizes are six 1-gal (3.8-l) containers per carton. Some imported oils are shipped in metric-size bottles.

Kitchen Yields
Varies depending on application.

AVOCADO OIL
A silky and mild oil with a high flash-point, but too expensive for deep-fat frying. Used in stir-frying or in salads.

CANOLA OIL
A cooking and salad oil developed in Canada from rapeseed oil. The word canola is an acronym from CANada, Oil, Low Acid. It contains healthy Omega 3 fatty acids, the same acids found in fish oil, while having only 7 percent saturated fat.

COCONUT OIL
An oil with a high level of saturated fats. It is seldom used in foodservice. Coconut oil was used in the production of margarine.

OLIVE OIL
Olive oil is the oldest manufactured oil and can range from rather bland and flavorless cooking oils to highly aromatic oils suitable for both cooking and flavoring. It contains monounsaturated fat.

Most olive oil is imported, and most imported olive oil comes from Italy and Spain, with some also coming from Greece, Algeria, Morocco, Tunisia, Turkey, France, and Portugal. A small quantity is manufactured in California.

Olive oil can be classified as:

Extra virgin:
From the first pressing of the olives. It has a full, fruity flavor and the lowest acidity level. The best grades of oil are greenish to green in color; the lesser grades are yellower. Young oil might have a slightly bitter taste which will mellow as it ages. Premium extra-virgin olive oil is grown on small estates at very high altitudes.

Virgin:
From the first pressing of the olives. Virgin olive oil has up to 1.5 percent acidity.

Pure olive oil:
Also comes from the first pressing, but has a lighter, less fruity taste and a higher acidity level. Pure olive oil has up to 3 percent acidity and is sometimes called *olio di oliva*, *huile d'olive*, or just *olive oil*.

Olive oil:
The usual name for a blend of refined olive oil and virgin olive oil. It has an acidity level of less than 1.5 grams acid per 100 grams of oil.

Olive pomace oil:
A lower grade oil, made from pressed olives with the aid of solvents.

PALM OIL (DENDE OIL)
Imported from Brazil and other tropical countries. This oil has a strong flavor and contains up to 51 percent saturated fat. Used in Brazilian dishes.

PUMPKIN OIL
A salad oil popular in some European countries.

RAPESEED OIL
Often sold as *canola oil*. It has only 7 percent saturated fat, but also has naturally-occurring erucic acid that must be removed by processing.

SAFFLOWER OIL

A cooking and eating oil derived from the seeds of the safflower plant. The oil is basically flavorless and high in polyunsaturated fat.

SESAME OIL

A flavoring oil used in combination with milder-flavored oils. The thicker, darker versions, from China and Japan, have the most intense flavor. The Middle-Eastern version is lighter and less aromatic.

SUNFLOWER OIL

An oil with mostly unsaturated fats.

TRUFFLE OIL

Oil which has been flavored with truffle peelings. The truffle itself has no fat content. Used as a flavoring oil.

WALNUT OIL

Salad oil popular in some European countries.

OKRA

Available canned, fresh, and frozen. It is also called *gumbo*.

CANNED OKRA

Available cut or whole.

Pack:
Six #10 cans, with a drained weight of 60 oz (1.7 kg); twenty-four #2½ cans, with a drained weight of 18 oz (500 g); twenty-four #2 cans, with a drained weight of 12 oz (340 g).

Kitchen Yields

Calories:
3¾ oz (106 g) cooked = 30 Calories.

FRESH OKRA

Long and short varieties are on the market in both green and yellow. Green okra is the most common variety.

Season:
Available year-round. Peak is from July to October.

Pack:
By weight in hampers, bushels, or baskets.

Kitchen Yields
Best size are pods 2 to 3½ in (50 to 89 mm) long. About 35 pods weigh 1 lb (450 g).

Calories:
8 pods, or ¾ oz (106 g) cooked = 30 Calories.

FROZEN OKRA

Available whole, cut, and breaded.

Pack:

Cut okra:
Twelve 3-lb (1.35-kg) boxes; individual 20-lb (9-kg) boxes.

Whole okra:
Twelve 2½-lb (1.1-kg) boxes; individual 20-lb (9-kg) boxes.

Breaded okra:
Individual 20-lb (9-kg) boxes, IQF.

OLIVES

Olives are available as green, ripe, and processed ripe olives. Because olives are an ancient food, many different styles are available in ethnic markets. Domestic and imported types are available. Ripe olives are cured by several processes.

CANNED BLACK OLIVES

The process of canning was developed in the United States. Large black olives in cans are made with unripe green olives and often lack flavor. Available whole pitted, whole unpitted, sliced, chopped, and in wedges.

Pack:
Six #10 cans.

CANNED PITTED BLACK OLIVES:
Table O-1 lists data for canned pitted black olives.

CANNED UNPITTED BLACK OLIVES:
Table O-2 lists data for canned unpitted black olives.

Table O-1 Yields for Canned Pitted Black Olives

Size	Drained Weight	Number per #10 Can	Number per 1 lb (450 g)
Small	51 oz (1.4 kg)	578	177 to 193
Medium	51 oz (1.4 kg)	486	150 to 165
Large	51 oz (1.4 kg)	430	123 to 126
Extra Large	51 oz (1.4 kg)	350	105 to 120
Jumbo	49 oz (1.39 kg)	245	69 to 90
Colossal	49 oz (1.39 kg)	199	54 to 70
Super Colossal	49 oz (1.39 kg)	163	44 to 56

Table O-2 Yields for Canned Unpitted Black Olives

Size	Drained Weight	Number per #10 Can	Number per 1 lb (450 g)
Small	66 oz (1.9 kg)	557	126 to 140
Medium	66 oz (1.9 kg)	466	106 to 121
Large	66 oz (1.9 kg)	404	91 to 105
Extra Large	66 oz (1.9 kg)	288	65 to 88
Jumbo	64 oz (1.8 kg)	228	51 to 60
Colossal	64 oz (1.8 kg)	192	41 to 50
Super Colossal	64 oz (1.8 kg)	126	26 to 40

SLICED, WEDGED, AND CHOPPED BLACK OLIVE PIECES

One #10 can of sliced olives weighing 55 oz (1.5 kg) drained yields 13 cups (3 l).
One #10 can of wedged olives weighing 55 oz (1.5 kg) drained yields 11¼ cups (2.6 l).
One #10 can of chopped olives weighing 90 oz (2.25 kg) drained yields 14½ cups (3.4 l).

Calories:
3 small or 2 large olives = 15 Calories.
1 cup sliced, or 4¾ oz (135 g) = 174 Calories.
1 cup wedged, or 5⅜ oz (150 g) = 193 Calories.
1 cup chopped, or 6⅞ oz (190 g) = 250 Calories.

CANNED OR PICKLED GREEN OLIVES

Most important varieties of green olives are Sevillano, Manzanillo, Ascolana and Mission olives. Olives are available unpitted, pitted, and stuffed with various foods.

Pack:
Many sizes are available. The label normally indicates drained weight.

Common drained weight:
½ pint (0.23 l) = 5 oz (140 g)
1 pint (0.47 l) = 10 oz (280 g)
1 qt (0.94 l) = 21 oz (600 g)
1 gal (3.8 l) = 88 oz (2.5 kg)

WHOLE UNPITTED GREEN OLIVES

Table O-3 lists data for canned unpitted green olives.

Calories:
4 medium, or 3 extra large, or 2 giant = 15 Calories.

CURED RIPE OLIVES

Cured ripe olives may range from brown to purple to black, and may be cured in brine, in oil, or by some other process.

IMPORTED OLIVES

Available canned, cured, and salted.

Table O-3 Yields for Canned Unpitted Green Olives

Size	Name	Count per 1 lb	Count per Kilo
00	Peewee	181 to 220	
0	Midget	141 to 180	
1	Small	126 to 140	280 to 300
2	Medium	106 to 127	220 to 240
3	Large	91 to 105	200 to 220
4	Extra Large	76 to 90	170 to 190
5	Mammoth	65 to 75	150 to 160
6	Giant	53 to 64	120 to 130
7	Jumbo	42 to 52	100 to 110
8	Colossal	33 to 41	80 to 90
9	Super Colossal	32 or fewer	70 to 80

IMPORTED CANNED OLIVES

Pack:
Three 10-lb (4.5-kg) cans; drained weight 5 lb 12 oz (2.7 kg).

Count:
2000 per can.

IMPORTED PICKLED AND CURED OLIVES
A large variety of loose black olives is available in ethnic stores. There are three varieties: olives shipped in brine, in oil, and dry cured olives. Dry cured olives can be very salty. All olives are processed with pits.

Pack:
Varies. Most olives are sold by weight.

Size:
Varies.

Kitchen Yields

Brine cured olives:
1 cup (0.23 l) weighs 6 oz (170 g).

Salted olives:
1 cup (0.23 l) weighs 7 oz (196 g).

Count:
1 cup (0.23 l) equals about 40 to 50 medium olives.

ONIONS

Onions are available canned, dried, fresh whole, fresh processed, and frozen.

CANNED ONIONS

PEARL ONIONS

Pack:
Six #10 cans.

Counts:
100 to 125, 200 to 250, 375 to 400, and 400 to 500.

Kitchen Yields
Use as is; there is no waste.

DEHYDRATED ONIONS

Pack:
Six #10 cans.

Net weight:
28 oz (800 g).

Kitchen Yields
1 lb (450 g) dry = 6¾ cups (1.4 l), or 13 cups (3 l) reconstituted onions.

FRESH ONIONS

BOILING ONIONS
See Pearl Onions, under this same heading.

CREAMER ONIONS
See Pearl Onions, under this same heading.

GREEN ONIONS (SCALLIONS)

Season:
Available year-round. Peak is in spring.

Pack:
15- to 25-lb (6.8- to 11.35-kg) cartons containing 48 bunches; 24- and 12-bunch cartons are also available.

Kitchen Yields

Waste depends on whether the green part, the white part, or both are used. If the whole vegetable is used, cleaning waste is about 10 percent by weight. The white and green parts comprise about 50 percent each.

Calories:

6 stalks, weighing 1½ oz (42 g) = 20 Calories.

MATURE ONIONS

Onions are classified as storage onions and fresh onions. Storage onions can be recognized by a darker-colored outer skin that is thicker than the skin of fresh onions. Storage onions are known for their firmness. Fresh onions can be recognized by their lighter color and thinner skin. They have a higher water and sugar content than storage onions, and they are more susceptible to bruising and decay. Both varieties are available most of the time in three colors: red, white, and yellow. Red onions are often referred to as Spanish or Italian onions. Bermuda onions are large white onions.

Sweet onions are sweeter than normal onions and do not irritate the eyes when being processed. They come from various growing regions. One of the best known varieties is Vidalia, named for the Georgia town of Vidalia, where it is grown. By Georgia law, only onions grown in 19 southeastern counties may be marketed as Vidalias. Sweet Spanish onions are large red storage onions from Idaho and eastern Oregon.

Fresh Onion Season:

Arizona:
May to June.

Imperial Valley Sweets, CA:
April to June.

San Joaquin Valley, CA:
May to August.

Colorado:
July to September.

Vidalia Sweets GA:
April to June.

Maui Sweets, Hawaii:
Year-round.

Los Cruces, NM:
June to August.

High Plain, TX:
July to August.

Rio Grande, TX:
March to June.

Trans Pecos, TX:
June to July.

Vidalia, GA:
April to June.

Winter Gardens, TX:
April to June.

Walla Walla Sweets, WA:
June to August.

Storage Onion Season:

July until April of the following year.

Pack:

5-, 10-, 25-, and 50-lb (2.2-, 4.5-, 11.2-, and 22.6-kg) bags; 40- and 50-lb (18.1- and 22.6-kg) cartons. Table O-4 lists colors, diameters, and weights for different sizes of mature onions.

Counts:

Table O-5 identifies counts of different sizes of mature onions, by pack.

Kitchen Yields

1 cup chopped weighs 6 oz (170 g); 1 cup sliced weighs 4 oz (112 g). One 50-lb (22.6-kg) bag yields 110 cups chopped, or 170 cups sliced.

Waste:

Peeling loss about 15 percent by weight.

Calories:

1 cup, or 6 oz (170 g), raw, chopped = 65 Calories.
1 cup, or 4 oz (112 g), raw, sliced = 45 Calories.

PEARL ONIONS

Also called *creamer* or *boiler onions,* these are small white onions used in stews and in vegetable preparations. They are also available canned, fresh, and frozen.

Table O-4 Trade Names and Average Sizes for Mature Onions

Trade Name	Color	Diameter	Weight
Colossal	yellow only	4 in & up (100 mm & up)	14 to 18 oz (400 to 500 g)
Jumbo	yellow & red	3¼ to 4½ in (82 to 112 mm)	8 to 10 oz (225 to 280 g)
Large Medium	yellow, white, & red	2¼ to 3¼ in (57 to 82 mm)	3 to 5 oz (85 to 140 g)
Prepack	yellow & white	1¾ to 2¼ in (45 to 57 mm)	3 to 1½ oz (85 to 45 g)
Boiler	yellow & white	½ to ⅞ in (12 to 22 mm)	1 to 1½ oz (28 to 45 g)
Creamer	yellow & white	½ in (12 mm)	1 oz or smaller (28 g or less)

Season:
Available year-round.

Pack:
28-lb (12.6-kg) lug. Other packs are available.

Count:
Varies.

Kitchen Yields

Waste:
15 percent peeling loss.

Serving size:
½ cup (0.12 l). 1 lb (450 g) yields 3½ servings.

SCALLIONS
See Green Onions, under this same heading.

Table O-5 Counts for Different Containers of Mature Onions

Container	Colossal	Jumbo	Large Medium	Pre-pack
50 lb (22.6 kg)	45 to 50	80 to 100	180	350
25 lb (11.35 kg)	22	45	90	170
10 lb (4.5 kg)	12	23	45	85
5 lb (2.25 kg)	6	11	22	44

SHALLOTS
See Shallots.

FRESH PROCESSED ONIONS
Available peeled, sliced, or diced.

Pack:
20-lb (9.1-kg) box containing four 5-lb (2.25-kg) bags; 20-lb (9.1-kg) box containing two 10-lb (4.5-kg) bags.

FROZEN ONIONS
Available diced or sliced, IQF, or as whole pearl onions. Many ready-to-use products are also on the market. For frozen pearl onions, see Pearl Onions, under this heading.

Pack:
12-, 16-, 20-, or 45-lb (5.4-, 7.3-, 9.1-, or 20.4-kg) boxes, loose or in 2-lb (0.9-kg) boxes.

ONION SOUP

See Soups.

ORANGES

See also Mandarin Oranges, Shamouti, Tangerines.

ORANGE JUICE
Available canned, dehydrated, freshly squeezed (in some markets), fresh, and as frozen concentrate.

CANNED ORANGE JUICE

Available sweetened and unsweetened.

Pack:
Twelve 46-oz (1.3-l) cans.

Kitchen Yields

Serving size:
6 oz (0.17 l).

Calories:
6 oz (0.17 l) unsweetened = 90 Calories.

DEHYDRATED ORANGE JUICE

Pack:
1-lb (450-g) jars. Other packs are available.

Kitchen Yields

Serving size:
6 oz (0.17 l); 1 lb (450 g) mixed with 1 gal (3.8 l) water yields 21 servings.

Calories:
One 6-oz (0.17-l) serving = 75 Calories.

FRESH ORANGE JUICE

Pack:
1-qt (0.94-l) cartons or bottles; ½-gal (1.8-l) cartons or bottles. Other packs are available.

Kitchen Yields

Serving size:
6 oz (0.17 l); thus, 1 qt (0.94 l) yields 5 servings, and ½ gal (1.8 l) yields 10 servings.

Calories:
6 oz (0.17 l) unsweetened = 90 Calories.

FROZEN ORANGE JUICE CONCENTRATE

Pack:
Various packs available. Common pack is a 12-oz (0.354-l) can.

Kitchen Yields

Dilute 1 part concentrate with 3 parts water; thus, one 12-oz (0.354-l) can mixed with 36 oz, or 4½ cups (1 l) water, yields 48 oz (1.4 l) juice.

Serving size:
6 oz (0.17 l); thus, one 12-oz (0.354-l) can diluted yields 8 servings.

Calories:
6 oz (0.17 l) = 90 Calories.

ORANGE SECTIONS

Available canned and fresh.

CANNED ORANGE SECTIONS

Pack:
Twenty-four #3 cylindrical cans; twenty-four or thirty-six #2 cans; twenty-four or thirty-six #303 cans.

Kitchen Yields

Serving size:
½ cup (0.11 l); 3½ oz (98 g).

Drained weights:
#3 cylindrical can weighs 30 oz (850 g) and yields 8½ servings.
#2 can weighs 12 oz (340 g) and yields 3½ servings.
#303 can weighs 10 oz (280 g) and yields 3 servings.

FRESH ORANGE SECTIONS

Pack:
Four 1-gal (3.8-l) jars.

Kitchen Yields

Serving size:
½ cup (0.12 l); 3½ oz (98 g).

Drained weight:
6 lb (2.7 kg); yields 25 to 26 servings.

WHOLE ORANGES

Marketing season is year-round, with a general peak from December through May. Valencia oranges from California and Arizona peak in

August to September. Oranges are produced in Florida, California, Texas, and Arizona.

Orange varieties include Valencia (good eating and juice orange), Navel (large, seedless, peels and sections easily), Hamlin (seedless, thin peel), Pineapple (juicy, has seeds), and Temple (few seeds, peels easily). Valencia is a summer orange; Navel is a winter orange. Blood oranges are in season during the spring and summer.

Seasons:

California and Arizona:
Navel: November to June.
Valencia: March to January.
Temple: November to February.

Florida:
Hamlin: October to January.
Navel: November to January.
Pineapple: December to February.
Temple: January to March.
Valencia: March to July.

Texas:
Valencia: February to June.
Temple: February to June.

Pack:

Varies, depending on growing area.

Florida:
37- to 45-lb (16.6- to 20.2-kg) cartons containing ⅘ bushel with counts of 64, 80, 100, or 125 oranges. Counts for navels are 32, 36, 40, 48, or 56.

California and Arizona:
37- to 45-lb (16.6- to 20.2-kg) cartons with counts of 48, 56, 72, 88, 112, 138, and 168 oranges.

Texas:
38- to 44-lb (17.1- to 19.8-kg) cartons with counts of 56, 64, 80, 100, 125, or 144 oranges; 82- to 87-lb (36.9- to 39.1-kg) cartons with counts of 100, 125, 163, 200, 252, or 288 oranges.

Sizes:

Florida sizes are based on the number of oranges in a 40-lb (18-kg) carton. Sizes and diameters are as follows:

125 size: 2½ in (63 mm) diameter.
100 size: 2¹¹⁄₁₆ in (68 mm) diameter.
80 size: 2¹⁵⁄₁₆ in (75 mm) diameter.
64 size: 3³⁄₁₆ in (81 mm) diameter.

Common hotel sizes for fruit baskets are sizes 56, 64, or 72.

Weights:

48 size: very large, 12 to 14 oz (360 to 400 g).
88 size: medium, 7½ oz (200 g).
163 size: small, 4 oz (112 g).

Kitchen Yields

For fruit baskets buy Navel or Valencia oranges. One large navel orange, weighing 13 oz (365 g), yields 8 oz (116 g) peeled fruit, 6 to 7 large slices, or 1 cup sections totaling 5 oz (140 g).
3 to 4 medium oranges yield 1 cup, or 8 oz (0.23 l) juice.
2 medium oranges yield 1 cup, or 5 oz (140 g), bite-size pieces.
1 medium orange yields 4 tsp grated peel.

JUICE ORANGES

Florida oranges have a higher juice content than do California oranges. The three best juice oranges are Valencia, Hamlin, and Pineapple. The best price is the lowest price per carton, regardless of size.

Seasons:

Florida:
Valencia: March to July.
Hamlin: October to January.
Pineapple: December to February.

California:
Valencia: March to January.

Arizona:
Storage oranges are available from July to October, but their juice yield is less.

Pack:

Florida:
size 125.

California:
size 112 or 138.

Kitchen Yields

The yield is influenced by the season, climate, count, and type of machine used. Higher-count oranges give slightly better yields.

One case of size 125 oranges yields 2¼ to 2½ gal (8.5 to 9.5 l) juice.

Calories:

1 cup, or 8 fl oz (0.23 l) = 110 Calories.

OREGANO

See Herbs & Spices.

OSTRICH

Ostrich meat is extremely low in fat and has become a low cholesterol alternative for other dark meats. Most meat is concentrated in the thighs and legs, as the breast muscle is rather small. Since the meat is dry, it is best to cook it medium rare. The eggs are edible and considered a delicacy.

Sizes and weights:

Eggs:

About 3 lb (1.35 kg) and larger.

Meat pack:

Eighty 2-oz (56-g) medallions in 10-lb (4.5-kg) cartons.
Forty 4-oz (112-g) medallions in 10-lb (4.5-kg) cartons.
Seventy 6-oz (170-g) medallions in 15-lb (6.75-kg) cartons.

Serving size:

6 oz (170 g).

Kitchen Yields

Meat is completely trimmed and there is little shrinkage.

Calories:

6 oz (170 g) = 194 Calories.

OTTAHITIA APPLES

Also spelled *otaheite apple*, this is a pear-shaped, tropical fruit (not a true apple) with a thin, edible skin.

Season:

Spring and fall.

Pack:

By weight.

Size:

About 2 oz (56 g).

Kitchen Yields

Serve raw or poached. Center pit is easily removed. About two fruits (four halves) per serving. Do not peel.

OYSTERS

CANNED SMOKED OYSTERS

Pack:

Forty-eight 3.6-oz (100-g) cans.

Count:

Varies; approximately 14 to 16 pieces.

FRESH OYSTERS

Many varieties of oysters are available from both the Atlantic and the Pacific Oceans. Atlantic oysters represent about 85 percent of all domestic production. Oysters are successfully cultivated. Imports from Canada, the Orient, and Europe are also available.

Oysters are sold whole, live in the shell, frozen IQF on the half-shell, and shucked fresh. Fresh oysters should be stored in a cool, dark place, covered with wet towels. Freshwater and ice kills oysters, because they are saltwater creatures.

ATLANTIC OYSTERS

Many communities produce oysters and they are marketed under the site name. The following is a listing of the major market varieties:

BELON OYSTER
European oyster, now grown in Maine.

Season:
Winter.

Pack:
144 per case.

BLUEPOINT OYSTER
Primarily harvested off Long Island, this variety is marketed whole, live in the shell, and fresh shucked with juice.

Season:
Cultivated oysters are shipped year-round.

Pack:
Bushel or cartons for whole live oysters in the shell; many food buyers purchase them by the piece.

Count:
220 to 230 medium oysters per bushel.

Sizes:
Some packers classify Bluepoints as medium or large; others use the term *select* for large oysters.

Kitchen Yields
About 10 percent to 15 percent are wasted for various reasons.

Serving size:
6 medium-size oysters in shell. 1 cup (0.23 l) shucked is equivalent to 13 to 19 select oysters.

Calories:
Six medium-size oysters = 65 Calories.
1 cup (0.23 l) shucked oysters = 160 Calories.

CAPE BRETON OYSTER

Season:
September to January.

Count:
425 oysters per bushel.

CAPE COD OYSTER

Season:
Available year-round.

Count:
150 oysters per bushel.

CHINCOTEAGUE OYSTER
Also called *Virginia oyster*.

Season:
Winter.

Count:
240 to 250 oysters per bushel.

DELAWARE OYSTER

Season:
Winter.

Count:
300 oysters per bushel.

GARDINERS BAY OYSTER

Season:
Available year-round.

Count:
250 oysters per bushel.

GREAT SOUTH BAY OYSTER

Season:
Winter.

Count:
250 oysters per bushel.

LYNHAVEN OYSTER

Season:
Available year-round.

Count:
125 oysters per bushel.

MALPEQUE OYSTER
Wild Canadian oyster.

Season:
September to January, and late spring.

Count:
225 oysters per bushel.

POCOMOKE SOUND OYSTER
Maryland oyster.

Season:
Winter.

Count:
300 oysters per bushel.

PRINCE EDWARD ISLAND OYSTER

Season:
September to January.

Count:
225 oysters per bushel.

WELLFLEET OYSTER

Season:
Winter.

Count:
150 oysters per bushel.

WHITESTABLE OYSTER
Imported oyster from the river Thames River estuary in England.

Season:
September to February.

Count:
250 oysters per bushel.

PACIFIC OYSTERS

KUOMOMOTO OYSTER

Season:
Fall and winter.

Count:
180 oysters per bushel.

OLYMPIA OYSTER
Also called *western oyster*, this oyster is very tiny. Available whole live in shell and shucked.

Season:
Available year-round.

Count:
400 oysters in shell per bushel; 500 to 600 shucked oysters per 1-gal (3.8-l) container.

PACIFIC GOLDEN OYSTER

Season:
Available year-round.

Count:
240 oysters per bushel.

FROZEN PROCESSED OYSTERS

BREADED OYSTERS
Commercially breaded oysters are available frozen from a number of manufacturers.

Pack:
3-lb (1.4-kg) boxes.

Kitchen Yields
Sizes range from 1 to 1⅓ oz (28 to 36 g).

OYSTER CRABS

See Crabs.

OYSTER PLANT

See Salsify.

P

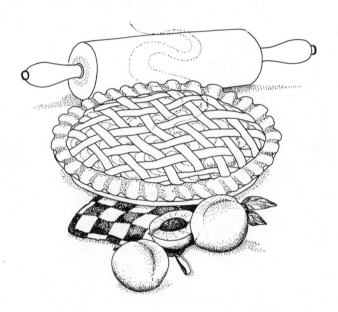

PANCAKES

See Griddle Cakes.

PAPADOM

Indian flat bread made with udad-dal flour in a number of flavors, some of them very hot.

Pack:
8¾-oz (250-g) packages.

Count:
16 to 17 pieces, each 7 in (177 mm) across.

Kitchen Yields
Papadoms must be fried quickly in very hot oil to puff up. For garnish with curry dishes, allow ½ piece per person.

PAPAYA

Also called *tree melon*, the oval to pear-shaped fruit varies greatly in size. The flesh is hard when the fruit is unripe, (indicated by green skin), but soft and very perishable when ripe (indicated by yellow skin). Papayas can reach 10 lb (4.5 kg) in some tropical countries, but Hawaiian papaya shipped to the mainland is uniform in size.

Pack:
10-lb (4.5-kg) containers.

Count:
8 to 12 fruits per container.

Kitchen Yields
Half a fruit, peeled, with seeds removed, weighs 5⅓ to 5¾ oz (150 to 160 g).

Calories:
1 cup cubed fruit, weighing 5⅓ oz (150 g) = 80 Calories.

PARSLEY

See Herbs & Spices.

PARSLEY ROOT

Also called *Hamburg parsley*, this vegetable looks like a yellow carrot and is used as a soup and stew ingredient.

Season:
Available year-round.

Pack:
By weight.

Size and Count:
Vary.

Kitchen Yields
Peeling loss is about 15 percent.

PARSNIPS

Root vegetable that tastes best when left in the ground until after the ground freezes.

Season:
October to January. A small amount is available until spring.

Pack:
25- and 50-lb (11.3- to 22.6-kg) bags; twelve 20-oz (560-g) bags.

Sizes:
Count varies. About four parsnips weigh 1 lb (450 g).

Kitchen Yields
Large parsnips can have a woody core, which reduces yields. 1 lb (450 g) fresh yields 2 cups cooked and diced.

Calories:
1 cup, or 6 oz (170 g), cooked and diced = 108 Calories.

PARTRIDGE

Chukar or Bartavelle partridge are two common varieties.

Size:
14 to 16 oz (400 to 450 g).

Kitchen Yields

Serving size:
1 bird.

PASSION FRUIT

Also called *grenadilla*. A purple-skinned fruit with yellow flesh and many edible seeds. Available from November to July.

Pack:
By weight.

Size:
3 oz (85 g), on average.

Kitchen Yields
Use the whole fruit.

Calories:
3¾ oz (100 g) = 75 Calories.

PASTA

Available canned, fresh, and dry. Canned pasta is of minor importance to foodservice and is not listed. *See also* Noodle Dough.

DRY PASTA
The quality of pasta depends on the quality of the flour used in making it. Since the base price of pasta is low, foodservice operators should only use high-quality products. There are hundreds of different pasta shapes on the market.

Pack:
1-, 10-, and 20-lb (0.45-, 4.5-, and 9-kg) boxes.

Kitchen Yields
The relation of weight to volume of cooked pasta varies according to shape and to the degree the pasta has been boiled. Large pasta such as rigatoni and rotini have a higher volume to weight ratio than do spaghetti, linguini, or elbow macaroni. Pasta cooked al dente (firm to the bite or undercooked) yields less than soft-cooked pasta.

Dry measures:
1 lb (450 g) medium size elbow macaroni equals 4 cups (0.9 l) and produces 7 cups (1.6 l) cooked pasta.
1 lb (450 g) noodles measures 7 cups (1.6 l) and produces 8 cups (1.9 l) cooked pasta.
1 lb (450 g) spaghetti produces 7 cups (1.6 l) cooked pasta.
1 lb (450 g) rotini equals 7 cups and produces 8 cups cooked pasta.

Serving sizes:
Dry pasta should be weighed for calculating portion size.
1 oz (28 g) side order.
2 oz (56 g) appetizer.
3½ to 4 oz (100g to 112 g) main course.
Typical serving sizes for cooked pasta are ½ cup (0.12 l) for side order; 1½ cup (0.35 l) for main course.

Yields for various pastas:

Elbow macaroni:
1 lb (450 g) produces 16 side-order servings or 4 main-course servings.
10 lb (4.5 kg) produce 160 side-order servings or 40 main-course servings.

Spaghetti or noodles:
1 lb (450 g) produces 16 side-order servings or 5 main-course servings.
10 lb (4.5 kg) produce 180 side-order servings or 50 main course servings.

Lasagna:
1 lb (450 g) lasagna consists of twenty-four 2¼ × 9½ in (57 × 240 mm) sheets.
1½ lb (670 g) lasagna fill one hotel pan 20 × 12 in (508 × 304 mm) with four layers.

Calories:
½ cup (0.12 l) cooked pasta without sauce = 200 Calories.

FRESH PASTA
Fresh pasta can be purchased in many shapes and flavors.

Pack:

By weight, often in 1-lb (450-g) and in 4-lb (1.8-kg) packages.

Kitchen Yields

1 lb (450 g) fresh pasta yields approximately 5 to 6 cups (1.1 to 1.2 l) cooked pasta.

1 lb (450 g) medium-size tortellini or small ravioli contains about 140 pieces.

Serving size:

For main course, 4 to 5 oz (112 to 140 g). Serving size varies according to pasta variety.

Filled fresh pastas, such as ravioli and tortellini are best calculated by the piece than by weight because the sizes vary. The fillings and dough flavors vary greatly.

PASTA DOUGH FOR RAVIOLI

Formula

    3 lb (1.3 kg) hard (bread) flour
    9 eggs
    ½ cup (0.12 l) oil
    ½ cup (0.12 l) water

Kitchen Yields

The total mix yields 4½ lb (2 kg).

PASTILLAGE

Formula

    1½ oz (42 g) plain gelatin
    6 lb (2.7 kg) confectioners sugar
    4 oz (112 g) cornstarch
    1 pint (0.47 l) warm water

Kitchen Yields

Total mix yields about 7 lb (3.1 kg)—enough to make four simple cookie stands.

PASTRY

See Danish Pastry.

PASTRY CREAM

Formula 1

    7½ qt (7 l) milk
    3½ lb (2.5 kg), or 7 cups or sugar
    36 (1 qt and 3 cups) whole eggs
    1 lb (450 g) corn starch

Kitchen Yields

Total mix yields 11 qt (10 l) or 44 cups pastry cream.

Formula 2

    10 qt (9.4 l) milk
    5 lb (2.2 kg) sugar
    50 (10 cups) whole eggs
    1 lb 6 oz (624 g) corn starch

Kitchen Yields

Total mix yields 15 qt (14 l) or 50 cups pastry cream.

PÂTE À CHOU

Also called *cream puff paste*.

Formula

    1 qt (0.94 l) milk
    1 lb (450 g) butter
    1¼ lb (560 g) patent flour
    ¼ oz (7 g) salt
    1 qt (32 oz or 0.94 l) or 20 eggs

Kitchen Yields

Total mix yields 3½ qt (3.2 l) pâte à chou.

PÂTÉ DOUGH

Formula

    3 lb 5 oz (1.5 kg) bread flour
    1 lb (450 g) shortening
    1 pint (0.47 l) warm water
    1 oz (28 g) salt

Kitchen Yields

The total mix yields 5 lb 5 oz (2.4 kg) pâté dough.

PEACHES

Available canned, dehydrated, fresh, and frozen.

CANNED PEACHES

Canned peaches are available packed in extra-heavy, heavy, or light syrup, or in water. They are packed whole, in halves, in quarters, in slices, and diced. Some varieties are marketed natural or spiced.

Pack:

#2½ and #10 cans. Many other packs are available.

Sizes:

Table P-1 identifies canned peach weights and volumes.

Counts:

For peach halves in #10 cans, counts are 25 to 30, 30 to 35, 35 to 40, and 40 to 50.

Kitchen Yields

Averages:

Halves:
#10 can: 35 to 40 pieces.
#2½ can: 10 to 12 pieces.

Slices:
#10 can: 6 lb 14 oz (4 kg) drained.
#2½: 1 lb 14 oz (840 g) drained.

Serving sizes:

Halves:
2 pieces fruit.

Table P-1 Weights and Volumes of Canned Peaches

Can Size	Net Weight	Total Contents	Drained Weight	Volume of Drained Fruit
#2½	1 lb 13 oz (820 g)	3½ cups (0.8 l)	18 oz (500 g)	2 cups (0.47 l)
#10	6 lb 12 oz (3 kg)	12 cups (2.8 l)	66 oz (1.87 kg)	8⅓ cups (1.96 l)

One #10 can yields 17 to 20 servings.
One #2½ can yields 5 to 6 servings.

Slices:
½ cup (0.12 l).
One #10 can yields 25 servings.
One #2½ can yields 7 servings.

Calories:

½ cup (0.12 l) or two halves syrup pack = 100 Calories.
½ cup (0.12 l) or two halves water pack = 38 Calories.

DEHYDRATED PEACHES

Dehydrated peaches are available as halves, pieces, dices, and slices, and as canned low-moisture slices.

Pack:

Regular dried:
10-lb (4.5-kg) lugs. Other packs are available.

Low-moisture slices:
Six #10 cans with a net weight of 3 lb (1.35 kg) each.

Count:

Varies.

Kitchen Yields

1 lb (450 g) dried peaches yields 5¼ cups (1.2 l) cooked fruit.
1 lb (450 g) low-moisture slices yield 4 cups (0.94 l) cooked fruit.

Serving size:

½ cup (0.12 l).
1 lb (450 g) dried peaches yields 10 servings; 5 lb (2.2 kg) dried peaches yield 50 servings.
1 lb (450 g) low moisture peaches yields 8 servings; 8 lb (3.6 kg) low moisture peaches yield 50 servings.

Calories:

½ cup (0.12 l) cooked, unsweetened fruit = 100 Calories.

NOTE: Calorie count for constituted dried peaches and for low-moisture peaches is about the same.

FRESH PEACHES

Two types of peaches are important: Clingstone and Freestone. Early-season fruits are often Clingstone peaches.

Season:

Domestic fresh peaches are available from late May until September, peaking in July and August. Imports are available during the winter. Many varieties are on the market.

Pack:

19- to 23-lb (8.6- to 10.3-kg) two-layer lugs with counts of 50, 56, 60, 64, 72, or 80; 17- to 18-lb (7.7- to 8.2-kg) boxes with counts of 40, 45, 50, 55, 60, or 65; 38-lb (17-kg) boxes of loose fruit in sizes of 2, 2¼, and 2½ in (51, 57, and 63 mm) diameter; 45- to 48-lb (20.2- to 21.6-kg) bushel baskets.

Common hotel size:

60-count lug.

Kitchen Yields

1 lb (450 g) is equivalent to 3 to 4 medium fruits, which yield 2 cups (0.47 l) sliced peaches or 1½ cups (0.35 l) pulp.

Calories:

One medium peach, weighing about 4 oz (112 g) with pit = 38 Calories.
½ cup (0.112 l) sliced peaches = 43 Calories.

FROZEN PEACHES

Frozen peaches are packed with approximately 25 percent sugar by weight. Available as halves and slices.

Pack:

1-gal (3.8-l) cans; 10-, 25-, and 30-lb (4.5-, 11.25-, and 13.5-kg) cans.

Serving size:

½ cup sliced peaches. One 30-lb (13.5-kg) can yields 100 servings.

Calories:

1 cup, or 9 oz (250 g), sliced and sweetened = 220 Calories.

PEARS

Available canned and fresh.

CANNED PEARS

Canned pears are available packed in extra-heavy syrup, heavy syrup, light syrup, slightly sweetened water, slightly sweetened fruit juice, or fruit juice.

Pack:

Cases of six #10 cans.

Counts:

Halves:
20 to 25, with a drained net weight of 66 oz (1.85 kg); 25 to 30, 30 to 35, 35 to 40, 40 to 45, 45 to 54, 50 to 60, or 60 to 70, each with a drained net weight of 67.5 oz (1.9 kg) or 2 qt (1.9 l).

Slices or pieces:
Drained net weight 70 oz (2 kg).

Diced:
Drained net weight 74.5 oz (2.11 kg).

Kitchen Yields

Serving sizes:

Use one #25 pear for stuffed pears; two #30 pears supply 1 portion for stewed fruit; three #35 pears supply 1 portion for pear salad.

Calories:

3½ oz (100 g) in fruit juice = 56 Calories.
3½ oz (100 g) in water = 35 Calories.
3½ oz (100 g) in light syrup = 75 Calories.
3½ oz (100 g) in heavy syrup = 92 Calories.

FRESH PEARS

Domestic pears are harvested green and ripened under controlled temperature conditions. Numerous varieties are on the market. Many pear varieties are available year-round. Table P-2 lists the seasons and primary uses of the most important varieties.

Table P-2 Pear Varieties, Availability, and Uses

Name of Variety	Peak Season	Uses
Anjou	October through May	Fresh and salads
Bartlett	August through December	Fresh and cooking
Bosc	September through May	Fresh and cooking
Comice	October through March	Fresh
Forelle	October through February	Fresh
Nelis	October through April	Fresh and cooking
Red Bartlett	August through December	Fresh and cooking
Seckel	August through January	Fresh

Pack:
44- to 46-lb (19.8- to 21.1-kg) layer-packed boxes; 36-lb (16.1-kg) cartons, tight-fill.

Counts:
70, 80, 90, 100, 110, 120, 135, 150, and 165 in layer-packed boxes. Carton counts roughly correspond to box counts and are 56, 64, 72, 80, 90, 96, 108, 120, and 125.

Sizes:
Large pear: 90 to 110 size.
Medium pear: 135 size.
Small pear: 165 size.
Not all varieties are available in all sizes.

Weights:
90 size: 8 oz (225 g).
135 size: 5½ oz (155 g).
165 size: 4½ oz (126 g).

Kitchen Yields
1 cup (0.23 l) sliced and peeled pear weighs 5½ oz (155 g). Three medium pears yield 2 cups sliced and peeled pears, and a 1-layer box of #135 pears yields 5½ gal (21 l) sliced, peeled, and cored pears.

Calories:
One whole medium pear, weighing 5½ oz (155 g) = 90 Calories.
1 cup sliced pear, weighing 5½ oz (155 g) = 90 Calories.

PEAS

Peas are available canned, dried, fresh, and frozen.

CANNED PEAS

BLACK-EYED PEAS
Black-eyed peas, closely identified with Southern cooking, are also called *cowpeas* and *black-eyed beans*. A number of varieties and combinations with other vegetables are on the market, canned.

Pack:
Six #10 cans, containing 13 cups (3 l) each.

Kitchen Yields
One #10 can contains 85 oz (2.4 kg) drained weight.

Serving size:
⅔ cups, or 4 oz (112 g); thus, one can yields 19 servings, and one case yields 115 servings.

Calories:
⅔ cups, or 4 oz (112 g) = 126 Calories.

GREEN PEAS
Canned peas are graded by size, as indicated by a sieve number. Sieve #1 is the smallest, and sieve #6 is the largest size. Many packers no longer indicate sieve size. The designation of Early or Fancy does not indicate size. Puréed peas are available from at least one packer in #303 cans.

Pack:
Six #10 cans (3.2 l) per case; twelve #303 cans (0.45 l) per case.

Kitchen Yields

Serving size:
½ cup (0.12 l). One #10 can contains 70 oz (2 kg) drained weight, and yields 18 servings. Thus, five #10 cans yield 100 servings.

Calories:
1 cup, or 6 oz (170 g) = 150 Calories.

DRIED PEAS

BLACK-EYED PEAS

Pack:
Twenty-four 1-lb (450-g) boxes; individual 25-lb (11.25-kg) bags.

Kitchen Yields
1 cup (0.24 l) weighs 7 oz (196 g).

Serving size:
½ cup (0.12 l) cooked.
1 lb (450 g) dried product yields 4½ cups (1.06 l) cooked or 9 servings.

Calories:
½ cup (0.12 l), or 4½ oz (127 g) = 95 Calories.

WHOLE AND SPLIT DRIED PEAS
Dried peas are classified as green or mature yellow peas. In most cases, the outer skin is removed during the drying process, and the peas split into two natural halves.

Pack:
Twenty-four 1-lb (450-g) boxes; individual 25-lb (11.25-kg) bags.

Kitchen Yields
1 lb (450 g) dried product is equivalent to 2¼ cups (0.5 l).

Serving size:
½ cup (0.23 l), cooked.
1 lb (450 g) produces 5 cups (1.1 l), cooked, or 10 servings; therefore, 10 lb (4.5 kg) produces 50 cups (11.75 l) or 100 servings.

Calories:
1 cup, or 7 oz (200 g), cooked = 230 Calories.

FRESH PEAS

BLACK-EYED PEAS
Available shelled.

Season:
Mid- to late summer.

Pack:
By weight.

Kitchen Yields

Serving size:
⅔ cups, or 3⅞ oz (108 g).

Calories:
⅔ cups, or 3⅞ oz (108 g) = 120 Calories.

GREEN PEAS
Green peas have large pods that must be shelled and discarded. The actual size of the peas can be seen through the pod, because they bulge out. The sizes of the kernels in a pack vary greatly; and for this reason, unshelled peas are seldom used in the food industry. Peas must be very fresh when used.

Season:
Available year-round, with peak in early summer.

Pack:
10- and 30-lb (4.5- and 13.5-kg) lugs.

Kitchen Yields

Waste:
1 lb (450 g) as purchased produces 10½ oz (300 g) loss.

Serving size:
⅔ cup, or 3⅝ oz (100 g).
1 lb (450 g) as purchased yields 1 cup, or 5½ oz (155 g) shelled peas. One 30-lb (13.5 kg) carton produces 30 cups (15 pints or 7 l) or 10 lb (4.5 kg) shelled peas, which yields 40 servings.

Calories:
1 cup, or 5¾ oz (160 g), cooked and drained = 110 Calories.

SNOW PEAS

Also called *mange tout*, snow peas are a cross between green peas and sugar snap peas.

Season:

Available year-round. Peak is in January to February and July to August.

Pack:

10- and 30-lb (4.5- and 13.6-kg) cartons.

Kitchen Yields

Serving size:

1¼ oz (35 g); 1 lb (450 g) yields 12 servings.

Waste:

Cleaning loss by weight is 5 percent.

SUGAR SNAP PEAS

Like snow peas, sugar snap peas are served whole; only the ends must be snapped off.

Season:

February to September.

Pack:

10- and 30-lb (4.5- and 13.6-kg) cartons.

Kitchen Yields

Serving size:

½ cup (0.11 l) or 2½ oz (71 g) untrimmed.
1 lb (450 g) contains approximately 120 pieces, which yield 6 portions.

Waste:

Trimming loss is 5 percent by weight.

FROZEN PEAS

BLACK-EYED PEAS

Frozen while still tender and green.

Pack:

Twelve 3-lb (1.35-kg) boxes; 20-lb (9.07-kg) bulk pack.

Kitchen Yields

Serving size:

½ cup cooked. 10 lb (4.5 kg) yields 110 servings.

Calories:

½ cup (0.12 l) = 80 Calories.

GREEN PEAS

Peas are graded by size and tenderness. They are marketed as Petit Peas, Small Peas, and under a number of other names. Size is an important quality factor. They are also on the market mixed with either pearl onions or cubed carrots.

Pack:

Twelve 2½-lb (1.12-kg) boxes; individual 20-lb (9.1-kg) cartons.

Kitchen Yields

Serving size:

½ cup cooked.
One 20-lb (9-kg) carton yields 100 servings.

Calories:

½ cup, or 3 oz (85 g) = 60 Calories.

SNOW PEAS

Frozen snow peas are now available. They overcook easily and loose crispness unless served right away.

Pack:

Twelve 2-lb (940-g) packages.

Kitchen Yields

Serving size:

3½ oz (100 g), as purchased; thus, one 2-lb (940-g) package yields 10 servings.

Calories:

3½ oz (100 g) = 55 Calories.

SUGAR SNAP PEAS

Sugar snap peas make a very practical banquet vegetable.

Pack:

Twelve 32-oz (900-g) bags, IQF.

Kitchen Yields

Serving size:
3½ oz (100 g), as purchased; thus, one 32-oz (900-g) bag yields 8 to 9 servings.

Calories:
3½ oz (100 g) = 50 Calories.

PECANS

Available shelled and in the shell. Pecan halves are graded by size; pieces are not graded by size.

Pack:
By weight.

Sizes:
Table P-3 lists pecan grades and numbers per 1 lb (450 g).

Kitchen Yields
1 cup (0.23 l) pecan halves weighs 4 oz (112 g).

PEPPERS

HOT PEPPERS
See Chiles, under Mexican Foods.

SWEET PEPPERS (BELL PEPPERS)
Available canned, often (under the name pimento), fresh, and frozen. Pickled red or green peppers are delicatessen items and are available in jars.

Table P-3 Pecan Grades and Numbers

Name	Numbers per 1 lb (450 g)
Mammoth	200 to 250
Junior Mammoth	251 to 300
Jumbo	301 to 350
Extra Large	351 to 450
Large	451 to 550
Medium	551 to 600

CANNED SWEET PEPPERS
Green and red peppers, normally diced.

Pack:
Six #10 cans. Other packs are available.

Kitchen Yields
One #10 can contains 70 oz (1.9 kg) drained, or 8 cups (1.8 l).

FRESH SWEET PEPPERS
Most sweet peppers are sold in the immature stage, which is green. All peppers turn red or yellow when they mature. A number of varieties have been developed, including red, yellow, purple, brown, and white. Some are imports from Holland and from Mexico. Some peppers loose their colors when cooked. The market differentiates between Choice and Fancy grades. The prices of colored peppers vary greatly according to season. Red sweet peppers are cheap and plentiful when in season, but can command a premium price when out of season.

Season:
Available year-round. Peak season is from July to October. Domestic red peppers are most plentiful in fall. Mexican peppers are available in winter in both green and red. Hothouse-grown peppers are European imports and are available year-round.

Pack:
26- to 30-lb (11.7- to 13.5-kg) bushels; 10-lb (4.5-kg) cartons. Specialty colored peppers should be purchased by weight.

Count:
Varies greatly. About 5 pieces per 1 lb (450 g).

Kitchen Yields
For chopping purchase Choice; for other applications, purchase Fancy.

Waste:
Cleaning loss is 20 percent by weight.
Ten medium peppers yield 5 cups (1.17 l) diced; 20 lb (9 kg) yield 40 cups diced and cooked.

Calories:
1 cup, or 4 oz (112 g), raw and diced = 28 Calories.

FROZEN SWEET PEPPERS

Green and red sweet peppers are available diced and in strips.

Pack:
Twelve 2½-lb (1.1-kg) packages.

Kitchen Yields
2½-lb (1.1-kg) package yields 9 cups (2.1 l).

PERSIMMONS

Two varieties of persimmons are marketed. The Fuyu persimmon has orange-colored skin and flesh. It should be eaten while still firm. The whole fruit is edible. The Hachiya variety is more pointed than the Fuyu variety and should be eaten when soft. Both varieties are used in salads and as a fruit garnish.

Season:
Fall and early winter.

Pack:
Flats with 24 or 30 fruits.

Kitchen Yields
1 fruit yields 4 oz (112 g) edible flesh.

Calories:
4 oz (112 g) edible flesh = 90 Calories.

PESTO

Pesto is an Italian pasta sauce made with basil. Prepared pesto sauce is available under a number of brand names. Since the supply and price of fresh basil varies according to season, it is often advisable to purchase a high-quality frozen pesto sauce.

Formula
>10 cups (2.25 l) basil leaves
>1 cup (0.23 l) chopped garlic
>2 cups (0.47 l) pine nuts
>3 cups (0.7 l) grated Parmesan cheese
>3 cups (0.7 l) olive oil

Kitchen Yields
The total mix yields 12 cups of pesto.

Serving size:
3 tb pesto with 1 cup cooked pasta. Therefore, the preceding formula yields pesto for 64 servings.

PHEASANT

This game bird in the poultry family has white meat and is available fresh or frozen. The birds develop their distinct flavor only by aging in their feathers.

Season:
Available year-round, because birds are farm-raised.

Average sizes:
15 to 18 oz (420 to 500 g); 20 oz (570 g); 1¾ to 2 lb (0.8 to 0.9 kg); 2 to 2½ lb (0.9 to 1.1 kg); 2½ to 3 lb (1.1 to 1.35 kg).

Kitchen Yields

Serving sizes:
15- to 18-oz (420- to 500-g) whole birds.
2-lb (0.9-kg) whole birds, when serving half-birds.
3-lb (1.35-kg) whole birds, when serving breast only.

SMOKED PHEASANT

Smoked pheasant is available as whole bird or as breasts in some markets.

Sizes:
For whole birds, 2¼ to 2¾ lb (1 to 1.2 kg).

PIE

CANNED PIE FILLING

Available are most fruit fillings, ready for baking.

Pack:
Six #10 cans.

Kitchen Yields
Varies, depending on fruit variety. One #10 can yields, on average, five 9-in (228-mm) pies.

PIE DOUGH

Formula
>3 lb (1.35 kg) pastry flour
>2 lb (900 g) shortening

1 pint, or 2 cups (0.47 l), cold water
1 oz, or 2 tb (28 g) salt

Kitchen Yields
Ten 9-in (228-mm) pie shells.

PINEAPPLE

Available canned, fresh, and fresh processed.

CANNED PINEAPPLE
Available sliced, in chunks, in tidbits, coarse-crushed, fine-crushed, and in broken slices. Most items are packed in choice of heavy syrup, light syrup, or juice.

Pack:
Six #10 cans. Table P-4 lists counts and weights for #10 cans of pineapple in different styles.

Table P-4 Counts and Weights for Canned Pineapple

Product Name	Can Weight	Drained Weight	Count
Sliced	108 oz (3.06 kg)		52
Sliced	108 oz (3.06 kg)		66
Sliced	108 oz (3.06 kg)		100 to 110
Chunks	109 oz (3.09 kg)	66 oz (1.87 kg)	
Small tidbits	108 oz (3.06 kg)	70 oz (2 kg)	
Coarse crushed	107 oz (3.03 kg)	90 oz (2.5 kg)	
Fine crushed	107 oz (3.03 kg)	90 oz (2.5 kg)	
Broken slices	107 oz (3.03 kg)	63 oz (1.8 kg)	

Kitchen Yields

Servings sizes:

Chunks:
4½ oz (126 g); therefore, one #10 can yields 22 servings.

Large slices:
1 slice; therefore, one #10 can yields 52 or 66 servings.

Small slices:
2 slices; therefore, one #10 can yields 50 to 55 servings.

Calories:
1 cup, or 9 oz (250 g) chunks in heavy syrup = 190 Calories.
1 large 3⅝-oz (105-g) slice, with 2¼ tb syrup = 80 Calories.

FRESH PINEAPPLE
Fruit should be picked almost ripe, and ripeness of fruit is difficult to judge. For this reason, brand is important. Domestic and imported fruit come to the market at various times. Baby pineapples, about 2½ to 3 in (63 to 76 mm) tall are available from Hawaii. They are used primarily for decorative purposes.

Season:
Available year-round. Peak is in April and May.

Pack:
20-lb (9.1-kg) half cartons; 40-lb (18.2-kg) full cartons.

Counts:

Half cartons:
4, 5, 6, or 7.

Full cartons:
8, 9, 10, 12, 14, 15, 16, or 18.

Kitchen Yields

Common hotel sizes:
#5 for salads; #14 for appetizer baskets.
One medium pineapple weighs 4 lb (1.8 kg) and yields 5½ cups diced pineapple.

One #5 pineapple yields 1⅓ lb (0.585 g) clean meat, which amounts to 17 slices when sliced with machine at #34 or to 68 sliced quarters.

Calories:

1 cup, or 5½ oz (156 g), raw and diced = 80 Calories.

FRESH PROCESSED PINEAPPLE

Available are chilled fresh pineapple chunks.

Pack:

5-lb (2.25-kg) pouches.

Counts:

Wedges:
23 to 32.

Spears:
10 to 12.

Tidbits:
139 to 153.

Kitchen Yields

Use in fruit salads. There is little juice in packages.

Calories:

4 oz (112 g) = 90 Calories.

PINEAPPLE JUICE

Available canned and fresh, sweetened and unsweetened.

Pack:

Forty-eight 6-oz (0.17-l) cans; twelve 46-oz (1.35-l) cans.

Kitchen Yields

6 oz (0.17 l) per serving; therefore, one 46-oz (1.35-l) can yields 7½ servings.
For fresh juice, one medium #5 pineapple yields 2½ cups (0.6 l) juice.

Calories:

6 oz (0.19 l) unsweetened = 110 Calories.

PINE NUTS

Also called *pignoli nuts*. Available shelled.

Pack:

By weight.

Kitchen Yield

1 cup dry measure weighs 5 oz (140 g).

PISTACHIOS

Available in the shell (often dyed red) and shelled. The shelled nuts can be purchased raw or roasted, salted or unsalted. They are usually still covered with a thin skin, which can be removed from raw nuts by blanching them with boiling water.

Pack:

Shelled nuts:
#10 cans with a net weight of 3½ to 4 lb (1.5 to 1.8 kg) each. 25-lb (11.25-kg) cartons.

Unshelled nuts:
By weight.

Kitchen Yields

1 lb (450 g) shelled nuts is equivalent to 6½ cups.

PITA BREAD

Flat round bread of Middle Eastern origin that forms a pocket inside.

Pack:

Plastic bags of 10 or 12 pieces.

Size:

2 oz (56 g) each, with a diameter of about 7 in (177 mm).

Kitchen Yields

One piece per person for sandwich. Product freezes well.

PIZZA

HOME-MADE PIZZA INGREDIENTS

PIZZA DOUGH

Formula

    50 lb (22.5 kg) high-gluten flour
    2 gal + 3 pint (9 l) water
    1 cup, or 8 oz (225 g), oil
    1 cup, or 8 oz (225 g), salt
    ½ cup, or 4 oz (112 g), sugar
    8 oz (224 g) fresh yeast

Kitchen Yields

The total mix yields 70 large 16-in (400-mm) pies scaled at 1 lb (450 g), or 110 medium 9-in (23-cm) pies, scaled at 10 oz (285 g), or 400 hors d'oeuvre pies, scaled at 1¾ oz (78 g).

PIZZA SAUCE

Formula

    Five #10 cans tomato sauce
    Three #10 cans crushed tomatoes
    One #10 can tomato ketchup
    ½ cup (0.12 l) oregano

Kitchen Yields

12 oz (0.7 l) sauce for one 16-in (400-mm) pie. The total mix yields sauce for 75 large pies.

PROCESSED PIZZA INGREDIENTS

FROZEN PIZZA CRUST

Frozen pizza crust is available as par-baked crust, and frozen and unbaked sheeted dough.

PAR-BAKED PIZZA CRUST

Sizes and packs:

Round:

Twenty-four 16-in (400-mm) pie crusts; twenty-four 15-in (375-mm) pie crusts; twenty-four or thirty 12-in (300-mm) pie crusts; thirty 10-in (250-mm) pie crusts; twenty-four or thirty 9-in (225-mm) pie crusts; sixty 6½-in (184-mm) pie crusts; one hundred twenty 5½-in (156-mm) pie crusts.

Rectangular:

Twenty-four 8- × 12-in (200- × 300-mm) pie crusts; twenty or twenty-four 9- × 10-in (225- × 250-mm) pie crusts; twenty 12- × 16-in (300- × 400-mm) pie crusts.

SHEETED DOUGH

Same sizes as par-baked crust.

Kitchen Yields

Common size for large pie is 16 in (400 mm). This requires a 14-oz (400-g) or 16-oz (450-g) crust. Individual pies are often scaled at 8 oz (225 g) dough.

PIZZA CHEESE

Mozzarella cheese is normally used.

Pack:

5- to 6-lb (2.2- to 2.7-kg) loaves; 20-lb (9-kg) loaves; 40-lb (18-kg) block; six 4-lb (1.8-kg) bags, shredded cheese.

Kitchen Yields

1 lb (450 g) cheese provides topping for one 16-in (40-0-mm) pie.
10 oz (280 g) cheese provides topping for one 10-in (25-cm) pie.

MOZZARELLA, FEATHERED

Shaved mozzarella cheese which is lighter than regular grated mozzarella cheese. As little as 5 oz (140 g) can be used to cover one 16-in (400-mm) pie.

PIZZA DOUGH BALLS

Available fresh and frozen.

Sizes:

4 oz (112 g), 6 oz (170 oz), 8 oz (224 g), 10 oz (280 g), 12 oz (340 g), 14 oz (400 g), 16 oz (450 g), 20 oz (570 g), and 22 oz (625 g).

Packs:

Twenty-four 22-oz (625-g) dough balls; twenty-four 20-oz (570-g) dough balls; twenty-four 16-oz (450-g) dough balls; forty 10-oz (280-g) dough balls; smaller sizes packed 48 dough balls per carton.

PIZZA SAUCE

Pack:
Six #10 cans.

Kitchen Yields

Serving size:
1½ cups (0.35 l) sauce for one 16-in (400-mm) pie.
One #10 can yields sauce for eight 16-in (400-mm) pies.

READY-TO-BAKE PIZZA
Ready-to-bake pizzas are available in many sizes.

Sizes and packs:
Forty-eight 4- × 6-in (100- × 150-mm) pies; forty-eight 4- × 6-in (100- × 150-mm) pies with extra cheese; forty-eight 4- × 5-in (100- × 125-mm) pies. Other packs and sizes are available.

PLANTAINS

Called *platanos* in Spanish, they are cooking bananas. The color ranges from green to dark yellowish brown (which indicates maturity).

Season:
Imports are available year-round.

Pack:
48-lb (21.6 kg) cartons.

Size:
Average 8 to 10 oz (225 to 285 g) each.

Kitchen Yields

Waste:
Peeling loss about 20 percent.

Serving size:
4 oz (112 g).

Calories:
8 oz (225 g) = 355 Calories.

PLUMS

Available canned and fresh.

CANNED PLUMS
Available canned varieties include Purple, Green Gage, Yellow Egg, and others, whole and in halves. Whole plums are usually not pitted. Canned plums may be packed in heavy syrup, light syrup, or in water pack.

Pack:
Six #10 cans; twenty-four #2½ cans; twenty-four #2 cans.

Kitchen Yields

Drained weights:

Whole plums:
#10 can weighs 60 oz (1.7 kg).
#2½ can weighs 15½ oz (440 g).
#2 can weighs 10½ oz (300 g).

Plum halves:
#10 can weighs 63 oz (1.8 kg).
#2½ can weighs 16¼ oz (460 g).
#2 can weighs 12 oz (340 g).

Serving size:
½ cup. One #10 can yields 16 servings, and one #2½ can yields 6 servings.

DRIED PLUMS
See Prunes.

FRESH PLUMS
The are two major varieties, Freestone and Clingstone. The Clingstone variety is marketed as plum for eating fresh, while the Freestone variety is marketed as fresh prune.

Varieties (by color):

> *Purple:* Italian or French, Damson.
> *Red:* Clayman, Climax, Hungarian, Santa Rosa, Beauty.
> *Yellow or green:* Yellow Egg, Wickson, Kelsey, Green Gage.

Season:
Domestic supplies peak during the summer and early fall. Various domestic and imported varieties are available year-round. Italian plums are available from late August to October.

Pack:
28-lb (12.7-kg) cartons or lugs.

Count:
Differs, depending on variety. Yellow Egg plums can be as large as 2 in (50 mm) across, while Damson plums can be as small as cherries.

Kitchen Yields

Quantities:

Large plums:
4 to 5 per 1 lb (450 g).

Small plums:
8 to 10 per 1 lb (450 g).

Calories:
4 oz (112 g) edible flesh = 50 Calories.

POLENTA

Polenta is yellow corn meal mush, sometimes flavored with grated Parmesan cheese.

Formula
    3 cups (0.7 l) coarse corn meal
    6 cups (1.4 l) chicken stock
    4 oz (112 g) butter
    ¼ cup (0.05 l) heavy cream
    Salt, nutmeg, and grated cheese to taste

Kitchen Yields

Serving size:
½ cup (0.12 l). The total mix yields 10 cups or 20 servings.

POMEGRANATES

Red-skinned fruit, used mostly in the manufacture of grenadine syrup.

Season:
August to December.

Pack:
22-lb (9.9-kg) lug.

Size and count:
3 to 4 in (80 to 120 mm) across.

Kitchen Yields
Primary use is for flavoring sauces and syrups, because numerous seeds are imbedded in the flesh.

Calories:
4 oz (112 g) edible flesh = 90 Calories.

POPCORN

Many different brands are available. Smaller kernels make better tasting popcorn than larger kernels. Natural blue popcorn and black popcorn have come on the market.

Pack:
By weight.

Kitchen Yields
Yield varies, as high-quality popcorn gives better yield than cheaper popcorn.
¼ cup (0.05 l) dry measure weighs 2 oz (56 g) and makes 9 to 10 cups (2 to 2.25 l) popped corn.
1 cup (0.23 l) dry measure weighs 8 oz (224 g) and makes 2¼ to 2½ gal (8.3 to 9.2 l) popped corn.

Calories:
2 oz (56 g), without fat, 9 to 10 cups popped = 220 Calories.
2 oz (56 g), with ⅔ oz (19 g) oil, 9 to 10 cups popped = 386 Calories.

POPOVERS

    24 whole eggs
    3 lb (1.35 kg) bread flour or 3 qts (2.8 l)
    2½ qt (2.25 l) milk
    1 oz (56 g), or 2 tb salt
    Nutmeg to taste
    Fat to fill muffin tins about one-quarter full

NOTE: Fat must be very hot when batter is poured in. Bake at 425°F.

Kitchen Yields
The total mix yields 60 pieces.

PORK

Pork products generally come from animals under 1 year of age, and for this reason all cuts are relatively tender. Pork parts are not graded, although the carcass is. Selection #1 is normally used for foodservice. For the sake of clarity, the *Meat Buyers Guide* (MBG) identification numbers established by the National Association of Meat Purveyors are used with some items.

LARGER CUTS OF PORK

BACK RIBS, MBG #422
Rib bones, with some loin meat still attached.

Weight ranges:
Under 1½ lb (0.6 kg).
1½ to 3 lb (0.6 to 1.35 kg).
Over 3 lb (1.35 kg).
Ribs weighing more than 3 lb (1.35 kg) can be tough.

Kitchen Yields

Serving size:
1 lb (450 g).

BUTT, MBG #406
Called the *Boston butt*, it is a piece from the shoulder, with the blade bone in.

Sizes:
4 to 8 lb (1.8 to 3.6 kg).
8 to 12 lb (3.6 to 5.4 kg).

Kitchen Yields
Meat for roasts, stews, or for use as ground pork.

Best size:
7 lb (3.1 kg).

Boned and trimmed:
6 lb (2.7 kg).

CAUL FAT
Thin, net-like covering of the lower part of the intestines; available fresh or salted. Keep caul fat in water in refrigerator.

Pack:
Sold by weight.

HAM, BONED AND NETTED, MBG #202B
Boneless ham, with all skin removed.

Sizes:
6 to 8 lb (2.7 to 3.6 kg).
8 to 10 lb (3.6 to 4.5 kg).
10 to 12 lb (4.5 to 5.4 kg).

Kitchen Yields
Smaller hams are generally leaner and easier to slice than larger ones.

Best size:
7 lb (3.1 kg).

Serving size:
6 oz (170 g) roast ham for main course, or 5 oz for sandwich meat. One 7-lb (3.1-kg) roast will yield 12 to 14 main-course servings, 15 to 16 sandwich servings.

HAM REGULAR, SHORT SHANK, MBG #401A
Basic ham with shank cut short.

Weight ranges:
10 to 14 lb (4.5 to 6.3 kg).
14 to 17 lb (6.3 to 7.6 kg).
17 to 20 lb (7.6 to 9.0 kg).

Kitchen Yields

Best size:
14 lb (6.3 kg).

Serving size:
6 oz (170 g) roast ham; thus, one 14-lb (6.3-kg) ham yields 16 to 20 servings.

HAM, SKINNED, SHORT SHANK, MBG #402A
Same items at regular ham, but skin and underlying fat is partly removed.

Kitchen Yields
The removed skin and fat accounts for about 8 to 10 percent of weight.

Best size:
12 lb (5.4 kg).

KNUCKLES

Average size:
12 oz (340 g).

Kitchen Yields

Serving size:
One knuckle.

LIVER

Weights:
3 to 4 lb (1.3 to 1.8 kg).

LOIN, MBG #410
Full split loin, including tenderloin and blade.

Weight ranges:
10 to 14 lb (4.5 to 6.3 kg).
14 to 17 lb (6.3 to 7.6 kg).
17 to 20 lb (7.6 to 9 kg).

Kitchen Yields

Serving size:
4 oz (112 g) cooked.

Best size:
12 lb (5.4 kg).
1 lb (450 g) as purchased yields 8 oz (225 g) bone-less cooked meat. One 12-lb (5.4-kg) loin roasted whole yields 8 lb (3.60 kg) raw boneless meat, or 20 boneless servings.

LOIN, BONELESS, MBG #413
Full loin, including end pieces, but fully boned.

Weight ranges:
6 to 8 lb (2.7 to 3.6 kg).
8 to 10 lb (3.6 to 4.5 kg).
10 to 12 lb (4.5 to 5.4 kg).

Kitchen Yields
Use boneless loin for roasting whole.

Serving size:
4 oz (112 g) cooked.

Best size:
8 lb (3.6 kg).
One 8-lb (3.6-kg) loin, yields 19 servings.

LOIN, CENTER CUT, MBG #412

Weight ranges:
4 to 6 lb (1.8 to 2.7 kg).
6 to 8 lb (2.7 to 3.6 kg).
8 to 10 lb (3.6 to 4.5 kg).

Kitchen Yields
Purchase this cut when there is no use for trimmings.

Best size:
8 lb (3.6 kg).
One 8-lb (3.6-kg) loin yields 6 lb (2.7 kg) raw boned meat.

RIBS, COUNTRY-STYLE, MBG #423
Basically a loin chop from the shoulder end, with chine bone removed, cut horizontally into two pieces—one piece containing the feather bones, the other containing piece the ribs.

Weight ranges:
1 to 2 lb (0.45 to 0.9 kg).
2 to 4 lb (0.9 to 1.8 kg).
4 lb (1.8 kg) and up.

Kitchen Yields

Serving size:
1 lb (450 g) and up.

SHOULDER HOCKS, MBG #417
Weights range upward from ½ lb (225 g).

SHOULDER, SKINNED, MBG #404
This is a bone-in shoulder, with most of the fat removed.

Weight ranges:
8 to 12 lb (3.6 to 5.4 kg).
12 to 16 lb (5.4 to 7.2 kg).
16 to 20 lb (7.2 to 9.0 kg).

Kitchen Yields
Use for stew meat and ground meat. For roasting, purchase Boston butt instead of whole shoulder.

Best size:

12 lb (5.4 kg).

12 lb (5.4 kg) skinned shoulder yields 7 lb (3.1 kg) boned meat, with skin, shank, and most fat removed.

Serving size:

For roast, 5 oz (142 g) roasted; thus, one shoulder, boned and tied, yields 12 lb (5.4 kg), as purchased, yields 15 servings. For stew, 8 oz (225 g) raw, or 5½ oz (156 g) cooked; thus, one 12-lb (5.4-kg) shoulder, as purchased, yields 16 servings.

SPARERIBS, MBG #416

Ribs from belly and breast.

Weight ranges:

1½ to 3 lb (0.6 to 1.35 kg).

3 to 5 lb (1.3 to 2.2 kg).

5 lb (2.2 kg) and up.

Kitchen Yields

Available as spareribs, breast off, MBG #416A, the weights are about 10 to 16 oz (280 to 450 g) less.

Serving size:

1 lb (450 g) and up.

SUCKLING PIG

Weights vary from 8 to 40 lb (3.6 to 18 kg).

Kitchen Yields

Best sizes:

Roasted whole pig for buffet:

25 to 30 lb (11.25 to 13.5 kg).

NOTE: This size pig will still fit in a convection oven.

Servings:

15 to 20 main-course servings, or 40 to 50 appetizer servings on buffet, from a 25- to 30-lb (11.25 to 13.5 kg) pig. Purchase 10-lb (4.5-kg) pigs for making galantine.

TENDERLOINS, MBG #415

Most commonly available frozen.

Weight ranges:

4 to 8 oz (112 to 225 g).

8 to 12 oz (225 to 340 g).

12 to 16 oz (340 to 450 g).

Kitchen Yields

Very little trim is needed. Roast or braise whole, or cut into small medallions.

Serving size:

Varies. For braising whole, use 8 to 10 oz (225 to 340 g) raw weight per person.

TRIMMINGS

Trimmings are available 90 and 80 percent lean. Good buy when making sausages.

POPULAR PORK DISHES

BARBECUED SPARE RIBS

Purchase Spareribs, MBG #416 (ribs from belly and breast), or Back Ribs, MBG #422 (rib bones with some loin meat still attached).

Best weights:

1½ to 3 lb (0.6 to 1.35 kg) for Spareribs, MBG #416; 1½ lb (1.35 kg) Back Ribs, MBG #422.

Kitchen Yields

Serving size:

1½ lb (675 g) raw weight, which yields 1 lb (450 g) cooked weight.

10-lb (4.5-kg) ribs yield 7 servings.

BROILED CHOPS

Purchase Loin, Center Cut, MBG #412.

Best weight:

8 lb (3.6 kg).

Kitchen Yields

Serving size:

Two chops, 5 oz (140 g) each, with only rib bones still attached.

One 8-lb (3.6-kg) loin yields 10 servings.

ROAST FRESH HAM

Purchase Ham, Boned and Netted, MBG #202B (boneless ham, with all skin removed).

Best size:
7 lb (3.1 kg).

Kitchen Yields
Smaller hams are generally leaner and easier to slice than larger pieces.

Serving sizes:
6 oz (170 g) roast ham for main course, or 5 oz (140 g) for sandwich meat.
One 7-lb (3.1-kg) ham yields 12 main-course servings, or 16 sandwich-meat servings

Calories:
6 oz (170 g) = 620 Calories.

ROAST FRESH SHOULDER
Purchase Butt, MBG #406. Also called *Boston butt* (piece from the shoulder, with the blade bone in).

Best weight:
7 lb (3.1 kg).

Kitchen Yields

Serving size:
6 oz (170 g) cooked meat.
One 7-lb (3.1-kg) butt yields 10 to 12 servings.

Calories:
6 oz (170 g) = 640 Calories.

ROAST LOIN
Purchase Loin, Boneless, MBG #413 (full loin, including end pieces, but fully boned).

Best size:
8 lb (3.6 kg).

Kitchen Yields

Serving size:
6 oz (170 g) cooked meat.
One 8-lb (3.6-kg) loin yields 16 servings.

PORTION CUTS OF PORK

BUTT STEAKS
Available bone-in and boneless. This is rather fatty meat.

Weight ranges:
4, 5, 6, and 8 oz (112, 142, 170, and 225 g).

Kitchen Yields
Braise with vegetables or with sauerkraut.

Serving size:
6 oz (170 g) raw weight.

CHOPS
Available in many sizes and configurations.

BONE-IN CHOPS:
Cut across the loin, with all bones still attached, starting at shoulder end. These are the least expensive chops.

Weights:
3, 4, 5, and 6 oz (85, 112, 142, and 170 g).

Serving size:
Two 4-oz (112-g) chops.

BONELESS CHOPS:
Cut from the boned full loin, from end to end.

Weights:
3, 4, 5, 6, and 8 oz (85, 112, 142, 170, and 225 g).

Serving size:
Varies.

CENTER-CUT CHOPS:
Available with or without the chine bone removed; and also available completely boneless. The completely boneless chops are the most expensive cuts.

Weights:
3, 4, 5, 6, and 8 oz (85, 112, 142, 170, and 225 g).

Serving size:
Varies.

CHOPS WITH POCKET:
Available as rib chops, or cut from the full loin. Rib chops have the incision made at the rib bone; the other chops have the incision made from the outside.

Weights:
5, 6, and 8 oz (142, 170, and 225 g).

Serving size:

One 6- or 8-oz (170- or 225-g) chop, stuffed.

SMOKED AND CURED PORK PRODUCTS

BACON

CANADIAN BACON

Cured and smoked boneless loin. Genuine
Canadian bacon is a product is its natural shape.
There is also a pressed and rolled product of the
same name on the market.

Weights:

Imported:
5 to 7 lb (2.2 to 3.1 kg).

Roll:
7 to 9 lb (3.1 to 4 kg).
Canadian bacon is also available sliced, in packages
of various sizes.

Kitchen Yields
The imported product is packaged on top of a thin
wooden board. Waste and trim loss amount to about
5 percent. The rolled product has very little waste.

Serving size:
Two 2-oz (56-g) slices, or 4 oz (112 g) total.
6 lb (2.7 kg) imported product yields 24 servings.
8 lb (3.6 kg) rolled product yields 30 servings/

IRISH BACON
Rolled belly bacon.

PANCETTA
Italian rolled bacon; used for cooking or eaten
uncooked.

Weight:
4½ lb (2 kg).

SLICED BACON

Pack:
10-, 12-, and 15-lb (4.5-, 5.4-, and 6.7-kg) boxes.
Other sizes are available. Layout bacon is placed on
oven-proof parchment paper.

Counts:

Regular bacon:
1 lb (450 g) consisting of 16 to 18 slices.
1 lb (450 g) consisting of 18 to 22 slices.

Special lean (no shrink):
1 lb (450 g) consisting of 30 slices.

Precooked:
1 lb (450 g) consisting of 50 slices.

Kitchen Yields

Serving sizes:
For breakfast, three slices regular bacon, 1 lb (450 g)
16 to 18 size bacon yields 5½ servings; 9 lb (4 kg)
yields 50 servings; and 18 lb (8.1 kg) yields 100
portions. 1 lb (450 g) 18 to 22 size bacon yields 6½
portions; 8 lb (3.6 kg) yields 50 portions; and
15½ lb (7 kg) yields 100 portions.
For salad garnish, three 18 to 22 size slices regular
bacon. This equals 1 oz (28 g) cooked bacon. 3¾ lb
(1.7 kg) uncooked bacon yield 25 servings.
For pasta, such as carbonara, 4 slices 18 to 22 size
regular bacon. This equals 1⅓ oz (37 g) cooked
bacon. 5 lb (2.2 kg) uncooked bacon provides
bacon for 25 servings of pasta carbonara.

Other yields:

1 lb (450 g) raw bacon equals 5 oz (140 g) cooked;
1 cup crisp bacon bits, chopped fine, weighs 4 oz
(112 g); 13 oz (364 g) raw bacon yield 1 cup (0.23 l)
chopped bits; 5 lb (2.25 kg) raw bacon yield 6 cups
bacon bits.

Calories:

16 to 18 size:
Three crisp 1-oz (28-g) slices = 175 Calories.

18 to 22 size:
Three crisp ¾-oz (21-g) slices = 130 Calories.

WHOLE OR SLAB BACON
Normally sold with skin on.

Purchase:
By weight.

Kitchen Yields
Trimming waste is about 5 percent.
Use for garnishes, or slice thick for special applications.

BOLOGNA (MORTADELLA)
See Sausages, under this same heading.

BRATWURST
White sausage, with smooth filling. Bratwurst with coarse filling is normally sold as Italian sausage. German bratwurst is also made with veal.

Pack:
10-lb (4.5-kg) cartons.

Count:
Forty 4-oz (112-g) pieces.

Kitchen Yields

Serving size:
One 4-oz (112-g) sausage.

BUTTS
Smoked boneless butts.

Weight range:
1½ to 2½ lb (0.6 to 1.1 kg).

Kitchen Yields
Shrinkage after boiling is 20 percent. Excellent braised with root vegetables, cabbage, or sauerkraut.

FATBACK
Available fresh (called *green*) or salted. The product is also called *larding pork*.

Weight range:
12 to 14 lb (5.4 to 6.3 kg).

Kitchen Yields
Weight of skin is about 8 to 10 percent of total weight. When product is used for pâté, make sure to specify unsalted fat back.

HAM

CANNED HAM
Available in natural shape, square shape, and rectangular shape (called *pullman ham*) in many quality levels, ranging from very lean to fatty. Pullman ham is available in 4 × 4 in (100 × 100 mm) blocks—the standard size of sandwich bread.

Sizes:
Vary greatly according to manufacturers.

Kitchen Yields
Basically there is very little waste.

Serving size:
3 to 4 oz (85 to 112 g) for sandwiches.

Calories:
4 oz (112 g) very lean = 260 Calories.

COOKED HAM
Boneless ham, fully cooked and wrapped. This ham is often used as breakfast ham. A number of manufacturers produce hams under trade names.

Sizes:
7 to 10 lb (3.1 to 4.5 kg).

Kitchen Yields

Trimming waste:
5 percent on most brands.

Serving sizes:
3 to 4 oz (85 to 112 g) for breakfast ham; 6 to 7 oz (170 to 200 g) for ham steak.
One 8-lb (3.6-kg) ham yields forty 3-oz (85-g) breakfast servings.

Calories:
4 oz (112 g), lean and fat = 325 Calories.

HAM STEAKS
Produced by many manufacturers. Fully trimmed and ready to eat, with center bone in.

Weights:
12 to 16 oz (340 to 450 g).

Packs:
15- or 30-lb (6.7- or 13.5-kg) boxes.

PICNIC HAM
Shoulder ham; often fatty.

Sizes:
From 2 to 6 lb (0.9 to 2.7 kg).

PROSCIUTTO HAM
Available bone-in, boneless in natural shape, and boneless shaped round. Available imported and domestic.

Sizes:

Bone-in:
11 to 14 lb (4.9 to 6.3 kg).

Boneless:
6 to 10 lb (2.7 to 4.5 kg).

Kitchen Yields
The waste factor of bone-in ham is high, because skin, shank, and bones (which have only limited kitchen use) must be removed. Boneless hams in natural shape also have high waste factor, because shank and skin must be removed. Fat cover can also be high in both ham varieties.

Serving size:
1½ oz (42 g)—about 2 large or 3 medium well-trimmed slices.
For a 12-lb (5.4-kg) bone-in prosciutto, the following weights and servings will be obtained.

> *Bones and trim:* 4 lb 6 oz (2.1 kg).
> *Usable meat:* 7 lb 10 oz (3.4 kg).
> *Servings:* 75, if slices of different sizes and shapes are used.

For a 9-lb (4-kg) boneless prosciutto in natural shape, the following weights and servings will be obtained.

> *Shank and trim:* 3 lb 3 oz (1.4 kg).
> *Usable meat:* 5 lb 13 oz (2.6 kg).
> *Servings:* 60, if slices of different shapes are used.

For a 7-lb (3.1-kg) round boneless prosciutto, the following yields will be obtained:

> *Usable meat:* 6¼ lb (2.8 kg).
> *Servings:* 60, if slices of different shape are used.

SMITHFIELD HAM
Another name for genuine Virginia ham.

VIRGINIA HAM
Genuine Virginia ham is from razorback hogs; it is air-dried and lightly smoked, then coated with pepper. Available raw or fully cooked, bone in or boneless.

Weights:

Whole, uncooked:
12 to 16 lb (5.4 to 7.2 kg).

Ready-to-eat, bone in:
10 to 12 lb (4.5 to 5.4 kg).

Ready-to-eat, boneless:
8 to 10 lb (3.6 to 4.5 kg).

Kitchen Yields
Soak overnight. Change water during boiling, if necessary, to remove salt.

Waste:

Uncooked Ham, bone in:
Waste is about 50 percent.

Cooked Ham, bone in:
Boning and trimming waste is about 40 percent.

WESTPHALIAN HAM
Smoked and dried ham that is served uncooked and sliced very thin. Available from specialty butchers.

Weights:
3 to 5 lb (1.3 to 2.2 kg) boneless. Other sizes are available.

Kitchen Yields
Better-quality hams have skin and fat layer still attached, and each piece has an irregular shape.

Trimming waste:
20 percent.

Serving size:
3 oz (100 g), for cold plate or sandwich.

WHOLE SMOKED HAM

Available both fully cooked (referred to as *ready-to-eat*) and uncooked. Most smoked ham on the market is fully cooked.

Pack and weights:

Ready-to-eat cooked Ham:
10 to 12 lb (4.5 to 5.4 kg).
14 to 17 lb (4.5 to 7.6 kg).

Uncooked Ham:
12 lb (5.4 kg) and up.

Kitchen Yields

Serving sizes:
4 oz (112 g).
One 14-lb (6.3-kg) ready-to-eat ham has the following yields:

> *Bone and trim:* 3 lb 5 oz (1.5 kg).
> *Usable meat:* 10 lb 9 oz (4.8 kg).
> *Servings:* 35.
> *Usable trimmings:* 1 lb 15 oz (0.9 kg).

One 15-lb (10.1-kg) uncooked ham undergoes a cooking loss of 2 lb 8 oz (680 g).

Calories:
4 oz (112 g) = 330 Calories.

KASSLER
See Smoked Pork Loin.

LOIN

Weights:
9 to 11 lb (4 to 4.9 kg).

Kitchen Yields
Product is normally sold as full loin, with all bones attached.

Serving size:
8 oz (225 g), consisting of 2 slices, boneless (except rib bones), cooked.
One 10-lb (4.5-kg) loin yields 10 servings.

LUNCHEON MEAT
Available canned in various sizes.

Kitchen Yields
There is no waste; use as is.

Calories:
4 oz (112 g) = 350 Calories.

MORTADELLA
See Sausages, under this same heading.

PANCETTA
See Bacon, under this same heading.

PROSCIUTTO
See Ham, under this same heading.

SALAMI
See Sausages, under this same heading.

SALT BELLY
Cured in salt only. Normally sold with skin on.

Weight:
12 to 14 lb (5.4 to 6.3 kg).

CORNED SALT BELLY
Cured with salt and saltpeter. Meat portion is slightly red. Normally sold with skin on.

Weight:
12 to 14 lb (5.4 to 6.3 kg).

SMOKED SALT BELLY
See Slab Bacon.

SAUSAGES

BREAKFAST SAUSAGES
Available in different sizes. Sausages made with other meats—without pork—are also available.

Pack:
5 lb (2.2 kg).

Sizes:
Eight pieces per 1 lb (450 g), or twelve pieces per 1 lb (450 g).

Kitchen Yields

The fat content of sausages varies greatly. Average shrinkage per weight is 35 percent. Precooked products with little shrinkage are on the market.

Serving size:
Three pieces, for breakfast. Thus, one 5-lb (2.2-kg) box, size 8, yields 13 servings; and one 5-lb (2.2-kg) box, size 12, yields 20 servings.

Calories:
6 oz (168 g), raw = 360 Calories.

ITALIAN SAUSAGES
Available mild (also called *sweet*) and sharp.

Pack:
By weight; normally 5-lb (2.2-kg) boxes.

Kitchen Yields
Sausages are available in different lengths or are portioned eight pieces per 1 lb (450 g) or larger.

Serving size:
Varies.

MORTADELLA
Large pork sausage, often sold as *Bologna sausage*.

Weights:
5 to 50 lb (2.2 to 22.5 kg).

SALAMI
Pork salami is often referred to as *Genoa salami*.

Weights
4 to 7 lb (1.8 to 3.1 kg). Smaller sizes are also available.

SAUSAGE MEAT
Breakfast sausage mix that is sold in rolls to be sliced or used in stuffing.

Pack:
By weight; usually in 3-lb (1.3-kg) rolls.

Kitchen Yields

Serving size:
Two 2-oz (56-g) pieces, raw weight; cooked weight is 2½ oz (70 g).

POTATO CHIPS

Available in many different shapes and flavors.

Kitchen Yields

Serving size:
1 oz (28 g) or less, as garnish with sandwich.

POTATO GNOCCHI

See Gnocchi.

POTATO LATKES

See Latkes (Potato Pancakes).

POTATOES

Available canned, dehydrated, fresh, and processed frozen.

CANNED POTATOES
Available whole, sliced, and diced.

Pack:
Six #10 cans.

Counts:
For whole canned potatoes, 130 to 150, 100 to 120, 80 to 100,and 200 and up.

Drained weight:
For diced and sliced potatoes, one #10 can weighs 108 oz (3 kg). Drained weight is 75 oz (2.1 kg).
NOTE: Counts and weights vary according to manufacturer.

Kitchen Yields

Serving size:
3 oz (85 g) each. One #10 can yields 25 servings.

DEHYDRATED POTATOES
Dehydrated potatoes are available as flakes, granules, slices, dices, hash browns, and french fry mix.

FLAKES

Pack:

For Idaho Instant Flakes:
Six 2-lb (0.9-kg) bags; six 2-lb (0.9-kg) #10 cans; six 2½- or 5-lb (1.1- or 2.2-kg) bags; twelve 1- or 2-lb (450- or 900-g) cartons. Larger packs are also available.

Kitchen Yields
Instant flakes produce mashed potatoes. Table P-5 lists ingredients and yields for two serving sizes (#10 and #8 scoops) of Idaho Instant Flakes.

Serving sizes:
#10 scoop equals ⅜ cup (0.087 l); #8 scoop equals ½ cup (0.12 l).

Method:
1. Bring water to boil, add butter or margarine.
2. Add cold milk and salt.
3. Add potato flakes. Stir gently; do not whip.

GRANULES

Pack:

For Idaho Granules:
Granules are available plain, seasoned, with milk and with vitamin C added. They are used to produce mashed potatoes. Table P-6 lists available forms of Idaho Instant Mashed Potatoes.

Table P-5 Ingredients and Yields for Idaho Instant Flakes

Ingredients	25/20	50/40	100/80
Water	1¾ qt (1.6 l)	3½ qt (3.2 l)	1¾ gal (6.4 l)
Margarine or butter	⅓ cup (74 g)	¾ cup (170 g)	1½ cups (340 g)
Milk	3 cups (0.69 l)	1½ qt (1.4 l)	3 qt (2.7 l)
Salt	1½ tsp	1 tb	2 tb
Potato flakes	1 lb (450 g)	2 lb (0.9 kg)	4 lb (1.8 kg)

Table P-6 Available Forms of Idaho Instant Mashed Potatoes

Granule Type	Packing Size	Yield per Can
Plain	Six #10 cans 6-lb (2.7-kg) can	5 gal (19.5 l)
With vitamin C	Six #10 cans 6-lb (2.7-kg) can	5 gal (19.5 l)
Complete	Six #10 cans 87 oz (2.4 kg) can	4½ gal (17.1 l)
Complete, with vitamin C	Six #10 cans	4½ gal (17.1l)
Seasoned, complete	Six #10 cans 5 lb 8 oz (2.4 kg) 3½ lb (1.5 kg)	4 gal (15.2 l)

NOTE: Flakes and granules cannot always be used interchangeably in recipes, because in dehydrated form they are not equal by volume measure. However, substitutions can be made based on weight measure. Follow directions on package.

SLICES
Slices are available plain or seasoned.

Pack:

Plain:
Six #10 cans; individual 5-lb (2.25-kg) bags; individual 1-gal (3.8-l) pour packs. Larger packs are available.

Seasoned:
Individual 2½-lb (1.1-kg) bags; six 2¼-lb (1-kg) cartons.

Kitchen Yields
Table P-7 lists rehydration and yields for slices, dices, and hash browns.

Serving size:
¼ cup (0.12 l).

Table P-7 Rehydration and Yields for Slices, Dices, and Hash Browns

Ingredient	25 Servings	50 Servings	100 Servings
Potato product	22 oz (616 g)	42 oz (1.1 kg)	5 lb 5 oz (2.25 kg)
Water 140 to 150°F	3 qt (2.7 l)	6 qt (5.5 l)	3 gal (11.4 l)

DICES

Pack:
Six 2½-lb (1.1-kg) #10 cans; individual 2½-lb (1.1-kg) bags; individual 5-lb (2.25-kg) and larger bags.

Kitchen Yields
Table P-7 lists rehydration and yields for slices, dices, and hash browns.

Serving size:
¼ cup (0.12 l).

HASH BROWNS
Six 2-lb (0.9-kg) pour packs; individual 5-lb (2.25-kg) bags.

Kitchen Yields

Serving size:
4 oz (112 g). One 5-lb (2.25-kg) bag, as purchased, yields 90 servings.
See also Table P-8.

FRESH POTATOES
Potatoes are classified into four broad groups:

> *Long Whites:* Boiling and salads.
> *Round Red:* Boiling and salads.
> *Round Whites (Irish potatoes):* Boiling, salads, and frying.
> *Russet:* Baking and frying.

Each group includes a number of varieties. Potatoes are available year-round, although fall is the harvesting season in most states. Potatoes are grown in most states. The main potato-producing states are Idaho, Washington, Colorado, and Maine.

Washington potatoes have a slighter higher nutrient content than the national average for American potatoes. Table P-8 lists purchasing requirements for unpeeled fresh potatoes.

A number of specialty potatoes have come on the markets, but they are not widely distributed. Their yield is about the same as for Irish potatoes. Some varieties are:

> *Cherries Jubilee:* Red and white striped.
> *Cowhorn, Peanut, Ozette, Ruby Crescent, Bishop* and *Tantillo.*
> *Kathadin and Green Mountain:* Old New England varieties.
> *Yellow Finn:* Resembles fingerlings, but with a higher starch content and can be baked
> *Yukon Gold:* A yellow-fleshed potato.

LONG WHITE POTATOES
Good variety for salads, hash browns, and home-fried potatoes.

Season:
Available year-round.

Table P-8 Yields for Unpeeled Russet Potatoes, 80 to 120 size

Form of Potato	25 Servings	50 Servings	100 Servings
¼-in fries, unpeeled	10¼ lb (4.6 kg)	21 lb (9.4 kg)	41½ lb (18.6 kg)
Jacket fries, skin on	9½ lb (4.2 kg)	18½ lb (8.3 kg)	37 lb (16.6 kg)
Shoestring fries, unpeeled	9½ lb (4.2 kg)	19 lb (8.5 kg)	37½ lb (16.8 kg)
¼-in fries, peeled	20 lb (9 kg)	40 lb (18 kg)	80 lb (36 kg)
Round fries	15¼ lb (6.8 kg)	30½ lb (13.7 kg)	61 lb (27.4 kg)
Shoestring fries, peeled	14¼ lb (6.4 kg)	28½ lb (12.8 kg)	57 lb (25.6 kg)

Pack:
50-lb (22.5-kg) bags.

Kitchen Yields
1 lb (450 g) raw, boiled in jacket, yields 14 oz (400 g) peeled, which produces 3 cooked portions of hash browns or home fries.

Calories:
One 6-oz (170-g) potato, cooked and peeled after boiling = 126 Calories.
5 oz (140 g) hash browns = 310 Calories.

ROUND RED (RED BLISS) POTATOES
Available small and large; in many markets, grade A indicates a larger potato than grade B. The small variety is often served whole as boiled potato, with only part of the peel removed before cooking.

Season:
Available year-round.

Pack:
50-lb (22.6-kg) bags.

Kitchen Yields
1 lb (450 g) is equivalent to approximately 6 to 7 small raw potatoes or 3 to 4 medium-sized potatoes.

Serving size:
5 oz (150 g) cooked, or 2 to 3 potatoes or one medium-sized potato, with peel partly removed.
1 lb (450 g) yields 3 restaurant servings; thus, one 50-lb (22.6-kg) bag yields 125 restaurant servings. For banquet servings, use two potatoes per person; thus, 50 lb (22.5 kg) yield 150 servings, and 30 lb (13.5 kg) yield 100 servings.

Calories:
Two small or one medium-sized potato, 5 oz (140 g), boiled = 105 Calories.

ROUND WHITE POTATOES (IRISH POTATOES)
Also called *chef's potatoes*.

Season:
Available year-round.

Pack:
50-lb (22.5-kg) bags.

Kitchen Yields
1 lb (450 g) is equivalent to 4 to 5 potatoes, which yield 3 to 4 portions boiled potatoes or 3 portions potato salad; therefore, 50 lb (22.6 kg) yield 150 portions potato salad.

Calories:
Two potatoes, 4¾ oz (130 g), boiled and peeled = 90 Calories.

RUSSET POTATOES
Most russet potatoes are grown in Idaho, Washington, and Colorado.

Season:
Fresh harvest in October; available year-round.

Pack:
50-lb (22.5-kg) cartons, net weight.

Count:
Ranges from 35 to 140 per carton, as detailed in Table P-9.
Most common restaurant sizes are from 80 to 100.

Table P-9 Counts and Weights of Russet Potatoes

Count	Average Weight per Potato
35	22 oz (638 g)
50	14 to 17 oz (400 to 475 g)
60	12 to 13 oz (335 to 365 g)
70	11 to 13 oz (300 to 320 g)
80	9 to 12 oz (250 to 335 g)
90	8 to 11 oz (225 to 300 g)
100	7 to 9 oz (200 to 250 g)
110	6 to 8 oz (170 to 225 g)
120	5 to 7 oz (140 to 200 g)
140	3 to 4 oz (85 to 110 g)

Shrinkage:

About 25 percent in weight after baking.

Kitchen Yields

Baked:

35, 50, and 60 size: Good for complete entrée.

80 size: Common hotel size.

90 size: Good for scooped out skins.

100 and 110 size: Good for commercial operations.

20 size: Perfect for elementary schools as side dish.

140 size: Weighs 3 oz (85 g) cooked; meets ⅔ cup vegetable requirement for school foodservice.

French-fried:

4 oz (112 g) cooked as side order.

Table P-10 gives weight yields for 4 lb (1.8 kg) of french-fried Idaho potatoes.

Mashed:

Table P-11 lists formulas for different yields of mashed potatoes.

Quantities:

1 lb (450 g) whole, unpeeled potatoes yields 2 cups (0.46 l) mashed potatoes; and 8 lb (3.6 kg) whole,

Table P-10 Weight Yields for 4 lb (1.8 kg) Fresh Idaho Potatoes

Form of Potato	Cooked Weight	Number of Servings
¼-in fries, unpeeled	44 oz (1.2 kg)	11
Jacket fries with skin on	42 oz (1.1 kg)	10
Shoestring fries, unpeeled	48 oz (1.35 kg)	12
¼-in fries, peeled	20 oz (560 g)	5
Round fries	26 oz (728 g)	6
Shoestring fries, peeled	28 oz (785 g)	7

Table P-11 Ingredients Needed for Different Quantities of ½-cup (#8-scoop) Servings Mashed Potatoes

Ingredient	25 Servings	50 Servings	100 Servings
Whole, unpeeled russet potatoes	6 lb (2.7 kg)	12 lb (5.4 kg)	24 lb (10.8 kg)
or			
Whole, peeled russet potatoes	5 lb (2.25 kg)	10 lb (4.5 kg)	20 lb (9 kg)
Milk, hot	3 to 4 cups (0.7 to 0.9 l)	1½ to 2 qt. (1.4 to 1.9 l)	3 to 4 qt (2.8 to 3.8 l)
Fresh butter	¼ lb (112 g)	½ lb (225 g)	1 lb (450 g)
Salt to taste			

unpeeled potatoes yields 1 gal (3.8 l) mashed potatoes or twenty #6 scoops.

Calories:

½ cup (110 g) mashed, with milk and butter = 100 Calories.

One #6 scoop, 6 oz (170 g) mashed, with milk and butter = 180 Calories.

One baked potato, #100, 6 oz (170 g) = 150 Calories.

FROZEN PROCESSED POTATOES

Many products are available in processed frozen form, such as french fries (in many cuts and styles), ranch or country fries, hash browns, ranch-style potatoes, and potato rounds.

Packs:

French fries:

Six 5-lb (2.25-kg) bags. Some varieties are also packed in 4- and 4½-lb (1.8- and 2-kg) bags.

Shredded hash browns:
Eight 2½-lb (1.12-kg) layers; ninety-six 3-oz (85-g) portions.

Long shredded hash browns:
Three 5-lb (2.25-kg) layers; eight 4-lb (1.8-kg) layers; six 3-lb (1.35-kg) bags, IQF.

Skin-on hash browns:
Six 5-lb (2.25-kg) bags.

Shells:
Six 5-lb (2.25-kg) bags, with 200 shells per case.

Wedges:
Six 5-lb (2.25-kg) bags.

Cubes:
Six 4-lb (1.8-kg) bags.

Kitchen Yields
Use as is; there is no waste.

Calories:
3 oz (85 g) french fries = 229 Calories.
¾ cup, or 4 oz (112 g), hash browns = 250 Calories.

POUSSIN

See Baby Chicken, under Chicken.

PRAWNS

See Shrimp.

PRICKLY PEARS (CACTUS FRUIT)

See Tunas, under Mexican Fruits.

PRUNES

DRIED PRUNES

Dried prunes are available in bulk packs, fully cooked, and canned. Prunes are dried plums, but not all varieties of plums can be dried. The most commonly used drying variety is the California French Prune. Prunes are available pitted and with pit in.

BULK-PACK DRIED PRUNES

Pitted prunes are classified in three types, which indicate size and quality. For restaurant foodservice, types I and II are used. The sizes of types I and II are identical.

Pack:
Table P-12 identifies sizes, counts, and servings in a 25-lb (11.25-kg) cartons of dried pitted prunes.
NOTE: Use Jumbo or Extra large sizes for stuffing. Table P-13 lists sizes, counts, and servings in 25- and 30-lb (11.25- and 13.5-kg) cartons of dried unpitted prunes.

Kitchen Yields
Average weight of one Extra Large prune is ⅓ oz (9 g).

Serving size:

Pitted Prunes:
Five large prunes; thus, 1 lb (450 g) Extra Large prunes yields 9 portions.

Whole Prunes:
Four to five large prunes; thus, 1 lb (450 g) 25 to 35 size yields 7 to 8 portions.

Table P-12 Sizes and Counts for 25-lb (11.25-kg) Cartons of Pitted Dried Prunes

Count per 1 lb (450 g)	Average Number per Case	Servings per 1 lb (450 g)	Servings per Case
Jumbo, 39 and larger	950	8 (5 prunes)	200
Extra Large, 40 to 49	1125	7½ (6 prunes)	150
Large 50 to 61	1375	9 (6 prunes)	229
Medium 62 to 79	1750	10 (7 prunes)	250
Small 80 and smaller	2000	10 (8 prunes)	250

Table P-13 Sizes and Counts for 25- and 30-lb (11.25- and 13.5-kg) Cartons of Unpitted Dried Prunes

Carton Weight	Count per 1 lb (450 g)	Average Number per Case	Servings per 1 lb (450 g)	Servings per Case
25 lb	20 to 30	625	6½ (4 prunes)	160
(11.35 kg)	25 to 35	800	8 (4 prunes)	200
	30 to 40	900	9 (4 prunes)	225
	40 to 50	1,125	9 (5 prunes)	225
30 lb	25 to 35	850	7 (4 prunes)	212
(13.5 kg)	30 to 40	1,080	9 (4 prunes)	270
	40 to 50	1,350	9 (5 prunes)	270

Calories:
Four Extra Large prunes with pits, uncooked = 110 Calories.
Five Large prunes with pits, uncooked = 110. Calories.

CANNED DRIED PRUNES
Canned prunes are available pitted and with pits in. There are three standard packs of canned prunes:

> *Regular:* Packed in syrup.
> *Nectarized:* Packed in water, with higher fruit count.
> *High-moisture:* No liquid added.

Pack:
Many can sizes are available. For institutional use, #10 cans are normally purchased. Table P-14 lists sizes, packs, and counts for pitted canned prunes. Table P-15 lists sizes, packs, and counts for unpitted canned prunes.

Calories:
7 to 8 extra-large prunes, 3½ oz (100 g), packed in syrup, drained = 110 Calories.

PRUNE JUICE
Canned or bottled prune juice is prepared from a water extract of dried prunes.

Pack:

Glass:
4 oz (0.12 l); 8 oz (0.23 l); 32 oz = 1 qt (0.94 l); 40 oz = 5 cups (1.15 l); 48 oz = 6 cups (1.4 l).

Cans:
5½ (0.16 l); 6 oz (0.17 l); 46 oz (1.3 l).

Kitchen Yields

Serving size:
5½ oz (0.17 l); therefore, 1 qt (0.94 l) yields 5½ servings, and one 46-oz can yields 8 servings.

Calories:
5½ oz (0.16 l) = 120 Calories.

PRUNE PASTE
Called *lekvar* on the East Coast, prune paste is used for baking—particularly in Danish pastries.

Table P-14 Sizes and Counts for Canned Prunes without Pits

Can size and Drained Weight	Type of Pack	Approximate Equivalent Size with Pit	Prunes per Can	Number of Portions
#10: 70 oz (1.9 kg)	Regular	20 to 30	140 to 160	30 (5 prunes)
#10: 92 oz (2.6 kg)	Nectarized	20 to 30	190 to 210	40 (4 prunes)
#10: 112 oz (3.1 kg)	High-moisture	40 to 50	330 to 365	70 (5 prunes)

Table P-15 Sizes and Counts for Canned Prunes with Pits

Can size and Drained Weight	Type of Pack	Prunes per Can	Number of Portions (and Portion Size)
#10: 70 oz (1.9 kg)	Regular	70 to 85	26 (3 prunes)
#10: 70 oz (1.9 kg)	Regular	115 to 135	32 (4 prunes)
#10: 70 oz (1.9 kg)	Regular	140 to 160	30 (5 prunes)
#10: 96 oz (2.7 kg)	Nectarized	155 to 175	40 (4 prunes)
#10: 7 lb (3.1 kg)	Moist pack	238 to 273	52 (5 prunes)

Pack:
25- to 40-lb packs (11.25- to 18-kg); six #10 cans of 7 lb (3.1 kg) each.

Kitchen Yields

Serving size:
1 oz (28 g) filling for one piece Danish; therefore, one #10 can yields 110 fillings.

Calories:
1 oz (28 g) = 70 Calories.

PULLED SUGAR

See Sugar.

PUMPKINS

Available as canned purée and fresh.

CANNED PUMPKIN

Primarily used in pies, but also in soups.

Pack:
Six #10 cans.

Kitchen Yields

Serving size:
½ cup. One #10 can contains 8½ cups (2 l) pumpkin purée, which yields 16 servings.

Calories:
1 cup, or 8¾ oz (245 g) = 80 Calories.

FRESH PUMPKIN

Weights:
Vary greatly.

Kitchen Yields

Waste:
Trimming loss is about 30 percent by weight.

Serving size:
½ cup (0.23 l), mashed.
50 lb (22.5 kg), as purchased, yield 3 gal (11.4 l) mashed.

Calories:
1 cup, or 7½ oz (210 g), baked and mashed = 130 Calories.

Q AND R

QUAIL

Farm-bred quail are available fresh or frozen in the following forms: whole, with bone in; whole, boned; and split.

Whole Quail:

Pack:
12, 24, 40, or 56 birds to a case; 4 or 6 birds per tray, with 72 per master.

Size:
4 to 5 oz (112 to 140 g) each, whole.
5 to 6 oz (140 to 170 g) each, whole.
4 oz (112 g) each, split.

Boned Quail:

Pack:
Eight 3½-oz (100-g) birds, with 40 per case.

Kitchen Yields

Serving size:
Two birds.
The meat stuffing needed to stuff one bird is 1½ oz (42 g).
The meat stuffing needed to stuff 50 birds is 3½ lb, (1.5 kg), or 7 cups (1.6 l).

QUAIL EGGS

Available fresh in flats and hard-boiled in jars and cans.

CANNED QUAIL EGGS

Packed in flavored or unflavored brine. Available domestic or imported.

Pack:
Twelve 15-oz (420-g) cans, with a drained weight of 8 oz (225 g) each.

Count:
30 eggs. Other packs are available.

Kitchen Yields
One egg weighs ¼ oz (7.5 g).

FRESH QUAIL EGGS

Pack:
30 eggs per flat, and 18 flats per case, or 540 eggs per case; 30 eggs per flat, and 6 flats per case, or 180 eggs per case.

QUICHE

QUICHE CUSTARD

Formula
>   6 qt (5.6 l) light cream
>   36 whole eggs
>   3 tb salt
>   1 tb white pepper
>   1 tsp nutmeg

Garnish for Quiche Lorraine:

>   ¼ cup chopped chives
>   8 cups (0.6 kg) diced Swiss cheese
>   4 lb (1.8 kg) raw bacon, cooked and diced

Kitchen Yields
Twelve 9-in (228-mm) quiches.

QUICHE DOUGH

Formula
>   3 lb (1.4 kg) pastry flour
>   2 lb (0.9 kg) shortening
>   14 oz, or 1¾ cup (0.4 l) cold water
>   2 oz (56 g) sugar
>   1 oz (28 g) salt

Do not overmix. Prebake shells at 375°F for 15 minutes.

Kitchen Yields
Twelve 9-in (228-mm) crusts.

QUINCE

Quinces are fruits that have a high pectin content and resemble yellow apples. They are used in making jams. Quinces are available fresh.

Season:
September to December.

Pack:
20-lb (9.1-kg) lug. Fruit is often sold in units of 1 dozen.

Average weight:
10 to 12 oz (280 to 340 g).

Kitchen Yields

Waste:
Peeling and coring loss is about 25 percent. One lug yields 15 lb (6.7 kg) peeled fruit.

Quince jam proportions:
Mix 1 lb (450 g) peeled and cored fruit with 12 oz (340 g) sugar.

QUINOA

High-protein grain that originated in the Peruvian Andes. Quinoa is used as a starch garnish, in place of rice or pasta.

Pack:
12 oz (340 g); 1 lb (450 g); and 25 lb (11.35 kg).

Kitchen Yields

Serving size:
1 cup, or 7 oz (200 g) cooked. 1 cup, or 6 oz (170 g), raw yields 3 cups cooked or 5 servings. 1 cup quinoa + 2 cups water = 3 cups cooked. NOTE: Rinse grain before cooking.

Calories:
1 cup, or 7 oz (200 g), cooked = 215 Calories.

R

RABBIT

Available fresh or frozen, whole or in pieces. Rabbit meat is white and can be dry.

Pack:

Whole skinless:
With head and feet off, eviscerated, 44-lb (19.8-kg) cases, in sizes 1¾ to 2½ lb (0.7 to 1 kg); 28-lb (12.6-kg) cases, in sizes 1½ to 3½ lb (0.6 to 1.5 kg); 26-lb (11.7-kg) cases in sizes 4 to 6 lb (1.8 to 2.7 kg).

Irregular pieces:
15-lb (6.7-kg) cases.

Boneless loins:
Pack is by weight and piece, in sizes 6 to 9 oz (170 to 250 g).

Kitchen Yields
One 2 lb (0.9 kg) rabbit yields two 8-oz (225-g) hind legs, one 8-oz (225-g) back piece, one 12-oz (340-g) shoulder, and trim of little value.

Serving size:
5 oz (140 g) cooked. One 2- to 2½-lb (0.9- to 1-kg) rabbit yields 3 servings.

Calories:
5 oz (140 g) cooked = 291 Calories.

RADICCHIO

See Lettuce.

RADISHES

Many varieties and types of radishes are marketed.

BLACK RADISHES

Black roots with white flesh; sharp and pungent when eaten raw. They are popular in Germany with beer. Black radishes can also be cooked as vegetable.

Pack:
Sold by weight.

DAIKON (JAPANESE RADISH)

See Japanese Foods.

HORSERADISH

See Horseradish.

LO BOK (CHINESE RADISH)

See Chinese Foods.

RED RADISHES

Available whole with the green leaves still attached, whole trimmed, and sliced.

Season:
Available year-round.

Pack:
12- to 14-oz (340- to 400-g) fresh bunches, including leaves, twelve cello packs in 30-lb (13.5-kg) cartons; sliced radishes in individual 5-lb (2.25-kg) bags.

Count:
Varies greatly.

Kitchen Yields
One bunch fresh contains 12 to 13 pieces in vastly different sizes. One bunch fresh, without leaves, weighs 8 oz (225 g); 1 cup sliced weighs 4½ oz (120 g).

Calories:
1 cup sliced, or 4½ oz (120 g) = 33 Calories.

RAISINS

Raisins are dried grapes. They are available seedless, made either from seedless grapes or from seeded grapes which have had their pits removed during processing. Unseeded raisins, which contain pits, are also on the market, but of lesser importance to foodservice. The color of raisins can range from golden yellow to dark brown. Very light raisins are often bleached during processing. The important varieties are Thompson Seedless and Muscat. Currants are small, dark raisins produced mainly in Greece. Sultanas are large, light-colored raisins.

Pack:
20-lb (9-kg) cartons, or 1-lb (450-g) boxes. Other packs are available.

Sizes:
Seedless raisins are sized as midget, small, or select. Unseeded raisins are sized from one to four crowns, four being the largest. The sizes vary according to variety, a select Thompson seedless is similar in size to a Muscat midget.

Kitchen Yields
1 cup (0.23 l) seedless raisins equals 5½ oz (154 g); 1 lb (450 g) seedless raisins equals 3 cups (0.7 l).

Calories:
1 cup (0.23 l) = 430 Calories.

RAMPS

Wild leeks with strong garlic smell, indigenous from Maine to Georgia. Bulbs and leaves are used. Harvesting plant with bulbs destroys plant.

Season:
From late March to June.

Pack:
By weight.

Size:
Varies.

Kitchen Yield
1 lb (450 g) with leaves yields 45 to 50 pieces. Waste about 50 percent by weight if leaves are discarded.

RAPINI

Bitter Broccoli. *See* Broccoli Rabe.

RASPBERRIES (BUSHBERRIES)

Available canned, fresh, and frozen.

CANNED RASPBERRIES

Pack:
Six #10 cans; twenty-four #303 cans.

Kitchen Yields

Serving size:
½ cup fruit and juice. One #10 can contains 6 cups drained fruit and yields 22 servings with juice. One #303 can yields 4 servings fruit and juice.

FRESH RASPBERRIES

Season:
June until November for domestically grown raspberries. Imports are available during the rest of the year.

Pack:
Flats of twelve ½-pint (0.23-l) baskets.

Kitchen Yields

There is basically no waste when merchandise is fresh.

Serving size:
For breakfast or dessert service, ½ pint yields 1⅓ servings, so 1 flat yields 16 portions. For garnish with desserts and ice cream, ½ pint yields 3 portions, so 1 flat yields 32 portions. There are about 60 to 75 berries in ½ pint.

Calories:
1 cup, or 4 oz (112 g) = 70 Calories.

FROZEN RASPBERRIES

Available straight and with sugar added at a ratio of 4 parts fruit to 1 part sugar.

Pack:
Six #10 cans, weighing 6½ lb (3 kg) each; 30-lb (13.5-kg) pack with sugar added, 4 to 1; 28-lb (12.6-kg) straight pack.

Kitchen Yields

Serving size:
½ cup fruit and juice. One #10 can yields 22 servings.

Calories:
½ cup, or 5 oz (140 g), with juice and sugar = 140 Calories.

RHUBARB

Rhubarb is available fresh and frozen.

FRESH RHUBARB

Season:
Spring to early summer and late fall. Hot-house rhubarb is often available from January to April.

Pack:

Hot-house:
5-lb (2.2-kg) cartons.

Regular:
15- and 20-lb (6.7- and 9.1-kg) cartons.

Kitchen Yields

Waste:
Cleaning waste is 10 percent by weight. Hot-house grown rhubarb might have a slightly smaller waste.

Serving size:
½ cup (0.12 l).
5 lb (2.2 kg) as purchased yield 17 servings.
30 lb (13.5 kg) as purchased yield 105 servings.

Sugar ratio:
1 lb (450 g) cleaned rhubarb to 8 oz (225 g) sugar.
NOTE: Cooked weight is same as raw weight on account of added sugar.

Calories:
½ cup (0.12 l), with sugar = 190 Calories.

FROZEN RHUBARB

Pack:
25-lb (11.25-kg) cans; twelve 2½-lb (1.1-kg) packages.

Kitchen Yields

Serving size:
½ cup (0.12 l). One 25-lb (11.25-kg) can yields 90 servings, and one 2½-lb (1.1-kg) package yields 9 servings.

Calories:
½ cup (0.12 l), with sugar = 192 Calories..

RICE

The leading varieties are Long Grain, Medium Grain, and Short Grain. Long Grain rice is commonly used in foodservice, except for some ethnic dishes. Rice has no gluten—not even glutinous rice. The following varieties of Long Grain Rice are available:

White rice: Polished rice; the most popular kind.

Converted rice: Rice steam-treated to retain vitamins.

Precooked rice: Fully cooked and then dehydrated rice; also called *instant rice.*

Brown rice: Whole, unpolished grains, with germ and bran intact.

Medium Grain and Short Grain Rice are also available white or brown.

The following specialty varieties are available:

Arborio rice or Pearl rice from California, used for risotto.

Basmati rice, used for Indian dishes.

Jasmine rice, for Thai dishes.

Thai Black or Japonica rice, for Thai desserts.

Texmati, Delta, Rosa, and Popcorn rice are American varieties.

Wild Pecan is a brown rice.

Granza is a Spanish rice used in Paella.

Sticky rice is used in Oriental dishes, especially sushi.

For other Oriental varieties, *see* Chinese Foods and Japanese Foods.

Many blends of rice and other grains or legumes have come on the market. The most popular are Long Grain and Wild rice blends and flavored rice mixes.

Pack:
2- to 10-, 25-, 50-, and 100-lb (2- to 4.5-, 11.3-, 22.6-, and 45.3-kg) bags. Special packs are available for flavored rice mixes.

Kitchen Yields

Serving size:
Between ⅓ to ½ cup.

White Rice:
1 cup (0.23 l) raw yields 3 cups (0.7 l) cooked.
1 lb (450 g) raw yields 6 cups cooked; thus, 10 lb (4.5 kg) raw yields 60 cups, or 3¾ gal (14.2 l), cooked. To make 1 gal cooked rice, use 3 lb (1.35 kg) raw rice. Table R-1 lists the proper formulas for different yields of white rice.

Converted Rice:
1 lb (450 g) uncooked yields 7½ cups cooked.
10 lb (4.5 kg) uncooked yields 75 cups, or 4⅝ gal (17.5 l), cooked.
To make 1 gal cooked, use 2 lb (0.9 kg) uncooked.

Brown Rice:
1 cup (0.23 l) raw rice yields 3 to 4 cups cooked. Use more liquid and longer cooking time than for white rice.
1 lb (450 g) raw rice yields 8 cups (1.9 l) cooked; thus, 10 lb (4.5 kg) raw rice yields 80 cups, or 5 gal (19 l), cooked.

Instant Rice:
1 lb (450 g) raw rice yields 14 cups cooked rice.

Wild Rice and Long Grain Blend:
1 lb (450 g) raw rice yields 12 cups (2.25 l) cooked.

Rice for stuffing:
2½ gal (9.5 l) cooked rice yields stuffing for 100 chicken breasts.

Table R-1 Ingredients for White Rice

Rice	Water	Fat	Salt	Yields	Portions
1 lb	5 cups	2 oz	1 tb	6 cups	10
5 lb	6½ qt	10 oz	½ cup	30 cups	50
10 lb	13 qt	1 lb 4 oz	1 cup	3¾ gal	100

Calories:
1 cup raw Long Grain, raw weighing 6⅝ oz (185 g) = 670 Calories.
1 cup boiled Long Grain, weighing 7⅓ oz (210 g) = 225 Calories.
1 cup cooked instant rice, weighing 5¾ oz (165 g) = 180 Calories.

RISOTTO

Also spelled *rizotto*, this is an Italian rice dish, flavored with meats or seafood, often with saffron; and always with grated Parmesan cheese, except with seafood. The dish should be soupy, yet the kernels should still be hard. Arborio rice is best.

BASIC RISOTTO

Formula
    1 pint (0.4 l) Arborio rice
    1 cup (0.23 l) chopped onion
    1 cup (0.24 l) melted butter
    1½ qt (1.42 l) chicken stock or other stock
    1 cup (0.23 l) Parmesan cheese
    4 oz (112 g) fresh butter

Kitchen Yields

Serving size:
1 cup (0.23 l) as appetizer. The total mix yields 6 servings.

ROUX

Roux consists of 3 parts bread flour to 2½ parts fat by volume, such as oil or clarified butter. White roux is heated long enough to cook the flour without causing it to change color. Brown roux is cooked slowly for a long time to produce its brown color.

Formula
    60 percent bread flour
    40 percent fat, such as oil or clarified butter

Kitchen Yields

Quantities:

White Roux:
3 oz (80 g) yield thickening for 1 qt (0.9 l) soup.

4 oz (100 g) yield thickening for 1 qt (0.9 l) medium-thick cream sauce.

Brown Roux:
Roux loses thickening power through roasting. Brown roux has approximately 25 percent less thickening power than white roux.

ROYAL ICING

Formula
    4 lb (1.8 kg) confectioners sugar
    ¾ lb (340 g) egg whites
    ½ tsp cream of Tarter

NOTE: Icing gets hard and brittle when dry. Use for decorative cakes only.

Kitchen Yields
The total mix yields royal icing for one 20-in (50.8-cm) cake dummy.

RUTABAGAS

Large, yellow root vegetable. Available fresh.

Season:
Fall and winter.

Pack:
50-lb (22.5-kg) bags or cartons.

Size and weights:
Vary.

Kitchen Yields

Waste:
20 percent, by weight.

Serving size:
½ cup (0.12 l) cubed and cooked. One 50-lb (22.5-kg) bag yields 6 gal (22.8 l) cubed and cooked rutabagas. One 4½-in (114-mm) diameter bulb yields 4¼ cups (1 l) cooked and diced rutabaga.

Calories:
⅔ cup, or 3½ oz (100 g) = 35 Calories.

S

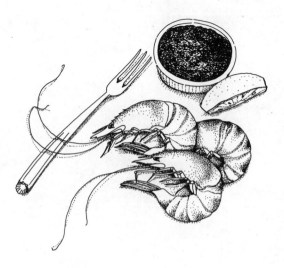

SAFFRON

See Herbs & Spices.

SALAD DRESSINGS

See Dressing Formulas.

SALAD GREENS

See also Cabbage, Lettuce, and Sprouts.

ALFALFA SPROUTS

See Sprouts.

ARUGULA

Salad plant with peppery mustard flavor. As a salad ingredient, arugula is always mixed with other greens, because it would be too sharp if served alone.

Season:
Available year-round.

Pack:
6- to 7-lb (2.7- to 3.1-kg) flats, 24-count bunches.

Kitchen Yields
Use one part arugala with three parts milder salad greens.

BEAN SPROUTS
See Sprouts.

BELGIAN ENDIVE
See Belgian Endive.

DANDELION GREENS
See Dandelion Greens,

SORREL
See Sorrel.

SPINACH
See Spinach.

WATERCRESS

Season:
Available year-round. Peak is from May to July.

Pack:
By the bunch.

Size:
Varies, but usually 4 oz (112 g) per bunch.

Kitchen Yields

Waste:
Trimming waste is about 10 percent by weight, if stems are cut 2 in (50 mm) from bottom.
1 lb (450 g) yields 10 cups (2.25 l) chopped.

SALSIFY

Available canned and fresh. Also called *oyster plant*, this vegetable is used most often canned. It resembles white asparagus in shape and parsnip in flavor, when cooked.

CANNED SALSIFY

Pack:
Six #10 cans, weighing 7 lb (3.1 kg) each; twenty-four 15-oz (420-g) cans.

Kitchen Yields

Serving size:
4 oz (112 g). One #10 can has a drained weight of 5 lb 10 oz (2.5 kg) and yields 20 servings. One 15-oz (420-g) can has a drained weight of 12 oz (340 g) and yields 3 servings.

FRESH SALSIFY
Available with white and black skin. The inside flesh is always white.

Season:
Fall and winter.

Pack:
By weight.

Kitchen Yields

Waste:
Peeling loss is 25 percent.

SALT DOUGH

Formula 1

> 2 cups (160 g) flour
> 1 cup (225 g) salt
> 1 cup (235 l) water

Dough can be dried or baked at low temperature.

Formula 2

> 1 pint (0.47 l) water
> 12 oz (340 g) corn starch
> ½ oz (14 g) gelatin
> 3 tb, or 1½ oz (42 g) water
> 2 lb (0.9 kg) extra-fine salt

Boil the starch with 1 pint water; add the gelatin (dissolved in 3 tb water) and the remaining ingredients. Dough will dry well.

SANDWICH FILLINGS

BUTTER OR MARGARINE
1 lb (450 g) softened product supplies spread for 70 slices of #2 bread.

CHEESE FILLINGS

Serving size:
2 to 3 oz (56 to 80 g) cheese per sandwich.

MEAT FILLINGS

Kitchen Yields

Serving size:
2 to 4 oz (56 to 112 g). Meat should be sliced very thin. Weight of meat varies according to moisture content.

Average yields:
1 lb (450 g) canned ham yields filling for 5 to 6 sandwiches.

1 lb (450 g) cold roast beef yields filling for 5 sandwiches.

SALAD FILLINGS

Kitchen Yields

Serving sizes:
For 2 oz (56 g), use #16 scoop; for 2½ oz (70 g), use #12 scoop; for 3½ oz (100 g), use #10 scoop; 4 oz (112 g), use #8 scoop.
For 30 tuna salad sandwiches, use the following recipe:

> 1 can tuna weighing 55 oz (1.5 kg) drained
> 1 pint (0.47 l) mayonnaise
> 1 pint (0.47 l) diced celery

Use #12 scoop to measure out filling.

SAPPODILLA

Known by its scientific name of *Achras sapota*, this tropical fruit is also called *chicle*, *chico*, *mammee sapota*, *marmalade plum*, and *naseberry*. An oval brown fruit that resembles a small football, it has a rough brown skin and dense, orange-pink pulp. Its seeds are arranged such that a star-shape is revealed in the center of the fruit when it is cut across its diameter.

The fruit's creamy, pudding-like flesh has a honey-sweet taste and is eaten raw or puréed into milk shakes. It is sometimes cut open and sold as a street snack in countries such as Peru.

Native to South America, it is also grown in the West Indies and the Philippines. Related varieties are the sapote (Calocarpum mamosum), which has a large central seed, the green sapote (Calocarpum viride), and the star-apple (Chysophyllum cainito). It is not related to the white sapote.

Season:
Available year-round.

Pack:
10-lb (4.5-kg) flats.

Sizes:
Large, medium, and small.

WHITE SAPOTA

See White Sapota.

SAUCES

BASIC SAUCE INGREDIENTS

BONNE FEMME SAUCE FOR FISH

Formula

>   One 3-lb (1.35-kg) basket sliced mushrooms
>   1 cup (0.23 l) chopped shallots
>   ½ lb (225 g) butter
>   1 pint (0.47 l) dry white wine
>   1 cup (0.23 l) cut chives
>   1 gal (3.8 l) heavy fish velouté (*see* Fish
>   Velouté, under this same heading)
>   1 qt (0.9 l) Hollandaise sauce
>   1 qt (0.9 l) heavy cream, whipped

Kitchen Yields

The total mix yields 1 ½ gal (5.7 l) sauce—enough for 100 portions of fish.

BROWN MUSHROOM SAUCE

Formula

>   One 3-lb (1.35-kg) basket sliced mushrooms
>   1 cup, or 8 oz (0.23 l) chopped shallots
>   ½ gal (1.9 l) white wine
>   1 gal (3.8 l) brown sauce
>   Herbs and spices to taste

Kitchen Yields

The total mix yields 1 ¼ gal (4.7 l) sauce.

BROWN VEAL STOCK

Formula

>   1 cup (0.23 l) oil
>   20 lb (9 kg) veal bones
>   ½ gal (1.9 l) mirepoix
>   4 lb (2.8 kg) tomato trimmings
>   10 gal (38 l) water
>   Salt, herbs, and peppercorns to taste

Kitchen Yields

The total mix yields 5 gal (19 l) sauce.

CHICKEN VELOUTÉ

Formula

>   4 gal (15.2 l) strong chicken stock
>   1 gal (3.8 l) light cream
>   3 lb (1.4 kg) mushroom trimmings
>   3 qt (2.8 l) white roux
>   1 lb (450 g) fresh butter

Kitchen Yields

The total mix yields 5 gal (19 l) sauce.

CREAM SAUCE (BECHAMEL)

Formula

>   2 large onions, studded with 8 cloves
>   4 bay leaves
>   4 gal (15.2 l) milk
>   1 gal (3.8 l) light cream
>   ⅛ cup (30 g) ground white pepper
>   2½ qt (2.37 l) white roux
>   1 lb (450 g) butter

Steep onions and bay leaves in hot milk; strain and pour over roux. Add cream; season and boil for 15 minutes.

Kitchen Yields

The total mix yields 5 gal (19 l) sauce.

CUMBERLAND SAUCE

Formula

>   Three #10 cans red currant jelly
>   3 qt (2.8 l) sweet port wine
>   3 cups (0.7 l) orange juice concentrate
>   1½ cups (0.3 l) lemon juice
>   1 cup (0.23 l) chopped shallots
>   3 tb dry mustard
>   ¼ cup (0.06 l) chopped ginger
>   1 pint (0.47 l) water

For garnish:

>   3 cups (0.7 l) orange zest
>   2 cups (0.47 l) lemon zest

Kitchen Yields

The total mix yields 5 gal (19 l) sauce.

DEMI-GLACE

Formula

        40 lb (18 kg) veal bones
        1 cup (0.24 l) oil
        ½ gal (1.9 l) mirepoix
        1 pint (450 g) tomato purée
        10 gal (38 l) brown veal stock
        2 lb (900 g) flour
        Thyme, peppercorns, and salt to taste

Simmer about 5 hours.

Kitchen Yields
The total mix yields 5 gal (19 l) sauce.

FISH STOCK

Formula

        25 lb (11.25 kg) fish bones and trimmings
            from saltwater fish
        6 gal (23 l) water
        ½ gal (1.9 l) dry white wine
        ½ gal (1.9 l) diced onions, leeks, celery, and
            parsley stems
        1 qt (0.47 l) fresh mushroom trimmings
        Salt, peppercorns, bay leaves, cloves, and
            thyme to taste

Simmer no longer than 30 minutes.

Kitchen Yields
The total mix yields 5 gal (19 l) sauce.

FISH VELOUTÉ

Formula

        3 gal (11.4 l) fresh fish stock
        1 gal (3.8 l) chicken stock
        1 bottle (0.75 l) dry white wine
        3 lb (1.4 kg) mushroom trimmings
        3 qt (2.8 l) white roux
        1 gal (3.8 l) light cream
        1 lb (450 g) fresh butter

Kitchen Yields
The total mix yields 5 gal (19 l) sauce.

GLACE DE POISSON (FISH GLAZE)

Formula

        5 gal (19 l) fish stock (made without salt and
            vegetables)

Reduce stock slowly; strain frequently and change
pots as the quantity reduces. Glaze freezes well.

Kitchen Yields
The total mix yields 2 qt (0.9 l) sauce.

GLACE DE VIANDE (BEEF GLAZE)

Formula

        5 gal (19 l) white meat stock (made without
            salt and vegetables)

Reduce stock slowly; strain frequently and change
pots as the quantity reduces. Glaze freezes well.

Kitchen Yields
The total mix yields 2 qt (0.9 l) sauce.

HOLLANDAISE SAUCE

Formula

        9 lb (4 kg) butter, when melted will yield
            3½ qt (3.2 l) clear butter fat
        24 egg yolks
        1 cup (0.23 l) water
        ¼ cup (0.06 l) vinegar
        ¼ cup (0.06 l) lemon juice
        Salt and cayenne pepper to taste

Kitchen Yields

Kitchen Yields
The total mix yields 1 gal (3.8 l) sauce.

LEMON SAUCE FOR DUCKLING

Formula

        3 cups (0.7 l) vinegar
        3 cups (0.7 l) sugar
        3 cups (0.7 l) frozen lemonade concentrate
        2 cups (0.46 l) red currant jelly
        8 lemons, cut into quarters
        2 qt (0.9 l) brown duckling stock
        ¾ cups (0.17 l) corn starch
        1 cup (0.23 l) dry sherry wine

For garnish:

2 cups (0.47) lemon peel, cut julienne style

Kitchen Yields
The total mix yields 1 gal (3.8 l) sauce.

MINT SAUCE

Formula
1 gal (3.8 l) white vinegar
1½ qt (1.4 l) sugar
1½ qt (1.4 l) water
2 qt (1.8 l) chopped mint leaves
1 pint (0.4 l) mint jelly

Kitchen Yields
The total mix yields 1½ gal (5.7 l) sauce.

NEWBURG SAUCE

Formula
1 pint (0.47 l) chopped onions
1¼ cup (0.3 l) Spanish paprika
2 lb (0.9 kg) butter
½ gal (1.9 l) dry sherry
1 gal (3.8 l) light cream
3½ gal (13.3 l) heavy cream sauce

Kitchen Yields
The total mix yields 5 gal (19 l) sauce.

ORANGE SAUCE FOR DUCKLING

Formula
3 cups (0.7 l) vinegar
3 cups (0.7 l) sugar
3 cups (0.7 l) orange juice concentrate
2 cups (0.46 l) red currant jelly
4 large oranges, cut into quarters
4 lemons, cut into quarters
2 qt (0.9 l) brown duckling stock
¾ cups (0.17 l) corn starch
1 cup (0.23 l) dry sherry wine

For garnish:

2 cups (0.47) orange peel, cut julienne style

Kitchen Yields
The total mix yields 1 gal (3.8 l) sauce.

SAUCE VERTE (GREEN SAUCE)

Formula
Purée in food processor:

1 bunch watercress, stems discarded
4 bunches chives
½ bunch parsley, stems discarded
1 bunch chervil
1 cup, or 6½ oz (180 g) cooked spinach
3 pieces anchovy fillets
1 tb chopped garlic
1 qt (0.94 l) mayonnaise

Kitchen Yields
The total mix yields 3 pints (1.4 l) sauce.

TARTAR SAUCE GARNISH

Formula
1 gal (3.8 l) coarse-cut onions
1½ gal (5.7 l) dill pickle, drained
½ bunch parsley
1 bunch watercress
1 pint (0.47 l) capers, drained
1½ tb chopped garlic

Grind all ingredients through medium plate of food chopper.

Kitchen Yields
The total mix yields 2½ gal garnish.
Blend 1 pint (0.47 l) with 3 qt (2.8 l) mayonnaise.

TOMATO SAUCE

Formula
2 lb (900 g) bacon (optional) *or* 1 qt (0.9 l) oil
½ gal (1.9 l) chopped onions
½ cup (0.12 l) crushed garlic
2 cups (350 g) flour
Four #10 cans tomato puree
Two #10 cans crushed tomatoes
1 gal (3.8 l) water
½ cup (0.12 l) sugar
Salt, basil, and oregano to taste

Kitchen Yields
The total mix yields 5 gal (19 l) sauce.

TONNATO SAUCE (COLD TUNA SAUCE FOR VEAL)

84 oz (2.25 kg), or two 42-oz (1.15 kg) cans tuna in oil
1 cup, or 8 oz (0.23 l) capers, drained
24 pieces anchovy fillets
2 tb grated lemon peel
2 cups (0.47 l) olive oil
2 pints (0.94 l) mayonnaise

Kitchen Yields
The total mix yields 1 gal (3.8 l) sauce.

SAUCES QUANTITIES

RESTAURANT USE

BROWN SAUCES

Serving size:
1½ oz (0.05 l).

BANQUET USE

BROWN SAUCES
5 qt (4.7 l) serves 100 covers.
2 gal (7.6 l) serves 200 covers.

CREAM SAUCES
1½ gal (5.7 l) serves 100 covers.
3 gal (11.4 l) serves 200 covers.

JUS (FOR ROAST BEEF)
3 qt (2.8 l) serves 100 covers.
1½ gal (5.7 l) serves 200 covers.

SAUERKRAUT

Available mostly canned, although fresh sauerkraut might be available locally. Varieties include shredded kraut, chopped kraut, sweet sauerkraut, and kraut with either celery seeds or caraway seeds. Kraut is the German name for cabbage.

Pack:
Six #10 cans, with a drained weight of 80 oz (2.25 kg) each. Smaller packs are available.

Kitchen Yields

Serving size:
With hot dog, 1½ oz (42 g); therefore, one #10 can yields 50 servings. As a vegetable, ½ cup cooked; therefore, one #10 can yields 20 servings.

Calories:
¾ cup, or 6 oz (170 g) = 30 Calories.

SAVOY CABBAGE

See Cabbage.

SCALLOPS

Available fresh, frozen, and processed. Scallops are classified as bay scallops, which have an edible muscle about ½ in (12.7 mm) across, and sea scallops, which can develop a muscle of up to 2 in (50.8 mm) across. Imported scallops are often shipped with the pink edible roe still attached. Domestic scallops are almost always fully cleaned and white. Small scallops are available still in the shell. They are sold by the piece as a specialty item.

Sea scallops are produced mostly in the North Atlantic. An important source of sea scallops are also the waters around Alaska and along the Pacific coast as far south as Oregon. Bay scallops are harvested in the estuaries along the Atlantic coast as far south as Florida. The southern variety is slightly larger than the genuine northern bay scallop, and is called a *calico bay scallop*.

FRESH BAY SCALLOPS
Bay scallops are sold shucked.

Season:
Available year-round, with peak season in the summer.

Pack:
Sold by 1-gal (3.8-l) cans. Net weight per can is about 8 lb (3.6 kg).

Kitchen Yields
There is no waste.

Count:
450 to 480 per gal (3.8 l).

Serving size:
For main course, 7 oz (200 g); 1 gal (3.8 l) yields 16 portions.
7 oz (200 g) raw scallops is equivalent to 4½ oz (127 g) cooked.

FRESH SEA SCALLOPS
Sea scallops are almost always sold shucked.

Pack:
Sold in 1-gal (3.8-l) containers. Net weight is about 7 lb 12 oz (3.5 kg).

Kitchen Yields
There is no waste.

Count:
Varies; about 160 to 240 per 1-gal (3.8-l) container.

Serving size:
For main course, 7 oz (200 g).

FROZEN SEA SCALLOPS
Available loose (IQF) or in frozen block.

Pack:

Block Scallops:
One case of ten 5-lb (2.25-kg) boxes.
One 50-lb (22.5-kg) individual case.

IQF Scallops:
One case of six 3-lb (1.4-kg) boxes.
One 30-lb (13.5-kg) individual case.

Kitchen Yields

Counts:
Up to 20, 20 to 30, 30 to 40, and 40 to 50 per 1 lb (450 g).

PROCESSED SCALLOPS
Frozen breaded scallops are available in two sizes: bay scallop size and sea scallop size. The breading is about 45 percent, by weight.

Pack:
Four 3-lb (1.4-kg) trays per 12-lb (5.4-kg) box.

Kitchen Yields

Serving size:
6 oz (168 g) uncooked; one tray 3-lb (1.4-kg) yields 8 servings.

Calories:
8 fried scallops, weighing about 4¼ oz (120 g) cooked = 240 Calories.

SCOOP SIZES

Scoops are classified according to the approximate number of scoops contained in 1 qt (0.47 l). Table S-1 lists scoop volumes and weights.
NOTE: Weight is approximate and depends on density of product.

SEAWEED

ASAKUSA NORI
See Japanese Foods.

DULSE
Purplish-red seaweed, available fresh and dehydrated.

Season:
April, May, and June.

Table S-1 Scoop Volumes and Weights

Scoop #	Measure	Approximate Weight
30	2 tb	1 oz (28 g)
24	2¾ tb	1½ oz (42 g)
20	3 tb	1¾ oz (49 g)
16	4 tb	2 oz (56 g)
12	5 tb	2½ oz (71 g)
10	6 tb	3 oz (85 g)
6	10 tb	5 oz (142 g)

Pack:
By weight.

KELP

Seaweed available fresh, dried, and pickled. Powdered kelp can be used as salt substitute.

Season:
April, May, and June.

Pack:
By weight.

KOMBU (DRIED KELP)

See Japanese Foods.

SEA BEANS

Seaweed available fresh year-round.

Pack:
By weight.

Kitchen Yields
Large stems are tough and must be discarded. Cleaning loss by weight is 20 percent.

SEA LETTUCE

Seaweed that has the texture of romaine and a spicy taste. It is available fresh.

Season:
April to August.

Pack:
By weight.

SEA PALM

Seaweed found on the Pacific Northwest coast. It is available fresh.

Season:
April to August.

Pack:
By weight.

WAKAME

See Japanese Foods.

SHALLOTS

Available fresh and processed, shallots are small bulbs that resemble onions but have a milder flavor. Used for flavoring sauces and as vegetable.

FRESH SHALLOTS

Season:
Available year-round.

Pack:
1-pint (0.47-l) cartons; 5-lb (2.25-kg) bags.

Sizes and counts:

Large:
40 to 50 pieces per 1 lb (450 g).

Jumbo:
20 to 25 pieces per 1 lb (450 g).

Kitchen Yields
1 cup chopped weighs 4 oz (112 g); 1 lb as purchased produces 2¼ cups chopped.

PROCESSED SHALLOTS

Chopped shallots have become available dehydrated, frozen, or packed in oil.

Pack:
Varies, depending on packer.

Kitchen Yields
Use as is. There is no waste.

SHAMOUTI

Also known as *Jaffa orange*, this fruit is now grown in limited quantities in the United States.

Season:
Domestic production in fall; imports in winter.

SHARON FRUIT

This fruit, which resembles a persimmon, is imported from Israel. It is seedless and can be eaten raw.

Season:

Winter.

SHELLFISH

See individual types, such as Crabs, Lobsters, and Shrimp.

SHRIMP

Shrimp are caught in most seas and come in many sizes and quality levels. There are three principal kinds of shrimp: white, pink, and brown. Large shrimp are often called prawns. Price depends on size. Pink shrimp are considered most desirable in foodservice. Shrimp are always shipped frozen, except in local markets. Shrimp, head-on, have become available in some markets.

COOKED SHRIMP

CANNED COOKED SHRIMP

Pack:

Six #10 cans. Other packs are available.

Kitchen Yields

Product is fully cooked and ready to serve. Drained weight varies, depending on the manufacturer.

Calories:

3 oz (85 g) = 100 Calories.

FROZEN COOKED COCKTAIL SHRIMP

These are fully cooked and peeled shrimp; most brands still have the tails attached for eye appeal. Only IQF shrimp should be purchased, because the glazing protects the product.

Counts:

Generally, 1 lb (450 g) green headless shrimp produces ½ lb (225 g) peeled cooked shrimp. For this reason, peeled cooked shrimp are often packed in 2½ lb (1.1 kg) boxes, so that the number of cooked shrimp corresponds roughly with the count of green, headless shrimp in 5-lb (2.3-kg) boxes. However, other packs are also available.

Pack:

Four 2½-lb (1.1-kg) boxes. Table S-2 identifies standard industry terms for shrimp sizes and compares counts of cooked cocktail and green headless shrimp. Terminology varies from one packer to another.

Table S-2 Size Comparisons between Cooked Cocktail and Green Headless Shrimp

Name	Tail Style	Cooked Count per 1 lb (450 g)	Raw Count (Green Headless) per 1 lb (450 g)	Cooked Count per 2½-lb (1.1-kg) Box
Super Colossal	tail on or off	18 to 25	10 to 12	52 pieces
Colossal	tail on or off	21 to 30	10 to 15	65 pieces
Super Jumbo	tail on or off	31 to 40	16 to 20	90 pieces
Jumbo	tail on or off	41 to 50	21 to 25	115 pieces
Extra Large	tail on or off	51 to 60	26 to 30	140 pieces
Large	tail on or off	61 to 70	31 to 35	165 pieces
Salad	tail off only	70 to 90, 110 to 130, 130 to 200, 200 to 300, or 300 to 500	36 to 42, 50 to 60	200 pieces or more

Kitchen Yields

Serving Size:
For shrimp cocktail, 5 pieces of size 31 to 40. One 2½-lb (1.1-kg) box yields 18 servings.

Calories:
5 oz (140 g) = 166 Calories.
4 oz (112 g), or 7 to 8 Super Jumbo pieces = 125 Calories.

FROZEN COOKED TINY SHRIMP
Alaska is the largest producer of these shrimp.

Pack:
Six 5-lb (2.25-kg) blocks or bags containing IQF shrimp. Other packs are available.

Counts:

Regular:
350 to 500 per 1 lb (450 g).

Medium:
250 to 350 per 1 lb (450 g).

Defrosted weight:
4 lb 13½ oz (2.2 kg).

Kitchen Yields
One regular block contains 2,250 shrimp; one medium block contains 1,500 shrimp.

Serving size:
6 oz (170 g) for shrimp cocktail; one 5-lb (2.25-kg) block yields 13 servings.

Calories:
6 oz (170 g) = 200 Calories.

PROCESSED SHRIMP

BREADED SHRIMP
Breaded shrimp are classified as hand-breaded and machine-breaded. Generally, the tails are left unbreaded on hand-breaded shrimp. On machine-breaded shrimp, the tails are usually breaded, although some brands of machine-breaded shrimp are available with unbreaded tails. Many different types of breading are available.

Pack:
Eight 3-lb (1.4-kg) boxes; four 3-lb (1.4-kg) boxes; twelve 8-oz (225-g) bags; twelve 6-oz (170-g) bags.

Kitchen Yields
Counts for breaded shrimp are basically the same as for green headless shrimp. The count on the box is the actual count. By government regulation, weight of breading can not exceed 50 percent. If breading exceeds 50 percent, the product must be labeled *Imitation Shrimp*. Miniature shrimp (very tiny shrimp) are available in 40 to 50 counts. Portion sizes vary according to count.

Calories:
6 medium shrimp, fried, weighing 6 oz (170 g) = 170 Calories.

RAW SHRIMP

GREEN HEADLESS SHRIMP
Green headless shrimp are uncooked shrimp in the shell, with the head removed. They are sold on the basis of count per 1 lb (450 g).

Pack:
5-lb (2.25-kg) boxes, frozen in a solid block. Table S-3 lists counts per 1 lb (450 g) and total number per box for green headless shrimp.

Kitchen Yields

Waste:

Peeling and deveining loss:
About 25 percent by weight.

Cooking loss:
25 percent by weight.

Total loss:
50 percent by weight.

Serving sizes:
For broiled stuffed shrimp served as main course, 4 shrimp of size Under 8; therefore, one 5-lb (2.2-kg) box yields 9 servings. For shrimp cocktail, 4 shrimp of size 16 to 20; therefore, one 5-lb (2.2-kg) box yields 22 to 24 portions. For shrimp salad course, 9 or 10 shrimp of size 21 to 25; therefore, one 5-lb (2.2-kg) box yields 13 servings.

Table S-3 Green Headless Shrimp per 1 lb (450 g) and per Box

Count per 1 lb (450 g)	Number per 5-lb (2.25-kg) Box
Under 8	36 to 38
Under 10	42 to 48
10 to 15	60 to 75
16 to 20	90 to 95
21 to 25	110 to 120
26 to 30	135 to 145
31 to 35	160 to 170
36 to 42	185 to 195
40 to 50	215 to 260
50 to 60	270 to 280

Calories:

5 oz (140 g) = 166 Calories.

P & D SHRIMP

P & D shrimp are peeled and deveined. They are normally shipped as individually quick frozen (IQF) shrimp. P & D shrimp are available by count per 1 lb (450 g), and by weight as broken pieces. Broken pieces are usable in salads and in shrimp dishes with sauce.

Pack:

Six 3-lb (1.4-kg) boxes, totaling 18 lb (8.2 kg); 12½-lb (5.6-kg) bulk pack. Other packs are available. Table S-4 compares counts of green headless and P & D shrimp.

Kitchen Yields

There is no peeling loss. Cooking loss is about 30 percent, because the IQF process involves glazing each piece with ice, which increases the water content of the product.

Calories:

5 oz (140 g) = 166 Calories.

Table S-4 Size Comparison between Green Headless and P & D Shrimp

Green Headless Count per 1 lb (450 g)	P & D Count per 1 lb (450 g)	P & D Count per 3-lb (1.4-kg) Box
10 to 15	18	54
16 to 20	23	69
21 to 25	28	84
26 to 30	32	96
31 to 35	38	112
36 to 42	44	132
40 to 50	53	159
50 to 60	63	190

SNAIL EGGS

Imported and domestic snail eggs have come onto the market. Some are flavored with saffron, ginger, or other flavorings.

Pack:

1-oz (28.4-g) jars, pasteurized.

SNAILS

See Escargots.

SNOW PEAS

See Snow Peas, under Peas.

SORREL (SOUR GRASS)

See Herbs & Spices.

SOUFFLÉ

Basic Mix Formula

    2 lb (900 g) flour

1¾ lb (790 g) butter
8 oz (225 g) sugar

Method:
Blend ingredients and store, scaled, in refrigerator.

Two-serving Soufflé Formula
3½ oz (100 g) basic mix
½ pint (0.23 l) boiling milk
4 egg yolks
3 egg whites
2 oz (56 g) sugar
½ oz (0.01 l) cordial or flavor

Forty-serving Soufflé Formula
Full basic formula mix
6 qt (5.6 l) milk
70 egg yolks
54 egg whites
2½ lb (1.1 kg) sugar
10 oz (0.30 l) cordial or flavor

SOUPS

BASIC SOUP INGREDIENTS
Only basic ingredients are listed in the formulas
presented under this entry.

BEAN SOUP WITH TOMATO
20 lb (9 kg) navy beans
12 gal (45.6 l) chicken stock
One #10 can chopped tomatoes
1½ gal (5.7 l) light cream

Kitchen Yields
The total mix yields 10 gal (38 l) soup.

BEEF CONSOMMÉ
10 lb (4.5 kg) clarification meat
30 egg whites, or 1 qt (0.9 l)
One #10 can peeled tomatoes
1 gal (3.8 l) mirepoix (diced soup vegetables)
12 gal (45.6 l) beef stock

Kitchen Yields
The total mix yields 10 gal (38 l) soup.

BLACK BEAN SOUP
15 lb (6.7 kg) black turtle beans
5 lb (2.2 kg) navy beans
1½ gal (5.7 l) light cream

Kitchen Yields
The total mix yields 10 gal (38 l) soup.

CHILLED CHERRY SOUP
6 gal (22.8 l) frozen pitted sour cherries
4 gal (15.2 l water
2 lb (0.9 kg) corn starch
2 lb (0.9 kg) sugar
4 cinnamon sticks
Peel from 8 lemons
1 tb cayenne pepper

Kitchen Yields
The total mix yields 10 gal (38 l) soup.

CRAYFISH BISQUE
10 dozen crayfish
¾ gal (2.8 l) roux
12 gal (45 l) strong chicken stock
1 gal (3.8 l) light cream
½ gal (1.9 l) white wine
1 qt (0.9 l) cream sherry
1 qt (0.9 l) brandy

Kitchen Yields
The total mix yields 10 gal (38 l) soup.

CREAM OF ASPARAGUS
10 lb (4.5 kg), or 6 boxes frozen asparagus
¾ gal (2.8 l) white roux
12 gal (45 l) strong chicken stock
1 gal (3.8 l) light cream

Kitchen Yields
The total mix yields 10 gal (38 l) soup.

CREAM OF BROCCOLI
7½ lb (3.3 kg), or 3 boxes frozen broccoli
¾ gal (2.8 l) white roux
12 gal (45 l) strong chicken stock
1 gal (3.8 l) light cream

Kitchen Yields
The total mix yields 10 gal (38 l) soup.

CREAM OF CAULIFLOWER

    7½ lb (3.3 kg), or 3 boxes frozen cauliflower
    ¾ gal (2.8 l) white roux
    12 gal (45 l) strong chicken stock
    1 gal (3.8 l) light cream

Kitchen Yields
The total mix yields 10 gal (38 l) soup.

CREAM OF CHICKEN

    ¾ gal (2.8 l) white roux
    12 gal (45 l) strong chicken stock
    1 gal (3.8 l) light cream

Kitchen Yields
The total mix yields 10 gal (38 l) soup.

CREAM OF CORN

    One #10 can creamed corn
    One #10 can kernel corn (for garnish)
    ½ gal (1.9 l) white roux
    12 gal (45 l) strong chicken stock
    1 gal (3.8 l) light cream

Kitchen Yields
The total mix yields 10 gal (38 l) soup.

CREAM OF CURRY

    ½ lb (225 g) curry powder
    ¾ gal (2.8 l) white roux
    12 gal (45 l) strong chicken stock
    1 gal (3.8 l) light cream

Kitchen Yields
The total mix yields 10 gal (38 l) soup.

CREAM OF MUSHROOMS

    9 lb (4 kg) fresh mushrooms
    ¾ gal (2.8 l) white roux
    12 gal (45 l) strong chicken stock
    1 gal (3.8 l) light cream

Kitchen Yields
The total mix yields 10 gal (38 l) soup.

CREAM OF TOMATO

    Three #10 cans tomato puree
    ¾ gal (2.8 l) white roux
    12 gal (45 l) strong chicken stock
    1 gal (3.8 l) light cream

Kitchen Yields
The total mix yields 10 gal (38 l) soup.

CUCUMBER SOUP

    25 lb (11.25 kg) potatoes
    20 lb (9 kg) peeled, seeded cucumbers
    2.5 gal (9.5 l) dry white wine
    2.5 gal (9.5 l) heavy cream

Kitchen Yields
The total mix yields 10 gal (38 l) soup.

FENNEL OR ANISE SOUP

    2 gal (4.6 l) chopped fennel, no greens
    ½ gal (1.9 l) chopped fennel, with greens
    ½ cup, or 2 oz (56 g) fennel seed
    ¾ gal (2.8 l) white roux
    12 gal (45 l) strong chicken stock
    1 gal (3.8 l) light cream

For garnish:

    ½ gal (1.9 l) diced fennel
    1 qt (0.47 l) chopped fennel

Kitchen Yields
The total mix yields 10 gal (38 l) soup.

GAME CONSOMMÉ

    15 lb (6.7 kg) browned venison or other game bones
    5 lb (2.2 kg) clarification meat (venison and beef trimmings)
    15 egg whites, or 1 pint (0.47 l)
    One #10 can peeled tomatoes
    1 gal (3.8 l) mirepoix (diced soup vegetables)
    ¼ cup, or 2 oz (56 g) crushed juniper berries
    12 gal (45.6 l) beef stock
    1 qt (0.9 l) dry sherry
    1 qt (0.9 l) cream sherry

Kitchen Yields
The total mix yields 10 gal (38 l) soup.

GAZPACHO

    10 lb (4.5 kg) onions
    10 lb (4.5 kg) seeded green peppers
    15 lb (6.7 kg) peeled, seeded cucumbers
    One #10 can peeled whole tomatoes

5 lb (2.2 kg) celery stalks
One #10 can tomato purée
Two 46-oz (2.6-l) cans tomato juice
2 qt (0.94 l) vinegar
1 qt (0.47 l) olive oil
½ cup crushed garlic
24 whole eggs
½ cup salt
¼ cup ground pepper
½ cup sugar
1 oz (28 g) dried tarragon

Kitchen Yields
The total mix yields 10 gal (38 l) soup.

GIBLET AND BARLEY SOUP

2.5 gal (9.5 l) ground raw giblets
½ gal (1.9 l) oil
5 lb (2.2 kg) pearl barley
½ gal (1.9 l) diced onions
½ gal (1.9 l) diced celery
½ gal (1.9 l) diced carrots
½ gal (1.9 l) diced turnips
1 qt (0.9 l) brown roux
12 gal (45.6 l) beef stock

Kitchen Yields
The total mix yields 10 gal (38 l) soup.

GUMBO

½ gal (1.9 l) diced green peppers
½ gal (1.9 l) diced onions
½ gal (1.9 l) diced celery
½ gal (1.9 l) diced cabbage
One #10 can chopped tomatoes
10 lb (4.5 kg) frozen diced okra
   or two #10 cans diced okra
1 gal (3.8 l) cooked rice
5 lb (2.2 kg) diced ham
½ gal (1.9 kg) cooked chicken
1 lb (450 g) file powder
3½ gal (11.4 l) chicken stock
3½ gal (11.4 l) beef stock

Kitchen Yields
The total mix yields 10 gal (38 l) soup.

JELLIED MADRILENE CONSOMMÉ

Four 46-oz (2.45-l) cans tomato juice
Two #10 cans peeled tomatoes
1 lb (450 g) plain gelatin
½ gal (1.9 l) chopped celery
10 lb (4.5 kg) clarification meat
30 egg whites, or 1 qt (0.47 l)
One #10 can peeled tomatoes
8 gal (30.4 l) beef stock

Kitchen Yields
The total mix yields 10 gal (38 l) soup.

LOBSTER SOUP

35 cooked lobster heads and carcasses from
   1¼-lb (560-g) lobsters, or 25 lb (11.2 kg)
   raw culls
One #10 can tomato purée
¾ gal (2.8 l) white roux
12 gal (45 l) strong chicken stock
1 gal (3.8 l) light cream
½ gal (1.9 l) white wine
1 qt (0.9 l) cream sherry
1 qt (0.9 l) brandy

Kitchen Yields
The total mix yields 10 gal (38 l) soup.

MINESTRONE

1 cup (8 oz) chopped fresh garlic
½ gal (1.9 l) olive oil
5 lb (2.2 kg) ham hooks
3 lb (1.35 kg) navy beans
½ gal (1.9 l) diced green peppers
½ gal (1.9 l) diced onions
½ gal (1.9 l) diced celery
½ gal (1.9 l) diced carrots
½ gal (1.9 l) diced cabbage
One #10 can chopped tomatoes
One #10 can tomato purée
3 lb (1.35 kg) broken spaghetti
7 gal (26.6 l) beef stock

Kitchen Yields
The total mix yields 10 gal (38 l) soup.

ONION SOUP

4 gal (15.2 l) sliced onions

½ gal (1.9 l) oil
12 gal (45 l) strong beef stock
¼ cup dried thyme
1 qt (0.9 l) apple jack

Kitchen Yields
The total mix yields 10 gal (38 l) soup.

PEA SOUP
20 lb (9 kg) green split or yellow peas
12 gal (45 l) chicken stock
1½ gal (5.7 l) light cream

Kitchen Yields
The total mix yields 10 gal (38 l) soup.

PHILADELPHIA PEPPER POT
1 gal (3.8 l) diced green peppers
1 gal (3.8 l) diced onions
1 gal (3.8 l) diced potatoes
1 gal (3.8 l) diced celery
1 gal (3.8 l) cooked spätzle
1 gal (3.8 l) cooked, diced tripe
8 gal (30.4 l) beef stock

Kitchen Yields
The total mix yields 10 gal (38 l) soup.

PUMPKIN SOUP
½ gal (1.9 l) white roux
Three #10 cans pumpkin purée
12 gal (45 l) strong chicken stock
¼ cup, or 2 oz (56 g) nutmeg
½ cup, or 4 oz (112 g) lemon juice
1 gal (3.8 l) light cream

Kitchen Yields
The total mix yields 10 gal (38 l) soup.

VEGETABLE SOUP
½ gal (1.9 l) diced green peppers
½ gal (1.9 l) diced onions
½ gal (1.9 l) diced potatoes
½ gal (1.9 l) diced celery
½ gal (1.9 l) diced carrots
½ gal (1.9 l) diced cabbage
One #10 can chopped tomatoes
7 gal (26.6 l) beef stock

Kitchen Yields
The total mix yields 10 gal (38 l) soup.

VICHYSSOISE (POTATO SOUP)
25 lb (11.25 kg) potatoes
8 lb (3.6 kg) onions
8 lb (3.6 kg) white of leeks
2 gal (7.6 l) light cream

SOUP QUANTITIES

Kitchen Yields

Serving size:
6 oz (0.17 l).
1 gal (3.8 l) yields 20 servings.
5 gal (19 l) yields 100 servings.
10 gal (38 l) yields 200 servings.
25 gal (95 l) yields 500 servings.
38 gal (145 l) yields 750 servings.
NOTE: Always make about 10 percent more soup than needed, to allow for spillage.

SOUR CREAM

See Cream.

SOUVLAKI

This is a Greek preparation of pork on skewers. It is available frozen, fully seasoned.

Pack:
15-lb (6.7-kg) cases.

Count:
Fifty-four 4-oz (112-g) skewers.

Kitchen Yields

Serving size:
Two pieces, as main course.

SOY BEANS

See Eda Mame, under Japanese Foods; *see also* Bean Curd.

SPÄTZLE

Small dumplings popular in southwestern Germany and neighboring Switzerland. Available dry, ready to use, or make fresh.

Pack:
1-lb (450-g) packages.

Kitchen Yields

Serving size:
4 oz (112 g).
1 lb (450 g) raw yields 2 lb (900 g) cooked product or 8 servings.

Formula

        3 lb (1.35 kg) bread flour
        12 eggs
        1 qt (0.94 l) milk
        ½ cup (0.12 l) oil
        1 tb salt
        1 tb baking powder

This formula yields forty ½ cup (0.12 l) servings. NOTE: To shape spätzle, use a food mill with very large holes. Some chefs shape spätzle on a wet, wooden board, then scrape them directly into the boiling water.

SPANISH LIME

This fruit resembles lychee nuts. It has a brown, tough skin. The fruit is eaten by sucking the milky flesh from the seeds.

SPAGHETTI

See Pasta.

SPICES

See Herbs & Spices.

SPINACH

Spinach is available canned, fresh, and frozen.

CANNED SPINACH

Available chopped and as whole-leaf.

Pack:
Six #10 cans.

Kitchen Yields

Serving size:
½ cup (0.11 l), weighing 3⅓ oz (93 g). One #10 can has a drained weight of 58 to 60 oz (1.6 to 1.7 kg) and yields 17 servings; one case yields 100 servings.

Calories:
½ cup (0.11 l), weighing 3⅓ oz (93 g) = 25 Calories.

FRESH SPINACH

There are two basic varieties: curly-leaf Savoy spinach and flat-leaf spinach, also called *broadleaf spinach*. Curly-leaf Savoy spinach ships better than the flat-leaf spinach. Semi-Savoy spinach is occasionally available. Loose spinach is shipped both clipped (with some stems removed) and in bunches.

Season:
Available year-round, with peaks in spring.

Pack:
20- to 22-lb (9- to 9.9-kg) bushels; cases with eight 10-oz (280-g) cello packs.

Kitchen Yields

Waste:
From bushel spinach, as purchased, ready-to-cook or serve as salad, the waste is 30 percent by weight. One 20-lb (9-kg) bushel as purchased produces 13 to 14 lb (5.8 to 6.3 kg) cleaned spinach.
From trimmed cello pack spinach, ready-to-cook or serve as salad, the waste is 15 percent by weight. One carton of eight cello packs as purchased produces 68 oz (1.9 kg) cleaned spinach.

Salad serving sizes:

For main course salad:
2 cups, or 4 oz (112 g).

For side order salad:

1 cup, or 2 oz (56 g).

One cello pack yields 2 main-course salad servings and 4 side-order salad servings.

One case yields 16 to 17 main-course salad servings or 32 to 34 main-course salad servings.

One bushel spinach yields 54 main-course salads or 100 side-order salads.

Serving size:

Cooked spinach:

½ cup (0.11 l).

One case cello pack spinach produces 7½ cups (1.7 l) cooked spinach, or 15 servings.

One bushel, as purchased, produces 10 lb (4.5 kg) cooked spinach.

10 lb (4.5 kg) cooked spinach equals 20 cups (4.6 l) or 40 servings.

Cooking losses:

10 lb (4.5 kg) trimmed spinach produces 7½ lb (3.3 kg) cooked spinach.

7½ lb (3.3 kg) cooked spinach equals 15 cups (3.5 l).

Calories:

1 cup, or 2 oz (56 g) raw, chopped = 15 Calories.
½ cup, or 4 oz (112 l) cooked, drained = 28 Calories.

FROZEN SPINACH

Available whole leaf, chopped, and IQF.

Pack:

Twelve 3-lb (1.35-kg) boxes, chopped or whole; twelve 2-lb (0.9-kg) bags, IQF.

Kitchen Yields

Serving size:

½ cup (0.23 l). One box yields 12 servings; therefore, one case yields 150 servings.

Calories:

½ cup, or 3⅓ oz (93 g), cooked, chopped, and drained = 28 Calories.
1 cup, or 6¾ oz (190 g), cooked leaf, = 45 Calories.

SPONGE CAKE

Formula

1 qt (0.47 l) egg yolks
3 qt (1.41 l) whole eggs
4 lb (1.8 kg) sugar
3 lb (1.35 kg) cake flour
1 lb (450 g) patent flour
8 oz (225 g) corn starch
1 lb (450 g) melted butter
Salt and lemon to taste

Kitchen Yields

The total mix yields twenty 8-in (200-mm) layer cakes.

SPROUTS

Sprout include alfalfa sprouts and bean sprouts. Brussels sprouts are listed separately; *see* Brussels Sprouts. Sprout varieties are available canned, cut, fresh, and live in planter boxes.

ALFALFA SPROUTS

Pack:

Twelve 4- or 6-oz (112- or 170-g) containers; 4-lb (1.8-kg) flats.

Kitchen Yields

There is no waste.

Serving size:

For salad garnish, 2 oz (56 g); one flat of 4-oz (112-g) containers yield 24 servings.

Calories:

2 oz (56 g) = 10 Calories.

BEAN SPROUTS

Bean sprouts are grown from mung beans.

CANNED BEAN SPROUTS

Pack:

Six #10 cans. Other packs are available.

Drained weight:

58 oz (1.6 kg).

Kitchen Yields
1 cup weighs 4 oz (112 g).

Calories:
1 cup, or 4 oz (112 g) = 35 Calories.

FRESH BEAN SPROUTS

Pack:
5- and 10-lb (2.25- and 5.5-kg) bags.

Kitchen Yields
There is no waste; use as is.
1 cup weighs 3½ oz (100 g).

Calories:
1 cup, or 3½ oz (100 g) = 33 Calories.

SQUAB

Squab is a young pigeon, and should not be confounded with the squab chicken, which is a baby chicken. Squab is available fresh and frozen and is shipped whole, bone-in and boneless. Fresh whole bone-in birds are often shipped with head on.

Season:
Available year-round, with a larger supply in spring.

Pack:
Twelve birds to a carton.

Sizes:

Whole:
12 oz (340 g), 14 oz (400 g), 16 oz (450 g), and 20 oz (560 g).

Boneless:
13 oz (365 g).

Kitchen Yields

Best size:
14 oz (400 g), with head.

Serving size:
One bird.

Breast only:
5 to 6 oz (140 to 168 g).
One 20-oz (560-g) bird will yield 2 breasts.

SQUASH

Available canned, fresh, and frozen. Squash is classified as soft-shell (also called *summer squash*) or hard-shell (also called *winter squash*).

FRESH SQUASH

Season:
Despite their classification into summer and winter types, many varieties are available year-round.

Pack:
25-lb (11.25-kg) cartons. Other packs are available.

Sizes:
Vary greatly. When sizes are indicated, they are the sizes most suitable for foodservice operators.

Kitchen Yields
Yields vary greatly, depending on season and size of vegetable. For summer squash, the smallest pieces are the best, because they give the highest percentage yield, are firm, and shrink little.

SUMMER SQUASH VARIETIES

BITTER MELON
Also called *Balsam Asiatic pear*, this squash has a sour/bitter taste. Seeds should be removed before cooking. Soaking in salt water removes some of the sourness. This vegetable looks like a crinkled cucumber.

Season:
Available year-round.

Pack:
By weight.

Size:
6 to 12 oz (170 to 340 g).

Kitchen Yields
Use with peel. Little waste.

Butternut

Season:
Summer for squash with soft edible skin and seeds. Winter for squash with harder shell.

Chayote

Also called *Mirliton squash*, this is a member of the melon family used for cooking. The squash is round to pear-shaped, and varies in color from light to dark green.

Season:
Available year-round.

Pack:
10- and 15-lb (4.5- and 6.8-kg) boxes.

Count:
Varies according to pack.

Sizes:
1 lb (450 g) average.

Kitchen Yields

Cleaning waste:
30 percent.

Custard Squash

Also called *Pattypan squash*.

Season:
Summer and fall.

Scallop Squash

Season:
Fall.

Yellow Crookneck

Season:
Summer and fall.

Average sizes:

Small:
4 oz (112 g).

Medium:
5 oz (140 g).

Yellow Straightneck

Season:
Summer and fall.

Zucchini

Season:
Available year-round.

Kitchen Yields

Trimming waste:
10 percent.

Serving sizes:
For restaurant service, 3 oz (85 g) sautéed or breaded; one 25-lb (11.2-kg) carton yields 120 servings sautéed or breaded.
For banquet service, 2½ oz (70 g); one 25-lb (11.2-kg) carton yields 140 servings, and 18 lb (8.16 kg) yield 100 servings.

Calories:
1 cup, or 7½ oz (210 g) cooked, drained, and diced = 30 Calories.

WINTER SQUASH VARIETIES:

Acorn Squash

Available green and gold.

Season:
Peak is from October to December.

Pack:
38-lb (17.1-kg) box.

Kitchen Yields
About 25 percent waste.

Banana Squash

Straightneck squash with a hard rind.

Season:
October to December.

Pack:
40-lb (18-kg) cartons.

BUTTERNUT

Season:
September to December.

Pack:
38-lb (17.1-kg) bushel.

CALABAZA

Spanish name for a number of hard shell varieties. Also called *Cuban squash*, the vegetable has a better yield than pumpkin. Buff color indicates maturity.

Season:
Available year-round. Some product is imported in the winter.

Kitchen Yields
1 lb (450 g) as purchased yields 11 oz (312 g) squash, ready to cook.

COCOZEALLA

Straightneck squash with hard rind.

Season:
September to December.

Pack:
40-lb (18-kg) cartons.

HUBBARD

Season:
September to November.

Average size:
4 lb (1.8 kg).

ORNAMENTAL SQUASH

Season:
October to December.

Pack:
By weight.

PUMPKIN

See Pumpkin.

SPAGHETTI SQUASH

Season:
September to December.

Pack:
35-lb (15.7-kg) carton.

Average sizes:
3 to 4 lb (1.3 to 1.8 kg).

WINTER MELON

Large vegetable, round or football-shaped, with green skin and white inner meat that contains many seeds. Must be cooked.

Season:
Available year-round; peak is in winter.

Pack:
By weight and piece.

Size:
Up to 20 in (500 mm) across.

PROCESSED SQUASH

CANNED PUMPKIN
See Pumpkin.

FROZEN SQUASH
Available are a number of varieties, including sliced zucchini and sliced yellow squash. Cooked squash purée is also available.

Pack:
Twelve 4-lb (1.8-kg) boxes squash purée; twelve 2-lb (0.9-kg) IQF zucchini or yellow squash; individual 20-lb (9-kg) IQF zucchini or yellow squash; twelve 2½-lb (1.1-kg) zucchini or yellow squash; twelve 3-lb (1.35-kg) yellow southern squash.

Kitchen Yields

Serving size:
½ cup, or 3¾ oz (106 g).
One 4-lb (1.8-kg) box squash purée yields 17 servings, so one case squash purée yields 212 servings. One 2-lb (0.9-kg) box IQF squash yields 7 servings, so one case IQF squash yields 84 servings.

One 2½-lb (1.1-kg) box squash yields 8 servings, so one case yields 100 servings.

Calories:
½ cup, or 3¾ oz (106 g) summer squash = 15 Calories.
½ cup, or 3¾ oz (106 g) winter squash = 60 Calories.

SQUID

Available fresh or frozen.

WHOLE SQUID

Squid, also called *calamare*, is normally sold fully cleaned, except for the center cartilage, which is easily pulled out.

Pack:
By weight.

Season:
Available year-round.

Kitchen Yields
Waste is about 5 percent by weight. Cleaned squid does not contain the squid ink, which is prized for pasta and sauce flavoring.

PROCESSED SQUID

Frozen breaded squid sections are available from specialty purveyors.

Pack:
Twelve 2½-lb (1.1-kg) boxes.

Kitchen Yields
Use as is. There is no waste.

STAR FRUIT

There are two varieties on the market: Green Star Fruit (also called *Cucumber Tree Fruit*) and a yellow variety called Star Apple. Both have the shape of a five-pointed star when cut across. The Green Star Fruit is sour and cannot be eaten raw. The Star Apple is slightly sweet.

Season:
Available year-round, with peak in fall and winter.

Pack:
By weight and by piece.

Size:

Green Star Fruit:
3 in (8 cm) long.

Star Apple:
4 in (12 cm) long.

STEAM TABLE PAN SIZES

Table S-5 lists sizes and capacities of different steam table pans.
NOTE: The capacities shown are to the rim of the pan. The effective capacity is considerable smaller when pans are filled and transported.

STRAWBERRIES

Available canned, fresh, and frozen.

CANNED STRAWBERRIES

Pack:
Six #10 cans; twelve, twenty-four, or thirty-six #303 cans.

Kitchen Yields
One #10, drained weight, is 74 oz (2 kg).
One #303 can, drained weight, is 11 oz (308 g).

Servings size:
½ cup (0.12 l) fruit and juice. One #10 can yields 25 servings, one #303 can yields 3½ servings.

FRESH STRAWBERRIES

Common cultivated strawberries are available year-round. Marshall strawberries are extra-large berries with the stem still attached. *Fraises de bois* is the French name for imported or domestic wild strawberries.

Table S-5 Steam Table Pan Sizes and Capacities

Size	Approximate Exterior Dimensions	Depth	Capacities	4 fl oz (0.12 l) Portions
Full	12¾ × 20¾ in (323 × 527 mm)	1 in (25 mm)	3½ qt (3.3 l)	28
		2 in (50 mm)	7 qt (6.5 l)	56
		2½ in (63 mm)	9 qt (8.4 l)	72
		3 in (76 mm)	11 qt (10.3 l)	88
		4 in (101 mm)	15 qt (14.1 l)	120
		6 in (152 mm)	22 qt (20.6 l)	176
		8 in (203 mm)	31½ qt (29.6 l)	252
Two-thirds	13¾ × 12¾ in (349 × 323 mm)	1 in (25 mm)	2¼ qt (2.1 l)	18
		2 in (50 mm)	4½ qt (4.2 l)	36
		2½ in (63 mm)	6 qt (5.6 l)	48
		3 in (76 mm)	7¼ qt (6.8 l)	58
		4 in (101 mm)	10 qt (9.4 l)	80
		6 in (152 mm)	14¼ qt (13.3 l)	112
		8 in (203 mm)	21⅜ qt (20.0 l)	171
One-half	10⅜ × 12¾ in (263 × 323 mm)	1 in (25 mm)	1½ qt (1.4 l)	12
		2 in (50 mm)	3½ qt (3.3 l)	28
		2½ in (63 mm)	4 qt (3.8 l)	32
		3 in (76 mm)	5 qt (4.7 l)	40
		4 in (101 mm)	7 qt (6.6 l)	56
		6 in (152 mm)	10 qt (9.4 l)	80
		8 in (203 mm)	15 qt (14.1 l)	120
One-third	6⅞ × 12¾ in (175 × 323 mm)	1 in (25 mm)	1 qt (0.9 l)	8
		2 in (50 mm)	2 qt (1.9 l)	16
		2½ in (63 mm)	2⅝ qt (2.5 l)	21
		3 in (76 mm)	3¼ qt (3.0 l)	26
		4 in (101 mm)	4½ qt (4.2 l)	36
		6 in (152 mm)	6½ qt (6.1 l)	52
One-quarter	10⁵⁄₁₆ × 6⁵⁄₁₆ in (261 × 160 mm)	1 in (25 mm)	⅝ qt (0.6 l)	5
		2 in (50 mm)	1¼ qt (1.2 l)	10
		2½ in (63 mm)	1⅝ qt (1.5 l)	13
		3 in (76 mm)	2 qt (1.9 l)	16
		4 in (101 mm)	3 qt (2.8 l)	24
		6 in (152 mm)	4¾ qt (4.5 l)	38
One-sixth	6⅞ × 6⁵⁄₁₆ in (174 × 160 mm)	1 in (25 mm)	½ qt (0.47 l)	4
		2 in (50 mm)	1 qt (0.94 l)	8
		3 in (76 mm)	1½ qt (1.4 l)	12
		4 in (101 mm)	2 qt (1.9 l)	16
One-ninth	6¾ × 4¼ in (171 × 108 mm)	1 in (25 mm)	⅜ qt (0.35 l)	3
		2 in (50 mm)	⅗ qt (0.70 l)	6

Season:
Available year-round. Peak is from March through June. Worst quality is in December. Imported strawberries come onto the market in the winter.

Pack:
Twelve 1-pint (0.47-l) baskets, with a total tray volume of 6 qt (5.6 l); 1-qt (0.94-l) baskets are also on the market.

Weights:
1 pint weighs 14 oz (400 g).
1 tray weighs 10 lb (4.5 kg).
1 qt weighs 1¾ lb (780 g).

Counts:
1 pint (0.47 l) contains 12 to 14 large berries or 20 to 25 smaller berries. Large berries are packed on top. One 12-pint tray contains 150 large berries or 240 to 300 small berries.

Kitchen Yields

Waste:
Cleaning loss is 10 percent by weight; percentage varies by season and size of berries.
1 pint yields 2 cups (0.47 l) whole berries, cleaned, or 1¾ cups (0.4 l) sliced berries.
1 cup whole berries, cleaned, weighs 5 oz (140 g), and one tray contains 24 cups.

Serving sizes:

Restaurants:
For breakfast or dessert (without ice cream), 1 pint yields 2 portions, and one flat yields 24 portions. For garnish with ice cream, mousse, or cake, 1 pint yields 3½ portions, and one flat yields 40 portions.

Banquets:
With ice cream, one flat yields 60 to 70 servings.

Calories:
1 cup, or 5½ oz (150 g) = 55 Calories.

EXTRA-LARGE STRAWBERRIES WITH STEMS
Sometimes called *Marshall strawberries.*

Season:
Available by special order. They are difficult to get in late fall and early winter.

Pack:
Tray or box with twelve 1-pint (0.47-l) baskets.

Count:
1 pint contains about 8 large berries.

Kitchen Yields

Serving size:
For garnish, 1 fruit; for dessert portion, 2 to 3 fruits. Therefore, 1 pint (0.47 l) yields 3 portions.

WILD STRAWBERRIES
Called *fraises de bois* in French, wild strawberries are available domestic and imported.

Season:
Spring and early summer.

Pack:
Twelve ½-pint (0.23-l) baskets.

Kitchen Yields
Berries are very small. Cleaning waste about 20 percent by volume.

FROZEN STRAWBERRIES
Available sliced, mixed with sugar, or IQF whole.

Pack:

Sliced, sweetened berries:
6½-lb (3-kg) can; 10-lb (4.5-kg) can; 30-lb (13.6-kg) tin.

Whole berries IQF:
30-lb (13.6-kg) carton.

Kitchen Yields
1 lb (454 g) canned fruit yields 1¾ cups.

Serving sizes:
½ cup (0.12 l) sliced fruit and juice for dessert;
¼ cup (0.05 l) as garnish with ice cream.
One 6½-lb (3-kg) can yields twenty-two ½-cup servings or forty-four ¼-cup servings.
One 10-lb (4.5-kg) can yields thirty-three ½-cup servings or sixty-six ¼-cup servings.

One 30-lb (13.6-kg) can yields one hundred ½-cup servings or two hundred ¼-cup servings. Serving sizes for whole berries IQF are about the same as for sliced berries, because berries will get very soft when defrosted.

Calories:
½ cup (0.12 l) sweetened, sliced = 118 Calories.

STRUDEL DOUGH

See Filo Dough, under Filo.

SUGAR

1 cup granulated sugar weighs 7 oz (200 g).
1 cup confectioners sugar weighs 4 oz (112 g).

PULLED SUGAR

Formula
    5 lb (2.25 kg) granulated sugar
    1 pint (0.47 l) water
    ¼ oz (6.75 g), or 2 tsp cream of tartar

Boil the mixture to 318°F (160°C).

Kitchen Yields
The total mix yields one medium-size basket.

SPUN SUGAR

Formula
    5 lb (2.25 kg) sugar
    1 lb (0.450 g) glucose
    1 pint (0.47 l) water

Boil ingredients to 320°F

Kitchen Yields
The total mix yields garnish for 50 desserts.

SUNCHOKES (JERUSALEM ARTICHOKES)

Pack:
12-lb (5.4-kg) carton.

Kitchen Yields

Waste:
20 percent by weight.

Calories:
3½ oz (100 g) = 75 Calories.

SURIMI

See Crab Meat Substitutes.

SWEET POTATOES AND YAMS

Available canned, fresh, and frozen. The names *yams* and *sweet potatoes* are often used interchangeably, although there is a difference between the two.

BONIATO
Sweet potato with red skin and white flesh.

Season:
Available year-round.

Kitchen Yields
Use as you would a sweet potato.

CANNED YAMS
Whole, cut, and mashed yams are available canned. Whole and cut sweet potatoes are available in syrup pack, vacuum pack, and dry pack.

Pack:
Six #10 cans; twelve #3 vacuum cans.

Kitchen Yields
Whole potato counts and weights in #10 can are as follows:
40 to 50: 2½ oz (70 g) each.
30 to 40: 3¼ oz (90 g) each.
20 to 30: 4½ oz (125 g) each.

Serving size:
½ cup (0.12 l). One #10 can syrup pack yields 20 servings; one #3 can vacuum pack yields 5 servings; one #10 can dry pack yields 25 servings.

Calories:
½ cup, or 5 oz (125 g), syrup pack = 177 Calories.

FRESH SWEET POTATOES OR YAMS

Little difference is made on the market between sweet potatoes and yams. Yams are considered to be more moist than sweet potatoes.

Season:
Available year-round, peak is in the winter months.

Pack:
Cartons with varying counts and weights.

Kitchen Yields
Shape is important for good yield. Look for clearly identifiable pieces.

Average weight:
5 to 6½ oz (140 to 185 g) for raw, unpeeled potato.

Serving size:

Baked:
½ medium potato.
1 lb (450 g) yields 11 oz (310 g) baked and peeled.

Mashed:
½ cup (0.12 l).
1 lb (450 g) yields 12 oz (340 g) mashed, or 2¾ servings.

Sliced:
½ cup (0.12 l).
1 lb (450 g) yields 12 oz (340 g) sliced, or 3 servings.

Calories:
4 oz (112 g), baked in skin = 160 Calories.
5 oz (140 g), boiled in skin = 160 Calories.
3¾ oz (106 g), candied = 175 Calories.

FROZEN YAMS

Available whole, sliced, and in patties.

Pack:
Twelve 2½-lb (1.1-kg) packages, whole or sliced; six 5-lb (2.2-kg) boxes, sliced; 24-lb case of 168 patties weighing 2 oz (56 g) each.

Kitchen Yields

Serving size:
½ cup (0.12 l). One 2½-lb (1.1-kg) package yields 11 servings; thus, one 5-lb (2.2-kg) box yields 22 servings.

Calories:
½ cup, or 3¾ oz (106 g), candied = 175 Calories.

SWISS CHARD

Vegetable in the beet family, grown for its leaves and stems, is available fresh.

Season:
Fall and winter, with some supplies available in early summer.

Pack:
20- to 25-lb (9- to 11.25-kg) bushel baskets; 30- to 35-lb (13.5- to 15.7-kg) cartons, by bunches.

Kitchen Yields
Trimming loss is about 30 percent. Yield depends to a large extent on how the vegetable is used. Some chefs braise the stems and cream the chopped leaves; others use the stems only.

T

Table T-1 Common Banquet Table Sizes

Shape	Size	Seating Capacity	Buffet Capacity
Round	2 feet (0.6 m)	2	n/a
	2½ feet (0.76 m)	3	n/a
	3 feet (0.91 m)	4	n/a
	4½ feet (1.36 m)	6	n/a
	5 feet (1.52 m)	8	n/a
	5½ feet (1.67 m)	10	n/a
	6 feet (1.82 m)	12	n/a
Rectangular	1½ × 6 ft (0.45 × 1.82 m)	4 schoolroom or theater style	10
	2½ × 4 ft (0.76 × 1.21 m)	6	20
	2½ × 6 ft (0.76 × 1.82 m)	10	25
	3 × 6 ft (0.9 × 1.82 m)	8	12
	3 × 8 ft (0.9 × 2.4 m)	12	30
Crescent	6 × 3 ft (1.82 × 091 m)	4	30

TABLE AND TABLECLOTH SIZES

Table T-1 lists the most common banquet table sizes.

The following is a list of table sizes and corresponding tablecloth sizes for standard banquet tables.

Round banquet tables:

Table Size	Tablecloth Size
2 ft (0.6 m)	72 × 72 in (1.82 m²)
2½ ft (0.76 m)	72 × 72 in (1.82 m²)
3 ft (0.91 m)	72 × 72 in (1.82 m²)
4½ ft (1.36 m)	90 × 90 in (1.82 m²)
5 ft (152 m)	90 × 90 in (1.82 m²)
5½ ft (167 m)	108 × 108 in (2.73 m²)
6 ft (1.82 m)	108 × 108 in (2.73 m²)

Rectangular banquet tables:

Table Size	Tablecloth Size
1½ × 6 ft (0.45 × 1.82 m)	two 62 × 62 in (1.57 m²) tablecloths
2½ × 4 ft (0.76 × 1.21 m)	72 × 72 in (1.82 m²)
2½ × 6 ft (0.76 × 1.82 m)	two 72 × 72 in (1.82 m²) tablecloths

Table T-2 Table Skirting Sizes

Skirt Length	Round Tables	Head Tables	Buffet Tables
12 ft (3.64 m)		2½ × 6 ft (0.76 × 1.82 m) *or* 3 × 6 ft (0.91 × 1.82 m)	
13 ft (3.9 meter)	4 ft diameter (1.2 m)	2½ × 8 ft (0.76 × 2.4 m)	
16 ft (4.8 m)	5 ft diameter (1.5 m)		
17½ ft (5.25 m)	5½ ft diameter (1.65 m)	two 2½ × 6 ft (0.76 × 1.8 m), side-by-side	2½ × 6 ft (0.76 × 1.8 m), freestanding
19 ft (5.7 meter)	6 ft diameter (1.8 m)		3 × 6 ft (0.9 × 1.8 m), freestanding
21½ ft (6.3 m)		two 2½ × 8 ft (0.76 × 2.4 m), side-by-side	2½ × 8 ft (0.76 × 2.4 m)

Crescent-shaped tables:

Table Size	Tablecloth Size
6 × 3 ft (1.82 × 091 m)	two 90 × 90 in (1.82 m²) tablecloths

To calculate the skirting length required for round tables, use the following equation:

$$\frac{\text{Diameter (in inches)} \times 1.14}{12} = \text{Length (in feet)}$$

Then round off to the next 6-in increment. Table T-2 lists skirting sizes for different tables.

TALLOW

Two varieties of tallow are used. One is pliable at room temperature. The other is hard enough to be carved.

Formula for Pliable Tallow
    5 lb (2.25 kg) shortening
    5 lb (2.25 kg) rendered beef fat
    4 lb (1.8 kg) paraffin

Formula for Carving Tallow:
    5 lb (2.25 kg) beeswax
    5 lb (2.25 kg) rendered beef fat
    5 lb (2.25 kg) paraffin

TAMARIND

The fruit, which resembles large, brown bean pods, is used for making syrups.

Season:
Available year-round.

Pack:
10-lb (4.5-kg) carton.

TANGELOS

A tangerine/grapefruit hybrid with thin skin, easily separated sections, and many seeds.

Season:
From October to May.

Pack:

Florida:
45-lb (20.2-kg), or ⅘-bushel cartons, with counts of 40, 48, 56, 64, 80, 100, or 125.

California:
27- to 32-lb (12.1- to 14.4-kg) cartons, with counts of 42, 54, 72, 84, 90, 100, 105, 135, or 165.

TANGERINES

See also Mandarin Oranges. Also called Temple oranges, these fruits have few seeds. They peel and section easily.

Season:
October to mid-May.

Pack:

Florida:
45-lb (20.2-kg) or ⅘-bushel cartons, with counts of 80, 100, 120, 150, 176, 180, or 210.

California:
27- to 32-lb (12.1- to 14.4-kg) cartons, with counts of 72, 84, 90, 100, 105, 135, or 165.

Kitchen Yields
Four #176 fruits weigh 1 lb (450 g).

Calories:
One 4-oz (12-g) tangerine = 40 Calories.

TARO ROOT

Potato-like root used in Oriental, Hawaiian, and South American cooking. Also called *poi* or *Hawaiian potato.*

Pack:
10-lb (4.5-kg) cartons.

Kitchen Yields

Waste:
25 percent by weight.

TEA

The best tea is grown on shrubs at high elevations. The smallest leaves are considered best; however, broken leaves are inferior. Fermented tea leaves are referred to as *black tea*. This tea has the typical tea flavor. Unfermented tea is called *green tea* and is the standard tea in Asia. Both black and green teas come from the same shrub. Almost all brands are blends, and the quality is dependent on where it is grown, the type of fermentation used, the size of the tea leaves, and the care exercised during packing, shipping, and storing.

Pack:

By weight. Many package sizes of loose or packed tea are available.

Kitchen Yields

For fermented (black) tea, 1 tsp yields 2 cups steeped tea; 1 oz (28.4 g) dry tea is equivalent to 12 tsp and yields 24 cups.

For green tea, 1¾ oz (50 g) dry tea yields 30 cups steeped tea.

TEMPEH

A soybean-derived food that resembles tofu. Firm, white cakes with chewy texture and mild flavor.

Pack:

By weight.

TEMPERATURE RANGES FOR BAKING

Heavy fruit cakes	325 to 350°F
Custards, quiche	325 to 350°F
Angel and sponge cakes	350 to 375°F
Cookies	350 to 375°F
Puff pastry	350 to 375°F
Eclairs, cream puffs	375 to 400°F
Danish pastry	375 to 400°F
Breads, rolls	400 to 425°F
Pizza	525 to 550°F

TEMPERATURE CONVERSION TABLE

Use Table T-3 for converting between Fahrenheit and Celsius (figures are rounded).

TERRAPIN

Small saltwater turtle. The diamondback is the best species. Only females should be used. Terrapins are sold live.

Table T-3 Fahrenheit to Celsius Conversion

Fahrenheit	Celsius
32°F	0°C
50°F	10°C
68°F	20°C
86°F	30°C
100°F	40°C
115°F	45°C
120°F	50°C
130°F	55°C
140°F	60°C
160°F	70°C
170°F	75°C
180°F	80°C
185°F	85°C
195°F	90°C
200°F	95°C
212°F	100°C
230°F	110°C
250°F	120°C
265°F	130°C
285°F	140°C
300°F	150°C
325°F	165°C
350°F	175°C
360°F	180°C
375°F	190°C
400°F	200°C
425°F	220°C
450°F	230°C
485°F	250°C
500°F	260°C
575°F	300°C

Season:
Summer and fall.

Sizes:
2 to 4 lb (0.9 to 1.8 kg).

Kitchen Yields

Serving size:
Average terrapin yields 4 appetizer servings.

TOFU

See Bean Curd.

TOMATILLOS

See Mexican Foods.

TOMATOES

Available canned and processed, fresh and frozen.

CANNED AND PROCESSED TOMATOES
A large variety of canned tomato products are on the market.

CHILI SAUCE
Tomato-based sauce flavored with chili peppers. Some brands contain seeds.

Pack:
Six #10 cans. Other packs are available.

Kitchen Yields
Sauce is often mixed with cocktail sauce. One #10 can contains 13 cups (3 l).

MARINARA SAUCE
Ready-to-use product.

Pack:
Six #10 cans.

SALSA
Available mild or hot, under many labels.

Pack:
Varies from portion pack to #10 cans.

TOMATO CATSUP

Packs:
Individual portion packs; twenty-four 14-fl-oz (0.4-l) bottles; six #10 cans; individual 3-gal (11.4-l) volume pack. Many other packs are available.

Calories:
¼ cup, or 2½ oz (70 g) = 72 Calories.

TOMATO JUICE

Pack:
Forty-eight 6-fl-oz (0.17-l) containers; twelve 46-fl-oz (1.33-l) cans.

Kitchen Yields

Serving size:
6 fl oz (0.17 l); therefore, one 46-fl-oz (1.33-l) can yields 7½ servings.

Calories:
6 fl oz (0.17 l) = 35 Calories.

TOMATO PASTE

Pack:
Six #10 cans. Other packs are available.

Kitchen Yields
Tomato paste is used in cooking, but can also be used reconstituted as tomato juice.

Serving size:
½ cup (0.12 l) reconstituted tomato juice. One #10 can + three refilled cans water produces 48 cups tomato juice or 96 servings.

TOMATO PIZZA SAUCE
Available are California plum tomatoes, prepared sauce, and other varieties.

Pack:
Six #10 cans, Other packs are available.

TOMATO PURÉE

Pack:
Six #10 cans. Other packs are available.

Kitchen Yields
Tomato purée has many uses in cooking, but can also be used reconstituted as tomato juice.

Serving size:
½ cup (0.12 l) reconstituted tomato juice. One #10 can + one refilled can water produces 24 cups tomato juice or 48 servings.

WHOLE OR CRUSHED TOMATOES
Available as solid pack with no added liquid, with juice added, and with purée added. Canned tomatoes may be whole or crushed.

Pack:
Six #10 cans. Other packs are available.

Kitchen Yields
Drained weight for grade A should be 66 percent of total can content.

Calories:
1 cup (0.24 l) solids and liquids = 50 Calories.

FRESH TOMATOES
Fresh tomatoes are available year-round. They are harvested green or turning and then ripened by exposing the fruits to carefully regulated temperatures and ethylene gas. Imports are available from a number of countries. Yellow tomatoes have come on the market as specialty item. Tomatoes with the vine attached are available as a premium specialty item.

Tomatoes are best when vine-ripened, but because tomatoes are very perishable when fully ripe, only locally grown fruits are marketed ripe. There is no comparison in flavor between vine-ripened tomatoes and warehouse-ripened tomatoes. There are many varieties on the market, including plum-shaped tomatoes (often referred to as *Italian tomatoes*). Tomatoes should not be stored in the refrigerator.

CHERRY TOMATOES
Available in yellow and red, round or teardrop-shaped.

Season:
Available year-round.

Pack:
Flats of twelve 1-pint (0.47-l) containers.

Count:
1 pint (0.47 l) contains 23 to 26, or 35 to 45 tomatoes; one flat of twelve 1-pint (0.47-l) or six 1-qt (5.6-l) containers, 312 pieces.

REGULAR TOMATOES
Tomatoes are shipped according to type. Mature, but still green tomatoes are shipped in cartons with volume-fill pack and locally repacked when red. Pink and vine-ripened tomatoes are shipped in one- or two-layer flats, lugs, loose-packed cartons, and basket-packed cartons.

Packs:
18- to 20-lb (8.1- to 9-kg) flats; 28- to 30-lb (12.6- to 13.6-kg) lugs; 25-lb (11.35-kg) cartons; 10-lb (4.5-kg) baskets.

Weights of individual tomatoes:

Maximum large:
8 to 10 oz (225 to 283 g).

Extra large:
5 to 7 oz (140 to 200 g).

Large:
3 to 5 oz (85 to 140 g).

Small:
Under 3 oz (85 g).

Counts:
Flats containing 40 (maximum large) to 60 (extra large) tomatoes; lugs with three layers contain 108 large, 126 medium, and 147 small tomatoes; cartons and baskets have varying counts.

Size classifications refer to the number of tomatoes packed in a carton or lug in rows. Thus, a straight-pack 6 × 6 lug contains 108 tomatoes. However, additional rows of the next size are permitted in lower layers, increasing the number of tomatoes in a carton. A lug of 5 × 5 tomatoes can contain 85 tomatoes. Table T-4 lists size classifications and corresponding diameters for tomatoes.

Kitchen Yields
1 lb (450 g) is equivalent to 3 to 4 medium tomatoes, or 1½ cups peeled, diced, and seeded tomatoes.

Serving size:
½ cup (0.12 l) raw diced or sliced tomato; therefore, 1 lb (450 g) yields 4½ servings.

Calories:
One raw, medium-size tomato, 5 oz (140 g) = 27 Calories.
3½ oz (100 g) raw tomatoes = 22 Calories.

SUN-DRIED TOMATOES
Available dry or packed in oil.

Pack:

Dry product:
By weight.

Wet product:
In jars.

Kitchen Yields
Yield depends on use. Good-quality sun-dried tomatoes have very concentrated flavor.

Table T-4 Size Classifications and Diameters

Size Classifications	Minimum Diameter	Maximum Diameter
7 × 7	2⁵⁄₃₂ in (54 mm)	2⁵⁄₁₆ in (58 mm)
6 × 7	2¼ in (56 mm)	2⁹⁄₁₆ in (64 mm)
6 × 6	2½ in (62 mm)	2¹³⁄₁₆ in (71 mm)
5 × 6	2¾ in (69 mm)	3³⁄₁₆ in (80 mm)
5 × 5	2⅞ in (72 mm)	3⅜ in (84 mm)
4 × 5	3 in (76 mm)	3⅝ in (91 mm)

TORTELLINI
See Pasta.

TORTILLA
See Mexican Foods.

TRUFFLES
See Mushrooms.

TURMERIC
See Herbs & Spices.

TURKEY

FRESH OR FROZEN WHOLE TURKEY
Available fresh and frozen, although most production is frozen.

Pack:

Fryers and roaster:
4 per carton.

Toms and hens:
2 per carton.
Weight varies according to sizes of birds.

Sizes:

Fryer/roaster:
5 to 9 lb (2.25 to 4.1 kg).

Hen:
8 to 16 lb (3.6 to 7.3 kg).

Tom:
16 lb (7.3 kg) and up.

Kitchen Yields
Whole turkeys have the following percentages of edible meat, before cooking:

> *Fryer:* 75 percent edible meat
> *Hen:* 78 percent edible meat
> *Tom:* 81 percent edible meat

Whole turkeys have the following percentages of edible meat, before cooking:

> *Breast:* 41 percent of weight
> *Drumstick:* 14 percent of weight
> *Thigh:* 17 percent of weight
> *Wings:* 11 percent of weight
> *Necks and giblets:* 8 percent of weight

The larger the bird, the higher the percentage of edible meat. The approximate edible yield after cooking is 55 percent. The usable yield after cooking is 40 percent of purchased weight. Cooking loss by weight is 27 percent.

Serving size:
6 oz (170 g) cooked meat. One 22-lb (10-kg) tom turkey, roasted, produces 12 lb (5.4 kg) meat, including all scraps, which yields 22 à la carte portions if hand-sliced directly from the frame or 24 portions if boned after cooking and sliced on machine.
For buffets, 12 lb (5.4 kg) meat yields about 40 portions when served with other meats and salads. For turkey galantine, one 25-lb (11.25-kg) turkey produces four 4-lb (1.8-kg) rolls.

Calories:
6 oz (170 g) roasted white meat only, without skin = 300 Calories.
5 oz (170 g) roasted dark meat only, without skin = 360 Calories.
6 oz (170 g) roasted diced, mixed meat, 1 cup = 320 Calories.

RAW TURKEY PARTS

BREAST

Weights:
8 to 22 lb (3.6 to 9.9 kg).

Pack:
2 to 8 pieces per case.

Kitchen Yields

Serving size:
3½ oz (100 g) cooked. Bone-in breast yields 2 to 3 servings per 1 lb (450 g). Boneless breast yields 3 to 3½ servings per 1 lb (450 g).

Calories:
3½ oz (100 g) cooked meat = 136 Calories.

DRUMSTICKS

Weights:
½ to 1½ lb (225 to 675 g).

Pack:
Bulk.

Kitchen Yields

Serving size:
10 oz (100 g). Purchase 10-oz (280-g) portions.

Calories:
10 oz (280 g) raw, or 3½ oz (100 g) cooked meat with skin = 200 Calories.

THIGHS
Normally available with bone in and skin on.

Weight:
½ to 1½ lb (225 to 675 g).

Pack:
Bulk.

Kitchen Yields

Serving size:
3½ oz (100 g) cooked. Bone-in thighs yield 2 to 3 servings per 1 lb (450 g).

Calories:
3½ oz (100 g) cooked meat without skin = 170 Calories.

WINGS

Weights:
¾ to 1¼ lb (337 to 560 g).

Pack:
Bulk.

Kitchen Yields

Serving size:
12 oz (336 g) raw, 3½ oz (100 g) cooked. Purchase 12-oz (336-g) portions.

Calories:
12 oz (336 g) raw, 3½ oz (100 g) cooked meat = 200 Calories.

TURKEY PRODUCTS

BREADED TURKEY PRODUCTS

BREADED TURKEY CUTLETS
Cut from whole-muscle breast meat, breaded or batter dipped. Precooked or fried.

Weight:
3.2 oz (90 g).

Count:
Five pieces per 1 lb (450 g).

Pack:
10-lb (4.5-kg) carton, containing 50 pieces.

Kitchen Yields
Ready-to-use product.

Serving size:
Two pieces.

BREADED TURKEY NUGGETS
Available batter-fried or breaded, fully cooked.

Weights:
½ to ¾ oz (14 to 20 g).

Pack:
8 to 12 lb (3.6 to 5.4 kg).

Count:
215 to 390.

Kitchen Yields
Ready-to-use product for buffets. Tastes best when heated.

Calories:
4 oz (112 g) = 328 Calories.

BREADED TURKEY PATTIES
Ground product, shaped into patties and precooked or browned.

Weights:
Five to seven pieces per 1 lb (450 g).

Pack:
48 to 72 lb (21.6 to 32.4 kg).

Kitchen Yields

Serving size:
One or two patties.

COOKED TURKEY PRODUCTS

BREAST AND THIGH
Boneless combination of natural proportions white and dark meat.

Weight:
7 to 10 lb (3.1 to 4.5 kg).

Pack:
Two to four pieces per case.

Kitchen Yields
Product is available flavored and browned. Economical, easy-to-slice white and dark meat. Shape of product varies and affects yield.

Calories:
4 oz (112 g) = 140 Calories.

FORMED BREAST
All breast meat, made with large sections and held together with a number of extenders, including ground meat, and water.

Weights:
4 to 10 lb (1.8 to 4.5 kg).

Pack:
Two to four pieces per case.

Kitchen Yields
Product is available flavored and browned. Economical, easy-to-slice all-breast meat. Shape of product varies and affects yield.

Calories:
4 oz (112 g), skinless = 125 Calories.
4 oz (112 g), skin on = 145 Calories.

PULLED OR DICED BONELESS MEAT
Frozen IQF.

Pack:
Normally, four 5-lb (2.2-kg) bags.

Kitchen Yields
Product can be used for any kind of hot turkey dish.

Serving size:
5 oz (140 g) frozen. Therefore, 5 lb (2.2 kg) yields 16 servings.

THIGH
Boneless, all-dark meat.

Weights:
4 to 10 lb (1.8 to 4.5 kg).

Pack:
Two to four pieces per case.

Kitchen Yields
Use for sandwiches.

Calories:
4 oz (112 g) = 144 Calories.

TURKEY ROLLS
Ground turkey, available as all-white meat or in combination of of white and dark meat. Can include extenders, binders, and extra water.

Weights:
7 to 10 lb (3.1 to 4.5 kg).

Pack:
Two to four pieces per case.

Kitchen Yields
Least expensive turkey for sandwiches.

Calories:
4 oz (112 g) = 168 Calories.

WHOLE-MUSCLE BREAST
Boneless, fully cooked and hand-packed. Available skin on or skinless. Up to 98 percent fat-free.

Weight:
2 to 10 lb (0.9 to 4.5 kg).

Pack:
Two to eight pieces per carton.

Kitchen Yields
Many brands are available from different packers. Product is available colored with caramel, browned, and with low salt content. Includes up to three breast muscles. This is the best-quality, but also the most expensive cooked breast.

Serving size:
2 to 4 oz (58 to 112 g) for sandwiches.

Waste:
There is about 3 percent cutting waste.

Calories:
4 oz (112 g), skinless = 125 Calories.

RAW PROCESSED TURKEY PRODUCTS

ALL-WHITE NETTED, BONELESS BREAST ROAST

Weights:
8 to 12 lb (3.6 to 5.4 kg).

Pack:
Four to six pieces per case.

Kitchen Yields

Serving size:
For sandwich, 3½ oz (100 g) cooked. Boneless breast roast yields 3 to 3½ servings per 1 lb (450 g).

Calories:
3½ oz (100 g) = 190 Calories.

ALL-WHITE NETTED, BONELESS SINGLE
BREAST ROAST
Injected with turkey broth. It is available skin on or skinless and is 99 percent fat-free.

Weight:
3.5 to 5 lb (1.6 to 2.3 kg), skin on or skinless.

Pack:
14- to 20-lb box.

BONELESS BREAST AND THIGH ROAST

Weights:
4 to 14 lb.

Pack:
Two to four pieces per case.

Kitchen Yields

Serving size:
For sandwich, 3½ oz (100 g) cooked. Boneless breast and thigh roast yields 3 to 3½ servings per 1 lb (450 g). Therefore, one 8-lb (3.6-kg) roast yields 26 servings.

Calories:
3½ oz (100 g) = 203 Calories.

DRUMSTICK STEAKS
Dark meat, skinless, whole-muscle, mechanically tenderized. Available IQF.

Weight:
4 oz (112 g).

Count:
40 pieces per pack.

GROUND TURKEY
Ground turkey is available in the following varieties:

> *All breast:* 99 percent fat-free.
> *Lean ground:* 93 percent fat-free, seasoned.
> *Ground flavored specialties:* Taco, Italian, or Sloppy Joe.

Weight:
3-lb (1.36-kg) chubs.

Pack:
Four chubs.

GROUND TURKEY
Mostly dark meat.

Weight:
10 lb (4.5 kg).

Pack:
Two to four rolls.

Kitchen Yields
This ground turkey is at least 85 percent lean, but the product can contain skin. Use for patties, meat sauce, and pizza.

Calories:
4 oz (112 g) cooked = 202 Calories.

RAW TURKEY BREAST SLICES/CUTLETS
All boneless and skinless meat, sliced across the grain. Available frozen.

Weights:
Approximately 2 oz (56 g) each, ⅛ to ⅓ in (3 to 8 mm) thick.

Pack:
30- to 40-lb (13.5- to 8.1-kg) cases.

Kitchen Yields
Product is packed with paper or plastic film between slices. It can be breaded or flattened for roulades or turkey scallopini.

Serving size:
Two pieces, breaded, for main course; one piece for buffet; two pieces, flattened, for scallopini. One 30-lb (13.5-kg) case yields 120 servings.

Calories:
4 oz (112 g) = 176 Calories.

BREAST CUTLETS
Available 99 percent fat-free in various sizes and packs.

Weights and packs:
3 oz (90 g) in 64-count packs; 4 oz (112 g) in 48-count packs; 6 oz (168 g) mechanically-tenderized cutlets in 32-count packs.

BREAST MEAT CUBES AND STRIPS
All natural, whole-muscle meat is 99 percent fat-free. Available as portion controlled IQF.

Weight:
5-lb (2.25-kg) bags.

Pack:
Two per carton.

BREAST STEAKS AND CHOPS

Breast steaks:
Whole-muscle breast meat, 99 percent fat-free. Available IQF.

Weights and packs:
6 oz (168 g) in 32-count boxes; 8 oz (225 g) in 24-count boxes.

Bone-in chops:
Breast meat, 98 percent fat-free. Available IQF.

Weights and packs:
4 oz (112 g) in 36-count boxes; 6 oz (168 g) in 24-count boxes; 8 oz (225 g) in 18-count boxes.

TURKEY TENDERLOINS
Whole muscle from inside the center of the breast.

Weights:
6 to 12 oz (170 to 340 g).

Pack:
20- to 40-lb (9- to 18-kg) cases.

Kitchen Yields
Frozen, with plastic film between layers. Cut pieces across grain into medallions, kebabs, or stir-fry dishes. There is some cutting waste, depending on portion size.

Serving size:
4 oz (112 g).

Calories:
4 oz (112 g) = 176 Calories.

TURKEY PATTIES
Turkey patties are available in the following varieties:

All-breast ground: 1 percent fat, 4-oz (112-g) portion IQF, one side scored.
Ground patty, lean: 7 percent fat, 4-oz (112-g) portion IQF, one side scored.
Seasoned patty: 7 percent fat, 4-oz (112-g) portion IQF, one side scored.
Taco/nacho: 4-oz (112-g) portion IQF.
Italian patty: 4-oz (112-g) portion IQF.

Weight:
4 oz (112 g).

Pack:
10-lb (4.5-kg) case of 40 patties.

TURKEY TENDERLOIN CUTS

Filet mignon:

Weights and packs:
3 oz (90 g) in 48-count packs; 4 oz (112 g) in 40-count packs.

Filet mignon butterfly:

Weight and pack:
40 patties.

Medallion:

Weight and pack:
1 oz (28 g) in 160-count packs.

TURKEY TENDERLOINS
Whole muscle from inside the center of the breast.

Weights:
6 to 12 oz (170 to 340 g).

Pack:
20- to 40-lb (9- to 18-kg) cases.

Kitchen Yields
Frozen, with plastic film between layers. Cut pieces across grain into medallions, kebabs, or stir-fry dishes. There is some cutting waste, depending on portion size.

Serving size:
4 oz (112 g).

Cooking loss:
75 percent.

Calories:
4 oz (112 g) cooked = 176 Calories.

TURKEY THIGH STEAKS
Boneless and skinless raw dark meat.

Weights:
3 to 4 oz (85 to 112 g).

Pack:
40 to 54 individual steaks.

Kitchen Yields
Thigh steaks can be braised, broiled, or baked.

Serving size:
One piece.

Calories:
4 oz (112 g) cooked = 232 Calories.

TURKEY DELICATESSEN ITEMS

SMOKED BREAST
Available boneless and on the frame.

Weights:

On frame:
6 to 12 lb (2.7 to 5.4 kg).

Boneless:
2 to 4 lb (0.9 to 1.8 kg).

Pack:
Two to ten pieces per case.

Kitchen Yields
Purchase bone-in breast for buffet display, boneless for slicing.

SMOKED WHOLE TURKEY

Weights:
8 to 10 lb (3.6 to 4.5 kg).
10 to 12 lb (4.5 to 5.4 kg).
12 to 14 lb (5.4 to 6.3 kg).
14 to 16 lb (6.3 to 7.2 kg).

Pack:
Four per case.

Kitchen Yields
Product is available fresh or frozen. It is best used as a display piece on buffets. If sliced meat is needed, purchase boneless breasts. Check quality carefully; some products are flavored with artificial smoke flavor and are boiled in the bag.

Serving sizes:
For buffet, 10 lb (4.5 kg) yields 20 servings.

TURKEY HAM
Available whole-muscle, chopped, as roll, pastrami-shaped, and as salami.

Weights:
5 lb (2.2 kg) and up.

Kitchen Yields
Ready-to-eat product, often less expensive than similar pork products. Items should be identified on menu as turkey products.

Calories:
4 oz (112 g) whole-muscle ham = 150 Calories.
4 oz (112 g) salami = 224 Calories.

WILD TURKEY

Available fresh or frozen.

Sizes:
10 to 20 lb (4.5 to 9 kg).

Kitchen Yields
1 lb (450 g) as purchased yields 35 percent usable cooked meat.

TURNIP GREENS

Available canned, fresh, and frozen.

CANNED TURNIP GREENS

Pack:
Six #10 cans, with a drained weight of 60 oz (1.7 kg).

Kitchen Yields

Serving size:
½ cup; thus, one #10 can yields 14 servings.

Calories:
⅔ cup (100 g) = 27 Calories.

FRESH TURNIP GREENS

Available with and without roots attached. Sometimes broccoli greens are shipped for turnip greens. Roots should be no larger than 1½ in (38 mm) across.

Pack:
By weight.

Kitchen Yields

Waste:
Trimming loss is about 40 percent.

Serving size:
½ cup; thus, 1 lb (450 g) as purchased yields 2 servings.

Calories:
⅔ cups, or 3½ oz (100 g), chopped with stems = 30 Calories.

FROZEN TURNIP GREENS

Available chopped, with or without diced turnips.

Pack:
Twelve 3-lb (1.35-kg) boxes.

Kitchen Yields

Serving size:
½ cup; one package yields 10 servings.

Calories:
⅔ cups, or 3½ oz (100 g), chopped = 28 Calories.

TURNIPS

Season:
Fall, winter, and spring. Smaller supply in summer.

Pack:
25- and 50-lb (11.25- and 22.5-kg) bags; 43- to 47-lb (19.3- to 21.1-kg) cartons containing 24 bunches, with greens still attached.

Counts:
Vary greatly.

Kitchen Yields

Smaller turnips are better than larger turnips. If vegetable is not fresh, regardless of its size, it can be spongy. This reduces yield considerable.

Best size:
About 2 in (50 mm) across.

Waste:
Peeling loss is 20 percent by weight for turnips without greens.

Calories:
1 cup, or 5½ oz (154 g), cooked and diced = 35 Calories.

U AND V

UGLY FRUIT

Ugly fruit is a juicy citrus hybrid with spotted, loose-looking skin.

Season:

Winter.

Pack:

By count.

Kitchen Yields

This fruit slightly smaller than a grapefruit, with thick skin. Use it as if it were a grapefruit.

UNIFORM SIZES

MEN'S SIZES

Table U-1 identifies uniform measurements for male personnel. This table is a general guideline for

Table U-1 Uniform Sizes for Male Personnel

Height	Weight	Chest	Coat Length	Waist	Trouser Inseam
5 ft 4 in (1.6 m)	120 lb (54 kg)	34 in (0.86 m)	27½ in (0.69 m)	36¾ in (0.93 m)	27 in (0.68 m)
	150 lb (67.5 kg)	38 in (0.96 m)	28 in (0.71 m)	37 in (0.93 m)	27 in (0.68 m)
	180 lb (81 kg)	42 in (1.06 m)	28 in (0.71 m)	37½ in (0.95 m)	27 in (0.68 m)
5 ft 6 in (1.67 m)	165 lb (74.2 kg)	40 in (1.01 m)	28½ in (0.72 m)	38 in (0.96 m)	27½ in (0.67 m)
	200 lb (90.0 kg)	44 in (1.11 m)	29 in (0.73 m)	39 in (0.99 m)	27½ in (0.69 m)
5 ft 8 in (1.72 m)	170 lb (76.5 kg)	40 in (1.01 m)	29½ in (0.75 m)	40 in (1.01 m)	29 in (0.73 m)
	185 lb (83.2 kg)	42 in (1.06 m)	30 in (0.76.2 m)	40½ in (1.02 m)	29 in (0.73 m)
5 ft 10 in (1.77 m)	175 lb (78.7 kg)	40 in (1.01 m)	30½ in (0.76 m)	41 in (1.04 m)	29½ in (0.75 m)
	190 lb (85.5 kg)	42 in (1.06 m)	31 in (0.78 m)	41 in (1.04 m)	29 in (0.73 m)
6 ft (1.82 m)	180 lb (81 kg)	40 in (1.01 m)	31½ in (0.80 m)	42 in (1.06 m)	30½ in (0.77 m)
	195 lb (87.7 kg)	42 in (1.06 m)	32 in (0.81 m)	42 in (1.07 m)	30 in (0.76 m)
6 ft 2 in (1.87 m)	198 lb (89.1 kg)	42 in (1.06 m)	33 in (0.84 m)	43½ in (1.10 m)	31½ in (0.80 m)

Table U-2 Uniform Sizes for Female Personnel

Dress Size	Height	Weight (Regular)	Bust Girth	Waist Girth	Hip Girth
4	5 ft 2½ in (1.58 m)	85 to 90 lb (38.3 to 40.5 kg)	30 in (0.76 m)	23½ in (0.60 m)	33 to 34 in (0.84 to 0.86 m)
6	5 ft 3 in (1.6 m)	95 to 100 lb (42.7 to 45 kg)	31 in (0.78 m)	25 in (0.63 m)	34 to 36 in (0.86 to 0.91 m)
8	5 ft 3½ in (1.61 m)	105 to 110 lb (47.2 to 49.5 kg)	32 in (0.81 m)	25½ in (0.67 m)	35 to 37 in (0.89 to 0.94 m)
10	5 ft 4 in (1.62 m)	115 to 120 lb (51.7 to 54 kg)	33 in (0.84 m)	26½ in (0.67 m)	36 to 38 in (0.91 to 0.96 m)
12	5 ft 4½ in (1.63 m)	125 to 130 lb (56.2 to 58.5 kg)	34½ in (0.88 m)	28 in (0.71 m)	38 to 39 in (0.96 to 0.99 m)
14	5 ft 5 in (1.65 m)	135 to 140 lb (60.7 to 63 kg)	36 in (0.91 m)	29 in (0.73.6 m)	39 to 41 in (0.99 to 1.04 m)
16	5 ft 5½ in (1.66 m)	150 to 155 lb (67.5 to 69.7 kg)	37½ in (0.95 m)	31 in (0.78 m)	41 to 42 in (0.99 to 1.06 m)
18	5 ft 6 in (1.67 m)	165 to 170 lb (74.2 to 76.5 m)	39½ in (1.0 m)	32 to 33 in (0.81 to 0.84 m)	43 to 44 in (1.09 to 1.11 m)

ordering uniforms. The chest size indicates the jacket size; the waist and inseam size indicates pant size. Most jacket sizes are 38, 40, 42, and 44. Most pant sizes are 37/27, 39/27, 40/29, 41/30, and 42/30.

WOMEN'S SIZES

Table U-2 identifies uniform measurements for female personnel. Note that the height varies between 2 and 4 in (50 and 100 mm).

VANILLA

Vanilla is available in whole vanilla pods, pure vanilla extracts, vanilla powder, and imitation vanilla concentrates.

IMITATION VANILLA CONCENTRATES

A number of imitation vanilla products are available in varying strengths, based on Vanillin, a synthetic product.

Pack:
1-qt (0.94-l) bottles; 1-gal (3.8-l) bottles. Other packs are available.

Kitchen Yields

Common dilution ratio is 1 part extract to 9 parts liquid.

PURE VANILLA EXTRACTS

Pack:
1-qt (0.94-l) bottle; 1-gal (3.8-l) bottle. Other packs are available.

Kitchen Yields
Use 4 oz (0.12 l) for 5 gal (19 l) ice cream mix or for 50 lb (22.5 kg) dough.

VANILLA PODS

The quality depends on the location where they were grown and on the care exercised in curing them. The best vanilla pods come from Mexico. The Bourbon grades are grown in Madagascar and other tropical islands. The best grades are the longest beans.

Pack:
By weight. Common pack is 8 oz (225 g).

Size:
Up to 10 in (254 mm) long for best grade.

Kitchen Yields
Difficult to determine, because pods can be used a number of times until all flavor is extracted.

VANILLA POWDER

Available pure or mixed with Vanillin, with or without ground bean specks.

Pack:
By weight.

Kitchen Yields
Strength varies according to product. With common-strength pure vanilla powder, use 3 oz (85 g) for 5 gal (19 l) ice cream mix or 50 lb (22.5 kg) dough.

VEAL

Animals up to three months of age are classified as veal; animals between three months and one year are classified as calves. For foodservice, veal is most likely to be specified, except in the case of liver, which comes from calves; veal liver is too small for commercial use.

Veal is normally not graded by the USDA. Some veal is raised and marketed with proprietary names, such as Plume de Veau and Provini. The animals are specially-raised and are heavy, but have light-colored meat. Nature veal is an industry term for heavy veal with light meat.

LARGER CUTS OF VEAL

When purchasing, make sure to specify veal, because some cuts are available in veal and calf weight ranges. Veal has soft, almost white meat; calf has redder and coarser meat. The *Meat Buyers Guide* (MBG) specification numbers are used to further identify the cuts.

BACK, MBG #341
Whole back with nine ribs, trimmed.

Weight ranges:
10 to 30 lb (4.5 to 13.5 kg).

Kitchen Yields
Use for buffet display.

Recommended weight:
18 lb (8.1 kg).

Serving quantities.
On buffet, one back yields 50 servings.

BONES
Bones from the neck and loin are soft and render flavor; knuckle bones provide gelatin for stocks and sauces.

Pack:
By weight.

Kitchen Yields
50 lb (22.5 kg) veal bones flavors 10 gal (38 l) brown stock.
NOTE: Judging the strength of stock is subjective. The preceding proportions are for good-quality stock.

BRAINS
Brains should only be purchased fresh, because the skin and membranes are difficult to remove from frozen brains.

Pack:
½ lb (225 g) per piece, in trays; 16 pieces per 10-lb (4.5-kg) box, with four boxes per 40-lb (22.5-kg) carton. Also available by weight.

Kitchen Yields
Soak in lukewarm water to remove skins.

Average size:
½ lb (225 g) per piece.

Usable meat:
12 to 13 oz (340 to 365 g).

BREAST, MBG #313

Weight ranges:
3 to 6 lb (1.3 to 2.7 kg).
6 to 8 lb (2.7 to 3.6 kg).
8 to 10 lb (3.6 to 4.5 kg).
10 to 12 lb (4.5 to 5.4 kg).

Kitchen Yields

Best use:
Bone and stuff, bone and roll, or braise with bones in.

ROLLED VEAL BREAST

Recommended size:
10 lb (4.5 kg).

Bones:
24 oz (670 g).

Trim, fat:
8 oz (225 g).

Breast, ready to roast:
8 lb (3.6 kg).

Weight after roasting:
5 lb 10 oz (2.5 kg).

Serving size:
Twelve 7-oz (200-g) servings.

STUFFED BREAST

Recommended size:
10 lb (4.5 kg).

Bones:
24 oz (670 g).

Trim, fat:
8 oz (225 g).

Breast, ready to stuff:
8 lb (3.6 kg).

Stuffing:
3 lb (1.35 kg).

Breast, ready to roast:
11 lb (5 kg).

Weight after roasting:
8 lb 5 oz (3.8 kg).

Serving size:
Fifteen to sixteen 8-oz (225-g) servings.

CHUCK, BONELESS, MBG #309B
Economical piece for cutting stew meat.

Weight ranges:
For whole or double chuck, 12 to 40 lb (5.4 to 18 kg).

Kitchen Yields

Trimming waste:
8 percent. 1 lb (450 g) produces 10 oz (280 g) cooked meat.

Serving size:
6 oz (170 g) cooked meat. Thus 20 lb (9 kg) yield 30 servings.

CHUCK ROLL, TRIMMED

Size:
3 to 4½ lb (1.3 to 2 kg).

Pack:
By weight. One purveyor offers a 22-lb (9.9-kg) case containing five 4½-lb (2-kg) pieces.

Kitchen Yields
1 lb (450 g) as purchased yields 11 oz (312 g) cooked meat.

Serving size:
5 oz (140 g) cooked. One 4½-lb (2-kg) piece yields 10 servings.

Calories:
5 oz (140 g) cooked = 380 Calories.

HEART

Average size:
1 to 2 lb (0.45 to 0.9 kg) per piece.

Pack:
By weight and piece. One purveyor offers 50-lb (22.2-kg) boxes, containing twenty-five to thirty 2-lb (0.9-kg) pieces.

Kitchen Yields
Braise or boil. Remove thin fatty top after cooking.

Serving size:
4 oz (112 g) cooked; one 1-lb (450-g) heart yields 2 servings.

Calories:
4 oz (112 g) cooked = 210 Calories.

HIND SHANK

Weight ranges:
1 to 4½ lb (0.45 to 2 kg).

Pack:
One purveyor offers 55-lb (24.7-kg) boxes of fifteen 3½-lb (1.5-kg) trimmed shanks.

Kitchen Yields
When purchasing, specify hook bone cut off. For osso buco, purchase 4½ lb (2 kg) or larger shanks, and cut each shank into four pieces. For roasting whole, purchase 3-lb (1.35-kg) shanks.

Serving size:
For osso buco, two pieces; for whole roasted shanks, one-half shank.

KIDNEYS
Available with the fat on or peeled and with fat removed. Most purveyors sell peeled kidneys only.

Size:
½ to ¾ lb (225 to 340 g) peeled.

Pack:
By piece and weight. One purveyor offers boxes of fourteen ¾-lb (340-g) pieces.

Kitchen Yields

Waste:
Trimming loss from peeled kidney is 5 percent. Purchase 10- to 12-oz (280- to 340-g) kidneys.

Serving size:
6 oz (170 g). One kidney yields one serving.

LEG, MBG #334
Legs are normally sold whole, bone in, in pairs. When a number of single legs are purchased, make sure that only every other leg has the tail still attached. The tails weigh about 8 to 10 oz (225 to 280 g).

Weight ranges:

For single legs, bone in:
12 to 20 lb (5.4 to 9 kg).
20 to 28 lb (9 to 12.6 kg).
28 to 35 lb (12.6 to 15.7 kg).
35 to 45 lb (15.7 to 20.5 kg).

Kitchen Yields
For boning and cutting into scallopini or cutlets, purchase the largest legs. For roasting whole, purchase smaller legs.

Recommended size:
For boning, 45 lb (20.5 kg).
The following are approximate weights of pieces, bones, and scrap from one 42-lb 12-oz (19.2-kg) leg:

Clean meat, ready-to-cut, fully trimmed, best quality:
6 lb 6 oz (2.8 kg)—15 percent.

Clean meat, good quality:
7 lb (3.1 kg)—16 percent.

Stew meat, second quality:
4 lb 5 oz (1.9 kg)—10 percent.

Scraps, useable for stock:
6 lb 10 oz (3 kg)—16 percent.

Fat:
6 lb 6 oz (2.8 kg)—15 percent.

Bones:
8 lb 9 oz (4 kg)—20 percent.

Shank:
3 lb 8 oz (1.5 kg)—8 percent.

Common uses for veal leg include scallopini, breaded cutlets, roast veal, stew, and veal strips sauté.

Scallopini:

Serving size:
Three 6-oz (170-g) pieces. The above leg yields 37 servings, providing all clean meat is used.

Breaded Cutlets:

Serving size:
5 oz (140 g). The above leg yields about 36 servings cutlets, and six servings scallopini.

Roast Bottom Round:

Serving size:
4 oz (112 g) cooked.

Cooking loss:
1 lb (450 g) produces 13 oz (365 g) cooked meat. One 4½-lb (2-kg) round, trimmed, yields 12 servings.

*Veal Strips Sauté (*eminc é *in French):*

Serving size:
For main course, 5 oz (140 g); for buffet, 3 oz (85 g).

Calories:
6 oz (170 g) scallopini, raw weight = 365 Calories.

BONELESS LEG, SHANK OFF, MBG #336

Weight ranges:
7 to 23 lb (3.1 to 10.3 kg).

Kitchen Yields
Good piece for roasting whole.

Recommended size:
12 lb (5.4 kg).

Serving size:
4 oz (112 g) cooked.

Cooking loss:
1 lb (450 g) reduces to 13 oz (365 g) cooked meat. Therefore, one 12-lb (5.4-kg) boneless leg yields 20 to 22 main-course servings, 25 banquet servings (if cut on machine), or 30 buffet servings.

LIVER (CALF'S LIVER)
On the New York market, the term *kosher calf liver* is used to indicate freshness, although the liver might not be certified kosher. The livers should be light in color and fresh. They may can come from heavy veal or from small calves.

Weight ranges:
2½ to 7 lb (1.1 to 3.1 kg).

Pack:
By the piece and by weight. One purveyor offers 55- to 65-lb (24.7- to 29.2-kg) cases of eight 7-lb (3.1-kg) whole livers.

Kitchen Yields
The liver must be skinned. There is a small flap, and some trimming waste, which can be used in pâté or as julienne of liver sauté.

Best size:
3 to 3½ lb (1.3 to 1.6 kg).

Serving size:
5 to 6 oz (142 to 170 g) in two slices; thus, one 3-lb (1.35-kg) liver yields 7 servings.

Calories:
5 oz (140 g) raw = 210 Calories.

LOIN, WHOLE, MBG #231
Whole loin, with two ribs, kidneys, and tenderloins. The same piece trimmed to 4-in (102-mm) flank, with kidneys removed, is called MBG #332. The same piece is also available boneless and rolled. The loin is the best part of the animal and very expensive.

Weight ranges:
6 to 10 (2.7 to 4.5 kg).
10 to 14 lb (4.5 to 6.3 kg).
14 to 18 lb (6.3 to 8.1 kg).
18 to 23 lb (8.1 to 10.3 kg).

Kitchen Yields

Recommended size:
22 lb (9.9 kg). One 22-lb (9.9-kg) piece consists of 7 lb (3.1 kg) usable meat.
Common uses of veal loins include loin chops, medallions, scallopini, and roasted and split loins.

Boneless Loin Chop:

Serving size:
One 6½-oz (180-g) piece per serving; thus, one 22-lb (9.9-kg) loin yields 16 servings.

Medallion (Completely Skinned):

Serving size:
One 5-oz (112-g) piece; thus, one 22-lb (9.9-kg) loin yields 16 servings.

Scallopini:

Serving size:
5½ oz (156 g); thus, one 22-lb (9.9-kg) loin yields 17 servings of three pieces per serving.

Roasted and Split Loin:

Serving size:
5 oz cooked meat; thus, one 22-lb (9.9-kg) loin yields 8 to 9 servings from each side.

Recommended size for roasted whole and presented cold on buffet, is 14 to 18 lb (6.3 to 8.1 kg). This size yields approximately 30 servings.

LOIN, BONELESS
Cap-on, 1-in (25-mm) flank.

Weight range:
3¼ to 4 lb (1.5 to 1.8 kg).

Pack:
One purveyor offers sixteen 3¼-lb (1.5-kg) loins in a 51-lb (23-kg) master carton.

Kitchen Yields
This is a boneless, well-trimmed piece of meat. It can be cut into boneless chops without additional trimming.

LOIN, BONELESS, TRIMMED

Weight range:
6 to 9 lb (2.7 to 4 kg).

Pack:
One purveyor offers seven 8-lb (3.6-kg) loins in a 56-lb (25.2-kg) master carton.

Kitchen Yields
Refer to yields for whole loins.

LOIN, TRIMMED TO SILVER SKIN

Weight range:
2½ to 3 lb (1.1 to 1.35 kg).

Pack:
One purveyor offers sixteen 2¾-lb (1.2-kg) loins in a 45-lb (20-kg) carton.

Kitchen Yields
Completely trimmed loin with no waste factor.

NECK, BONELESS

Weight range:
9 to 11 lb (4 to 4.9 kg).

Kitchen Yields
Good piece for cutting stew meat.

Trimming waste:
5 percent.

Cooking loss:
1 lb (450 g) stew meat reduces to 11 oz (312 g) cooked meat.

Serving size:
8 oz (225 g) raw meat, or 5½ oz (150 g) cooked meat, for main course; 5 oz (140 g) raw meat, or 3½ oz (100 g), for buffet. Thus, 10 lb (4.5 kg) raw stew meat yields 20 main course servings or 30 buffet servings.

RACK, MBG #306
Racks with seven ribs are standard.

Weight ranges:
5 to 20 lb (2.2 to 9.0 kg).

Kitchen Yields
The piece provides very low yield on account of the bone structure it contains. The proportion of usable meat to bone is better in larger pieces. However, chops cut from 16-lb (7.2-kg) and larger racks are very heavy due to the large rib bone.

Recommended size:
16 to 18 lb (7.2 to 8.1 kg).

Breakdown of one 19-lb 4-oz (8.6-kg) rack:

Fat:
1 lb 8 oz (0.6 kg)—8 percent.

Bones:
4 lb 4 oz (1.9 kg)—22 percent.

Scraps:
2 lb 8 oz (1.1 kg)—13 percent.

Stew meat:
3 lb 8 oz (1.5 kg)—18 percent.

Rack, two pieces, frenched (with rib bones):
7 lb 8 oz (3.3 kg)—39 percent.

Serving size:

Rib chop, bone in:
9 oz (250 g).
The above rack yields ten rib chops, and two 6-oz (170-g) servings scallopini.

Roast rack of veal:
7½ oz (210 g) including rib bone. The above rack yields 12 servings.

ROASTED LOIN, SPLIT, BONE IN, AND FRENCHED

Recommended size:
16 lb (7.2 kg).

Serving size:
For main course, 8 oz (225 g) cooked. Thus, one 16-lb (7.2-kg) loin yields 14 servings.

RIB-EYE
New way of cutting the carcass. This piece is available from at least one packer.

Size:
3 lb (1.35 kg).

Pack:
Ten 3-lb (1.35-kg) pieces in 30-lb (13.5-kg) cartons.

Kitchen Yields
The piece is boneless and well-trimmed. It can be cut into boneless steaks, or it can be roasted whole.

RIBLETS

Pack:
40-lb (18-kg) case.

Count:
Varies; about four pieces per 1 lb (450 g).

Kitchen Yields
Short-cut riblets, ready to use.

Serving size:
12 to 16 oz (340 to 450 g) raw weight.

SCOTCH TENDER
Fully trimmed piece from the shoulder.

Size:
1-lb (450-g) piece, vacuum-packed.

Pack:
Sixty 1-lb (450-g) pieces per 60-lb (27-kg) box.

Kitchen Yields
Relatively new and convenient piece. It can be used for roasting or braising whole, or it can be cut for stew. The piece is very practical for banquet or buffet use.

Cooking loss:
1 lb (450 g) roasted whole reduces to 11 oz (312 g) cooked meat.

SHOULDER, BONE-IN

The shoulder is cut from the chuck. The best part is the clod, which can be rolled and tied for a roast.

Weight:
16 to 20 lb (7.2 to 9 kg).

Kitchen Yields
Use for stew meat or roast clod.

Recommended weight:
16 lb (7.2 kg).

Weight of parts:

Usable meat, including shank, cubed:
8 lb 11 oz (3.93 kg).

Scraps and bones:
7 lb 5 oz (3.33 kg).

Cooking loss:
1 lb (450 g) stew meat reduces to 11 oz (312 g) cooked meat.

Serving size:
8 oz (225 g) raw meat, or 5½ oz (154 g) cooked meat, as main course; 5 oz (140 g) raw meat, or 3½ oz (100 g) cooked meat, as buffet. Therefore, 10 lb (4.5 kg) raw stew meat yields 20 main-course servings or 30 buffet servings.

SHOULDER CLOD, BONELESS, MBG #310

Weight ranges:
4 to 9 lb (1.8 to 4 kg). Fully trimmed pieces weigh 3 to 4 lb (1.3 to 1.8 kg).

Pack:
By piece and weight. One purveyor offers five 4-lb (1.8-kg) pieces in 20-lb (9-kg) boxes.

Kitchen Yields

Serving size:
5 oz (140 g) cooked meat; thus, one 4-lb (1.8-kg) piece yields 8 servings.

STEW MEAT
Purchase by weight.

Kitchen Yields
Refer to Neck or Shoulder under this same heading for yield information.

SWEETBREADS
Make sure to specify veal sweetbreads, because calf's sweetbreads can be very tough. Specify fresh when possible. Veal sweetbreads are lighter in color than calf's sweetbreads.

Pack:
By weight; usually 5-lb (2.2-kg) baskets or 40-lb (18-kg) boxes.

Sizes:
1 lb (450 g) average, per pair.

Kitchen Yields
Sweetbreads pairs consist of two uneven parts. They are often sold separated.

Trimming waste:
10 percent by weight.

Cooking loss:
15 percent by weight.

Serving size:
8 oz (225 g) cooked, as main course; thus, 5 lb (2.2 kg) sweetbreads yield 7 servings.

TENDERLOINS
Short, fully trimmed tenders.

Size:
½ lb (225 g) each.

Pack:
Sixty-four ½-lb (225-g) pieces in a 37-lb (16.6-kg) master carton.

Kitchen Yields
Very tender pieces. Best use is for scallopini or for breaded cutlets.

TONGUE

Size:
1 to 1½ lb (450 to 675 g).

Pack:
By piece and weight. One purveyor offers thirty-two 1½-lb (675-g) pieces in a 40-lb (18-kg) case.

Kitchen Yields

Cooking loss:
1 lb (450 g) as purchased reduces to 10 oz (280 g).

TOP ROUND, FULLY TRIMMED

Pack:
Eight 4½-lb (2-kg) pieces in a 37-lb (16.6-kg) master case.

Kitchen Yields

Meat can be cut into cutlets or scallopini. There is little trimming waste. For portion sizes, refer to Leg, MBG #334.

PORTION CUTS OF VEAL

CUBED STEAKS

Boneless slices that have been mechanically tenderized. The meat can be dry.

Sizes:
3, 4, 5, 6, and 8 oz (85, 112, 142, 170, and 225 g).

Kitchen Yields
Best use is breaded.

Serving size:
4 oz (112 g) lunch size, when breaded.

CUTLETS

Boneless slices made from leg meat only. The meat is cut against or with the grain. Slices must be pounded before use in order for meat to be sufficiently tender.

Sizes:
2, 3, 4, 5, and 6 oz (85, 112, 142, and 170 g).

Pack:
256 pieces of 2 oz (56 g) each in four 8-lb (3.6-kg) boxes; 170 pieces of 3 oz (85 g) each in four 8-lb (3.6-kg) boxes; 126 pieces of 4 oz (112 g) in four 8-lb (3.6-kg) boxes.

Kitchen Yields

Meat can be tough and dry on account of the loss of juices after thawing. Best use is breaded, but the product can also be used as veal marsala or for scallopini.

Serving size:
One 4-oz (112-g) slice, cut in half, for reception; one 5-oz (145-g) slice for braised roulade.

GROUND PATTIES

Available in different sizes. Low cholesterol substitute for beef hamburger patties. Available plain and breaded.

PLAIN PATTIES

Sizes:
3 oz (85 g); 4 oz (112 g).

Packs:
170 pieces of 3 oz (85 g) each in four 8-lb (3.6-kg) boxes; 126 pieces of 4 oz (112 g) each in four 8-lb (3.6-kg) boxes.

BREADED PATTIES
4 oz (112 g).

Pack:
126 pieces of 4 oz (112 g) each in four 8-lb (3.6-kg) boxes.

LIVER (CALF'S LIVER)

Calf's liver is available sliced. Not to be confused with baby beef liver.

Weights:
3- and 4-oz (85- and 112-g) slices.

Pack:
170 pieces of 3 oz (85 g) each in four 8-lb (3.6-kg) boxes; 126 pieces of 4 oz (112 g) each in four 8-lb (3.6-kg) boxes.

LOIN CHOPS

Cut from the loin, with bones still attached. Up to 3 in (75 mm) of flank can be left on.

Sizes:
3, 4, 5, 6, 8, and 10 oz (85, 112, 142, 170, 225, and 280 g).

Kitchen Yields
This piece is rather expensive and is best used as a dinner item.

Serving sizes:
One 8- or 10-oz (225- and 280-g) piece; two 5-oz (140-g) pieces.

OSSO BUCO
Cut veal shank, available pre-cut.

Weights:
6- to 8-oz (170- to 225-g) pieces.

Pack:
Four 10-lb (4.5-kg) cartons.

Count:
80 to 90 pieces.

RIB CHOPS
Cut from the rack. All bones are still attached, but the blade is removed.

Sizes:
3, 4, 5, 6, 8, and 10 oz (85, 112, 142, 170, 225, and 280 g).

Pack:
Varies, depending on size and packer.

Kitchen Yields
This item is rather expensive and is best used as a dinner item.

Serving size:
8 or 10 oz (225 and 280 g).

SHOULDER CHOP
Cut from the chuck, with bones still in.

Sizes:
3, 4, 5, 6, 8, and 10 oz (85, 112, 142, 170, 225, and 280 g).

Kitchen Yields
Best used for braising. Shoulder chops make a good lunch item.

Serving size:
6 oz (170 g).

YIELDS OF POPULAR VEAL DISHES

FRICASSEE
Use high-quality stew meat from the shoulder.

Serving size:
7 oz (200 g) raw meat for lunch.

LOIN ROAST
Can be stuffed with any stuffing or with kidneys. It can be made with loin halves, flank still attached, or with the whole, small loin.

Kitchen Yields

Best sizes:

Half loin roast:
4 lb (1.8 kg) boneless, oven-ready meat plus stuffing. This size yields 10 servings.

Full loin roast:
7 lb (3.1 kg) boneless, oven-ready meat plus stuffing. This size yields 16 servings.

OSSO BUCO
Purchase large shanks of about 4 lb (1.8 kg) each. Cut the center of the shank into four pieces. There will be about 1½ lb (680 g) bone without meat left over.

Serving size:
Two 8- to 10-oz (225- to 280-g) pieces.

PAILLARD
Very thin, pounded cutlet, grilled or sautéed to order. Use best-quality leg meat.

Serving size:
5 oz (140 g).

PICCATA

Veal scallopini served with lemon juice and sliced lemon.

Serving size:
Three pieces per serving, with a total weight of 6 oz (170 g). One 45-lb (20.2-kg) leg yields 40 to 42 servings scallopini.

ROASTED VEAL SHANKS (HAXEN)

Haxen is the German word for whole roasted shanks. Use 3-lb (1.35-kg) shanks, untrimmed.

Serving size:
One-half shank.

ROGNONNADE

French name for roast loin stuffed with kidneys. *See* Loin Roast, under this heading.

ROLLATINE

Italian name for stuffed, rolled cutlet. It is often sliced for service. Use thin cutlets.

SALTIMBOCCA ALLA ROMANA

Veal scallopini with prosciutto and sage.

Kitchen Yields

Serving size:
Three 2-oz (56-g) pieces, plus 1 oz (28 g) prosciutto sliced in 3 pieces, for a total of 6 oz (170 g).

SCALLOPINI

Scallopini, cut from leg.

Kitchen Yields

Serving size:
Three 2-oz (56-g) pieces, for a total of 6 oz (170 g).

VEAL BIRDS

Rolled, stuffed, and braised cutlets. Cubed cutlet can be used.

Kitchen Yields

Serving size:
For main course, 6 oz (168 g) meat plus 1 oz (28 g) stuffing; for buffet, 3 oz (85 g) meat plus ½ oz (14 g) stuffing.

VEAL MARSALA

Scallopini flavored with marsala wine. *See* Scallopini.

VEAL OSCAR

Veal cutlet topped with asparagus, crab meat, and Hollandaise sauce.

Kitchen Yields

Serving size:
6 oz (170 g) boneless cutlet, plus 1 oz (28 g) crab meat, plus 3 asparagus tips.

VITELLO TONNATO

Cold veal roast covered with cold tuna fish-based sauce. Any roast can be used. Tonnato sauce formula is given elsewhere; *see* Tonnato Sauce, under Sauces.

Serving size:
For main course, 4 oz (112 g) cooked roast, sliced thin, with 2 oz (0.06 l) sauce.

WIENER SCHNITZEL

German name for boneless breaded cutlet.

Serving size:
4 oz (112 g) for lunch; 5 oz (140 g) for dinner.

VEGETABLE BURGERS

Burgers made with vegetables, legumes, and grains. Available in 2, 4, and 6 oz (50, 112, and 170 g) sizes.

Packs:
Varies.

Kitchen Yields

There is little shrinkage and a 4-oz (112-g) burger is adequate as a diet main course.

VENISON

Available fresh, frozen, or smoked, domestic and imported.

FRESH OR FROZEN VENISON

Pack:

Whole animal, hide on:
80 to 180 lb (36 to 81 kg).

Hind leg, shank cut short:
16 to 25 lb (7.2 to 11.25 kg).

Saddles:
10 to 14 lb (4.5 to 6.3 kg). Boneless, fully-trimmed loins are also available.

Boneless stew meat:
10-lb (4.5-kg) bags.

Also available are fully trimmed hind leg and shoulder cuts.

Kitchen Yields

Leg:

Best size:
16 to 18 lb (7.2 to 8.1 kg); this yields 14 to 16 servings when roasted medium, or 12 to 14 servings when braised.

Rack:

Best size:
12 lb (5.4 kg); this yields 20 servings of two 2½-oz (70-g) boneless filet steaks, or 16 servings roasted whole, on the bone.

SMOKED VENISON LEG
Available as a specialty item. Serve sliced very thin, like prosciutto ham.

VIANDE DE GRISON

See Bündnerfleisch, under Beef, Smoked and Cured.

VESIGA

Gelatinous sturgeon marrow; available dried and frozen.

Pack:
By weight.

Kitchen Yields
Use in soups and in coulibiac (baked salmon loaf). Soak and boil.
3 oz (85 g) dried vesiga produces 15 oz (420 g) cooked vesiga.
NOTE: Soak dried vesiga for at least 5 hours.

VINEGAR

Vinegar is available as plain white or as specialty vinegar, such as balsamic, cider, raspberry, rice, tarragon, or wine vinegar (red and white).

Balsamic vinegar is an aromatic vinegar, normally made with condensed grape juice mixed with wine vinegar and vinegar "mother" (culture) and aged in wooden barrels. The aging process can take many years. Most balsamic vinegar is imported from Italy.

Cider vinegar is made from apple cider. It is slightly brown.

Raspberry vinegar is made by fermenting raspberry juice and wine.

Rice vinegar (*su* in Japanese) is a mild, aromatic vinegar.

Tarragon vinegar is made by steeping tarragon herbs in mild vinegar.

Wine vinegar is made by fermenting wine. Red wine vinegar is more common than white wine vinegar.

Pack:
Four 1-gal (3.8-l) packs; twelve 1-qt (0.95-l) bottles.

W, Y, AND Z

WAFFLE BATTER

Available as dry mix or made fresh.

Pack:
Six 5-lb (2.25-kg) bags.

Kitchen Yields
Follow instructions on bag.

Formula
    30 eggs
    1½ lb (675 g) sugar
    8 lb (3.6 kg) cake flour
    2½ lb (1.1 kg) melted shortening
    5 qt (4.7 l) milk
    2 oz (56 g) salt
    8 oz (225 g) baking powder
    Vanilla flavor to taste

Kitchen Yields

Serving size:
For 7-in (177-mm) waffles, use 4 oz (112 g) batter. The total mix yields 80 servings.
NOTE: Batter will get stiff when stored in refrigerator. It can be diluted with milk. Additional baking powder must be added if diluted and stored longer than 24 hours.

WALNUTS

Available in shell and shelled. Shelled walnuts are sold as halves and as pieces.

Pack:
By weight.

Kitchen Yields
1 cup halves consists of 60 pieces.
1 cup chopped consists of 4½ oz (126 g).
1 cup ground consists of 3½ oz (100 g).

Calories:
1 cup, or 4½ oz (126 g) chopped = 790 Calories.
1 cup, or 3½ oz (100 g) ground = 620 Calories.

WATER CHESTNUTS

Available canned, fresh, and as flour. In Oriental cooking, a number of different varieties are clearly distinguished. Fresh water chestnuts are available only in ethnic markets. The canned product is the accepted foodservice standard.

CANNED WATER CHESTNUTS
Available sliced or whole.

Pack:

Whole:
Six #10 cans; twenty-four 10½-oz (300-g) cans.

Sliced:
Six #10 cans. Other packs are available.

Kitchen Yields
One #10 can whole nuts weighs 35 oz (1 kg) drained.
One 10½ oz (300 g) can whole nuts weighs 5 oz (140 g) drained.
One #10 can sliced nuts weighs 40 oz (1.1 kg) drained.

FRESH WATER CHESTNUTS
Brown bulbs with white interior.

Season:
Available year-round.

Pack:
10-lb (4.5-kg) lugs.

Size:
1 to 2 in (25 to 50 mm) across.

Kitchen Yields

Cleaning waste:
30 percent, by weight.

WATERCRESS

See Salad Greens.

WATER ICE

See Granite.

WATERMELON

See Melons.

WATER WEIGHTS

1 cup (8 oz) weighs 0.23 kg
1 pint (16 oz) weighs 0.47 kg
1 qt (32 oz) weighs 0.94 kg

½ gal (64 oz) weighs 1.9 kg
1 gal (128 oz) weighs 3.8 kg

WHEAT CAKES

See Griddle Cakes.

WEIGHT AND VOLUME EQUIVALENTS

WEIGHT EQUIVALENTS

Table W-1 lists common avoirdupois and metric weight equivalents.

Table W-1 Weight Equivalents

Avoirdupois Weight	Metric Equivalent	Avoirdupois Weight	Metric Equivalent	Avoirdupois Weight	Metric Equivalent	Avoirdupois Weight	Metric Equivalent
22½ lb	10.00 kg	4 lb	1.80 kg	14½ oz	400 g	4½ oz	125 g
20 lb 1½ oz	9.00 kg	3 lb 14½ oz	1.75 kg	13⅓ oz	375 g	4½ oz	120 g
18 lb 4¾ oz	8.20 kg	3 lb 9 oz	1.60 kg	13 oz	360 g	3½ oz	100 g
17 lb 4 oz	8.00 kg	3 lb 6 oz	1.50 kg	12½ oz	350 g	3½ oz	90 g
15 lb 10 oz	7.00 kg	3 lb 2 oz	1.40 kg	11½ oz	320 g	3 oz	80 g
13 lb 6½ oz	6.00 kg	2 lb 14½ oz	1.30 kg	10¾ oz	300 g	2¾ oz	75 g
11 lb 2½ oz	5.00 kg	2 lb 11 oz	1.20 kg	11¾ oz	275 g	2½ oz	70 g
10 lb 2 oz	4.50 kg	2 lb 7½ oz	1.10 kg	9 oz	250 g	2⅓ oz	65 g
9 lb	4.00 kg	2 lb 3¾ oz	1.00 kg	8⅓ oz	240 g	2 oz	60 g
7 lb 13½ oz	3.60 kg	2 lb	900 g	8 oz	225 g	1¾ oz	50 g
7 lb 13 oz	3.50 kg	1 lb 14⅓ oz	850 g	7 oz	200 g	1½ oz	40 g
7 lb 1 oz	3.20 kg	1 lb 12½ oz	800 g	6½ oz	180 g	1½ oz	35 g
6 lb 11 oz	3.00 kg	1 lb 10¾ oz	750 g	6½ oz	175 g	1 oz	28 g
5 lb 13½ oz	2.60 kg	1 lb 9 oz	700 g	6 oz	170 g	¾ oz	20 g
5 lb 10 oz	2.50 kg	1 lb 7½ oz	650 g	5¾ oz	160 g	½ oz	15 g
5 lb 6½ oz	2.40 kg	1 lb 5½ oz	600 g	5⅓ oz	150 g	⅓ oz	10 g
5 lb	2.25 kg	1 lb 2 oz	500 g	5 oz	140 g	½ oz	7 g
4 lb 7½ oz	2.00 kg	1 lb	450 g	4½ oz	130 g	⅛ oz	3½ g

VOLUME EQUIVALENTS

Table W-2 lists liter to fluid ounce conversions. Table W-3 lists conversion factors for common volume equivalents.

WILD BOAR

See Boar.

WHITE SAPOTA

Known also as *custard apple*, this tropical fruit can be eaten raw, or cooked. The skin is edible and should be light yellow when mature.

Season:
April to November.

Pack:
10-lb (4.5-kg) flats.

Count:
Varies. Average is the size of a large orange.

WHITE STURGEON

Farm raised; also sold under the trade name of Belusa.

Size:
11½- to 14-lb (5.17- to 6.3-kg) bullets (gutted, headless fish, with fins and tail off).

Table W-2 Conversion from Liters to Fluid Ounces

Liter	Fluid Ounces	Liter	Fluid Ounces	Liter	Fluid Ounces
0.01 l	⅓ oz	0.35 l	11½ oz	2.50 l	2 qt 22 oz
0.02 l	¾ oz	0.40 l	13¾ oz	3.00 l	3 qt 7½ oz
0.025 l	1 oz	0.45 l	1 pint	3.50 l	3 qt 24½ oz
0.03 l	1 oz	0.50 l	1 pint 1½ oz	4.00 l	1 gal 10 oz
0.04 l	1½ oz	0.55 l	1 pint 3 oz	4.50 l	1 gal 27 oz
0.05 l	1¾ oz	0.60 l	1 pint 4 oz	5.00 l	1 gal 44½ oz
0.06 l	2 oz	0.65 l	1 pint 5¾ oz	6.00 l	1 gal 78 oz
0.075 l	2½ oz	0.70 l	1 pint 8 oz	6.50 l	1 gal 3 qt
0.08 l	2¾ oz	0.75 l	1 pint 9¾ oz	7.00 l	1 gal 113⅓ oz
0.10 l	3⅓ oz	0.80 l	1 pint 11½ oz	8.00 l	2 gal 20 oz
0.12 l	4½ oz	0.85 l	1 pint 13⅓ oz	9.00 l	2 gal 54⅓ oz
0.15 l	5 oz	0.90 l	1 pint 15 oz	10.00 l	2 gal 90 oz
0.175 l	6 oz	1.00 l	1 qt 2½ oz	12.00 l	3 gal 30 oz
0.20 l	6¾ oz	1.20 l	1 qt 9⅓ oz	14.00 l	3 gal 100 oz
0 225 l	7¾ oz	1.50 l	1 qt 20 oz	15.00 l	4 gal 5½ oz
0.25 l	8½ oz	1.80 l	62 oz	20.00 l	5 gal 50 oz
0.30 l	10 oz	2.00 l	2 qt 5 oz	24.00 l	6 gal 60 oz

Table W-3 Common Volume Equivalents

Level measure	Equivalent
1 gal (3.886 l)	4 qt (8 pints)
1 qt (0.946 l)	4 cups (2 pints)
1 pint (0.473 l)	2 cups (16 fl oz)
1 cup (0.237 l)	8 fl oz (½ pint or 16 tb)
2 tb (28.35 ml)	1 fl oz
1 tb (15 milliliter)	3 tsp
1 l	1.05 qt or 1 qt + 1.9 fl oz
1 l	4 cups + 2 tb

Pack:
By weight, often 100-lb (45-kg) boxes.

Kitchen Yield
Each fish yields two 4- to 5-lb (1.8- to 2.25-kg) fillets. Sturgeons have soft cartilage instead of bones. Sturgeon marrow is called vesiga.

WILD RICE

Water grass seeds, still growing wild in Minnesota, Wisconsin, California, and Canada. The quality is determined by the number of broken kernels per pound and by the size of kernels. Uniform kernel size is important, to insure even cooking. Precooked wild rice has become available.

Pack:
100-lb (45-kg) bags or boxes; 25-lb (11.35-kg) pails; six 5-lb (2.25-kg) boxes or tins; twelve 1-lb (450-g) boxes or tins. Other packs are available.

Kitchen Yields
Long Grain blends require three times their own volume in liquid. Cooking time is 60 minutes. Medium grain blends and cracked blends require two and one-half times their own volume in liquid. Cooking time is 50 minutes. NOTE: Yield is increased if product is soaked overnight. Soaking water should be used in cooking to preserve nutrients.

Serving size:
½ cup (0.12 l); 1 lb (450 g) produces 10 cups cooked product.

Calories:
½ cup, or 3 oz (85 g) cooked = 73 Calories.

WILD TURKEY

See Turkey.

WINE

Calories:
4 oz (0.12 l) dry wine = 100 Calories.
4 oz (0.12 l) sweet wine = 160 Calories.

WONTON WRAPPERS

See Chinese Foods.

Y

YAMS

See Sweet Potatoes and Yams.

YEAST

Available dry and fresh.
½ oz (14 g) fresh yeast is equivalent to 1 envelope dry yeast.
1 oz (28 g) fresh yeast is equivalent to 2 envelopes dry yeast.
Fresh yeast weighs twice as much as dry yeast.

Proofing Temperatures:
Sweet dough: 95 to 98°F, humidity of 80 percent.
Bread dough: 80 to 82°F, humidity of 80 percent.
NOTE: Yeast dies at 138°F.

YOGURT

Fermented milk product available with varying fat content and with different fruit flavors.

Pack:
8-oz (225-g) packages; 16-oz (440-g) packages. Other packs are available.

Kitchen Yields

Serving size:
8 oz (225 g). Foodservice operators should only purchase individual 8-oz (225 g) servings, which should then be served in the original container.

Calories:
8 oz (225 g) plain and fat-free = 110 Calories.
NOTE: Calorie count depends on fat content and fruit or flavor additives. Refer to package label for additional information.

YUCA ROOT

Also called *cassavas*, it is a starchy root used in many tropical countries. There are many varieties.

Season:
Available year-round.

Pack:
By weight.

Kitchen Yields

Peeling loss:
25 percent, by weight.

Z

ZUCCHINI

See Summer Squash, under Squash.

CREDITS

Abigail Kirsch Culinary Productions; Bedford, New York

Alaska Seafood Marketing Institute

Amendola, Joseph, *The Bakers Manual* (New York: Ahrens Publishing, 1960)

American Agri-Mushroom Business Enterprises; New York City

American Dairy Association

American Lamb Council

American Mushroom Institute

Apollo Foods, Inc.; Cleveland, Ohio

Bartolotta, A.C., Research Chef, Sexton & Co.; Elk Cove Village, Illinois

Batter Bake; Parsippany, New Jersey

Beatrice/Hunt Wesson, Inc.; Fullerton, California

Belgian Endive Marketing Board

Betelson Company; San Francisco, California

Berliner & Marx, Inc.

Blue Anchor, Inc., Seafood

Blue Diamond Almond Growers; Sacramento, California

Bruce Church, Inc., Produce

Bud of California

Bush Agricultural Resources; Jonesboro, Arkansas

Bush Brothers and Company; Dandridge, Tennessee

Butler, Kevin, Director of Purchasing, Hilton Hotels Corp.; New York City

Calavo Growers of California

California Apricot Advisory Board

California Artichoke Advisory Board

California Avocado Commission

California Fresh Market Tomato Advisory Board

California Iceberg Lettuce Commission

California Kiwi Fruit Commission

California Olive Industry; Fresno, California

California Pistachio Commission

California Prune Board

California Raisin Advisory Board

California Strawberry Advisory Board

California Table Grape Commission

California Tree Fruit Agreement

Carrer, Michel, Executive Chef, Hotel St. Regis, New York City

Carr's Classic Game

Castle and Cooke Foods

Castroville Artichoke People

Caviarteria, Inc.; New York City

Certified Angus Beef

Chiquita Brands, Inc.

Clay Center KS

Coco Lopez, USA; Columbus, Ohio

Consolidated Wild Rice Co.

Corrin Produce Sales, Inc.

Country Skillet Catfish Co.

Culinary Institute of America, *The Professional Chef* (Boston: CBI, 1979)

Czimer Foods, Inc.; Lockport, Illinois

Dahlen, Martha, and Phillipps, Karin, *A Popular Guide to Chinese Vegetables* (New York: Crown Publishers, 1983)

D'Artagnan, Inc.; Jersey City, New Jersey

Del Monte Fresh Fruit Co.

Dionne, René, Director of Purchasing, Johnson & Wales University; Providence, Rhode Island

Doherty, John, Executive Chef, The Waldorf Astoria; New York City

Dutch Valley Veal; South Holland, Illinois

Egg Nutrition Center; Washington, D.C.

Enfant Riant Escargots; Petaluma, California

Erman, Kurt, retired Executive Chef, The Waldorf Astoria; New York City

Fink Baking Corp.; Long Island City, New York

Fishery Products, Inc.; St. John's, Newfoundland, Canada

FLAV-R-PAC Frozen Foods
Florida Avocado Administrative Committee
Florida Celery Exchange
Florida Department of Citrus
Florida Lime and Avocado Administrative
    Committee
Florida Tomato Exchange
Food and Wines from France; New York City
Freshco, Inc.
Fresh Produce Foodservice Directory (Shawnee
    Mission, Kansas: Vance Publishing)
Fresh Western Marketing
Frieda's Finest/Produce
Friedrich, Frank, retired Chef Gardemanger, The
    Waldorf Astoria; New York City
Frionor Norwegian Frozen Fish, Ltd.; New
    Bedford, Massachusetts
Gamekeeper's Choice; Laburnum, Victoria,
    Australia
General Foods Corp.; White Plains, New York
Gilroy Farms, McCormick & Co., Inc.
Golden Dipt Co.; St. Louis, Missouri
Green Valley Meats
Gourmet Fresh; Kennewick, Washington
Hazelnut Marketing Board; Tigard, Oregon
Idaho Potato Commission
International Apple Institute
Irongate Products Co.; New York City
Jac Creative Foods. Inc.; Los Angeles, California
J.R. Simplot Company
Kaufco Sales; West Nyack, New York
Kellogg's; Battle Creek, Michigan
King and Prince Seafood Corporation; Brunswick,
    Georgia
Kitchen Ready Foods; Great Neck, New York
Koegler, Jean, Executive Chef, Canteen Company,
    New York City
Kona Coffee Council
Kotschevar, Lendal H., *Quantity Food Purchasing*
    (New York: John Wiley & Sons, 1970)
Kronos Gyro Products; Astoria, New York
Lamb Weston; Portland, Oregon
Landreth Wild Rice Co.; San Antonio, Texas
Larsen Co.; Green Bay, Wisconsin
Levie, Albert, *The Meat Handbook* (Westport,
    Conn.: AVI Publishing, 1967)
Liberty Ramsey Imports; Carlstadt, New Jersey

Lo Presto, Butcher; New York City
Louisiana Crawfish Promotion and Research Board
Mann Packing Company, Inc.
Maple Leaf Farms; Milford, Indiana
Mash's, Inc., Meat Company
McQuail; Miami, Florida
Meat Buyers Guide, National Association of Meat
    Purveyors (Tucson, Ariz.: 1980)
Metropolis, George, Pastry Chef and Instructor,
    retired, Culinary Institute of America, Hyde
    Park, N.Y.
Michigan Apple Committee
Michigan Bean Commission
Michigan Blueberry Growers Association
Michigan Marketing Association
Michigan Plum Advisory Board
Mitsui Foods, Inc.; Hackensack, New Jersey
Muscovy Grove Duck Farm
Nabisco Brands, Inc.
National Association of Meat Purveyors, *Meat
    Buyers Guide* (Tucson, Ariz.: 1980)
National Onion Association; Greeley, Colorado
National Peach Council
National Pecan Marketing Council
National Pork Producers Council
National Restaurant Association, *Fresh Fruits
    Technical Bulletin*
National Turkey Federation; Reston, Virginia
New York Times; New York City
New Zealand Farm-Raised Venison Council
New Zealand Fishing Industry Board
New Zealand Kiwifruit Authority
New Zealand Lamb Company; Elmsford, New
    York
Nicolas, Jean, *American Fish and Shellfish* (Boston:
    CBI, 1981)
Noeth, Guenther, Banquet Service Director, Hotel
    Pierre; New York City
North American Blueberry Council
North Carolina Yam Commission, Inc.
North Star Foods, Inc.
North West Cherries; Yakima, Washington
Nova Scotia Food Products
Ocean Spray Cranberries, Inc.
Oregon, Washington, California Pear Bureau
Ore-Ida Foods, Inc.
Oscar Mayer Foodservice

Ostrich Information

Ottman Custom Processors, Inc.; Wilkinsonville, Massachusetts

Pacific International Rice Mills; Woodland, California

Pacific Pearl Seafoods-Wakefield; Bellevue, Washington

Papaya Administrative Committee

Pet Incorporated; St. Louis, Missouri

Pollio Dairy Products Corp.; Mineola, New York

Potato Board of Colorado

Reiner, Hermann, formerly Executive Chef, Windows on the World and Inhilco, World Trade Center; New York City

Revsin, Leslie, Executive Chef, New York City

Ritz, Willy, retired Pastry Chef, The Waldorf Astoria, New York City

RLB Food Distributers, West Caldwell, New Jersey

Salmon Institute

Schmidt, Arno, *Notes from the Chef's Desk* (Boston: CBI, 1977)

Seald-Sweet Growers, Inc.

S & H Organic Acres; Montgomery Creek, California

Singelton Seafood Company; Tampa, Florida

Sonnenschmidt, Fredric, and Nicolas, Jean, *Art of Gardemanger* (Boston: CBI, 1982)

Steinke, Klaus, formerly Banquet Service Manager, The Plaza, New York City

Sunkist Growers, Inc.

Sun World International, Inc.

Tarantino, Joseph, Pastry Chef and Instructor, New York Technical College; New York City

Texas Sweet Citrus Advertising, Inc.

Trombetti, Joseph, retired Executive Chef, The Plaza Hotel, New York City

Uncle Ben's, Inc.; Houston, Texas

Universal Frozen Foods; Twin Falls, Idaho

U.S. Department of Agriculture, "Food Buying Guide"

U.S. Department of Agriculture, "Fruits in Family Meals"

U.S. Department of Agriculture. "Nutrition: Food at Work for You"

U.S. Department of Agriculture. "Nutritive Value of Foods"

Virga's Pizza Crust Company; Bronx, New York

Virginia Dare Extract Company; Brooklyn, New York

Walker Foods; Springfield, New Jersey

Washington Asparagus Growers Association

Washington State Apple Commission

Washington State Fruit Commission

Washington State Potato Commission

Western Growers, Inc.

Wisconsin Milk Marketing Board

INDEX